Oŕ

M. J. MOLLOY

Irish Drama Selections

General Editors
Joseph Ronsley
Ann Saddlemyer

IRISH DRAMA SELECTIONS
ISSN 0260–7962

Each volume contains a representative selection of plays by the playwrights, together with a critical introduction and a checklist of works. Available in hardcover and paperback.

All titles contain a Bibliographical Checklist. For details of the plays, see the advertisement at the back of this book.

SELECTED PLAYS
OF
M. J. MOLLOY

chosen and with an introduction by
Robert O'Driscoll

Irish Drama Selections 12

1998
COLIN SMYTHE
Gerrards Cross, Bucks.

THE CATHOLIC UNIVERSITY
OF AMERICA PRESS
Washington, D.C.

First published in Great Britain in 1998
by Colin Smythe Limited, Gerrards Cross, Buckinghamshire

British Library Cataloguing in Publication Data
A catalogue record for this book is available from the British Library
ISBN 0-86140-148-4
ISBN 0-86140-149-2 pbk

First published in North America in 1998 by
The Catholic University of America Press, Washington, D.C.

Library of Congress Cataloguing-in-Publication Data
Molloy, M. J. (Michael Joseph)
 [Plays. Selections]
 Selected plays of M. J. Molloy / chosen and with an introduction by Robert O'Driscoll.
  p. cm.—(Irish drama selections, ISSN 0260-7962 : 12)
 Includes bibliographical references.
 Contents: The king of Friday's men—The paddy pedlar—The wood of the whispering—Daughter from over the water—Petticoat loose—The bachelor's daughter.
 ISBN 0-8132-0933-1.—ISBN 0-8132-0934-X (pbk.)
 1. Ireland—Drama. I. O'Driscoll, Robert. II. Title.
III. Series.
PR6025.020846 1998
822'.914—dc21   98-40761
                                                        CIP

Produced in Great Britain
Typeset by Art Photoset Ltd, Beaconsfield, Buckinghamshire
Printed and bound by T. J. International Ltd, Padstow, Cornwall

CONTENTS

INTRODUCTION:
The Folk Realm of M. J. Molloy

The creation of art out of the great residue of Celtic myth, folklore, and history constitutes the main substance of Ireland's contribution to twentieth-century literature. We know, in this respect, the work of Yeats, Synge, O'Casey, Lady Gregory, and others. We are less familiar with a dramatist who has for the last forty years been hailed as the greatest master of Irish folk theatre since Synge, M. J. Molloy, but whose work is as significant as Synge's in that it is a full and authentic representation of the survival of ancient Celtic customs and wisdom in the modern world.

Synge, we must remember, is an outsider to the Irish world he presents in his work. He visited Connemara, Wicklow, and West Kerry, but lived merely for some months at a time on the Aran Islands. 'I got more aid than any learning could have given me,' Synge writes in the Preface to *Playboy of the Western World,* 'from a chink in the floor of the old . . . house where I was staying, that let me hear what was being said by the servant girls in the kitchen.'[1] One might say, in fact, that Synge was an outsider trying to get in. Molloy, on the other hand, is an insider getting out. 'Does Synge influence me?' Molloy asks: 'Not directly, but the people who gave him his material do. My neighbourhood at home is full of Synge characters.'[2] Molloy is unique among modern Irish dramatists in that he has been immersed all his life in the folk world he presents in his work: he was not only born into that world in 1917, but for almost fifty years spent a portion of each week meticulously collecting and scrupulously recording the folklore of the area in County Galway where he was born and was living. Molloy's folk realm is rooted in a reality that he not merely knows, but which he has experienced, first in imagination through the particular folk story or tale that he has collected, and then in the corroboration he deliberately seeks in the facts of social and cultural history. His folk realm is at once imaginative and real.

Molloy was born and 'will die', he tells us, with 'a strange craving for every kind of history.' A mere hundred yards from his front door in Milltown, County Galway, the heart of the folk world presented in his plays, stood a famous Visiting House owned by a local blacksmith, Michael Silk; there every evening neighbours gathered to exchange stories, songs, wit and conversation. The Visiting House was the institution in Irish life that had kept folklore and history a living presence in the minds of the people for hundreds of years, and in Silk's Visiting House, which Molloy began to frequent at the age of twelve or thirteen (and which became the model for his second play, *The Visiting House*, with Broc Heavey being modelled on Silk himself), his interest in folklore, history, and racy dialogue was fed.

In art the imagination often expresses the contrary of the conditions that define us in real life. In his noble stylized drama Yeats presents on the stage the opposite of the heterogeneous activity that characterizes waking life. Synge's vibrant characters, his playboys and his tragic queens, contrast with his own early death of Hodgkins disease. M. J. Molloy, a neat, delicate, undemonstrative man, represents the contrary in physical appearance of the bullymen, randy bachelors, and ribald women that dominate his plays. As well as this, his casual, off-hand manner of speaking is in marked contrast to the fantastic, free-flowing speech of his characters. His mother was a church organist and National School teacher, his father a commercial traveller, and in his youth, after completing his Leaving Certificate at St Jarlath's College in Tuam, he spent three years training for the Chinese Missions in St Columban's College, Dalgan Park, completing two year's philosophy and classics and one year's theology. But in 1937, at the age of twenty, he was stricken with an extremely painful disease, bone tuberculosis, and he spent the next five years fighting for his life through a series of operations that left him with a permanently short left leg and stiff knee.[3]

One evening a friend invited him to the Abbey Theatre, and this became the second event that contributed to his becoming a playwright. Standing on crutches and covered in plaster, Molloy viewed Shaw's *Village Wooing* and *Candida*: 'I was entranced. It was like your man looking at Chapman's Homer. I never got over that night.'[4] He always had had an interest in writing; now it turned to playwriting. The next four years were spent reading every play he could, going to the theatre as often as possible, writing a farce which was produced by his fellow patients in a tuberculosis sanatorium in County Wicklow, and, when he returned home to

Milltown, writing concert sketches and producing plays for local amateurs.

Milltown, and indeed the rest of Ireland, possessed an amateur theatrical tradition that stretched back for at least two generations before Molloy's time. 'My farthest back memory of drama', Molloy writes, 'is of one scene from an old melodrama played locally. The old landlord is seated in a chair in front of his mansion, and he is dying of old age or illness, because he keeps saying, "My sweet woodlands, must I leave ye!" to which the faithful retainer replies with a grin and a wink at the audience, "You're going to a better place, your honour".'[5] In its early days, the Abbey Theatre was, of course, an amateur theatre, and in the country it was the amateur tradition that influenced in one way or another most twentieth-century Irish dramatists, actors, and producers. Molloy is fond of quoting Shaw, who, when asked if there would always be great acting talent in Ireland, replied, 'I'm afraid so!' 'Drama is to Ireland', Molloy says, 'what opera is to Italy – we take to acting naturally. The amateurs . . . are the salvation of drama through the country.'[6]

As well as the production in Dublin, London, New York, and elsewhere, Molloy's plays have been the staple diet of rural amateur companies, and this in turn has contributed to their durability: 'The rural Irish audience is an Elizabethan audience', Molloy has said, 'They're very tough – they come out for a night's fun, and if they don't get it from the stage they'll make it for themselves in the auditorium. That's why the first question asked after a production in my part of the country is "Did ye get good silence?" or "Did they give ye a hearing?"'[7] In addition to their insistence on entertainment, the rural Irish audience of Molloy's time has the same credulity and involvement in the action as Shakespeare's audience, carrying the willing suspension of disbelief to the furthest point, reacting to events on the stage as if they were events in real life.

Still, though, until the end of the 1930s, Molloy confesses: 'I had no vision. I had nothing to say.' Then, in 1940, in the National Library of Ireland he came upon an unpublished thesis that showed that rural Ireland has passed through some very romantic periods, characterized by runaway matches and a high marriage rate. 'I got the impression that the Irish were the most romantic people in the world, and always had been.' Without this discovery, Molloy says, he would probably have written 'bitter, rather cynical, and satirical plays like those of George Sheils', but with the discovery, the corroboration in social and cultural history of the poetic and romantic image of the Irish he was receiving in folklore, his direction becomes clear, for he finds a double authority, in history as well as in folklore, for the 'romantic and outlandish characters and situations' of a hidden, pre-famine Ireland with which he became increasingly fascinated.

In 1941 he began the writing of *Old Road*, a play which subsequently won the Abbey Playwriting Competition of the year. On one level, the play is a protest against forced emigration and the cautious matchmaking mentality that had supplanted the romanticism of pre-famine Ireland – a romanticism resulting in early marriages and large families. On another and more important level, *Old Road* introduces to the Abbey stage a new type of character: farm labourers and retainers who earn their living in the most menial fashion but who possess a rich interior life. They are open, generous, warm-hearted, capable of fine deeds, at once tricky and gallant, and possessing at all times a capacity for love. They set off at the end of the play on the old road of emigration, but carrying to their new homes in foreign slums a bright vision of realized love. In *Old Road*, therefore, Molloy accomplishes the first task to which an original dramatist must address himself: the creation of a world of his own. It is this world that is revealed more fully in his subsequent folk plays: *The Visiting House* (1946), *The King of Friday's Men* (1948), *The Paddy Pedlar* (1952), *The Wood of the Whispering* (1953), *Daughter from Over the Water* (1963), *Petticoat Loose* (1979), and *The Bachelor's Daughter* (1985). Molloy himself notes the exigencies that determined his personal and professional choices between the early fifties and the late sixties:

The burning of the old Abbey and the sixteen years at the Queen's Theatre was a disaster for me as for other dramatists. The Queen's was a music-hall theatre, and farce like *The Will and the Way* did very well there. But the poetic play like *The Wood of the Whispering* or *Friday's Men* did not draw good audiences, and straight tragedy spelled box-office ruin. So I began to stock my farm with sheep and cattle because the income from playwriting was falling. But the stock-managing and farming took up more and more of my time and left me with insufficient energy for good playwriting. When I finally realised this I sold the stock and the land. By this time the new Abbey had opened.

Folk life provides new characters and situations for drama, situations and characters that lie beyond the pale of strict classical comedy and tragedy. A folk world is a loose, almost anarchic one, allowing uninhibited opportunity for the development of a theme or the presentation of an unusual configuration of characters, a world beyond social custom or expectation in which the dramatist can concentrate on the unchanging passions of human nature without regard to the forms in which these passions have been traditionally expressed or contained. Characters seem to be encountered rather than created. With the authority, too, of a tradition that can be documented in cultural and imaginative history, the dramatist is released from the demands of strict morality and convention, while at the same time he is anchored against the potential excesses and eccentricities of the individual imagination. The static conventions of the naturalistic stage are shattered; verisimilitude is no longer required; the imagination of the audience is transported to a remote, timeless world where anything is possible.

In a folk world, Molloy indicates, stories and poetry are preferred to 'philosophy or theology or science.'[8] The folk dramatist tends not to intellectualize a situation or concern himself with the psychological motivation behind character; characters and situations are presented as they are found, without judgment or condemnation. Action – those distinctive yet revealing emanations of the will – is found to be more significant than psychological probing. In a folk world, therefore, the dramatist finds manifested correspondences for emotions, archetypes of human experience, fables that illustrate conclusions of modern psychology. Molloy's *Petticoat Loose* embodies something that modern medicine is beginning to acknowledge: that physical ailments often result from spiritual causes. Emotional equivalents can be found in folk motifs for deeply suppressed fears and anxieties, superstitions, the irrational and subconscious, as in *Paddy Pedlar* and *The Bachelor's Daughter*. At the same time, a preconscious, pre-scientific world makes for an atmosphere of innocence, of credulous characters, bringing, as in *Petticoat Loose*, an urban audience dangerously close to a state of detached condescension, while *Bachelor's Daughter* needs the credulity of the characters to make acceptable to the audience the dramatic representation of a poltergeist phenomenon that sustains the action.

Language in folk drama is released from stereotype, cliché, and the burden of meaning placed on it by logic and plausibility. It glitters with vitality, engaging the imagination of the audience, becoming the mediating force between the world that the dramatist reveals and the world the audience has left. A patterned rhythmic language, as occurs in all of Molly's plays, is therefore integral to the very fabric of folk drama.

The romantic and poetic past Molloy regards as 'a hill' from which to view the harsh social and economic realities of contemporary Ireland. In considering the social backdrop to the plays, the modern Irish people, Molloy believes, were prisoners of history, free politically, but not free in 'their own souls and minds from the ill effects of having been born in slavery.'[9] In the country sufficient land existed, but because of the connection between sub-division of the land in the past and the horrors of the famine, contemporary owners were unwilling to subdivide again. The result was that the young were forced to emigrate or to live out futile lives waiting for the death of a parent or older sibling. Depopulation in the country affected the towns, which were in turn dependent on country folk for survival, forcing further emigration, and thus a chain reaction set in.

To these farm-villagers could be added a further group, a class which has disappeared from Ireland during Molloy's lifetime, the landlord's villagers, a group which provides, in a way, a mirror image of the occupants of the Big House – gardeners, carpenters, gamekeepers, cooks, maids, butlers, *etc* – craftsmen and retainers who were in many instances abandoned to old age, semility and sometimes lunacy, when the Parnellite Land Wars ruined the landlord, and he could no longer employ them. Molloy writes of this group:

They had very little land, so these villages became doomed warrens of old bachelors and old maids and childless couples. Poverty had made them more primitive in some ways than the ordinary farm villages. They never went to Church except for Baptism and Marriage, but they went thirty miles in carts every year to St Bernard's Well. It was supposed to give fertility to women. They brought their cows thirty miles to Co. Mayo every year to another holy well on its Pattern Day. Apart from this, their only religious practice seemed to be that they did not play cards during Lent. Their contacts with the landlord's books and culture and morality made them cynical and anarchic in their outlooks on life, philosophy and religion. Some could talk about literature like professors, others could talk about religion and philosophy like agnostic theologians. They were skilful carpenters and builders, who repaired other people's houses and let their own houses fall down. ... They were great talkers and local historians, especially about the history of their own landlords. They were influenced in their characters and habits by the character and habits of their landlords.[10]

The Wood of the Whispering, set in 1950 and played out before the crumbling stone and weed-choked gardens of a fading eighteenth-century mansion, evokes with Chekhovian delicacy the marginal life of this class and the despoliation of a once wooded countryside, focusing on the silent figure of Sadie. Her spirit, suspected to have been stolen by the fairies, brooding and introspective, becomes a haunting symbol – perhaps like the dead woman in the Paddy Pedlar's sack – of Ireland itself:

> ... then she was left alone and the lonesomeness and the darkness and the trees defeated her at last. 'Tis two years now since she spoke to anywan or went out amongst the neighbours. She spends the day and the night within there thinking and ever thinking about how she lost herself.[11]

M. J. Molloy is an original and significant dramatist. *Wood of the Whispering* (1953), with its portrait of a vanished class, anticipates in terms of character, treatment, and theme, much that is moving and profound in the plays of Samuel Beckett, a survivor of another doomed class, the Anglo-Irish. *The Visiting House* (1946) dramatizes an aspect of Irish rural life that had never been dramatized before, while his masterpiece of farce, *The Will and the Way* (1955), documents another disappearing class, the old-time amateur actors of the countryside, or 'playboys' as they called themselves. *Old Road* (1941) reveals the type of warm-hearted emigré who joins the proletariat in Britain and America. *Daughter from Over the Water* (1964), a light comedy which focuses on the emigrée returning to Ireland, anticipates the theme popularized in Brian Friel's *Loves of Cass Maguire* (1966). *The King of Friday's Men* (1948) documents the *droit du seigneur* and faction-fighting of a hidden pre-famine Ireland. *The Paddy Pedlar* (1952) is a powerful dramatization of what must be, when set side by side with another work drawing on a Scots-Irish tradition surviving in the American South, William Faulkner's 1930 novel *As I Lay Dying*, a very ancient burial ritual.[12] *Petticoat Loose* (1979) is a ribald representation of the sexual and religious practices of a pagan world totally untouched by orthodox Roman Christianity (the world 'pagan' comes from the Latin word 'paganus', which originally meant 'country dweller', but it entered the English language with the meaning of 'heathen' or 'non-believer'). *The Bachelor's Daughter* (1985), treating the phenomenon of the poltergeist, opens up new possibilities for drama in the communication it engineers between visible and invisible characters on the stage.

It is not merely as a representation of a lost folk world, nor as cultural or social documents, that Molloy's plays are ultimately significant, but as contemporary examples of an unusual dramatic art. The first point to notice is that the plays resist classification into the common classical genres, comedy and tragedy, but are more in the tradition of the forms of drama developed in the Middle Ages: morality and farce. A morality play is one, usually with an edifying end, in which a lesson is worked out about the nature of life. *The King of Friday's Men, The Wood of the Whispering*, and *Petticoat Loose* are moralities. In *Wood of the Whispering* a whole community comes to realize that it is the duty of one generation to bring into being the generation that is to succeed it, a fairly obvious proposition, but in the 1950s, which witnessed the greatest exodus from rural Ireland since the famine, the proposition needed to be re-stated. *The Paddy Pedlar* reveals how an encounter with the unexpected and irrational, with indeed a kind of grace operating through the unlikely figure of a pedlar carrying the body of his dead mother on his back in a sack, brings about the sudden conversion of a petty thief. *The King of Friday's Men*, Molloy's finest play, elucidates the Christian belief that suffering is a noble vocation. The victims and the sufferers are glorified at the end, with the eloquent and compassionate outcast, Bartley, concluding that the task given him by God is to help those more unfortunate than himself. In contrast, the morals elucidated in *Petticoat Loose* are not even Christian, and are only to be understood in the context of a wild, romantic, pre-famine pagan world.

A critical failure to understand the structure and substance of these moralities can lead to misinterpretation and confusion. Characters that may appear marginal, if examined in terms of classical genres, become recognizable. In a morality, as in a farce, character is subservient to situation and message. They are, as a consequence, not fleshed out, thin, almost but not quite one-dimensional: out of that comedy is generated, as in most of the characters in *Petticoat Loose* or with Nan in *Bachelor's Daughter*. With regard to plot, the ingenious twists and turns in the third acts of the plays – the virtuoso displays of stage dexterity which is a Molloy characteristic – become intelligible in terms of morality and farce. Once one can perceive, as in a flash, the end, then one can acknowledge how and why the plot is designed to reach that end. Bartley tries on many occasions to duck his fate: he desires the girl as a mate and companion. Only through repeated disappointments does he realize that love, marriage, and family are not meant for him, that his apparent misfortunes are heaven-sent, to test him, to reveal his vocation as one of the King of Friday's men whose destiny is to wander and suffer.

Of the remaining two plays in this collection, *Daughter from*

Over the Water is what Molloy calls a 'religious problem play' (it was, Molloy claims, rejected by the Abbey because 'the directors were worried that the fake miracle would cause offence amongst Catholics'), and *The Bachelor's Daughter*, which, like *The Visiting House*, is an example of what is called nowadays 'documentary drama', or more precisely documentary comedy. In *The Visiting House* Molloy seems intent on presenting the manners of a vanished social world. The play suffers as drama, the love situation between Tim and Mary possessing a dramatic potential that is not developed or satisfactorily resolved. *The Bachelor's Daughter* is a strange type of documentary in that it attempts to use an invisible force, a poltergeist, as an agent in the play. So successful is this invention that the invisible force takes over the whole direction of the play, the 'documentary form' being taken to such a point of exaggeration that the form through which the meaning is communicated is itself parodied.

One might even say with relation to Molloy's work that the methods of farce, the comedy of situation rather than the comedy of character, the one consistent strain through the moralities as well as the documentaries, are used to educe a greater morality. The first two acts of *Wood of the Whispering*, for example, are deeply pathetic, but the farcical action of the third act, as well as of the third acts of most of the other plays, seem introduced to show the characters stripped of everything except their vivid language and their ingenuity in manipulating the immediate circumstances of their lives, in creating out of the deeper resources of the human spirit some sort of life over the abyss, a vivid and humorous expression that somehow renders their material deprivation irrelevant. Language and laughter become the only bulwarks, though sometimes as short-lived as the running time of the play itself, against the forces that threaten all life and all art: despair, desolation, and death. To language and laughter Molloy adds the transmogrifying power of love. "All of my plays," he has said, 'are a protest against the cruel, unromantic, mechanistic mentality of modern times.'

The following are the dates of the first productions of plays by Molloy at the Abbey Theatre: *Old Road* on 26 April 1943; *The Visiting House* on 18 November 1946; *The King of Friday's Men* on 18 October 1948; *The Wood of the Whispering* on 26 January 1953; *The Paddy Pedlar* on 5 September 1953; *The Will and the Way* on 5 September 1955; *A Right Rose Tree* on 10 February 1958; *The Wooing of Duvesa* during the 1964 Dublin Theatre Festival; *Petticoat Loose* on 16 May 1979. *Daughter From Over the Water* was given its first professional production in the Gaiety, Dublin, on 13 April 1964. *The Bitter Pill* is a one-act play which has so far been only produced by amateurs. *The Bachelor's Daughter* received its first production on 3 March 1985 by the Tuam Theatre Guild.

Molloy also has been fortunate in his interpreters: Cyril Cusack as the young Myles in *Old Road*, F. J. McCormick and Harry Brogan in *The Visiting House*, M. J. Dolan and Bríd Ní Loinsigh in *The Wood of the Whispering*, Walter Macken as Bartley Dowd in *The King of Friday's Men*, Siobhan McKenna in *Daughter From Over the Water*, etc., and, on the amateur level, there have been inspired productions of *The Paddy Pedlar* by the Ballina Players and the Listowel Drama Group. Molloy's work has also been presented on radio and television. The BBC Third Programme has adapted and broadcast *Old Road, The King of Friday's Men,* and *The Paddy Pedlar,* and *Old Road* was presented on BBC Television during the late fifties. Radio Telefis Eirean has adapted and broadcast *The King of Friday's Men, The Paddy Pedlar,* and *Bachelor's Daughter.* Professional productions outside Ireland include *The King of Friday's Men* in London, Cambridge, Cardiff and Brighton in 1949, and in Boston and New York in 1951; *The Wood of the Whispering* in Stratford, England, in 1963; and *The Paddy Pedlar* in London in 1957.

With relation to the texts, I have used the most recent published version of the particular play, to which Molloy has made some revisions, slight in some cases, more extensive in others. *Bachelor's Daughter* is published here for the first time. Some mention should also be made of plays that have not yet been published in any edition: two historical plays, *A Life for Bamba* (first produced at the Abbey under the title *A Right Rose Tree*), set during the first days of the Irish Free State and the subsequent civil war, and *Delilah* (first written in 1981 under the title *The Turning Tide,* and so far unproduced), set in an English house in London during the Land War of the 1880s. While Molloy does evoke in these plays the suspicion, bitterness, recklessness, and mindless intimidation of warfare, it could be said that the exuberant language, credulous characters, lack of philosophic probing, and manipulation of situations, all so characteristic of Molloy's plays, seem unsuitable for the treatment of historical situations. *The Wooing of Duvesa,* also unpublished, moves easily between the historical plays, which demand a certain verisimilitude and fidelity to fact, and the folk play, where anything becomes possible.

Robert O'Driscoll

xvi

[1] *Plays, Book Two,* ed Anne Saddlemyer (London, 1968), *Collected Works IV,* 53.
[2] *The Irish Times* (10 September 1955).
[3] Programme for *The Wood of the Whispering,* Druid Theatre Company (Galway, 1955), p. 7.
[4] Undocumented quotations are statements made by Molloy to me in conversation.
[5] Druid Programme, p. 5.
[6] *The Irish Times* (10 September 1955).
[7] Ibid.
[8] Introduction to *Petticoat Loose.*
[9] See below, p. 111.
[10] Druid Programme, p. 7.
[11] See below, p. 119.
[12] When I drew Molloy's attention to the similarity of the action in *The Paddy Pedlar* and Faulkner's *As I Lay Dying,* he wrote to me as follows: 'I think it inevitable rather than surprising that different countries would have stories about corpses being carried on the back for burial. In primitive societies and at the lowest level of poverty the human back was the beast of burden. Accounts of the Irish famine give many examples. The story was not told to me as anything very extraordinary.' It is true that in Faulkner's novel the corpse is carried in a horse-drawn wagon rather than on anyone's back, and apparent that Molloy had not read *As I Lay Dying,* but the general similarity of situation is striking. The story that forms the substance of *The Paddy Pedlar* was told to Molloy about Billy Doogan, one of the most famous fighting men of the Tulrahan Pattern area between 1830 and 1870:

A travelling man with a bag on his back came the way and asked for a night's lodgings. Billy treated him well, and gave him his supper. After they went visiting, came home and slept the night. In the morning when the travelling man was setting out, Billy said to him, 'That's a very heavy bag you have. What's in it?' 'My mother', said the travelling man. 'When she was dying she commanded me to carry her up to County Sligo, and bury her with her husband.'

The King of Friday's Men

A PLAY IN THREE ACTS

Preface

The play opens in the year 1787 with the French Revolution a couple of years ahead. One of the abuses that provoked that bloody outbreak of vengeance was the *droit du seigneur*: the old fuedal rule or custom, whereby the landed aristrocrats could compel the prettiest daughters or wives of their tenant farmers to become their mistresses for a night, or for a lifetime. The *droit du seigneur* was practised in many countries besides France. Mozart's opera *The Marriage of Figaro* had its run terminated by order of the Austrian Emperor, because he knew that the variety of *droit du seigneur* satirised in the opera was standard practice amongst his nobility. The English landlord in Goldsmith's novel behaved as badly as his contemporary landlord in my play.

But nowhere, except probably Tsarist Russia, was the *droit du seigneur* practised more openly and brutally than in Ireland. In Ireland the landed aristrocats were backed by the English army of occupation, and enjoyed the rights of conquerors as well as the old feudal rights of great land-owning aristocrats. They were also the local magistrates with powers of life and death, as the only police force was their own servants. Their tenant farmers had to sign farm leases acknowledging that their landlords owned everything on their farms except two things: sunlight and air. The threat of eviction from their farms and homes always hung over them, as they could be evicted for no reason. So the tenant farmers had a proverb: "Never fear the winter till the snow is on the blanket" – that is, until you are evicted. Yet like war-time soldiers on leave, they flung themselves recklessly into every kind of wild merrymaking they could think of and half afford. If security is bad for us, as some philosophers say, security was an evil from which they were wholly free.

In a new country like North America, feudalism never became established; neither did its usual by-product, the *droit du seigneur*. But it is a mistake for North Americans to suppose that other older countries were so fortunate: countries held in the iron grip of feudalism for a thousand years. And yet feudalism had developed

3

as a very necessary protection against the Viking raids and invasions. In the same way that Communism developed in our day as a reaction against the excesses and failures of Capitalism. The French Revolutionaries cared nothing about poverty but everything about individual liberty. The Communists care everything about poverty and nothing about individual liberty. So mankind has fetched the full circle in less than two hundred years.

CHARACTERS

GAISCEEN BREHONY, Huntsman to Caesar French.
UNA BREHONY, His niece.
OWEN FENIGAN, Son of one of Caesar's tenants.
MAURA PENDER, Daughter of one of Caesar's tenants.
BARTLEY DOWD, The Man from Tyrawley.
BOORLA, Caesar's Bailiff.
RORY COMMONS, Son of Cormac Commons, last of the bards.
KITTY, A peasant girl from a neighbouring estate.
BIDDY, Caesar's Housekeeper.
MURTY, A stable-hand of Caesar's.
CAESAR FRENCH, Norman-descended landlord of Kilmacreena, a
    large estate on the Mayo-Galway border.

ACT I

The bedroom of Gaischeen's cottage on the Kilmacreena Estate
about ten o'clock on one of the last nights in January of the year
1787.

ACT II

SCENE I. A hillside on the Co. Galway side of the river. Twenty-
four hours later.

ACT II

SCENE II. The same. Thirty-six hours later; about noon of St.
Brigid's Day.

ACT III

Living-room of French Hall half an hour later. Nightfall of St.
Brigid's Day.

5

The King of Friday's Men

ACT ONE

The place is the bedroom of a cottage near the village of Kilmacreena, in the remote and hilly corner where the counties Mayo, Galway and Roscommon meet. The room is fairly large, whitewashed, high-roofed and thatched. There is only one window in the middle of the back wall, and it is extremely small. The only door is in the middle of the left wall (from the actor's point of view) and leads into the kitchen. A small table stands in the middle of the room, with two home-made chairs drawn up to it. A big locked wooden chest stands just inside the door. Men's hats and coats, and women's shawls are hung on the wooden pegs stuck in the walls. On a second small table placed against the right-hand wall, are sundry bottles and kegs and mugs, also some cakes of oaten bread, and some long-shanked pipes of the period. Under this table is thrown a bundle wrapped and knotted in a coarse linen cloth. There is a fireplace in the left hand wall, with a turf fire burning.

The great glory of the room, however, is the bed, a mighty, high-posted, canopied, curtain-hung bed of the period. Everything about this bed suggests aristocratic wealth and luxury, and it stands out in contrast to the solid comfortable plainness of the rest of the room and furniture. It runs at right angles to the right wall. As the curtains are drawn, one cannot see whether there is anyone in the bed.

When the curtain rises, the stage is empty. From the kitchen can be heard an Irish jig played on the bagpipes, and the stamping and shouting of many dancers. Suddenly the door is opened, and the music and tumult can be heard at full strength. Shouts ring out, such as "More power to you, piper!" "Faster, lads!" "Round the house, and mind the dresser!" In a moment Gaisceen (pronounced Gosh-keen) struggles in, freeing himself from many detaining hands, and beset by cries of "Wait, Gaisceen." "Give us Cormac's new song." "Don't refuse us Cormac's new song."

GAISCEEN. (*good-humouredly*). I will; I'll sing it for ye as soon as I rhyme it over to myself first, and see have I it off right.

6

(*He closes the door, and comes over to the table. He is small but wiry; probably nearer sixty than fifty, but lively as a bee, and sprightly as a youth. Every Spring* GAISCEEN *works hard for a few weeks sowing potatoes in the half-acre* CAESAR *has allotted to him; in the Autumn he works for another couple of weeks digging and pitting these potatoes. On this sole food, the fruit of a few weeks' labour, he lives very contentedly throughout the year; so he has plenty of time for more congenial work. The rent for his potato patch he pays by serving his landlord* CAESAR FRENCH *as huntsman, also as gillie on his fowling and fishing occasions. As a poteen-maker he is in much demand, his brand being famous. So between all his various occupations and hobbies he has never found time to marry or keep his cabin or clothes in repair. But he is quite happy. For* GAISCEEN *is a good-humoured simple soul, who seems never to have been troubled by the fiercer, baser passions that drive and rend the common run of men. In short, he is nature's gentleman, that rare phenomenon. He is dressed in a swallow-tailed frieze coat, knee-breeches, home-knitted stockings and buckle shoes.*)

GAISCEEN (*to himself*). Now, Gaisceen, if you can rhyme it through wance without a stumble, you have it good enough.

> *One morning in June, when I chanced to go wandering,*
> *I met a maiden, and so handsome was she,*
> *Nothing could save me, I fell wild in love with her*
> *Wounded to death, for she smiled charmingly,*
> *I asked her her name, and "What happy fit was it*
> *Turned your steps this way, my bright love so fair?*
> *My heart it will break if you don't come along with me.*
> *Farewell for ever to sorrow and care.*

(*Rubbing his hands with satisfaction.*) More power to you, Gaisceen. You're not too decayed yet to master a new song.

(*The door opens, and* UNA (*pronounced Oona*) *runs in, closing the door behind her. She is not more than seventeen, and somewhat small and frail, but very pretty with her dark eyes, and her innocent, almost child-like smile. She is the pretty child blossoming into pretty womanhood, but shy as yet and timid, easily blushing, easily thrilled, easily frightened. In company she still has not yet broken off her childhood's habit of sitting and looking in front of her, and listening silently while her elders carry on the conversation. But she is quiet and shy rather than serious-minded. She has seen little of the world yet, and has no*

7

comprehension of its grimness. She is dressed surprisingly well, in a dress of that new and expensive material: English cotton from Lancashire. The dress is not new; nevertheless it becomes her very well.)

UNA (*running to him radiant and breathless with excitement*). Gaisceen Gaisceen, d'ye know the tidings I have?

GAISCEEN (*smiling*). I do, and well. He has you asked to wed him?

UNA (*amazed*). Why, Gaisceen? How did you guess?

GAISCEEN (*rising*). Sure lately anywan could see 'twas on the tip of his tongue to ask you, and tonight he was sure to on account you have that grand dress of Biddy D'Arcy's on. (*He sets out for the other table where the bottles and mugs are left.*)

UNA. You reckoned so? And myself never thinking he would yet on account the two of us are so young.

GAISCEEN (*uncorking a bottle*). What young? Isn't he nineteen years, and isn't yourself crushing up to eighteen? Aren't they all wedding as young as that these late years since the tillage came in, and gave work for all in Ireland?

UNA. Very near my eyes fell out with surprise. All I could think to say was that I should ask yourself first.

GAISCEEN (*picking out three mugs*). Never mind Gaisceen's advice. Please your mind about him. Do you like him good enough for marriage?

UNA. I like him very good, and he likes me very good too.

GAISCEEN (*coming back to the table with the bottle and the three mugs*). Well, wance ye like each other that good ye must wed, for ye'll not be contented till ye do.

UNA (*her eyes sparkling*). We can marry now so! . . . Gaisceen, I'm partly afeard – but altogether rejoiced. (*Running to the door.*)

GAISCEEN (*pouring out the drinks for the toast*). And on account I'm huntsman and poteen-maker to Master Caesar he'll give ye leave to cut the makings of rafters and a door for yere cabin from his woods.

UNA (*radiant*). I'll bring him in, and you can tell him all. (*She runs out, closing the door behind her.*)

GAISCEEN (*singing, bottle in hand*).

> *But I being so airy for such was my nature,*
> *It made my own parents and me disagree.*
> *Then my darling asthore, if you'll listen a whileen,*
> *I'll tell you a story very pleasant, you'll see,*
> *That I'm a young man that's doughtily in love with you,*

And surely my heart is from roguery free.

(*He goes back to the other table with the wine bottle, and as he reaches it the door opens, and* OWEN *runs in, followed by* UNA, *who closes the door behind them. He is a tall but lightly built youth of nineteen, boyishly impetuous, eager, excitable. He is not particularly good-looking, nor particularly intelligent, but his alertness, wild idealism, his headlong enthusiasm and do-or-die earnestness are both amusing and engaging. He has fallen in love with all the wild undoubting romanticism of the Ireland of his day and, after the fashion of that time, will be satisfied with nothing but marriage immediate and glorious. He runs in defiantly.*)

OWEN (*wildly*). I don't care Gaisceen. I don't care what you or anywan says. We're wedding in spite of all Ireland.

GAISCEEN (*smiling*). May the roof of yere house never fall in, and may those under it never fall out!

OWEN (*overjoyed*). Gaisceen! You're on our side then!

GAISCEEN. To be sure. (*Coming to the middle table and taking up a mug.*) And now I'll not take right or wrong till a good luck toast is drunk to ye.

OWEN (*wildly enthusiastic*). Here, Una! (*Handing her one mug and taking up the third himself.*) We'll drink that toast no matter if 'tis poison he has in the mugs.

UNA. Sound the toast, Gaisceen.

GAISCEEN. Here's good health to ye; and long life and happiness; with crops rich and high; a landlord without cruelty; the rent money without fail, and a cradle with something new every year in it.

OWEN (*delighted*). Good, Gaisceen! I'd drink the blood of the devil to that.

(*They touch mugs and drink.* OWEN *then looks at his drink with surprise.*)

OWEN. What's it? 'Tisn't poteen whatever.

GAISCEEN. 'Tis what you never tasted before: Wine from France — all the way from Brandy Harbour. Captain O'Malley's smugglers gave it to me tonight for a jar of my best poteen.

OWEN. Whatever it is, 'tis so pleasant you'd drink it out of a tinker's apron. (*With enthusiasm.*) Sit down now, let ye, till we settle up about the wedding. (*The sit down.*) Gaisceen, we were reckoning up how soon we could wed, and the soonest'd be four days from now, that'd be the day after the Pattern.

9

GAISCEEN (*smiling*). God help yere foolish heads! Is it go wedding the day after St. Brigid's Pattern, when the men of the country, and yourself with them, 'll be stiffened with sore heads and broken bones after the shillelagh fighting at the Pattern? Ye'd have no wan at yere wedding.

OWEN. The divil a lie you have, Gaisceen. (*To* UNA.) Our bones'll be caked from beating that day, so we'd best not wed for two days after the Pattern whatever.

UNA (*pleading*). Owen, maybe you could avoid fighting altogether this year at the Pattern.

OWEN (*shocked*). Is it me to desert my neighbours in their challenge fight against the Tulrahans? And they reckon this'll be the finest day's fighting that ever was seen at St. Brigid's Pattern.

GAISCEEN (*beaming at the prospect*). They tell me the Tulrahans 'll have five hundred great skelpers against us this time, and ourselves'll have equally as many, so win or lose we'll have a grand evening's fighting.

UNA (*uneasy*). But, Owen, is there any fear you'd take great hurt in the fighting?

OWEN. Not me. I'll have my fine oak shillelagh, and my hat with the double crown, and I have three years' practice at shillelagh fighting. He'll be a good man that'll soften my head.

GAISCEEN (*arising*). Kithogue Flynn is the most man of the Tulrahans that has death in his blow; and I doubt we have Kithogue's match at last. (*He crosses to the bed.*)

OWEN. Is it Bartley Dowd the great fighter that's after coming down from Tyrawley to challenge Kithogue at the Pattern?

GAISCEEN. 'Tis. He's here.

(*He draws back the bed curtains and* BARTLEY *can be seen lying on his left side fast asleep with his back to the audience. His shoes are off, but otherwise he is fully dressed, his clothes being rather worn and ragged. He is obviously a big and powerfully built man.* OWEN *and* UNA *come over, and all look down at him.*)

GAISCEEN. He was fatigued out after two days hard walking from Tyrawley, so I sent him in to rest a while. If he whips Kithogue at the Pattern, we'll defeat the Tulrahans ready and easy. 'Twas Kithogue won the day for them each year, slashing gaps through every rank we made.

UNA (*admiring the curtains, etc.*). Isn't it a wonderful fine bed, Owen? Like what you'd hear tell'd be in a gentleman's house.

OWEN. 'Twas a gentleman built this house, sure. Wasn't it Master

10

Caesar's father, Gaisceen? (*He surveys the high, strongly-raftered roof with admiration.*)

GAISCEEN. Master Hubert, God rest him, that built it for his tallywomen in the times when his wife was still living, and he daren't go sleeping with them at French Hall.

OWEN. He behaved a decent man to give his tallywomen such a princely bed, and house, and it greatly furnished and all. (*He examines one of the chairs.*)

UNA. And talk about fine blankets and linen sheets! Look, Owen!

GAISCEEN (*proudly*). Is it that much costs to hurt the frenches of Kilmacreena, and they owners of seven villages and ten thousand acres of prime land? (*He pulls back the bed curtain, and sets out for the wooden chest.*) Come here till I show ye.

OWEN (*following him*). She tells me the box is as heavy as a chapel with fine dresses Master Hubert gave his tallywomen.

GAISCEEN (*kneeling beside the chest, and taking a key from his pocket*). 'Tis; and she can keep the lot.

UNA (*running over with a cry of joy*). Gaisceen, is that the truth? Can I keep this dress then, for the wedding, and for evermore?

GAISCEEN (*unlocking chest*). After Sarah D'Arcy, the last of Master Hubert's tallywomen, died last week, Master Caesar commanded me to live here any more, and keep the house mended for him. When we seen this box was full of Sarah's clothes, I ses to him very fast: "Your Honour," I ses, "Myself has a young niece, and she's very raggedy and poor in the world." "Give her the lot," ses Master Caesar, and threw the key down. So here's the lot. (*He throws back the lid of the chest.*)

UNA (*enraptured, pulling up dress after dress*). Look, Owen, look! Now haven't I a fortune for you! . . . Owen, what ails you? (*For* OWEN *has walked away looking seriously disturbed and displeased.*)

OWEN. Gaisceen, that the divil may give you oats and small stones through it! You have a most dangerous act done.

GAISCEEN (*rising amiably*). Why so, man?

OWEN. To go drawing down her name to Master Caesar, a man that every girl on his property runs a-hiding from!

GAISCEEN. But sure, I didn't give her name. And I never told him she comes visiting to me, or to anywan on this estate. (*He comes over to the table, and takes up his mug again.*)

OWEN (*somewhat relieved*). Didn't you! Still, she'd be safer him not to know her like was in the world at all. (*He sits at the table, still*

11

looking disturbed.)

UNA (*alarmed*). And is Master Caesar taking girls for tallywomen the same as his father?

OWEN (*gloomily*). To be sure he is. What would the cat's son do but kill a rat?

GAISCEEN (*shaking his head gravely*). That was the way with the gentry ever more. Any tenant's daughter they'd want they'd have to get her. 'Tis having too much money, and too little work, and power to do what they like – that's what ruins the poor fellows. ... (*To her, reassuringly,*) But wance you're married, you're safe. Caesar never troubles married women at all.

OWEN (*jumping up with great relief*). Right enough, Gaisceen; he never took a married woman yet. (*Coming to her.*) So you'll be exempt, Una, only to keep out of his sight till we're married. (*The door-latch rattles suddenly, this being the local equivalent of knocking.* GAISCEEN *runs to the door, calls out.*)

GAISCEEN. Who's there?

A GIRL'S VOICE. Maura Pender.

GAISCEEN (*pleased*). Maura, is that yourself? (*To* UNA.) 'Tis Maura Pender that's tallywoman to Master Caesar with a long time.

UNA. D'ye think he is sending her to lodge here?

GAISCEEN. Not him. Evermore Master Caesar kept his tallywomen in French Hall, on account he has no wife to scold him. Maybe Maura has some trouble or question for me to riddle, so let ye go dancing for another whileen. (*He shoots the bolt.*)

OWEN (*wildly enthusiastic*). We will. We'll have another spatter of a dance. (*He whirls her out calling to* MAURA *as he passes her.*) You're in luck, Maura. Gaisceen has wine that'd make a saint hop! (*He pulls open the door, and out they go.* MAURA *comes in, closing the door after her. She is a remarkably fine-looking girl, of considerable natural dignity, refinement and intelligence. She is twenty years of age, but somewhat less blooming and more mature in manner than one would expect in a girl of her age. She is obviously possessed of considerable spirit and strength of character; but there is an air of disillusionment about her, with, at times, a hint of suppressed bitterness. She is very well dressed in the fashion of a lady of the day; and over all she wears the long hooded cloak of the period.*)

GAISCEEN (*warmly*). Maura, 'tis news to see you at a dance.

MAURA (*having closed the door*). What business had I at dances

12

when the lads wouldn't dance with me for fear Caesar'd hear, and turn jealous? (*As he sets a chair near the table for her, she silently takes off her cloak and hangs it on a peg.*)

GAISCEEN (*with admiration*). Maura, you're looking more like a real lady every day. 'Tis a pity you're only wan of ourselves. If you were a lady, I'd venture to say he would marry you.

MAURA (*quietly*). Caesar'll never marry anywan, lady or no. He'd eat his clothes before he'd marry. (*She sits down at the table.*)

GAISCEEN (*going to the other table*). Before now when he wasn't keeping any girl beyond a few weeks I was afeard too he'd never marry, but he has kept you two years all out, and when he contented himself with the same girl that long, maybe he'd soon settle down his mind for marriage. (*He comes back with the wine bottle and a mug, pours her a drink.*)

MAURA (*quietly*). I'm as well to give you the truth first at last. (*She takes the mug, looks down at it a moment absently.*) Half an hour since he told me he was done with me, and to clear out.

GAISCEEN (*stunned*). By the elevens! Did you give him impudence, or the like?

MAURA. I'll tell you all, from the root to the blossom, another time, but not now. At finish he told me to flit off, and sent for Boorla and the Press-gang to bring another girl for him. (*She sips the wine; and seems neither dejected at her dismissal nor elated over her liberation.*)

GAISCEEN. By the elevens! And tell me: did he give you a hansel, and you going?

MAURA (*quickly*). That's what brought me here. Gaisceen, you'll keep it safe for me? (*She takes a knotted handkerchief from her pocket and gives it to* GAISCEEN.)

GAISCEEN. To be sure. I'll dyke it under the floor where I do have the poteen a-hiding from the Revenue men. (*He tosses it in the air, and the clink of guineas is heard.*) Yellow guineas, I'll go bail. Is there a good count in it?

MAURA. Fifteen.

GAISCEEN. Fifteen! And they tell me that's more than ten!

MAURA. 'Tis very near twice more.

GAISCEEN (*impressed*). By the lands! But sure I wouldn't doubt Master Caesar. (*Proudly.*) Evermore the Frenches led all Ireland for decency. I'll dyke it in here for a whileen. (*He goes to the chest, and unlocks it again.*)

MAURA (*with sudden bitterness*). What good are his guineas now when my character is broken over him?

13

GAISCEEN. Why would it? Don't all know Boorla and his Press gang brought you to Caesar against your will, and your people could say no word on account they were Caesar's tenants?

MAURA (*gloomily*). No matter; when the decent lads are looking out for the wife they duck their eyes past any girl that has another man's brand on her.

GAISCEEN. Still, money is nice company, and where else would they get a girl that'd have fifteen guineas for a fortune? (*He puts the money in the bottom corner of the chest, closes and locks it again.*)

MAURA. No doubt I'd get the clever greedy kind that'd wed anything for money. I'd die in a ditch before I'd marry them.

GAISCEEN. You came hoping my dance 'd draw stranger lads that wouldn't know you were a tallywoman?

MAURA. I did, but my side-eye coming in didn't spy any faraways.

GAISCEEN. The floods stopped them. Except one hardy chuck here. (*He draws bed curtain.*)

MAURA. He has shoulders like Goll McMorna.

GAISCEEN. He's the champion fighter of the Barony of Tyrawley, and he came down to lead us against the Tulrahans on the Pattern Day, and to challenge fight Kithogue, the best man of the Tulrahans.

MAURA. I heard all right that Sally Blake's tenants are offering ten acres to the man that'd whip Kithogue and win the day for ye against the Tulrahans.

GAISCEEN. Just overside the river from here the ten acres is. He came this way to cross by the stepping stones, but the flood was man high, so I coaxed him to wait here tonight.

MAURA. He must be a fearless man to challenge Kithogue, that has severals killed in challenge fights. . . . But is he civil?

GAISCEEN. As mannerly as a priest, and decent moreover.

MAURA. You wouldn't say he's greatly set on riches.

GAISCEEN. I ses to him: "When you'll have ten acres won, you'll be out for a girl with a fine lot of money that'll help you to stock it." "Not me," he ses, "If I could chance on a nice girl and she to have a true wish for me, I didn't care if she hadn't a farthing piece itself. "My plan," he ses, "is the new plan: to marry for love and work for riches."

MAURA. Wance he said that, the decent drop is in him, and I like him very good; I don't care if his youth is past, and his countenance wrecked with shillelagh fighting.

GAISCEEN. In a while's time when he has a good 'nough of sleep got

14

I'll make ye acquainted.

MAURA. But I'll give him fair warning that Kithogue Flynn has several killed in challenge-fights.

GAISCEEN. I drank before you there. I told him all Kithogue killed, but I didn't tell him about the candle. (*He goes over to the candle lighting on the table.*)

MAURA. Why? Is there a death token in the candle?

GAISCEEN. A secret wind is spluttering the candle-grease and making a white shroud of candle-grease on one side of the candle. A sure-death-token for someone that slept in this house, or used it, or that owns it.

MAURA (*fingering around the candle*). It must be a fairy wind. It wouldn't stir a hair on an old man's head. It'd be a world's pity if such a great bullyman as Bartley Dowd is killed at this Pattern.

GAISCEEN. It would be a shame to kill him ... (*Cheering up.*) But, maybe, and likely, it's only myself will be killed in the fighting.

MAURA. God forbid!

GAISCEEN. Will I make Bartley Dowd the wiser of your while as tallywoman?

MAURA. Do not. Keep that news in your pocket.

GAISCEEN. But it's sure to be upcasted to him at shillelagh battles after ye're wed.

MAURA. By that time he might love me well enough not to care what I was or wasn't before I got married. (*She opens the door a little, peers out.*)

GAISCEEN. Well, you're right to behave as cute as all the marrying women. And hide your faults till the reins are in your hands.

MAURA. Bless my life! Gaisceen, d'ye know who're landed now? Boorla and the Pressgang!

GAISCEEN (*dismayed*). The villains! They'll drink all that's in the house on me! (*He hides the wine bottles.*)

MAURA. 'Tisn't for that they came this time. Didn't I tell you? Caesar sent them to capture another girl for him.

GAISCEEN. By the elevens! Right enough! And they reckoned a great pick of girls'd be here for the dance. (*He comes to the door.*)

MAURA. The Pressgang are flocked just inside the kitchen door so as no girl'll get chance to escape.

GAISCEEN. And look at Boorla and Kippen looking over each girl in turn, and whispering judgments to each other. No wan but the flower of the flock'll do them.

15

MAURA (*at the crack*). The Pressgang have their shillelaghs hidden under their coats so as no wan'll know what they come for.

GAISCEEN (*in consternation*). By the lands! D'ye know who they're judging now? Young Una Brehony, my own young niece! Oh, God save us, they're eyeing her with admiration, and nodding their heads! Sarah D'Arcy's grand dress has her looking too handsome. By the elevens! Here's Boorla making in to us.

MAURA. Then I'll be off. 'Tisn't me he wants this time.

(*She slips out.* GAISCEEN *runs behind the table and pretends to be busy.* BOORLA *comes in quietly and closes the door behind him. He is a middle-sized, powerful-looking man of forty-five, bull-necked, with massive, forward hanging head. He has the keen, unresting eyes of the Bailiff, and there is something deliberate, determined and inexorable about his movements. For him,* CAESAR FRENCH *is the Law and the Prophets; for* CAESAR *he is willing to undertake any villainy and undergo any risks. In this he is the typical Irish gentleman's retainer of the period, but on his own account he is not particularly villainous and, in fact, is generally cheerful and friendly, although in his own quiet, watcful fashion. He takes in the room with one quick glance; pulls his shillelagh from under his coat and puts it under his arm.*)

BOORLA (*in quite good humour*). Where have you the great bully-man from Tyrawley that got benighted here? (*He sets out for the bed, without waiting for a reply.*)

GAISCEEN (*heartily, as if surprised*). Boorla, man, is that yourself? (*Crossing to the bed.*) He's stretched back sleeping his 'nough. (*They draw back the curtains, and survey* BARTLEY.)

GAISCEEN. Isn't that a great piece of a man?

BOORLA (*coming alongside, and lifting* BARTLEY'S *arm*). Without no lie, he's a powerful man. Look at his wrist!

GAISCEEN. I reckon he'll wallop water out of Kithogue.

BOORLA. 'Twill be a wonderful great fight. For ten years the birds'll be afeard to sing over the place. (*He sets out for the door.*)

GAISCEEN (*closing the bed curtains*). Boorla, man, wait a whileen till you taste a new keg of poteen I'm after making.

BOORLA (*smiling*). Not tonight, Gaisceen; I'm in a hurry tonight. I have a girl to bring to Caesar.

GAISCEEN (*as if surprised*). D'ye tell me so? And have ye her picked yet?

BOORLA. They tell me she's wan Una Brehony from Shanballard.

GAISCEEN. Thunder and turf! Boorla, man, she's a niece of my own!

16

BOORLA. You're in luck, Gaisceen. When you have a niece up at French Hall you'll be the top dog of French's country in earnest. (*He sets out for the door again.*)

GAISCEEN. But the girleen is on the border of marrying young Owen Fenigan. Wance His Honour takes her, her marriage'll be baulked.

BOORLA (*sincerely enough*). 'Tis a pity; still she's the flower of the flock, and 'tis the flower of the flock His Honour should get. None of us'd be in the world at all but for the land and goodness of the Frenches. (*He sets out for the door again cheerfully.*)

GAISCEEN (*following him*). But, Boorla, she'll be crying like a banshee and in an awful way. The dance'll be quenched, everywan'll be that grieved for her.

BOORLA. Not it. We'll stifle her from screeching, and have her whipped away before they understand rightly what 'tis about. (*He unlatches the door.*)

GAISCEEN (*desperately*). Boorla, stand a minute till you see what I have for you.

BOORLA (*smiling indulgently*). What's it? (*He makes a practice swing or two with his shillelagh, while* GAISCEEN *disappears behind the bed, and returns a moment later with about a pound of tobacco.*)

GAISCEEN. As good tobaccy as ever the smugglers carted from Brandy Harbour, and you can have the biggest divide you like out of it.

BOORLA (*smiling*). Going childish, you are, Gaisceen, or you'd know Boorla wouldn't betray Master Caesar for tobaccy, or for all the gold of King Louis of France.

GAISCEEN. Man alive, sure all I'm asking is you to puff tobaccy in the kitchen for a fistful of minutes while I bring her in here and tell her what a fine and decent gentleman Master Caesar is. Then she'll go with ye contented enough maybe, and ye'll have no bother at all.

BOORLA. Well, right; I'll wait that length. 'Tis early, and Caesar'll not be going to his bed yet. (*He cuts off a big chunk of tobacco, and opens the door.*)

GAISCEEN. As you're passing her by, whisper Gaisceen wants her.

BOORLA. I'll do that too. (*He hides the shillelagh under his jacket, and goes out, closing the door.* GAISCEEN *throws the tobacco on the lid of the chest and paces about distractedly.*)

GAISCEEN. What'll you tell her? How will you acquaint her in such a way as she won't lose her life with fear? (*Suddenly he has an idea, hastily unlocks the chest, and rummages out a fancy hair ribbon.*)

UNA (*running in excitedly*). Gaisceen, more great tidings for us. Several of the lads have Owen promised a day's help at building our cabin, if Master Caesar'll let them off task work.

GAISCEEN (*a little grimly*). I never seen such a night for tidings. Here's a ribbon I chanced upon in Sarah's box, and I'd reckon 'twould be a great addition to your hair. (*He gives her the ribbon.*)

UNA. Gaisceen! Now I'll be a lady from my head to my heels! (*She runs to the mirror on the left wall and tries on the ribbon. GAISCEEN bolts the door, takes out his snuff-box, and takes snuff rapidly. He is evidently at a loss for words.*)

GAISCEEN. Did you remark a lot that came in a short while since?

UNA (*turning*). I did that, and they looked as wild as heroes. D'ye think it is for ructions they came?

GAISCEEN. They're working evermore in Master Caesar's corn mills. Boorla, the bailiff, is their captain and they'd do any mortal thing for Master Caesar. The Pressgang we do call them. . . . It appears Master Caesar sent them down for the loan of a girl.

UNA (*alarmed*). For what? Is it for a tallywoman?

GAISCEEN (*taking snuff, and trying to appear casual*). I believe it is for a tallywoman. He has Maura freed out at last.

UNA (*jumping up in sudden terror*). For a tallywoman? And is there any fear they'd pick me?

GAISCEEN (*parrying this with forced enthusiasm*). The girl they choose'll be lucky. 'Tis she'll have the lady's life, with quality clothes, quality eatables and drinkables, a quality feather bed to sleep in, and no work, only as much bossing of the house sluts as ever she'll like.

UNA. Gaisceen, d'ye hear me? Is there any fear they'd pick me?

GAISCEEN. If Master Caesar takes you itself; 'tis maybe only for a few weeks.(*With a sudden impulse of terror, she runs to the door. He cries out in alarm.*) Stop, girl! They'll take you directly you step outside that door.

UNA (*turning slowly*). Then it is myself is picked? (*Reading final confirmation in his face, she crumples up with a moan.*) Mother of God! (*She falls on her knees beside the chest, and buries her face in her hands.*)

GAISCEEN (*still doing his best*). Master Caesar isn't half as severe as you'd judge from his countenance. Obey all his commands

18

directly, and let on you're proud and glad to be with him, and you'll find him the decentest gentleman in Ireland.

UNA (*beating the chest with her hands frantically*). Gaisceen, "tis the last stone in my beads to go to him.

GAISCEEN. Sure, don't I know well; but what can you do now but make the best of it?

UNA. And will you not raise a hand to save me?

GAISCEEN (*horror-struck, as if he had heard a blasphemy*). Is it raise my hand against the Frenches of Kilmacreena, that all belonging to me are serving since the foundation of the world? I couldn't do it, girl, if he was going to strike me dead itself. My arms'd refuse to rise against him.

(OWEN *rushes in, banging out the door behind him.*)

OWEN. Darby Kelly has promised me enough rushes to thatch our cabin!

UNA (*jumping up and running to him*). Owen, you must save me. The Pressgang are going to take me for Caesar.

OWEN (*stunned*). What's that?

GAISCEEN. There's no lie in it. He has Maura freed out.

OWEN (*hoarsely*). Gaisceen, I'll not stand this. If Caesar was our landlord a score of times over, still and all he'll not ruin her.

GAISCEEN. What can you do, man?

OWEN. What can I do? (*Runs and picks up a chair.*) The first that lays a hand on her I'll split his skull like a swallow-tailed coat. (UNA *goes behind him; he stands facing the door, the chair held aloft for action.*)

GAISCEEN (*gravely*). Boorla has six great men and himself the seventh. He has Mickle More that's the third best fighter in the parish, and Kippen, the worst man he has, is accounted the twelfth best. Any man of them fighting single hands'd easy thrash a young slip of a lad such as you.

OWEN (*despairing*). Gaisceen, you have the truth. I'll do my whole endeavour; I'll fight while there's any dash of breath left in me at all, but I stand no chance against them. (*He puts down the chair, and wanders downstage distractedly.*)

UNA. Owen, wouldn't your comrades help you?

OWEN (*bitterly*). There isn't a man at the dance but is a tenant of Caesar's and they'll be afeard to go against their landlord, that can make tramps and beggars of all belonging to them. (*Turning in desperation.*) What'll we do, Gaisceen?

GAISCEEN (*shaking his head*). 'Twill fail you to save her with strength, and the law'll not save her on account Caesar is a

19

magistrate and all the magistrates are gentlemen, and the lawyers'd be afeard to take her case, Caesar has so many duels fought and won. . . .

UNA (*suddenly*). Let ye tell them I escaped someway, and I'll be a-hiding under the bed. (*She runs to the bed, pulls back the curtains, and* BARTLEY *can be seen, sound asleep as before.*)

GAISCEEN. They'd search under the bed, and dig up the ground down as far as hell.

UNA (*crying out*). Gaisceen! The great bully-man from Tyrawley! Maybe he'd fight for me!

OWEN. As true as living he would! He isn't Caesar's tenant, and the ten acres he's aiming to win aren't on Caesar's property. (*He crosses to* BARTLEY.)

GAISCEEN. He'd fight for her if ye stood any chance at all. But against seven fearful fighters, and yourself only a slip of a lad! They'd slash ye to death the same as if ye were mad dogs, and then take her. 'Tisn't likely he'd go throwing his life away for no benefit.

OWEN. Still, 'tis her last chance, and I'll make a trial of it. (*Shaking* BARTLEY *vigorously.*) Rouse up, let you.

GAISCEEN (*stopping him*). Wait, Owen; don't rouse him yet till we compose some way of coaxing him so as he might fight for her. Give Gaisceen a whileen now. (*He walks across the room, taking snuff rapidly.*)

UNA. Hurry, let ye, before they break in for me.

GAISCEEN (*soberly*). Sure enouth the Pressgang spied Owen coming in. You should go out, Owen, or they'll doubt you're scheming some escape for her, and they'll break in directly. (*He goes to the door, and starts.*) By the elevens! Already the Pressgang are flocked together, and looking this way, and talking very lively. Outside, man, quick. (*He pulls back the bolt.*)

OWEN (*indignantly*). Is it me to leave her side, and she in such jeopardy?

GAISCEEN. You must go out directly, and sit by yourself looking very mournful, and broken down. The divil a wan of them'll doubt any trick then, and she'll get time to rouse and coax him.

OWEN. And d'ye reckon she's the best wan to coax him?

GAISCEEN. 'Tis what I'm sure. He's greatly respecting women. He declares a woman is a different person. (*He looks out again, and jumps.*) They're leaning this way greatly! Jog out, Owen Fenigan, or I'll curse the three pains of death into you.

UNA. Una, he's right: I must quit ye. Wheedle the bully-man the best you can. I'll sit by the fire, and snap down the tongs the minute the skelping begins. (*He goes out, closing the door.*)

GAISCEEN. Now he's out of the way, and I can talk straight-forward.

UNA. Quick, Gaisceen, what'll I say to him?

GAISCEEN. Bartley Dowd is a fearless bully-man and decent, moreover, and when you tell him your pitiful case, maybe he would strip his teeth, and fight the best he can for you. But he has seven great slashers to overthrow, and if he only fights his best he stands no chance at all.

UNA. Sure, how could any man fight beyond his best?

GAISCEEN. It happens an odd time for a fighter that has the real spirited red tint of blood in him, and his whole heart set on some wan thing. If that thing is of a sudden put in jeopardy or insulted, he'll go altogether wild: he'll fight the same as he had seven divils in him; he'll fear no odds, and feel no blow, and he'll slash five times harder than he'd be fit to do in an ordinary fight where he'd be only fighting his best. (*Rising and crossing to the bed.*) The champion bully-man of Tyrawley is here. If you could coax him out of his seven senses; if you could win him so as he'd fight beyond his best – that's your last and only chance.

UNA (*dumbfounded*). But how could I do the like, Gaisceen?

GAISCEEN. 'Tisn't riches his heart is set on, but a nice young girl of a wife, wan that'd have a true wish for him moreover. He's understanding well he'll hardly get the like on account he has his youth lost, and his looks, too, with shillelagh batterings. If you let on you have a great fancy taken for him, and let on you'd marry him, he'd go out of his senses with joy, and fight for you such a fight as wasn't seen since the giants were shaking the world,

UNA (*stunned for a moment*). Let on I'd marry him! (*Then, desperately.*) Gaisceen, I'll do the like. I'll do anything before I'll be dragged to Caesar.

GAISCEEN. Owen and yourself can make up to him for the trick after.

UNA. The best way we can we will. (*She runs to* BARTLEY.) I'll waken him.

GAISCEEN. Wait yet till I have all ready. (*He brings mugs and the poteen from the side table to the middle.*) Let on I sent you in to rouse him for the dance; then spread before him the drinkables and eatables, and a pipe of tobaccy and keep him here, rummaging his mind about marriage, and making up to him, till

21

at last myself'll pop in, and draw down a marriage between ye. (*He brings half of an oaten cake, and a knife from the side table to the middle table.*)

UNA. But the Pressgang, Gaisceen; when'll I make known to him about them?

GAISCEEN (*alarmed*). Never tell him about the Pressgang at all; for if you did, he'd know you were pledging marriage only so as he'd save you, and you having no wish for him at all. When the Pressgang break in for you, let on to be surprised beyond measure, and leave the rest to Gaisceen. (*He brings a pipe and tobacco from the side-table to the middle table; then sets out for the door.*)

UNA. Gaisceen, are you sure and certain 'tis the best plan?

GAISCEEN (*solemnly*). As sure as there's a gun in London it is. I'll tell the Pressgang you're like wan that'd be taken out of the river with tears, so they'll give you a good spell. Good luck to you, now. (*He slips out, and she closes, and bolts the door after him.*)

UNA (*blessing herself*). God help me, and guide me now. (*She runs across to* BARTLEY, *puts her hand on his shoulder and shakes him, but rather gently and timidly. Then suddenly she stands up again.*) I must brighten up first, or he'll not like me good enough. (*She runs back to the mirror, smoothes her hair and dress, rubs her − by this time − somewhat tear-stained woebegone eyes and cheeks. Finally, she succeeds in mustering up a semblance of a smile; this done, she returns to* BARTLEY. *She shakes him, at first gently, then more boldly.*) Bartley, Bartley, rouse, up let you. . . . Is it dead he is? . . . Rouse up, Bartley! (*Suddenly his hands go to his face, and he rubs his eyes sleepily, and rolls over on his back.*)

BARTLEY. Is it rousing time? Is it breaking day? (*He rolls over on his right side, and at last is facing the audience. He raises himself on his elbow; but is still bleary-eyed with sleep. Drowsily, to himself.*) That sleep was very sweet. Now I'll be in high fettle for the day. (*He blesses himself, and concentrates devoutly for a few moments. Then he suddenly realises that he is looking down at something unfamiliar.*) A mattress and a bed in place of rushes! Where am I at all? (*He looks round wonderingly, and sees* UNA *for the first time, standing near the foot of the bed.*)

UNA (*smiling nervously*). You're in Gaisceen's house on the boundary of Galway.

BARTLEY (*sitting up excitedly*). Right enough; And there's the piper

22

hard at it still!

UNA. Gaisceen sent me to rouse you. He reckoned you'd be rested good enough.

BARTLEY (*heartily*). I'm greatly obliged to the two of ye. Now I'm mended up and I'll enjoy the dance in earnest. (*He swings his legs out of the bed, and begins with vigour to put on his shoes. He is a big fellow of swift and powerful movement. In his youth, he might have not been unhandsome in a vigorous masculine way; but now his face is ravaged by shillelagh scars and worn and lined from dawn to dark labour in wind and sun and rain. His clothes are patched and worn. His most striking feature is his great, grave and somewhat wistful eye. He is meditative, at times absent-minded; at all times serious; but his vigour and interestedness save him from any surrender to gloom. His speech and manner are corresponding: grave, but interested and vigorous. His age might be anywhere between thirty and forty.*)

BARTLEY (*tying his shoes*). Let you not delay from the dance. Myself'll be after you directly.

UNA. I'm soon enough going out yet. (*She moves to the table, and pretends to be busy there.*)

BARTLEY (*setting out for the door vigorously, buttoning his jacket as he walks, and not even looking in her direction*). Now we're ready for all.

UNA. (*hastily*). Wait yet; wait a whileen. I have a thing for you here.

BARTLEY (*at the door, turning in surprise*). You have, girl! What's it?

UNA. I wheedled Gaisceen, and look! He gave me choice poteen and oaten bread, and a pipe and tobaccy for you.

(*He comes over, and looks down at the table in surprise.*)

BARTLEY (*half to himself*). No lie in the world you have!

UNA. I was afeared the best'd be gone on you in a while's time when the drinking begins.

BARTLEY (*looking at her for a moment gravely*). No doubt at all you're a very decent young girl; and I'm heartily thankful to you. But the way it is Gaisceen gave me a great 'nough of eatables and drinkables not two hours since. (*He is moving off again.*)

UNA. Still, this heel of poteen'd stir you nicely for the dance.

BARTLEY (*turning back*). You could be right. I'll take it so, if you please. (*He sits down, takes the glass in his hand.*)

UNA. Go easy now, let you, till I pour a sup out for myself. (*She crosses to the other table.*)

23

BARTLEY. No doubt at all you'd be in want of it. The kitchen is that thronged and warm as 'twould train wan for hell.

UNA. 'Tis warm, surely.

BARTLEY (*gravely, taking up his mug*). Your good health, now.

UNA. And yours. (*She takes a small sip. Not so he; he finishes his drink at a draught, and rises.*)

BARTLEY. My thanks to you again. (*He is half-way to door.*)

UNA (*hastily, in alarm*). Wait; let you stop another whileen till we have a conversation.

BARTLEY (*turning in surprise*). Why so? D'ye not want to go dancing a while yet?

UNA (*nervously*). Not yet for a small whileen. . . . I'm fatigued out.

BARTLEY (*coming back and looking at her with his immense seriousness*). I understand you now. 'Tis how you'd like to have company and conversation while you're taking your ease.

UNA (*smiling*). That's it.

BARTLEY. To be sure I'll wait for you. (*He sits down.*) Sure the night is long; the night is long. (*Vigorously.*) It is, girl. (*He sits looking in front of him thoughtfully.*)

UNA (*rising*). Maybe you'd take another heel of poteen?

BARTLEY. No, girl; I'm challenge-fighting the king bully-man of the Barony of Costelloe on St. Brigid's Day, so I'm dipping very little into the poteen till that fight is won.

UNA (*sitting down again*). Very well, so.

(*There is another pause. He is still preoccupied in his grave, and, at the same time, vigorous fashion. There is nothing listless or dejected about this man. So far, he has looked at her only when speaking to her, and then briefly. When he does speak, it is with his grave and natural courtesy, but there is no evidence that she has made any impression upon him, and, obviously, he is making no attempt to make an impression upon her. It is as if he cannot conceive that so young and pretty a girl could have any interest in him, apart from a little curiosity of the gossiping sort. She, for her part, is becoming uneasy about her failure to make any impression. After some hesitation, she sets the conversation going again.*)

UNA. They tell me you have the sway won from all the fighters of Tyrawley.

BARTLEY (*briefly – this is a subject he hears too much of*). This start I had over them all. My father made me extra strong.

UNA. And they tell me you have a great shillelagh.

BARTLEY. Blood and 'ouns! (*Jumping up in alarm.*) I was

24

forgetting. (*He runs to the bed, pulls his shillelagh from under the mattress and brings it back to the other table at the left wall.*) I'm with six months seasoning this in the chimney, swamping it in goose-grease, polishing it, balancing it with lead and all. I'd be nicely pickled if some vagabone had it fetched away on me while I was sleeping.

UNA. You have it grandly dressed all right.

BARTLEY (*taking from his pocket a wrist-thong with a new green tassel at one end*). While you're resting your bones, I'll be putting on this new wrist-thong which was given me for a present by my comrades in Tyrawley. (*He takes off the old wrist-thong and puts on the new one.*)

UNA. Like all men, very apt you get great glee out of fighting.

BARTLEY (*with the matter-of-factness of that age when shillelagh fighting was the national pastime of Ireland*). Shillelagh fighting is fine sport all right. The wan drawback that was in it, every time we'd fight for Errismen, the Errismen'd have the same plan: "Man to man, and three on Bartley!" That's what has my face in tatters the same as you see.

UNA. The lads around here'd think themselves in Heaven if they were fighters as good as you.

BARTLEY (*almost gloomily*). They're the same in Tyrawley. They reckon the finest thing in the world wide is to be the best fighter.

UNA. And isn't that your thinking?

BARTLEY (*vigorously*). 'Tis not my thinking. ... (*Rising, and speaking half to himself, but passionately.*) My thinking is this: the finest thing in this world of God is a nice young girl, a nice young girl – and she to have a true wish for you ... (*Doggedly.*) That's my thinking evermore, and I'll alter it for no man. (*He takes two practice strokes, one backhand and one forehand with the shillelagh; then he contemplates the wrist thong a moment.*) A shade nearer the butt'd be something better. (*He sits on the stool again and proceeds to make the necessary adjustments.*)

UNA. 'Tis a great wonder you never married.

BARTLEY (*vigorously*). I had no ways, girl; I had no ways.

UNA. That's a wonder.

BARTLEY. Well, so long as I'm gabby at all I'm as well to tell you the lot. The eldest brother I had was the best fighter in Tyrawley before myself took the sway in it. But at last he did what no man should do: by himself he fought four hardy men. While he was downing the two facing him, th'other two swung from behind, and pounded out his brains. His widow and batch of children were left, and there wasn't wan but myself to work their patch of land, and pay the rent for them. So for thirteen years hard running I was altogether baulked from marrying.

UNA. And was there ever any girl you had a wish for?

BARTLEY. There was girls in Tyrawley so nice they'd draw the two eyes out of your head. And some of them had a wish for me, too, on account I was the best bully-man, and that time hadn't my youth and looks lost.

UNA. But you couldn't propose for any of them.

BARTLEY. I could not; and wan after another my comrades soon had them swept away ... That's the most grieving thing in this world of God: to have great wish for a girl, but no ways of marrying her, and to see her at the height of her bloom swept in marriage with another. That way I many a time supped sorrow with a long spoon.

UNA. You had misfortune for a comrade so.

BARTLEY (*gravely*). I had that. (*Rises.*) And there's one thing I questioned my brains about many a time. Was it God sent the misfortune to correct me, or was it the devil sent it to tempt me? ... But I'll not find out that till the Judgment Day ... (*He puts the shillelagh back under the mattress again. He sits down at middle table and sets to work filling the pipe with tobacco.*)

UNA. You're freed out at last from working for your brother's family?

BARTLEY. Since the back end of the year. Her eldest lad has enough muscle made to knock out a living for them any more.

UNA. Who brought you the tidings of the ten acres prize for defeating Kithogue?

BARTLEY. Slash Morgan the pedlar brought it. Just the time I was free to go at last, he came peddling to Tyrawley for the first time in many a year. Maybe 'twas God put it into his heart to come. Everywhere Slash goes, his delight is to challenge the best fighter, so he challenged me. We fought it out at the Fair of Cloonkeely and, as soon as he got his senses back again, he up and told me about Kithogue and the ten acres.

UNA. When you have ten acres you'll soon raise yourself up to be well off and well dressed.

BARTLEY. In the run of a few years; but what good will it be to me if I fail to win a nice girl? The girls that are going lately don't want any fellow that's past twenty-three or twenty-five at the most. And look at me: I'm thirty-three all out!

UNA (*genuinely surprised*). Are you that old?

BARTLEY (*grimly*). A cat that'd be as old as me wouldn't go playing with a wisp. And there's another thing that's greatly against me. The girls that's going now are all flocking fast after lively lads with humour and wit in them. And that's where my father wronged me. He made me very strong, but too serious – away too serious.

UNA. Some girls, all right, do prefer lads that'd be humorous.

BARTLEY (*vigorously*). All of them, man; and they like lads to be middling handsome too. That's where I'm lost altogether. (*Brightening up a little.*) Though d'ye know a plan I'm making a trial of with a good while?

UNA. No.

BARTLEY. They reckon the best time to ask Our Saviour for anything is at the Mass just as the Chalice is rising; so with a long time at the Mass, just as the Chalice is rising, I do ask Him to allot for me a nice young wife – wan with a wish for me. He can do it ready and easy; but He won't unless He'll judge it to be for my good, and the good of the world. (*Suddenly the door latch rattles, and* GAISCEEN'S *voice is heard.*)

UNA (*jumping up*). Gaisceen! (*She runs to the door, unbolts it, then runs back to table.* GAISCEEN *can be heard calling loudly above the clamour of that thronged kitchen.*)

GAISCEEN. Mickle Bawn a penny; Sally Beg a penny-farthing; Shawn Holihan a penny-halfpenny. (*Appearing in the doorway carrying a hat.*) Is there any here didn't give yet to the piper?

BARTLEY (*calling out promptly*). Here's wan, Gaisceen! (*He begins to rummage in the lining of his coat.*)

GAISCEEN (*loudly*). Here's two that didn't! Out with yere purses directly. (*He closes the door behind him.*) The finest musicianer since Turlough O'Carolan, so open yere purses wide. (*He comes over, and stands between the pair of them.*)

GAISCEEN (*heartily, clapping* BARTLEY *on the shoulder*). Tell me again: aren't you wishing for a nice girl of a wife?

BARTLEY (*briefly*). That is so. (*He has taken a small knotted cloth from his coat and is busy untying it.*)

GAISCEEN. Well, you needn't go a step further for wan. Here she is within a hen's kick of you. (*He points to* UNA, *who at this moment drops a couple of coppers into the hat.* BARTLEY *looks around quickly, but upon seeing him indicate* UNA, *he quietly ignores both her and the suggestion.*)

BARTLEY (*dropping a couple of coins into the hat*). A penny half penny is the lot I can spare. You see for yourself the rag is very slack with me. (*And he holds up the "rag" for* GAISCEEN'S *inspection.*)

GAISCEEN. I see it well, and never mind that. But what about herself for you? All give in she's the cream of this quarter of the country.

BARTLEY (*again quietly, but reproachfully*). Gaisceen, leave it so. (*He rises, and sets about reknotting the "rag."*)

GAISCEEN. But I'm telling you, man, she's just the girl you're seeking, for she has great wish for you.

BARTLEY (*grimly*). I"m going out to the dance. (*He sets out for the door.*)

GAISCEEN. But, man, 'tis the truth. Girl, didn't you run to me, and your heart panting to know was he wedded, or looking out for a wife?

UNA (*nervously, her eyes cast down*). 'Tis the truth.

BARTLEY (*grimly*). No doubt when ye're young and extra handsome 'tis yere delight to mock a middling old ugly fellow that his father made too serious. But 'tis a sport that gives more stabs to me; so I bid ye good-day. (*He moves to the door.*)

GAISCEEN. Quick, girl!

UNA (*running to stop him*). As true as God, Bartley, I'd give all the world to marry you.

BARTLEY (*turning at the door, his face dark with anger*). Didn't I see you abroadside dancing always with the lad in the green coat, and wasn't I told for true he was your bachelor and ye were on the border of marrying?

GAISCEEN. Sure we're not denying it, man. But then she heard the king fighter of Tyrawley was in the house.

BARTLEY (*startled, the anger vanishing from his face*). Blood and 'ouns! Is it a bully-man she's looking for?

GAISCEEN. That's it. A craze for a hero is stuck in her evermore. Isn't that so, girl?

UNA. 'Tis so.

BARTLEY. And was that why you were lagging here, and digging my mind to the root, about fighting and marriage and all?

UNA (*nervously*). 'Twas, Bartley. . . .

BARTLEY. 'Tis past believing. (*He strides up to her sternly.*) Girl, let me look into the ball of your eye. (*He tips back her head and looks down into her eyes sternly for several seconds; then his expression changes to wonder and joy.*) No doubt in the world! You're as honest as the day! There's no lie in you! (*He turns to* GAISCEEN, *his voice husky with emotion.*) Gaisceen, at last! − as nice a young girl as ever a man got! – and she with a true wish for me!

GAISCEEN. What did I tell you?

(*But* BARTLEY *has not waited for any reply. With his two hands to head he wanders across the room like a man dazed. They watch him, she with a mixture of uneasiness and remorse, but* GAISCEEN *with great relief and joy.* BARTLEY *comes to the chest, and sits on the edge of it.*)

BARTLEY (*looking up at last gravely*). Gaisceen, whenever you want anything from Our Saviour, ask Him at the Mass when the Chalice is rising. Praised be the Hand of God.

GAISCEEN. And she declares she'll wed you no matter if you fail to win the ten acres.

BARTLEY (*almost fiercely*). Is it me not to whip Kithogue now? (*He runs to the bed, pulls out the shillelagh and brandishes it fiercely.*) Is it Kithogue to stand long against my undersnouting stroke, or my back-hand? 'Twill be like a fight between a hawk and a thrush!

GAISCEEN (*delighted*). More power to you, Bartley Dowd! And now myself must fetch the piper his dues. (*He sets out for the door.*)

BARTLEY. Well do, for I have a hat-full of things to say to herself.

GAISCEEN (*opening the door, and calling out, hat in hand*). Bartley Dowd from Tyrawley a penny halfpenny! (*He goes, closing the door behind him, and* BARTLEY *comes up to* UNA *apologetically.*)

BARTLEY. I made you afeard that time when I took two holds of your head.

UNA. Not you. (*She is smiling, but nervously, there is something almost overpowering in the vitality of the man now that he is fully roused.*)

BARTLEY. The way it was that time between doubting and hoping, the soul was shaken in me. But let you not be afeard I'd ever use rough hands. In shillelagh fighting I'm fiery; but in the house, you'll see, I'll be as kind as a woman. And wait now till I show you a thing I have. (*He throws his shillelagh on the bed and takes down a heavy but somewhat battered cloak from the wall.*)

BARTLEY. They tell me your father is the same as myself, as poor as a crow, and couldn't afford you a penny fortune. No matter; if we haven't costs for a blanket itself, still and all the frost'll never pinch us. Feel the weight of this.

29

UNA (*weighting it*).'Tis as heavy as a coachman's cloak.

BARTLEY. A coachman in Tyrawley gave it to me for saving him from robber men. While we have this, we'll never famish if we can afford no blanket itself. (*He restores it to its peg.*)

BARTLEY. And maybe your father, like some, is priding out of his blood, and wants no son-in-law only wan that'd be from the real good stock. Well, if he's so, all right. (*He moves left, then turns again.*) I know my genealogy, and 'tis wan would suit him. My family were chief fighters from the O'Dowds of Tyrawley, and were captains over hundreds when Ireland was in its hey-day. . . . (GAISCEEN *runs in, leaving the door open behind him.*)

GAISCEEN. Bad tidings for ye! – the worst in the world! His honour's bailiff tells me Master Caesar wants the loan of herself!

UNA. He does! Gaisceen, I'll not go to him. (*She runs to the far side of the table, where she shelters behind* BARTLEY.)

BARTLEY (*dismayed, though surprisingly calm in the circumstances*). Blood and 'ouns! And us on the brink of marrying!

GAISCEEN (*very loudly, as if amazed at this*). What's that? Is it going marrying? (*To* BOORLA, *who has just entered and closed the door behind him.*) Boorla, d'ye hear this? Herself and this lad have a match made!

BOORLA (*coming up with his friendliest smile*). What harm? (*To* BARTLEY.) You can have her agian, to be sure, as soon as Master Caesar is done with her.

BARTLEY (*urgently*). But can't you take wan of the girls abroadside that's idle presently and won't mind? You know yourself 'tisn't lucky to postpone a wedding.

BOORLA (*smiling, but inflexibly*). 'Tis herself was picked, so no other'll do. Very apt he'll not keep her long.

BARTLEY (*turning to her sorrowfully*). Una, girl, I wouldn't wish this for many a round guinea. Still, he'll maybe not keep you passing a few days, so you should humour him. 'Tis always safest to keep to the west side of the gentry.

UNA (*in consternation*). Is that all you care about me? Or d'ye know what he wants me for at all?

BARTLEY (*blankly*). For task-work? What else?

UNA. 'Tis not. Tis for tallywoman.

BARTLEY. What's that? (*He stares at her.*)

BOORLA (*drawing his shillelagh from under his coat*). Master Caesar is a thoroughbred gentleman. He'll fill her fists with bright guineas. He'll give her a fortune for you.

BARTLEY (*turning to* BOORLA). Does he want to ruin her?
BOORLA (*genuinely sorry to see a great fighter court destruction*). I
have six great wipers, their shillelaghs in their fists. Any man
that stands against Master Caesar they'll slash him to death like
a rat in a haggard. (*Suddenly* BARTLEY *leaps to his feet, and
backs away from* BOORLA. *He drags the chair by its back, and
swings it into the air as a useful weapon against* BOORLA'S
shillelagh.)
GAISCEEN (*as if horrified*). Sit down, Bartley! Have sense, man.
BARTLEY (*between his teeth, fiercely but not loudly*). Hi for Bartley!
Hi for Tyrawley! (*He retreats to the bed, never once taking his
eyes off* BOORLA.)
BOORLA (*shouting*). Hi for French! Hi for Kilmacreena! (*His eye on
BARTLEY likewise, he retreats rapidly to the door.* BARTLEY
*arrives at the bed, throws the chair into it, and quickly pulls his
shillelagh from under the mattress. As he does so,* BOORLA
opens the door, roars out.) Shillelaghs, men, quick; and clear the
kitchen out. Hi for French! Hi for Kilmacreena! (*He runs out,
closing the door behind him.* GAISCEEN *runs to the door, peeps
through the crack,* BARTLEY, *however, has paid no attention to*
BOORLA'S *final exit. He prepares for battle with a silent, fierce
efficiency. He peels off his jacket, tightens his belt, and puts on
his old battered hat.*)
GAISCEEN (*at the door*). They're clearing the kitchen out for yere
fight. They're putting all out. . . . Oh, murther! Owen is refusing
to go! He has the tongs snapped up! Murther! Mickle More
stretched him senseless with a forehand blow.
UNA (*running towards the door the minute he mentions* OWEN).
Owen! Owen! Save him, let ye. They'll have him killed!
BARTLEY (*in a voice of thunder*). Come back, girl. Come back here.
(*She turns.*) Go a-hiding behind that bed till this fight is over.
Don't stir from it at all. (*There is no questioning that fierce eye
and tone; she obeys hurriedly.* BARTLEY *is nearly ready. He
takes his jacket by the end of the sleeve and, drawing it after him
along the floor, advances to the middle of the room with the
shillelagh in his right hand.*)
GAISCEEN. They're making two ranks across the kitchen. (*Coming
over to* BARTLEY.) You're ready?
BARTLEY (*briefly*). The wrist-thong. (*He holds out his right fist and
the shillelagh to* GAISCEEN, *who ties the wrist-thong of the
shillelagh around* BARTLEY'S *wrist.*)
GAISCEEN (*apologetically*). Bartley, I must let on to strike a blow

for my landlord.

BARTLEY. To be sure.

GAISCEEN. I'll let on to charge you now, and you'll let on to stun me against the ground with wan stroke.

BARTLEY. Very well. The undersnouting stroke.

GAISCEEN. Right. I'll be ready for that. (*He takes up the stool and runs to the door roaring "Hi for French! Hi for Kilmacreena!" He flings open the door, shouts out "In men, till we powder his bones. Hi for* GAISCEEN*!" He runs around the table and charges at* BARTLEY *from the left.* BARTLEY *swings his shillelagh groundwards and thence upwards again like lightning in the undersnouting stroke.* GAISCEEN *is ready and holds the stool at chin level in anticipation. Shillelagh meets stool leg with a crack, and* GAISCEEN *staggers and falls into the bed, howling like a desperately injured man.* BARTLEY *bounds to the door, draws himself up, and surveys his opponents a moment fiercely.*)

BARTLEY (*loudly*). Hi for Bartley! Hi for Tyrawley!

THE PRESSGANG (*in thundering unison*). Hi for French! Hi for Kilmacreena!

BARTLEY. Faugh a ballagh!

(*And with the word, charges fiercely, and the battle begins. The uproar is terrific; yells of pain and fury, the cracking of the shillelagh, and forearms and skulls.* BOORLA'S *voice is heard – "Round about him, men. Kill him from behind! Other-hand him, Mickle!" "Ooch!" There is a howl of pain, and a crash as the first man goes down. "Mickle is down! Into him, men!" "Blacken him!" "Stun his elbows!" "Knock his life out."* GAISCEEN *grabs some big potatoes from the corner and throws them at the Pressgang every time their backs are turned.*)

GAISCEEN (*excitedly, but not loudly*). Good, Tyrawley, give them stick. Draw fast raps on them.

UNA (*running out from behind the bed*). How is he fairing?

GAISCEEN. He's greatly cut. He's all blobbed with blood, but he has two of them down. By the elevens! God save us, he's giving ground! They have him flocked in a corner. He's done!

(*The shouting offstage reaches a triumphant climax. "He's failing! We have him! After him, lads! Kill him against the wall! Hi for French! Hi for Kilmacreena!"*)

GAISCEEN (*turning away sadly*). Don't look, girl. The poor fellow'll get a dirty fate.

(*Suddenly there is a roar of "Hi for Bartley!" "Hi for Tyrawley!" followed by a crack, a howl and a crash, as a man goes down.*

Immediately afterwards there is a second howl of pain and terror. "I'm kilt – save me!" and a crash as a second man goes down, followed by another bull roar of "Hi for Tyrawley!")

GAISCEEN (*in amazement*). Two more down! He's breaching through them again.

UNA. God be praised, he is! (BOORLA *is heard "Stand yere ground, men. We'll whip him yet. Hi for French!" Another voice: "Spare me!" "Ouch! I'm done."*)

GAISCEEN (*awestruck*). He's driving them before him like sheep!

UNA. He is! (*She approaches the door.*)

(BOORLA'S *voice is heard – "We're bet. Run, Thady, for your life."*)

GAISCEEN (*sharply*). Watch out, girl! (*She turns to fly, but too late.* BOORLA *runs in followed by a battered, bloody and ferocious* BARTLEY. *With a roar of "Hi for Tyrawley!" he swings up his shillelagh for the finishing blow. But, quick as lightning,* BOORLA *drops his shillelagh, seizes* UNA, *and swings her in front of him, ducking his head behind hers.*)

BARTLEY (*fiercely, his shillelagh aloft*). Down, woman; down to the ground. (*Suddenly* BOORLA *lifts* UNA *off her feet and swings her against* BARTLEY *with such force that he staggers. Before he can recover his balance,* BOORLA *runs past him, and out the door.*)

BARTLEY. Stand aside, woman, till I put him into eternity. (*He runs after* BOORLA, *roaring, "Hi for Tyrawley!"*)

GAISCEEN (*sitting on the floor with an expression of awe on his face*). 'Tisn't as strong as a man he is, but as strong as a stallion horse! Their shillelaghs were no good to them, for his made dust of them above on their heads.

UNA. I can hear no stir from them. (*She advances cautiously towards the door.*)

GAISCEEN (*rising*). And for quickness, too, he flogs all the bully-men ever I seen. The wind from his blows'd give you a cold for a week.

UNA (*peeping out*). Six of them are stretched back, and not a single move or stir. God save us! Look at Owen, and he soaking in his blood!

GAISCEEN. Oh, murther! I had him forgotten! Ready the bed, child. (*He runs out, and returns carrying* OWEN, *who is senseless and bleeding from the head. He lays him on the bed.*)

GAISCEEN. Only stunned he is. He'll be as right as nine-pence.

UNA. Are you sure the death isn't in him?

GAISCEEN (*feeling* OWEN'S *skull with practised fingers*). His skull is

33

nowhere softened. 'Tis sound as bell metal.

UNA. Thanks be to God! (*Then agitatedly.*) Gaisceen, Bartley's blood is wild now from the fighting. I daren't tell him yet how we deceived him.

GAISCEEN (*alarmed*). Let you not tell him at all till he has you brought across the river to Blake's country, where you'll be safe from Caesar's dogs and guns.

UNA. Easy! This is him coming! (*She runs over to beside the bed, and a moment later* BARTLEY *appears in the doorway, wild-eyed, and blood-spattered. One hand trails his jacket, the other swings his shillelagh.*)

BARTLEY (*fiercely*). Gaisceen, has Caesar any more ruffians that might fancy a while's skelping with Bartley?

GAISCEEN (*humouring him*). Why so, man?

BARTLEY. Go out, and tell them Bartley'll be rejoiced to see them. Tell them he isn't threshed half good enough yet. (*He throws his jacket across the chair, and begins to tighten his belt, in preparation for further battle.*) Go directly, Gaisceen.

GAISCEEN. I will, I will. (*He makes no move to go, though.*) Did you catch Boorla?

BARTLEY. I lost him in Caesar's wood, else he'd steal girls no more. (*He strides up to* OWEN, *looks down at him sternly.*) Your bachelor. . . . Is he badly?

UNA (*nervously*). He's only stunned, Gaisceen reckons.

BARTLEY (*grimly but sincerely*). Good! The Pressgang ruffians, I must view them over. (*He strides out to the kitchen, shillelagh in hand.*)

UNA (*in sudden agitation*). Gaisceen, how'll I ever tell him I tricked and made a fool of him before all the country? And himself as gallant and honest a man as ever buckled a shoe!

GAISCEEN (*solemnly*). If you'll be said by Gaisceen, you'll never tell him at all, but marry him in place of Owen.

UNA (*staring*). Marry him! Gaisceen, are you away from your right mind?

GAISCEEN (*vigorously*). Why would I? That man is the king fighter of Connacht. He'd give you a son that could murder the country. (*He goes to the door.*) How are they, Bartley?

BARTLEY (*coming in*). None of them are suffering death, whatever.

GAISCEEN (*urgently*). Ye'll want to make yere ground off across the river. Boorla'll have Master Caesar told, and he'll put his horse under him and come against ye with sword and gun. (*He takes a rope from a peg on the wall.*)

BARTLEY. Then we must cross the river. The shillelagh is no match for the gun. (*He takes down his top-coat and hat from the wall.*) We'll roll our cloaks around two flags of stones, and throw them across.

GAISCEEN (*offering the rope*). Tie an end of this around your waist, and if the flood stumbles you itself, the lads'll pull you back safe. Then you can draw herself across.

BARTLEY. That way she'll be safe. (*He ties the rope around his waist.*

GAISCEEN (*to* MAURA, *who enters at this moment*). He's on the bed beyond. (MAURA *crosses to the bed, and looks at her patient.*)

BARTLEY (*coming over to her earnestly*). You're going minding the poor lad for us?

MAURA (*quietly*). That is so.

BARTLEY. God spare you the health. You're a decent girl. (*Turning to* GAISCEEN.) The hard tidings that she's to wed me instead, give him no wrinkle of it till he's well improved. The poor lad might lose heart and make a bad stand against the death. (*He comes back to the door, takes up his bundle, overcoat and the rope in one arm, while his right fist carries the shillelagh, free and ready for action.*) I'm ready whatever. (*He looks at* UNA *inquiringly.*)

UNA. I'm ready, Bartley. (BARTLEY *goes to the door, followed by* UNA. *He looks out carefully, but there is no one in sight.*)

BARTLEY (*turning*). Good luck to ye now till the Pattern Day. (*They go out.*)

GAISCEEN (*calling after him*). If the river is drowning ye, let ye be sure to say, "God is good, and the Divil himself isn't bad." Then neither'll be too hard on ye, maybe. (*Comes in again.*) I was the father of a plan tonight, and I'm afraid 'twill come out bad at finish.

MAURA. What was it?

GAISCEEN. She let on she'd marry him so as he'd save her from the Pressgang, and now she must make the truth known to him some way.

MAURA. You didn't get chance to draw down my name to him?

GAISCEEN. No; but maybe another time I will. (*Putting on his old battered hat and taking his shillelagh from under the bed.*) Now I must leave you and set off for French Hall. I have a plan made and it might halt Master Caesar from going after them.

MAURA. Let you flit away fast, or Caesar'll be gone after them already.

GAISCEEN (*going to the door*). I'll not take while a cat'd be licking his ear. God bless ye, now. (*He hurries out.*)

MAURA. Good luck, Gaisceen. (*She looks at her patient a moment, goes to the table, and brings back the mug of poteen* BARTLEY *had not time to touch. She is holding this to his lips carefully when the curtain falls.*)

CURTAIN

ACT TWO

Scene 1

SCENE. *A hill-side on the County Galway side of the river.*

TIME. *Twenty-four hours later.*

It is a fine starry winter's night, about nine o'clock. One end of a squat, mud-walled cabin occupies the extreme right of the stage. Its one and only door is in the gable wall. At one time apparently the cabin had a second room or kitchen, but all that remains of it now is five or six feet of crumbling back wall. The nook which this wall makes with the gable has been roughly roofed with branches and scraws. A turf fire stands in the outer part of the nook, and several rough stools, which are simply blocks of wood, are in the inner part. Some potatoes are heaped on the ground beside the fire. By the light of the fire, UNA is mending a patch in BARTLEY'S cloak. From time to time she looks towards the left into the darkness anxiously. Suddenly the sound of rapid footsteps is heard, and KITTY runs around the end of the wall and comes to the fire carrying a pot. She is a lively, bouncing coquettish young girl with a humerous bantering way about her. She is coquettishly be-ribboned, but her present homespuns cannot compare with the more expensive tallywomen's clothes of UNA and MAURA.

KITTY (*merrily*). Here's another loan of the pot to ye to boil the spuds for yere breakfasts. (*She puts the pot on the fire.*) I have water in it and all, so now amn't I good?
UNA. Kitty, you're as good as ninety-nine. (*She rises and hangs BARTLEY'S cloak on a peg in the wall.*)
KITTY. Let ye boil them to-night, then ye'll only have to warm them in the morning. (*She builds the fire around the pot carefully.*)
UNA. That's what we'll do.

37

(*She goes on her knees beside the fire, and the two of them proceed to throw the potatoes into the pot.*)

KITTY. Where's Bartley?

UNA. He's gone viewing the river to see is the flood reduced any piece since the morning.

KITTY. Tell me here: did you make Bartley the wiser yet that you're going marrying Owen, and only promised himself so as he'd fight for you?

UNA. No, Kitty; I didn't mention a word about that big, little or small, I'll not tell him till after the Pattern for fear it might upset him, and lose him his fight against Kithogue.

KITTY (*chuckling*). But if he's believing you'll marry him, as sure as the day he'll set into making love to you at last. (*She sits down again.*)

UNA. He will not, Kitty, and I'll tell you why. I'm behaving very shy with him, not meeting his eyes, or having much to say about marriage, or such things at all.

KITTY. All reckon Bartley is the king fighter of Connacht and as decent a man as ever stepped it, moreover. They reckon you have poor taste in your mouth if you'd prefer a young skelp of a lad such as Owen Fenigan.

UNA (*earnestly, and even a little troubled*). God's truth Kitty, I'm fully knowing Bartley at last, and I'd like him greatly for company, or conversation,or story telling – or for marriage, too, maybe.

KITTY. Still, 'tis Owen you're to wed.

UNA. Owen ventured his life for me, too, and he'll surely lose his holding of land for striking out against his landlord's men. How could I desert him when he ruined himself for me? And my hand was pledged to him first, moreover.

KITTY (*nodding*). There's weight in what you say all right. . . . Which is yourself or Bartley to stop up watching to-night?

UNA. I was craving him to let me watch to-night, and let himself sleep within, but he wouldn't agree at all.

KITTY. Between watching all night and working in the day, he'll not be fit to draw a herring out with the tongs.

UNA. I told him so sure, but "With the first dawning of the day," he said, "I'll rouse you with a shout that'd bring deaf cows out of a wood. Then you can watch out, and myself'll sleep sound till noon."

KITTY. Well, wance he has a few hour's sleep he'll be all right. 'Tisn't much work he has to do to earn yere day's 'nough of spuds. (*She rises.*)

UNA. Are you off, Kitty?

KITTY. The dark night is the likeliest time they'll come against ye, and 'twould never do me to lose the life, and good people so scarce. (*She skips to the left and looks towards the river again.*) The minute ye hear any plunges from the river, let ye flit off, for the Pressgang with their guns 'd give ye the life of a spud in the mouth of a pig. (*She crosses towards the village.*)

UNA. Good-night, Kitty.

KITTY. God be good to ye. (*She runs off. UNA continues sewing for a minute or so. Then suddenly she starts, looks towards the river, jumps to her feet, runs around the corner of the cabin, and flattens herself against the wall. In a moment, BARTLEY comes in, walking briskly, and carrying his shillelagh. He seems surprised and disappointed at not finding her.*)

BARTLEY. Una, are you gone sleeping for the night?

UNA (*running to him with great joy*). Bartley! 'Tis yourself is in it!

BARTLEY (*surprised*). 'Tis to be sure.

UNA (*checking herself*). You were that long as I grew afeard.... How is the river?

BARTLEY (*throwing down his shillelagh*). The flood is reducing; still, no wan could cross tonight. (*He sits down on one of the stools, and holds his hands out to the blaze. He is much as in the last Act; still serious and vigorously thoughtful.*)

UNA (*sitting down likewise*). We're safe for tonight so – unless Caesar'd cross over by Frenchbridge.

BARTLEY. If he comes against us by Frenchbridge, he'd likely be seen by the whole country, and that'd put him in danger from the law. The wan place a gentleman can do openly what he likes is on his own property and to his own tenants.

UNA (*smiling with relief*). Maybe in God we're safe enough so, till the flood goes down. (*She rises.*)

BARTLEY (*quickly*). Are you going sleeping?

UNA (*returning with his cloak*). No, Bartley, 'tis early yet, and I'd fall off asleep easier if you'd put my mind in good cheer first with a story. (*She sits down, and resumes the mending of his cloak.*)

BARTLEY (*pleased in his grave way*). No lie; the stories are a great warrant to banish trouble. I heard th' oul' men to say how in the bad times when the Irish were losing every war they couldn't put up with the world at all only they had the story-telling every night.

39

UNA. Wance you'd take the habit of them, you'd be awful lost for them.

BARTLEY. I'll tell you wan that's something shorter than last night's. 'Twill only take while two fires'll be wearing. But (*Very gravely.*) before I dip into it I should tell you thing I heard today. . . .

UNA (*uneasily*). What's it?

BARTLEY (*looking at her*). They reckon Caesar never troubled a married woman yet, and your best chance to be safe is to marry me directly.

UNA (*alarmed*). They told you that?

BARTLEY (*watching her gravely*). Without no lie, they did.

UNA (*agitated*). But, Bartley, we couldn't marry that quick. We aren't above wan day acquainted yet.

BARTLEY (*gravely*). You're too shy of me yet for marriage so, I could see that well. No matter; on account you have a true wish for me the shyness'll steal away from you at last; never fear.

UNA (*avoiding his eyes*). In the run of a few days . . . .

BARTLEY. A good piece longer maybe, and if it takes a fair while itself, still I'd sooner wait, for 'tis well known that the hardest work in all the world is making love to a girl against her will.

UNA (*very ill at ease*). We should follow what the rest of the couples do; be friends a while first.

BARTLEY (*eagerly*). That's it. Friends a whileen first; lovers a whileen more; then marriage at last. . . . But, Una girl, you must make known to me when your shyness is gone at last, and you'd like us to be lovers. (*He takes a coin from his pocket.*) Here's a money piece my grandfather had ever; it went astray on the King of Spain's men in the wars long ago. (*He puts it into her hand.*) When you'd like us to be lovers at last, you need say no word, only hand it back, and Bartley'll know. Won't you be sure and do that?

UNA (*smiling a little at this*). I will, Bartley.

BARTLEY (*vigorously*). Well, do, and now that all is put right, I can rattle ahead with the story. In the good times long ago, before the Divil pelted the English villains at Ireland, there was a king in it, and he had no family only the Queen and wan young lad of a son. It fell out wan year that the Queen got into diseases, so the doctors came, and judged her body, and said she had no longer to go, When she heard that, she gave a sigh that near broke wan of the rafters, and called the King and said to him, "I'm going making the long journey now; and I'll die happy if you'll promise you'll bring no stepmother in till my son is hardy enough to mind himself." So the King promised her he never would marry till his son'd be twenty-wan years, and he made a faithful vow there by the bedside to the Father, the Son and the Holy Ghost, the Three that never got vexed. With that the Queen was content, and tussled no more, but went directly out of the world.

(*He has scarcely finished the first paragraph of the story when the head of a man appears around the end of the wall almost at* BARTLEY'S *elbow. Quickly the rest of him comes into view. He is a man of fifty-five to sixty, a wild unearthly looking creature, skeleton thin, haggard, stooped, ragged, with a vast tattered cloak swinging about him. One eye is half closed through some defect or other; his graying hair and beard are long and wild as that of a rambling madman; his movements are spasmodic and unsteady. A man less favoured by nature and fortune one could hardly imagine, yet his whole aspect and behaviour is one of the wildest, most touchy and arrogant pride. In one hand he carries something or other in an old dirty coarse linen bag.*)

RORY (*jumping in fiercely*). The story of the King of Ireland's son and the eight-legged dog! My father has that story as good as you. (UNA *leaps up with a cry of fear. But* BARTLEY *merely turns round quite calmly, shillelagh, however, as always in hand.*)

BARTLEY (*mildly*). God save you.

RORY (*fiercely*). D'ye know who I am, Bartley Dowd?

BARTLEY. Well, not to tell you a lie, I don't.

RORY (*with crazy pride*). I'm Rory Commons, the son of the chief composer of Ireland.

BARTLEY (*eagerly*). Is it Blind Cormac's son?

RORY. Who else? (*peremptorily.*) Let me in that seat, Bartley Dowd. (*He throws the bag on the ground beside it.*)

BARTLEY (*very willingly*). Here you are, and welcome. (*He gives his seat to* RORY *and sits on a vacant stool on* RORY'S *left.* UNA *returns to her seat on* RORY'S *right.*)

RORY (*fiercely*). Have ye any spuds to put in my bag? (*He lifts the lid off the pot and looks in.*) Ye must put a share of them in my bag, or my father'll compose a song that'll scold ye out of the country.

BARTLEY (*alarmed*). No, Rory, he'll have no occasion. There's three hatfuls of spuds in the cabin within, and all you want you can have, with a heart and a half.

RORY (*glaring dimly at him*). Rory'll take the lot. Three hatfuls is a shabby share enough for the chief composer of Ireland.... A

41

shabby hansel it is. (*He snatches up the bag and stumbles into the cabin, muttering to himself.*)

BARTLEY. Is he Cormac's son for sure?

UNA. I doubt so. Their cabin is within a gunshot of this townland. Cormac's big age has him as weak as a June robin, and he isn't fit to go travelling through the country no more; but Rory scours east and west with his bag, and none dare refuse him, so they're not getting hunger.

BARTLEY (*gravely*). If I was suffering death with the hunger still and all I wouldn't refuse a composer. When a composer throws a slur on you in a song, 'tis remembered against all belonging to you till the end of the world.

RORY (*re-emerging, grumbling loudly*). Three poor hatfuls! Still, I'll do with it. My father'll not scold ye this time. Rory'll see to that. (*He throws his bag on the ground, sits down and takes out his snuff-box.*)

BARTLEY (*sincerely*). There'll be no day but I'll earn something above our needs of spuds, so let ye not be short.

RORY (*taking snuff fiercely*). The chief composer of Ireland should have enough for eating and drinking and spending and giving away so as to keep his spirits high. Isn't that so, Bartley Dowd? (*He offers* BARTLEY *his snuff-box.*)

BARTLEY. To be sure, Rory. (*He takes a pinch of snuff affably.*) How is Cormac this while back?

(RORY *leaps up, then confronts* BARTLEY *in a towering rage.*)

RORY. For why do you ask how he is? Like more are you longing for him to die so as you could take vengeance on Rory for all?

BARTLEY (*astonished*). Not me, Rory.

RORY. Let this knowledge to ye. My father is to leave me his gift when he's dying, then I'll be a composer as good as him, and away better. Any man that looks crooked at me then I'll compose a song against him that'll rank him for ever with Judas that's in Hell.

BARTLEY. Rory, you have judged us wrong. 'Twas never in us to grudge his share to a composer, or to wan belonging to him.

RORY (*grimly*). And would ye say when I amn't a composer yet I should go working in the fields the same as I was an ass or a man?

BARTLEY. No so, Rory. Our thinking is you should idle your body so as you'll have long life as a composer.

RORY (*to* UNA). And is that your thinking?

UNA. 'Tis, Rory. A man that's to be a composer should do no work.

RORY (*Sternly, but much mollified*). Very well, then; I'll give ye yere pardons this time. (*He re-seats himself, and begins to take snuff again.*) In my heyday I very near did go working. Wan time – when I was to go soldiering for King Louis, and another time when a widow with six acres was wishing to marry me – she could get no better on account she had two humps on her back the same as a dog that'd be licking a pot. But always Cormac'd say to me, "Rory, don't leave me, don't desert your poor blind father, and when I'm dying I'll leave you my gift as good and as fresh as the day God of Heaven gave it to myself." (*Looking around at them sternly.*) So his word is pledged, and, if he broke that on his dying bed, he was in Hell directly, and spread-legs on a red beam in it.

BARTLEY (*reassuringly*). The divil a fear of Cormac to betray you. They tell me he's the fairest man of the day, only not to vex him.

RORY (*bitterly*). Bartley Dowd, my father is not a fair man. He's with ten years badly, and hundreds of times God sent him enough sickness that'd give him full liberty to die. But evermore he's refusing the death. Right well he knows I'll make a better composer on account I have sight, and seen the wonders and sceneries of the world, so he's keeping the gift from me as long as he can. (*He resumes his seat gloomily.*)

BARTLEY. D'ye reckon so?

RORY. He's bedsick presently with a sickness that'd slay ten men; but he'll not give in; not him! He'll stagger out for ten years more, then myself'll be a stale oul' man, and too decayed to make a great composer. He knows that well, that's why he's refusing his death.... (UNA *has been anxiously watching a chance to get a word in, and at this point the chance presents itself.*)

UNA (*quickly*). Rory, what were you at to-day?

RORY (*gloomily looking into the fire*). The same as every day; swapping talk for potatoes.

UNA. But where were you?

RORY. In Caesar French's country up and down a-through the hills and hollows.

UNA (*eagerly*). In French's country! Then maybe you seen Gaisceen?

RORY. I did that. (*Taking a bottle from his coat pocket and uncorking it.*) 'Tis good poteen, too, up to his best. (*Handing it to* BARTLEY *commandingly.*) Put the lot down into your belly, Bartley Dowd. My father has full and plenty of everything.

43

BARTLEY. Ye're very decent, like all true composers; still, I'll leave a small drop in the bottom for Cormac (*Unperceived, he corks the bottle without tasting it, and slips it back into the pocket of* RORY'S *coat.*)

UNA (*anxiously*). Rory, did Gaisceen give you any tidings?

RORY (*drowsily*). I believe so.

UNA. What were they?

RORY. He ses he'd be at the brink of the river aout this time with tidings for ye. (BARTLEY *and* UNA *jump to their feet on the instant.*)

BARTLEY. He did!

UNA. Where did he say?

RORY. Just opposite the lone bush, and, if he wasn't there, not to wait, for 'twould be a sure sign the Pressgang were thereabouts with their muskets and blunderbusses, watching for a shot at ye.

BARTLEY. Let you stop here so. You mightn't be nimble enough at dodging the shots.

UNA. D'ye think, Bartley?

RORY (*rounding upon her*). Take your seat, woman. Gaisceen ses you were by no means to go.

BARTLEY. I'll bring you full tidings. I'll be there and back while you'd be striking your two hands together. (*He hurries out, shillelagh in hand.*)

RORY (*taking snuff fiercely*). Ten years time! What good'll the gift be to me then? And my strength getting a little exhausted already!

UNA. Rory, did you hear any tittle about Owen Fenigan?

RORY. Master Caesar has him under lock and key in the lowest cellar he has for fear he'd steal you from Bartley Dowd, and run away with you to a far district where Caesar couldn't trace you.

UNA. God save us! Poor Owen!

RORY (*sternly*). Never think you have all fooled. They're doubting well you only promised Bartley so as he'd fight for you.

UNA. Ssh! Take care would Bartley hear you. I never told him yet.

RORY (*fiercely*). You aren't to tell him at all. You're to marry him directly, for until you do Owen Fenigan'll be barrelled in the cellar with no comrades only the blackness and the rats and the cold.

UNA (*horrified*). God preserve him! But are you sure Caesar'd free him out wance I wedded Bartley?

RORY. Why wouldn't he, woman? Doesn't he know well Owen Fenigan wouldn't go stealing a wedded woman?

44

UNA. What did Gaisceen say?

RORY. To wed Bartley Dowd, for Owen'll never be freed out till you do.

UNA (*slowly*). It appears it musn't be for me ever to wed Owen Fenigan, so I'll wed Bartley Dowd now the soonest day I can.

RORY (*gloomily looking at the ground*). Your wish is for young Fenigan still?

UNA. I have great wish for Bartley too, but I was putting him off evermore before now.

RORY (*rising, and taking up his bag*). If my father dies in time, I'll compose a song for yere wedding. But he's refusing the death this time too. He has no more regard for God's Will than the Serpent that doomed Eve. (*He stumbles out right, going in the direction of the village.*)

UNA (*calling after him*). I hope your father dies soon. (*She takes the Spanish coin from her pocket, considers and nods her head slowly. She transfers her stool besides* BARTLEY'S, *finds this too daring, retreats a yard or so and, finally, halves the distance again. She has the coin in her hand, and is considering how best to return it, when she hears* BARTLEY'S *footsteps, and hides it hastily.*)

BARTLEY. Gaisceen isn't in it presently whatever. The Pressgang must be abroad, or the water bailiff.

UNA (*smiling*). No matter. Sure we'll meet Gaisceen at the Pattern in two days.

BARTLEY. To be sure we will. . . . Rory wouldn't wait?

UNA. He would not. Off he flew like a fly from a butter pot.

BARTLEY. Every year longing for the gift, and never getting it, have his wits cracked at last, or very near it, the poor fellow.

UNA. He's punished surely for want of the gift.

BARTLEY (*sitting at the fire again*). Will I rattle ahead with the story?

UNA (*hastily*). No, Bartley; the night is too far reduced now for starting a story.

BARTLEY. Please yourself. Maybe you'd sooner go sleeping directly?

UNA. Not for another small whileen.

BARTLEY. Suit yourself. (*He lifts the lid off the pot, and looks in.*) Last year's spuds had more fight in them. A few minutes boiling, and they'd be throwing their jackets off. (*He replaces the lid, and pokes the fire vigorously.*)

UNA (*nervously*). Bartley. (*He is so busy that he does not hear her, so she tries again a little more loudly.*) Bartley!

BARTLEY (*turning in surprise*). What's it?

UNA (*smiling, with a mixture of shyness and nervousness*). I have

45

thing for you. (*She take his hand, places the coin in it, closes his hand again, and looks away shyly.*)

BARTLEY (*opening his hand, then with astonishment*). The Spaniard's money! So soon! (*He jumps to his feet in his excitement.*) Una, girl, d'ye mean this for true? (*As her eyes are still cast down, but smilingly, he puts his hand under her chin and raises her head. Then immediately he is overjoyed.*) You do then! 'Tis in your countenance. You need say no word – no word at all. Bartley'll do all. (*He transfers his stool to beside hers.*) And I was afeard your shyness might stand for a long month yet! God be praised! (*Then apologetically.*) But this I must tell you first about pleasing girls; 'tis the same as every other trade, a man wants practise at it, and myself had none on account hard fortune blighted me in my youthful days. Still, I'll do the best I can. (*She remains half turned away from him, and still smiling. He considers her and his course of action gravely for a moment or two.*)

BARTLEY. I understand ye do all like this much whatever.... (*He puts his arm round her waist carefully.*) Maybe that's too tight? Tell me the truth out: is it?

UNA (*smiling at him*). No, Bartley.

BARTLEY (*gravely*). Maybe you'd like it a piece tighter?

UNA (*smiling, and more at her ease now*). Please yourself, Bartley.

BARTLEY. Is it please myself, and my arm extra strong? Not me. I'll be ever careful not to hurt you with too much strength.... But d'ye know what'd please me greatly, and do you no hurt?

UNA (*shyly*). What, Bartley?

BARTLEY (*gravely*). This, what I'll show you. (*He raises her head a little, and looks into her eyes, while she looks into his.*) Th' oul' lads that rose up in the bad times when land and money were more valued than women in Ireland'd always reckon you can see nothing in a woman's eye, only her eye, and not herself. But they were as far out as a lighthouse there. If a fellow'll look close in her eyes he'll surely see her mind darting here and there, odd times when she'll forget herself.... I never seen your eyes so soft before, as soft as water, I declare.... And I never felt your cheeks before.... They're as smooth as new silk. My curse on the fighting that has my own face crusted enough to bleed you!

UNA (*smiling*). Not it, Bartley. 'Tis priding out of your wounds I'll be, for they're showing for true how you fought great men, and refused none.

BARTLEY (*fervently*). God be praised! That was the most thing I was

46

afeard of. (*He looks away a moment, then back again, and raises her head again. He looks into her eyes again, and suddenly his strict self-control seems to fail. His eyes kindle, and his voice changes as he whispers urgently.*) I'd like greatly to kiss you now. Have I your leave?

UNA (*in a whisper*). Yes, Bartley. (*He kisses her slowly and warmly, then looks at her eagerly.*)

BARTLEY. Did that please you?

UNA. It did, Bartley.

BARTLEY. And your mind didn't say – "He's rough and awkward anear Owen Fenigan?"

UNA. Not it, Bartley.

BARTLEY. You didn't think of him at all?

UNA. I didn't think of him at all.

BARTLEY. Then maybe we can marry any day. D'ye reckon so?

UNA (*smiling*). I'm sure so, Bartley.

BARTLEY (*overjoyed*). Una, girl! We're in God's pocket from now!

CURTAIN

ACT TWO

Scene 3

SCENE. *The same.*

TIME. *Thirty-six hours later; noon of St. Brigid's Day.*

The scene is the same; and it is thirty-six hours later; a little before noon of St. Brigid's Day. It is a beautiful sunny morning, such as you will sometimes get at that time of year, and usually after a particularly savage spell of storm and rain. A couple of miles away across the valley can be seen a range of great hills. A road winds its way across the valley and out between two of the hills. Tiny peasant villages dot the hill-sides, for the great population increase is now well under way, that amazing increase, which, in ninety years, quadrupled the population on the land, reclaimed millions of acres of bog, and swamp and rocks and heather, and made the peasantry of that period a race of bold pioneers, and lighthearted improvisors despite their state of slavery. The three essentials of food, shelter and marriage they enjoyed and so, despite their subjection, were much happier than their descendants, who are denied the last of the three.

A small turf fire is burning, and the pot is on as usual. A tub of clear water is set down on the open ground on the right; and here UNA *is trying on her bonnet with the aid of her reflection in the water. She is bending over the tub when* GAISCEEN *comes in from the left, dressed in his best for the Pattern and carrying his shillelagh. He comes right up to her unnoticed, and looks down at her a moment humorously.*

GAISCEEN. Have you the Prayer against Drowning said?
UNA. Gaisceen! You crossed the river!
GAISCEEN. Why not, girl? The flood is melted down to the stepping-stones to-day. Where's himself?

48

UNA. He's sleeping yet. He was up watching all night.

GAISCEEN. Troth, 'tis high time now to give him a stir. (*He crosses to the door, shouts in.*) Bartley Dowd! Bartley Dowd! Out with you, man. All are on their ways off to the Pattern. (*He goes to the brow of the hill, and looks down towards the road. With enthusiasm.*) The road'd scatter your sight to see it! Pipers, fiddlers, pedlars, hucksters, pilgrims, beggarmen, tinkers, and the big and the little of the country all drawing fast to the Pattern. Hi for Kilmacreena! (*This, and a shillelagh flourish to some passers-by, who respond in like manner.*)

UNA (*hanging her bonnet on the wall, and setting to work to ready* BARTLEY'S *breakfast*). I'm in hopes he'll have time to eat a bit whatever. Sure the fighting won't be till the evening time of the day? (*She takes roasted potatoes from the ashes, sets them on a stool, fills a wooden mug with water from the tub, and sets it beside them.*)

GAISCEEN. The usage of Tulrahan Pattern is the same as the usage of yere own Pattern in Shanballard. (*He comes back to the fire, sits down and takes out his pipe.*) First all'll do the Stations around St. Bridid's Well, then they'll go buying and selling, and dancing and drinking and singing till about the hour of five o'clock, when we'll fight the Tulrahans and beat them out of face at last, with the help of Bartley and of St. Patrick's Curse − for the Tulrahans stole his goat while he was preaching to them. . . . But, tell me, will you wed Bartley?

UNA. We are wedding, and the soonest day we can so as Owen'll be freed out. The day after to-morrow if all thrives for us.

GAISCEEN. There isn't any enormous great hurry like that. Owen's head is mending nicely again, they tell me. D'ye reckon you have a true wish for Bartley at last?

UNA. I reckon so. And d'ye know a thing I'm remarking. Ever since I gave in to wedding him, he's growing less serious.

GAISCEEN. To be sure he is. Sure what had that man so serious he was full sure God had no good fortune allotted for him in this world.

UNA (*hopefully*). When he's lighthearted for a few months maybe it might make him witty as well.

GAISCEEN. Very apt it will. For already he's a sound talker that's able to put the world through and fro.

(BARTLEY *comes out in his shirt sleeves. He has changed, although not very markedly as yet. The old intense seriousness and wistfulness is gone, and is replaced by an expression of quiet,*

49

deep happiness and confidence. On occasion, too, he can be humorous, but in a quiet, unassuming way. He is very pleased to see GAISCEEN.)

BARTLEY. Gaisceen, how did you venture to cross?

GAISCEEN. Venture, man! I come at Caesar's bidding. He sent me to make you the wiser of Kithogue's fighting tricks, and how best you'd exceed him.

BARTLEY (*amazed*). D'ye tell me Caesar is wishing me to win?

GAISCEEN. He has a score of guineas bet on you with Colonel Browne, Kithogue's landlord.

BARTLEY. Well, that beats cock-fighting! And us expecting him to come against us with death in his fist! (*He sits down and takes up the mug of water.*)

GAISCEEN. The night ye fled off I flew to Master Caesar, and told him you thrashed seven. "Here's your chance, your Honour," I ses, "to win back the twenty guineas you lost when Kithogue killed Shawn More." I coaxed, and wheedled, and with every hook and crook weaned him out of his temper at last. He flung aside whip and sword and, like a true sportsman, said he'd leave ye without punishing till you'd have your challenge-fight with Kithogue fought and won.

UNA. After to-day, we'll be in jeopardy.

GAISCEEN (*gravely*). Ye will, for he'll spare neither earth nor air till he takes vengeance on you for defying him, and leaving six of his men to this day half-grogged with beating.

BARTLEY (*anxious*). Will they live?

GAISCEEN. They will, but every time they think of the blows they got, they fall again.

UNA. Take your breakfast, Bartley; or the men'll be gone on you.

BARTLEY (*cheerfully*). Not them. I'll only down this sup now, and the spuds I'll lodge in my pockets, and be eating them on the way.

UNA. I'll fill your pockets up, so. (*She goes into the hut for his jacket.*)

BARTLEY (*putting on his cravat*). They tell me Caesar is leading all the gentlemen of the barony at hospitality and fighting and hunting, and good to his tenants, too only for that wan divilment for the girls that's stuck in him.

GAISCEEN (*sadly*). Wan of Colonel Browne's tallywomen that ruined the poor fellow. He was a young man and lodging a night in Browne Hall, and they made him reckless with drink; then wan of Browne's tallywomen made a blackguard for life of the poor fellow.

(UNA *comes out with* BARTLEY'S *coat, and the subject is quickly changed.*)

BARTLEY (*to* GAISCEEN). No lie; you couldn't ask a nicer day for shillelagh fighting. (*To* UNA, *with a smile.*) I'm thankful to you. A small batch of spuds'll do. I was as dry as a hawk, but noways hungry.

(BARTLEY *and* UNA *set into picking the best potatoes, and putting them into his jacket pockets. A moment later* KITTY *runs in from the village.*)

KITTY (*excitedly*). Bartley, the finest of tidings for you from Kithogue.

BARTLEY (*eagerly*). Is he taking my challenge?

KITTY. He's agreeing to fight you single hands in sight of all!

BARTLEY. More power to Kithogue, and long life to him! Now the ten acres is safe in the middle of my fist!

KITTY. The men want you at the village to talk up the day's fighting, and how you'll lead them.

BARTLEY (*jumping up*). You'll come, Gaisceen?

GAISCEEN (*cheerfully*). The divil a wan but I will.

(*As* BARTLEY *is hastening out, he is seen from the road below and loud shouts are heard. "Hi for Bartley," "Hi for Tyrawley," "More power to Bartley," etc.*)

GAISCEEN. 'Tis the men from Cloonkeen village, where Cormac is living of late.

BARTLEY (*waving his shillelagh*). Hi for Cloonkeen! Hi for Kilmacreena!

A VOICE. Bring us victory to-day, Bartley.

BARTLEY. I'll do my level best for ye. I'll take the sway from Kithogue whatever.

GAISCEEN (*shouting*). Let ye sing yere composer's new song for him in proof ye have welcome before him in this country.

VOICES. We will. Directly.

BARTLEY. A grand hearty song it is, too. We'll chorus it with them. (*He goes out right.*)

GAISCEEN. Kitty, girl, you'll chorus it with Gaisceen.

KITTY (*mischievously*). Gaisceen, you're a great warrant to make poteen. I'm thinking I'll toss aside my own bachelor, and wed you instead.

GAISCEEN (*entering into fun*). Let you not think at all I'm old. My hair is grey only because my mother weaned me too young. (*They all go out except* UNA, *and the singing can be heard in the distance, during the next scene between* MAURA *and* UNA.*)

51

"One morning in June when I chanced to go wandering,
I met a maiden, and so handsome was she,
Nothing could save me, I fell wild in love with her,
Wounded to death, for she smiled charmingly.
I asked her her name, and "What happy fit was it,
Turned your steps this way, my bright love so fair?
My heart it will break if you don't come along with me,
Then we'll goodbye to all sorrow and care."

2.

"I'm a young girl from the coast far meandering,
Who has honestly reared, though of no high degree,
But I being so airy, for such was my nature,
It made my own parents and me disagree."
"Well, my darling asthore, if you'll listen a whileen,
I'll tell you a story very pleasant you'll see.
I'm a young man who's doughtily in love with you,
And surely my heart is from roguery free."

3.

"Go, you bold rogue, sure you want to delude me,
A bird in the hand is worth two on a tree.
I have neither wheat, potatoes, nor anything,
Nor a blanket itself for cold nights that will be."
"Never mind that, I'll buy tea and a dress for you,
A gown of English cotton, the best in the fair,
So powder your hair, love, and come away 'long with me,
Then we'll goodbye to all sorrow and care."

4.

"There's an alehouse nearby we'll spend till daybreak in,
If you are satisfied, my bright love, with me,
Early next morning we'll send for the clergyman,
Who'll bind us as close as the bark and the tree,
We will stay drinking as long as the money lasts,
And after reel homewards with hearts light as air,
When the reckoning is paid, who cares for the landlady?
Farewell for ever to sorrow and care!"

(UNA *puts the remaining potatoes into the pot, then carries both pot and mug into the hut. She comes out, and proceeds to "rake" the fire by covering it with ashes. She is on her knees at this work when* MAURA *enters swiftly from the direction of the river. She is*

52

dressed in her best for the Pattern.)

MAURA (*quickly*). Where is Bartley?

UNA. Maura Pender! . . . He's gone to the village. He'll be back directly.

MAURA. I must tell you fast, so, and not lag. (*She sits down.*) Caesar is gone to the cock-fighting at Galla to-day, and the Pressgang are gone off to the Pattern. Murty is the only servant left to guard French Hall, and I have him bribed with two guineas to give Owen his chance to escape.

UNA (*delighted*). You have!

MAURA. I didn't see Owen himself, but Murty brought me his message. Owen ses you were to stop home from the Pattern, and when all'd be gone he'd come to you here, and ye'd scour off to the mountains before Bartley or Caesar'd hear a thing.

UNA (*rising in agitation*). But Bartley and myself are pledged to wed in two days!

MAURA. Sure that was only because Owen was jailed up. Now Owen'll be at large again, so you have no occasion to wed Bartley.

UNA. But, Maura, I'm knowing Bartley right now, and I'd like him greatly for marriage.

MAURA (*taken aback*). You do! Would you prefer him to Owen, then?

UNA. I have a great wish for Owen, too. He ventured his life for me, too, suffered wounding and jailing, and I was pledged to him first moreover. (*She crosses, and looks down towards French's country distractedly.*)

MAURA (*gloomily*). It makes no matter to me which you wed. 'Tis hardly likely Bartley'd wed a tallywoman the like of me. But I'd say Owen has suffered the keenest for you, for he has his fine farm and means lost. If you leave Bartley he'll not be so badly; he'll have his ten acres whatever.

UNA. 'Tisn't broad acres or riches Bartley was ever hungry for, and he all his lifetime as lonesome as a crane at a lake. He's wild for me now the same as if 'twas from Heaven I fell to him, and if I steal away from him 'twill sicken his heart all out.

MAURA. Maybe the fittest thing for you so'd be to steal away from neither; but honestly to flatten out the whole case for them, and see what themselves'll say. (*She crosses to the back, and looks towards the village.*)

UNA (*sitting down gloomily*). I have no other choice. . . . But I'll not tell Bartley yet for fear 'twould upset him for his challenge fight.

I'll make an excuse to stop home from the Pattern, meet Owen, and make all known to him first, and when the two of them are told neither of them'll want me likely.

MAURA (*suddenly*). Here's Bartley drawing this way from the village. (*Quickly.*) Did you make him the wiser yet of my two years as a tallywoman?

UNA. I never did, Maura.

MAURA. Let you take a canter off to the village for a whileen, till I draw out his thinking about girls that were tallywomen.

UNA (*mournfully*). Bartley'll have no more to do with me wance he hears how I made a flaming fool of him the night of the dance. He'll not be able to put trust in me again evermore. (BARTLEY *enters, carrying some wool in his hand and, in his grave way, he is very pleased to see* MAURA).

BARTLEY. By my hand! Maura Pender! The very girl I was praising oftentimes for your goodness to Owen Fenigan that night.

MAURA (*quietly*). Wouldn't any girl do as much?

BARTLEY (*vigorously*). They would not, in troth. They'd be afeard to go minding a lad that struck a blow against his landlord! (*He takes his old hat from the wall, sits down, and begins to pad it with wool.*)

UNA (*rising*). Bartley, I have my mind changed. I'm reckoning now I'll stop home from the Pattern to-day.

BARTLEY (*dismayed*). You will! Why so?

UNA. I'm thinking now I'd sooner not be a witness to the fighting. Every stroke you'd get'd go through me greatly.

BARTLEY. But my father made me able to bear a power of beating. And I'll have my cap thickened with wool, moreover.

UNA. Still, Bartley, 'twould frighten me greatly, so the Pattern'd be no pleasuring place for me at all.

BARTLEY. Please your mind whatever. Yourself is the best judge.

UNA. I must make know to Kitty that I'll not be with her to-day. (*She takes the tub and runs out.*)

BARTLEY (*nodding*). You should do. (*When she is gone, he turns to* MAURA *gravely.*) Isn't it surprising how a girl could have a great wish for a good fighter, and still'd sooner not see him fighting? But I heard tell of her kind before. (*He is busy lining his cap with wool.*)

MAURA. I'd like greatly to have your advice about a thing. 'Tis about misfortune my sister had.

BARTLEY. Well, misfortune is wan thing I might have middling valuable things to say about; for misfortune had hooks in me from my youthful days till two nights back.

MAURA. Caesar took her, and held her two years.

BARTLEY (*looking at her*). Blood and 'ouns! Is it as tallywoman?

MAURA (*avoiding his eyes*). Yes.

BARTLEY. She's greatly to be pitied. She's greatly to be pitied. But they reckon that was the way ever since Adam's sin. They reckon there was never a time in the world since that the divil hadn't a bigger following than God.

MAURA. D'ye think any decent man'd marry her after Caesar?

BARTLEY (*gravely*). They'd have the greatest pity in the world for her; but their drawing is for a girl that wasn't for a man before. They can't help that: 'tis in a man's nature.

MAURA (*gloomily*). She must bear to stop single, so; or take the kind that'd marry anything for gold.

BARTLEY. It could happen that misfortune only is allotted for her in this world. If it happens so, d'ye think will she be fit to bear it, and not go reckless?

MAURA (*darkly*). I couldn't be sure about that.

BARTLEY (*reminiscently*). That's the most jeopardy that's in misfortune. 'Twould be ever and always tempting you to say there must be no God at all, or else a cruel wan, and wance we give in to that we go reckless.

MAURA (*morbidly*). They reckon the divil'll do all for you if you'll give him a lease of yourself.

BARTLEY. Let her have no truck with him at all. Instead let her not halt from asking Our Saviour, and every Sunday without fail at the Chalice time of the Mass. Look at the fine young girl He sent me when my looks and youth and all hope was lost!

MAURA (*bitterly*). But if my sister is without chance. If no decent man'd have her.

BARTLEY. You could never tell. Some decent fellow might that met great misfortune himself, and that way'd have pity for her misfortune.

MAURA (*her eyes lighting up with hope*). D'ye reckon so?

GAISCEEN (*running in*). Bartley, me bold son of Erin! Cormac, God bless him, has another new song composed!

BARTLEY. He has! Who told ye?

GAISCEEN. The divil a wan; but I see Rory coming up the Mass-path, and he prancing and dancing and singing like a merry-man.

BARTLEY. Well, Cormac is a powerful composer.

MAURA (*rising*). I have tidings for Una that I should give her, so I'll bid ye farewell for a while. (*She goes out towards the village, and looks more hopeful than she has done so far.*)

GAISCEEN (*taking up the poteen bottle and uncorking it*). The men are all ranked and ready at the village below, with their shillelaghs in their fists. (*Looking out back.*) Here they're stepping out and coming.

BARTLEY (*putting on his hat*). I'm ready whatever.

GAISCEEN (*excitedly*). Here's Rory passing by. We must stand him, and coax the new song from him. (*Brandishing the bottle, and calling.*) Rory Commons! Rory, draw this way a whileen. (RORY *is heard laughing wildly off stage.*) Here's poteen good enough to make a cat talk! (RORY *staggers in, wildly excited, singing and laughing with his high, windbroken laugh.*)

RORY.

"Oro, my thousand loves, oro my thousand loves,
Here's oro in to bother you until the bright day comes."

GAISCEEN (*disappointed*). Rory, never mind that old song. Give us your father's new song.

RORY (*wildly hilarious*). Gaisceen Brehony and Bartley Dowd, 'tisn't a new song I have but the finest tidings since Cromwell went to Hell. Before duskus today I'll be the best composer was ever reared on Irish soil.

GAISCEEN. Oh, God bless us! Is Cormac giving in to death at last?

RORY (*delightedly*). He hasn't two choices this time. The death is in his eyes and throat and heart, and no mistake. For the priest he sent me in hurry. Before the stars are winking Rory'll be left his gift. . . . Give me that bottle, Gaisceen, or I'll compose then a song scolding you.

GAISCEEN (*hastily*). Not you, Rory. Here's the lot, and welcome.

RORY (*taking up the bottle triumphantly*). Bartley Dowd, if you'll take the sway from Kithogue and the Tulrahans this day, I'll compose a praising song for you directly.

BARTLEY (*eagerly*). Maybe you'd have a share of it composed for my wedding in two days.

RORY. I'll have a song as long as the river composed for it. Wance I get the gift I'll be composing fast, not the same as my father. Praising songs without stint for the generous and the gallant; and scolding songs without mercy for the niggardly that'd grudge the black of their nails to a composer.

GAISCEEN (*with enthusiasm*). And love songs, Rory! The love song is the longest that lasts.

RORY. Love songs of the two kinds; the pitiful and the cheering;

and praising songs for the young women that'll set them coaxing Rory with soft kisses and all. I tell ye Rory'll be like a king going.

BARTLEY (*suddenly grave*). Without no lie you will, Rory; but let you go ahead now, and have the priest in time to help your father home.

RORY (*pocketing the bottle*). Rory'll not lag. He'll keep ever going at a good hand-trot. (*He sets out, then turns again ecstatically.*) When ye lay eyes on Rory again, ye'll not know his countenance with the dint of composer's brightness. (*He goes towards the exit, and shouts down to the crowd below.*) Great tidings for ye all. Cormac is for the ladder. (*Pointing to Heaven.*) To-night ye'll have a new composer. Hi for Rory, the brightest composer since Turlough O'Carolan! (RORY *runs off, waving his hat in the air.* GAISCEEN *runs to the back, and looks down.*)

GAISCEEN. The men are belowside, waving and calling us.

BARTLEY (*following him*). Here's herself coming, and I must leave her farewell. Let you be posting ahead.

GAISCEEN. Let ye not lag. (*Shouting down joyously.*) We're coming, men. Hi for Kilmacreena! (*He runs out, waving his shillelagh.* UNA *comes in, and* BARTLEY *takes her two hands earnestly.*)

BARTLEY. Una, let you keep out of sight in Blake's wood, for fear Caesar's men might make any poke for you while I'm far away.

UNA. I will, Bartley, and let you take good care of your life in the fighting.

BARTLEY (*cheerfully*). Never fear. The divil's iron flail'd hardly be fit to kill Bartley. (*Shouts are heard, calling "Bartley!" Bartley!"*) They're for off! Farewell a whileen.

UNA. Farewell, Bartley. (*They kiss.*)

BARTLEY (*to* MAURA *who enters*). Are you coming?

MAURA. I'll be after ye directly.

BARTLEY. Good yourself. (*Shouting as he goes.*) Wait, men. Hi for Kilmacreena!

MAURA (*hurriedly*). This I must tell you before I take my road. Murty is a lackey of Caesar's so you couldn't trust a bone in him if it was behind the rafter. Maybe he has it fairly in the head to let Owen go, or maybe he's only watching his chance to set a snare for you. So lie a-hiding in Blake's wood, and never stir from it only if Owen himself comes.

UNA. I'll give no glimpse of myself to anywan only Owen; and, Maura, I'm judging now, 'tis Bartley I'll be loyal to and wed. Owen'll easy get a wife, on account he's so young and lively.

But if I desert Bartley now 'twould be a fearful throw to him, and he'd never be able to put trust in a woman again.

MAURA (*suppressing her disappointment*). . . . You must please your mind about it. You'll wait and tell Owen all?

UNA. I'll wait in Blake's wood for him. I'll be that far with you. (*A mighty chorus is heard of men singing.* MAURA *runs to the back and looks down.*)

MAURA. They're off – at the rate of a fox-hunt! Run, or they'll be gone on me. (*They run out right together. The last verse of Cormac's song is heard as the men pass by.*)

> "There's an ale-house nearby we'll spend till daybreak in,
> If you are satisfied, my bright love, with me,
> Early next morning we'll send for the clergyman,
> Who'll bind us as close as the bark and the tree.
> We will stay drinking as long as the money lasts,
> And after reel homewards with hearts light as air.
> When the reckoning is paid, who cares for the landlady?
> Farewell for ever to sorrow and care."

(MURTY *comes in from the left, bending low and looking ahead cautiously. He is a reckless, ruthless-looking young fellow, more or less of* OWEN'S *height and build, and dressed in* OWEN'S *clothes and hat. He peeps round the corner of the hut; then he turns and waves to someone waiting near the river. In a few moments, that someone appears. It is* BOORLA, *shillelagh in hand, and bending double so as not to be seen from the village.*)

MURTY (*pointing*). There she is driving fast for the wood! I'll go after her.

BOORLA. A small piece only, so as she'll see Owen's clothes, but not your face. Keep your hat well down over your eyes. Don't give her your voice. Whistle only.

MURTY (*pulling his hat over his eyes*). I'll whistle my upmost. I don't care if it wakens the dead.

(*He goes out left towards the village. A moment later a long whistle is heard, followed by a second, and a third, each louder than the last.* BOORLA *takes a look at the inside of the cabin. The whistle is heard again.* BOORLA *looks round the corner, and grins with satisfaction.* UNA'S *voice is heard calling "Owen!"*)

BOORLA. Good boy! You have her drawn! Now for the net! (*He moves back into the shelter of the hut, and stands in readiness. A moment later* MURTY *appears, running rapidly in the direction of the river, and waving urgently for* UNA *to follow him.*)

MURTY (*to* BOORLA). I have her hooked. Now let you gaff her. (*Waving vigorously, he disappears in the direction of the river.* BOORLA *runs into the cabin and closes the door. In a few moments,* UNA *is heard calling "Owen, come back; wait for me." She appears, running breathlessly. "Owen, I'll not cross the river. Why don't you answer me? Owen!" She slows down, but still continues in the direction of the river.* BOORLA *comes out, and sets out swiftly and stealthily after her.*)

CURTAIN

ACT THREE

The living-room at French Hall. It is a large, fine-looking room with massive doors and furniture. A door in the middle of the back wall opens into the entrance hall. The window in the left wall overlooks the front grounds and avenue. A door in the right-hand wall leads to the middle hall, and through that to the kitchen and the back of the house. Large ancestral portraits hang on every wall. A small mahogany table is on the left, with a leather upholstered chair behind it, and a big armchair a little to its left-hand side and facing the audience. A sofa is still further to the left, likewise facing the audience. Various other chairs are along the walls, and here and there. Against the right-hand wall is a bulky, many-drawered cabinet. Against the back wall on the left is a sideboard, on which are placed decanters and glasses, together with a punch-bowl and ladle. Against this wall on the right is another massively fine cabinet. The room is well carpeted and papered, and the window is richly curtained. So far, the room's contents have been orthodox; but there are some further items which reflect the bachelor tastes and habits of CAESAR FRENCH. *Over the sideboard two duelling-swords lie side by side supported by wall brackets. On two wall-brackets over the second cabinet on the other side of this wall are two fowling-pieces; while beside them there hangs from a nail an ornamental powder-horn. Over the doorway are stag horns. Against the other wall, near the footlights, stand a fishing-rod and net.*

The time is the evening of the same day. The darkness is falling swiftly now, and in a few minutes it will be night.

CAESAR *being away,* BIDDY, *his housekeeper is relaxing. She is a woman of fifty, lean, hardy, leathery-skinned, of leisurely and phlegmatic disposition. She is not gloomy, but her nearest approach to joy is a smile which is as faint as it is rare. For the rest, her calm lack-lustre eyes wander here and there with a kind of dull reflectiveness. Her speech is in keeping; slow, slightly drawling, eventoned, imperturbable. In sum, a stupid, leisurely woman, not unkindly, unswervingly loyal to her lord and master, but stolidly unafraid of him, or of anybody, or of anything.*

As the curtain goes up, she is sitting in the armchair smoking and ruminating in her dull way. Suddenly steps are heard of a man running, and BOORLA *flings open the door on the right and runs in. He is breathless, anxious, angry.*)

BOORLA. Is Caesar home yet? He's not, or you'd not be in here. Where's Mehaul?

BIDDY. In the dark cellar, bracing young Fenigan with a jorum of punch.

BOORLA (*grimly*). Faith, I'm presently in want of a little courage myself. (*Hurriedly he takes a glass from the sideboard, pours out a half glass for himself.*) Biddy, all in this house are in jeopardy from Bartley Dowd. We were spied making a prisoner of her.

BIDDY. Ye bungled yere plan, so?

BOORLA (*vigorously*). We did not, Biddy; we done everything rightly according to Master Caesar's commands. We made a prisoner of her in the morning, and locked her in the water-bailiff's house; then off with us to the Pattern to enjoy the day's fighting. 'Twas in the morning when we were netting her that God tripped us. We were reckoning Murty could draw her across the river into Caesar's woods. He couldn't be seen capturing her there, so all'd believe 'twas Owen Fenigan was in it, and she ran away with him. But would she Hell's fire cross the river! (*He pauses for breath and a gulp at his glass.*)

BIDDY (*stolidly*). So yourself had to drag her across in sight of all.

BOORLA (*rising agitatedly*). The village hags heard her screeches and came spying out from their cabins. They'll make all known to Bartley directly he comes from the Pattern, and he'll come at French Hall as savage as black Cromwell up from Hell. (*He pulls back the curtains, closes and bolts the window shutters.*) We must bolt all doors, and load all guns, too. Short the shutters'll halt him. He'll pull a gate-post up, and breach through them in no time. (*He takes down one of the guns and the powder-horn, carries them to the table, pulls out the ramrod and begins to load feverishly.*)

BIDDY (*composed*). That's sure. How did Bartley fare against Kithogue?

BOORLA. Left him lying low, and then led us against the Tulrahans, flattening them all roads till they ran from us at last, the few of them that were able.

BIDDY (*taking down two swords from the rack*). 'Tis a pity to shoot to death such a good fighter. Maybe Murty and yourself could defeat him back with swords and avoid killing him. (*She draws the swords from their scabbards*).

BOORLA. He's a match for ten men with any fair weapons. Our wan chance is the guns.

BIDDY (*matter-of-factly*). Ye'd better shoot him, so. For fear the guns'd miss fire I'll leave these handy. (*She leaves the swords on the sideboard with their hilts projecting conveniently.*)

BOORLA. I'd sooner Caesar'd have the shooting of Dowd. He'd be safer from the Law on account the Grand Jury and Sheriffs are all gentlemen like himself.

BIDDY (*taking the shot-pouch from one of the drawers*). Here's the shot-pouch for you. He said he'd be back from the cock-fighting at duskus, but maybe he'll forget all about her with the pleasuring he'll be having.

BOORLA. Hell's cure to him that won't marry in place of jeopardising us all. (*The door on the right is flung open, and MURTY enters dragging UNA violently after him by a rope tied around her wrists. A sack is pulled down over her head, and tied around her neck to smother her cries. MURTY drags her across the room, and flings her on to the sofa.*)

MURTY (*savage and scared*). Biddy, watch over this rap, you. (*To BOORLA.*) I'm going to turn loose the mastiffs. (*He makes for the door, then turns again.*) Boorla, bar all the doors and windows first. They'll give us time to load the guns.

BOORLA. The divil a lie they would. I'll bolt them directly.

(*MURTY goes out of the door on right to the main hall, and BOORLA goes out the back door to the front hall. BIDDY taps out her pipe, and looks down at UNA a moment.*)

BIDDY (*casually*). How are you going on? (*But the half-stunned UNA does not reply, or move. BIDDY begins to untie the cord which binds the sack around her neck.*) You have no occasion to be afeard. Master Caesar has no mind to put you to death or thrash you itself. He ses he'll only keep you wan week or two, as a parable for any other girls that'd go defying him. Then he'll give you a fine batch of guineas, and you can go east or west with young Owen Fenigan or Bartley Dowd, or whoever is your fancy. (*She pulls the sack up from UNA'S head.*) Now I'll free your hands out, and you'll have ease.

UNA (*desperately*). You're Biddy Hartigan, his housekeeper, and I've heard tell you're kindly. Give me chance to escape from him, Biddy, and I'll pray for you till my dying day.

BIDDY (*stolidly*). Child, how could I betray the Frenches, that all belonging to me served evermore?

UNA. But in the honour of God, Biddy! You're breaking God's law when you hold me for Caesar.

BIDDY (*placidly*). Our Saviour understands well we have no choice but to obey the gentlemen. And, if I don't do it, Caesar can find plenty that will. Stop there, and I'll give you a fine hooker of claret that'll warm your blood, and dull your brains, so as you'll not be fretting at all.

UNA. I'm lost so, unless Bartley comes. . . . (*Despairingly she buries her face in her hands*).

BIDDY (*pouring out a big glass of wine*). In the bad hungry times before now, the tenant girls were glad and willing to be tallywomen, for the hunger'll do anything. Master Caesar isn't rightly understanding why the girls are not so willing these late years. He's doubting 'tis because ye reckon him to be too old, and that vexes him beyond measure. If you'll be said by Biddy Hartigan, you'll not let him see you're afeard of him or unwilling at all. (*Taking the glass, she tries to raise* UNA'S *head*). Tipple this back your throat, and then you'll be bold and cheerful facing him.

(*Suddenly the fierce barking of the mastiffs is heard just outside the window.* BIDDY *leaves the glass back on the table, takes up one of the guns, and resumes the loading it.* MURTY *bursts in from the main hall.*)

MURTY. D'ye hear the mastiffs? There's some wan coming up the avenue. (*He takes the second gun and hurriedly sets to work loading it.*) Bear in mind the rule, Biddy –

> "If you want to shoot your enemy dead,
> Ram the powder, but not the lead"

(*The howling of the dogs grows louder and nearer, then a fierce knocking is heard at the front hall door.* BOORLA *runs in from the front hall in great alarm.*)

BOORLA. D'ye hear that? Nowan'd dar' knock like that only Bartley Dowd, or Master Caesar himself.

MURTY. I sent Mehaul to the highest window to watch out. (*To* BOORLA.) Load the guns you till I ask him who's in it.

(MURTY *runs into the main hall, and* BOORLA *takes over his gun, while* BIDDY *continues readying the other. The knocking is resumed again, this time with even greater violence.* UNA, *in*

63

terror, moves towards the window as if hoping to find safety behind its curtains.)

BIDDY (*stolidly*). If 'tis Master Caesar he'll flog all before him for the delay.

BOORLA. I hope in God the powder is dry! (*Carrying the gun at the ready, he approaches the door leading into the front hall. Suddenly a new sound is heard, the savage lashing of the door with a heavy stick.* BOORLA *turns to* BIDDY.)

BOORLA. D'ye hear that?

BIDDY. 'Tis either a riding-whip, or a shillelagh.

MURTY (*running in*). 'Tis Master Caesar.

BOORLA. Quick, you divil, and open the door for him.

MURTY. Wherever a skelping is sure – Murty is sent there! (*He goes out to open the main door.*)

BIDDY. 'Tis time for me to be leaving ye.

(*She goes out door right.* BOORLA *empties the wine glasses on to the floor, puts the glass back on the side-table, takes the second gun from the table. There is a rattle of heavy chains as* MURTY *opens the door, then* CAESAR *is heard shouting fiercely, "Take that and that, you drone you!" Through the library door* MURTY *can be seen as he flees howling from* CAESAR'S *riding whip.* CAESAR *attired in hat and cloak chases him past the doorway, then can be heard shouting, "Have my horse stabled in two minutes, or I'll cut the flesh off your bones."* UNA *runs across stage, and out the side door after* BIDDY, *but* BOORLA *catches her, and hauls her back.*)

BOORLA. Don't try running away ever in this house. Always we'll catch you fast, and hurt you sore.

(*As he is throwing her down on the sofa again* CAESAR *enters taking off his sword belt. His hat and cloak he has taken off, and left in the hall apparently. In build he is the typical Norman-descended West of Ireland aristocrat for the period, being a huge man, muscular and hard as iron from a life-time of dare-devil horsemanship on and off the hunting field, of fowling, fighting and general outdoor activity. He has, likewise, the big-bridged nose of his race, and the black hair, which is now well tinged with grey. He is obviously a man of fierce pride, and of enormous energy and determination. But he feels very bitterly the loss of his youth and good-looks, and the imminent loss of his powers. As he has no intellectual or family interests, old age will have few compensations for him, and he knows it. The bold cynicism of his youth has developed into pessimism; and the most striking thing about the man is his air of fierce gloom and disillusion. But its very intensity and genuineness almost ennobles him: at least it redeems him from mere common-place arrogance and brutality.*)

BOORLA. Your honour, here she is, the wan that refused you!

CAESAR (*after a brief and grim look at her*). I'll deal with her later. (*To* BOORLA.) What do you mean standing me like a beggar on my own doorstep?

BOORLA. Your honour, we were afeard 'twas Bartley Dowd. The village hags spied us making a prisoner of her.

CAESAR. So you bungled matters, you blockheads! Serves you right if he cracks your empty skulls. (*He hands* BOORLA *his sword and belt, drawing the sword from its scabbard, and looking at the point as he does so.*)

BOORLA. Your honour, there's blood on your sword!

CAESAR. Yes, Blake of Lowberry's. (*He draws up his left sleeve disclosing a bandaged and bloody forearm. He pours some brandy on the wound.*)

BOORLA. Ye had a variance! And your honour is wounded, too!

CAESAR. Before the whole company he sneered at me, "Well, Caesar, I hear your peasant wenches are turning up their noses at you." I knocked him down, he drew his sword, and we fought until they came between us. (*He opens his pistol case, rams powder and shot into one of the pistols.*)

BOORLA. So he heard tell about her refusing you! Bartley's fearful fight against us has that news spread far and near.

CAESAR (*with a savage look at her*). No matter; I'll make an everlasting example of the slut. Open the window for a fireoff, and I'll see if the powder is dry in case Dowd should lead a drunken Pattern day mob against the house.

BOORLA. But, your honour, if I open the shutters and the window we'll be in jeopardy from Bartley Dowd. Maybe he's outside watching a chance to spring in at us.

CAESAR. You blockhead, do you suppose I'm afraid of a single peasant ragamuffin with a shillelagh?

BOORLA. But, all reckon he's in league with the divil for fighting, and he has a shillelagh like a young tree.

CAESAR. Open the window directly!

BOORLA (*hastily*). Yes, your honour. (*He opens the shutters, raises the window half way, and* CAESAR, *pistol in hand, takes up his stand facing it.*)

CAESAR. Ready, Boorla?

BOORLA. Yes, your honour. (CAESAR *fires. There is a flash in the*

65

pan, but no report; the pistol has missed fired.)

CAESAR. Missed fire, by George!

BOORLA. The powder must be damp, your honour!

CAESAR (*drawing back the cock of the pistol again*). If Murty has neglected the powder again, I'll flog him into Hell. (*He pulls the trigger, and again there is merely a flash in the pan.*)

BOORLA. The powder is damp, your honour!

CAESAR (*in a fury*). Damp as the bog! I'll flog his living heart out. (*He pulls the kitchen bell rope violently.*)

BOORLA (*taking the powder horn*). I'll set the powder near the fire, and 'twill dry the run in a few minutes.

(BOORLA *hurries out.* CAESAR *takes the riding whip from the cabinet, and walks up and down muttering to himself.*)

CAESAR. Scoundrels and fools. Laziness and impudence. (*With a look at* UNA.)

BIDDY (*entering, smoking as usual*). Murty neglected the powder again.

CAESAR. Bid them tie the blackguard to the yard gate, and bring me word directly it is done.

BIDDY (*nodding*). 'Tis the only way you can make Murty have memory of his duties. He's the same as the ass: he has to be bet. (*She goes out.* CAESAR *brings a huge old ledger from the cabinet to the table. As he does so he notices blood streaming down his arm again.*)

CAESAR. Bloody again. Curse it. (*He unties the bandage, and begins to unwind it. He turns to* UNA *sternly,*) Come here, girl. (UNA *backs away in terror.*)

CAESAR. Where are you going, wench?

UNA (*halting at the wall*). Nowhere, your honour.

CAESAR. Come back here. (*Menacingly, as she does not move.*) Will you come back, or won't you? Very well then. . . . (*He rises.*)

UNA. I'm coming, your honour. (*She comes back to the end of the table. He puts his bare and wounded arm in front of her on the table.*)

CAESAR. Bind that; and bind it tightly above the stab.

UNA. Yes, your honour. (*She begins with trembling hands to rebandage his arm. After a moment,* CAESAR *pulls over the ledger with his right arm, and slaps it.*)

CAESAR. I have here the rent book for my Shanballard estate. I have looked over your father's accounts. In the last seven years, he has been late with his rents five times. Three times he did not pay in full, and once he did not pay at all.

UNA. Of late, your honour, he isn't getting the health so good.

CAESAR (*grimly*). Bad health! The stock excuse of the idler! As you know very well, such excuses are not accepted in Connacht. Pay up or quit, is the rule. I could have flung your father out years ago, but I didn't. Did you think of that the night you refused me? Answer, wench!

UNA. No, your honour.

CAESAR. You would never have been born at all, if my father hadn't leased two acres of our land to your parents to marry and live upon. Did you think of that the night you refused me?

UNA. No, your honour.

CAESAR. Wench, answer directly: why did you refuse me?

UNA (*shaking*). I was afeard, your honour, on account you were a stranger man.

CAESAR (*fiercely*). A stranger! Your landlord a stranger! God damn your impudence! How often have I passed your door on my way to my bailiff's house?

UNA. Our cabin is a piece back from the road. I only seen you a good way off.

CAESAR. Nevertheless, you saw and heard enough to know I was neither dwarf nor giant, pig-face, savage, or idiot. Then what did you dislike in me?

UNA. Nothing, your honour, only I was shy on account you were a great high-up gentleman, and I was never in conversation with the like before.

CAESAR. So now the story is that you were shy! But you weren't too shy to elope with a runaway robber and murderer from Tyrawley.

UNA (*with some spirit*). Your honour, Bartley was never a robber or a murderer.

CAESAR. For all you know, he may be; yet you went with him. (*Rising to his feet in final fury.*) Do you suppose I'm a fool? Do you suppose I don't know why you refused me? It was because you were seventeen years and, like every young slut nowadays, you suppose a man is nothing but a crippled grandfather at two score. And because I am easy-going, and don't evict ye directly for non-payment of rent, ye suppose I am an idiot in second childhood. I'll show you, by George, I'll show you. (*He is beginning to handle her, when* BIDDY *comes in, still smoking.*)

BIDDY. Your honour, they have Murty tied to the gate, and ready for you.

CAESAR (*taking the riding whip from the table*). Very well.

(*Indicating* UNA.) Take her to the kitchen for the present. (*Suddenly the dogs begin to bay fiercely.*)

BIDDY. Very apt 'tis Bartley this time. I'll shutter the window, your honour. (*She moves towards the window.*)

CAESAR (*taking up his sword*). You will not, woman. I'll not have any peasant ruffian besiege me in my own house. If he wants fight, he'll find Caesar obliging. (*He strides up to the window.*)

BIDDY. We'll be making out, girl. (*She marches* UNA *out.* CAESAR *does not bother to watch them go. In a moment or two,* BOORLA *runs in much relieved.*)

BOORLA. 'Tis all right, your honour. 'Tis only Gaisceen on his way from the Pattern.

CAESAR (*nodding*). Yes, I told him to come up as usual, and tell me about the day's fighting. Send him up directly.

BOORLA. Your honour, will you not thrash Murty yet? We have him grandly tied up and all.

CAESAR (*irascibly*). The blackguard will wait until I am ready. Send up Gaisceen.

BOORLA. Yes, your honour. (*He runs out.* CAESAR *carries a bottle of wine and two glasses from the sideboard to the wine table.* GAISCEEN *staggers in, muddy and bloodstained from the evening's fighting, but waving the broken remnant of his shillelagh triumphantly.*)

GAISCEEN. Master Caesar, we beat the Tulrahans! And Bartley knocked the senses out of Kithogue, and won your twenty guineas back from Colonel Browne.

CAESAR (*his sombre face breaking into something like a smile*). Yes, the wager; I had forgotten. (*He pours out two glasses of wine.*) But sit down, and tell me about the fighting. (*He sits down in the chair behind the wine table, and pushes a glass in front of* GAISCEEN, *who sits in the armchair.*)

GAISCEEN (*with enthusiasm*). They fought, your honour, for all the world like two of the giants that used to come against Ireland long ago from the East. Up and down, toe to toe, backhand and forehand, head blows and body blows for half and hour, till their two shirts were running all roads over with blood. But Bartley wore him out with strength and quickness, and when Kithogue was driven against the ground for the last time, the women had to roll him in a sheet, and carry him home.

CAESAR (*watching him with affectionate amusement*). Then ye thrashed the Tulrahans for the first time in nine years?

GAISCEEN (*solemnly*). Bartley sent a man to the ground with every blow, and every man of them'll have to wait in bed a day. He breached through every rank they made and broke their hearts at last.

CAESAR (*his eyes glistening*). I'm sorry I missed that. No doubt about it, he's a splendid fighter. (*Gloomily.*) It will be a pity if I have to kill him, a great pity.

GAISCEEN (*in horror*). Kill him! Your honour, are you going capturing her to-night?

CAESAR. No need for that. Biddy has her safe in the kitchen. (*He tosses off the glass of wine, while* GAISCEEN *stares at him dumbfounded.*)

GAISCEEN. She's in the kitchen, your honour!

CAESAR. The slut tried to betray this Dowd fellow. She stayed home from the Pattern so as to run away with young Fenigan, who was to meet her. However, it was Murty met her in Fenigan's clothes, and netted her neatly enough.

GAISCEEN (*rising to his feet in dismay*). Bartley'll come against this house, your honour, the minute he hears she's vanished away.

CAESAR (*lifting his sword, and feeling the point of it gloomily*). Very likely; It will be a pity if I have to kill him. (*Rising and walking about.*) But there will be no need. All we have to do is tell him how she tricked and betrayed him; then he'll wish her to the devil, and go about his business without more ado.

GAISCEEN. Maybe in God the poor fellow will turn against her, and not go throwing his life away. . . . D'ye think, your honour, will you keep herself long?

CAESAR (*walking up and down grimly, and slapping his boot with the flat of his sword*). Long enough to teach her a lesson; and after that we'll see.

GAISCEEN (*mournfully*). You'd be a great deal a better man to marry, your honour. The same as most of the bachelors when their youth is past you're turning dark in your mind and cross. A wife, if you'd chance on a right wan'd make a kind man of you again.

CAESAR (*with grim conviction*). This is the way the world was made: all the men scoundrels and all the women fools. None of them is content with living with a man. They aren't satisfied until they are interfering and ruling him, and I'm not a man to brook ruling. When I've had enough of a peasant wench I give her ten guineas, and with that she can get a husband and a home. But a wife, a woman of my own class, I couldn't get rid of even if she proved the most interfering slut since Eve. The man is an ass who marries when he can get women otherwise. (*He goes to the cabinet, takes a cloth from one of the drawers, and sets to work cleaning and polishing his sword blade.*)

GAISCEEN (*grieved*). But the estate, your honour. What'll it do for an heir?

CAESAR. I can leave it to one of my nephews, and, if I fancy none of them, I can leave it to one of my bastards.

GAISCEEN (*nodding gravely*). Right enough. The same as Colonel Bourke did, and Lord Brackloon and several gentlemen more.

CAESAR. Yes. Have you kept an eye on the bastards as I told you?

GAISCEEN. To be sure, your honour. Every two months or three I do call on them all to make sure their mothers and stepfathers are giving them good looking after.

CAESAR (*tossing sword onto the sideboard*). Any promising lads among them?

GAISCEEN (*with enthusiasm*). Your honour, they're as gallant a batch of young bastards as ever a gentleman had.

CAESAR. Good. Then one of these days we'll ride over the estate, look them over, and pick out the most promising for schooling and rearing. (*He takes up one of the pistols, and sets to work drawing out the lead, and the charge of damp powder. As he does so, the baying of the dogs is heard again, but more faintly, as if from the back of the house. Continuing to unload calmly.*) See if you can see anyone.

GAISCEEN (*running to the window*). Yes, your honour. . . . No wan; but from the barking I'd say 'tis somewan at the back of the house.

BOORLA (*running in excitedly*). The powder should be dry, your honour. Will we reload the guns? (*He takes the two muskets from their racks.*)

CAESAR. Do. Gaisceen, help him to draw the damp charges and reload.

GAISCEEN. Yes, your honour. (BOORLA *and* GAISCEEN *run out left with the two muskets.* CAESAR *takes up his sword, and moves to the window, looking quite unconcerned.*)

BIDDY (*entering*). 'Tis only Maura Pender, and she wants to see your honour.

CAESAR (*very grimly*). She wants to see me! And I want to see her. Send her in, by George.

(BIDDY *goes out*, CAESAR *comes back to the table, and throws his sword upon it. He takes up one of the pistols and, with the aid of its ramrod, proceeds to draw the damp charge from it. He*

THE KING OF FRIDAY'S MEN — ACT III

tosses some of the damp powder out of the window, and is at this when MAURA *enters from the main hall. She is flushed and eager. Her manner towards* CAESAR, *whose mistress she had been for so long, is unafraid; but not bold or aggressive. She speaks as to one with whom she has lived on terms of intimacy and equality.*)

MAURA (*eagerly*). Caesar. . . .

CAESAR (*with marked hostility*). I told you never to cross my threshold again.

MAURA. I came begging a last favour.

CAESAR (*fiercely*). Favour, by George! I paid you fifteen guineas for two years here, and gave you a life lease of Sarah D'Arcy's cottage and four acres. Your thanks for all that was to bribe my own lackey to betray me!

MAURA (*earnestly*). Caesar, 'twasn't to spite you I did that, but because 'twas the only way of saving the life of Bartley Dowd, that I was in hopes of marrying. Wance she was gone with Owen Fenigan, Bartley might wed myself and with my money rent a few acres far away from this estate and the Pressgang.

CAESAR (*grimly*). So that was the plot! And you're setting your cap at this Dowd! Well, he is more likely than ever to lose his life now. (*He comes back to the table, leaves down the pistol, takes the second one and proceeds to draw the charges from it, and empty the damp powder out of the window as before.*)

MAURA. I know. He's sure and certain to come saving her any minute at all; and the favour I'm asking is you to spare his life. There's only one way to save him, and that's to let her go free, with Owen Fenigan, or whichever of them she wants.

CAESAR. I'll free that wench for nobody – least of all you.

MAURA (*smiling slightly*). You're vexed still because I behaved so insolent to you that night.

CAESAR (*fiercely, coming back to the table*). I gave you regard and trust such as I never gave to a woman before; and directly you felt sure of me you set about ruling me. I'll never forgive you for that after my two years of true regard for you. (*He throws the second pistol upon the table, then rings the servants' bell, and roars out the main hall door.*) One of you there. The gunpowder, and quick about it. (*He comes back and sits at the table.*)

MAURA. I knew as well as yourself you wouldn't stand insolence. I behaved insolent so as you'd order me from your house.

CAESAR. What the devil? What d'ye mean?

71

MAURA. I was many a month begging you to let me go, before my youth was past, but no good. At last my wits nudged me to behave all out impudent of a sudden, and vex you that much as you'd order me out. (CAESAR *looks at her hard for a moment or two; then turns away and grins ruefully.*)

CAESAR. So that was it! You baggage! And I thought you took me for a fool! (*He thumps the table vigorously, and is obviously much relieved.*) By George, you were right there. You fooled me to the eyes.

MAURA. Will you do me the favour? Will you spare his life?

CAESAR. Girl, pitch him to the devil. You're not going with him, you're stopping here with me. I cannot marry you: my own class would shun me if I did; but neither will I marry anyone else. I'm forty-five, and at that age a man doesn't tire of a girl so quickly. I'll not tire of you; don't you fear it.

MAURA (*quietly*). You mean what you say, no doubt; but, Caesar, it isn't in you to be loyal to a girl wance she has her looks lost.

CAESAR (*striding up and down*). That has yet to be tested, and proved. All my wenches so far proved fools, so I got rid of them long before they lost their looks; but you have enough brains to stick to your own business, and leave a man to mind his. So there will be nothing to sour us, or separate us. . . . Well, will you take your chance with me?

MAURA. 'Tis against God's law; and, moreover, too many young handsome girls are rising up on your property. In a few years you'd be cursing your pledges to me, or breaking them. So 'tis best for us to part now.

CAESAR (*bitterly*). So you're afraid to take your chance with me. Very well then; marry some ragamuffin with a few acres; and as for this Dowd fellow, I'll avoid killing him, if I can.

BOORLA (*entering with a plate of gunpowder*). The gunpowder, your honour, and I'm after reckoning up a plan that'd save the bother of fighting and killing Dowd.

MAURA. There's only wan way: to let her go free. (*She goes.*)

CAESAR (*grimly setting to work to reload the pistols*). Well, Boorla?

BOORLA (*urgently*). Your honour, Bartley Dowd'll not believe she tricked and deserted him on our word; he'll believe it only from herself; and she'll deny it hard and fast. Then he'll fight for her as savage as ever.

CAESAR. Well, if he won't believe us, more fool he.

BOORLA. There's wan plan, your honour. You to promise her her freedom if she'd tell Bartley to his face how she fooled him.

Then he'd not fight for her.

CAESAR. Understand, Boorla; I'll not let the wench go free if it was to save fifty lives.

BOORLA. Sure you'll only pretend to let herself and Owen Fenigan go free, and then, when they're a piece down the avenue, two or three of us'll spring on them from the trees, and retake them. Dowd'll never hear, or find out. You can keep him here in conversation.

CAESAR (*after walking up and down for a few moments*). Yes; that will save killing him, and give us another way of punishing him well for his attack on my men. Bring her in.

BOORLA. Yes, your honour. (*He hurries out.* CAESAR *paces the room planning hard.* BOORLA *and* BIDDY *come in with* UNA. CAESAR *sits at the table, surveys her.*)

CAESAR. I have made up my mind to let you go, on condition that you leave my property directly and never set foot on it again; secondly, that you confess to Dowd to his face how you tricked him and deserted him; thirdly, that you confess you cared only for young Fenigan all along.

UNA. But then I'd be talking liary, your honour. For I have true regard for Bartley, and I waited for Owen this day only to tell him so.

CAESAR. So, even when you're offered release, you won't tell the truth! Very well, back with her to the kitchen.

UNA (*desperately*). Your honour, I'll say anything ye like if ye'll spare Bartley's life.

CAESAR. Will you tell him you tricked him, and never cared two straws for him?

UNA. I will, your honour, though 'tis false.

CAESAR. Liar again! And will you choose young Fenigan to leave here with to-night, and to wed?

UNA. I will, your honour, if that'll save Bartley.

CAESAR. Very well. In that case – and in that case only – we will spare him. Take her away, Biddy, and send Gaisceen up with hot water and lemons for the punch.

(BIDDY *leads her out.* CAESAR *goes to the sideboard, sets upon it the punchbowl and ladle, also three glasses, and a bottle of brandy.* GAISCEEN *comes in with a tray containing a steaming kettle, a sugar bowl, and some lemons.*)

GAISCEEN (*about to go*). Is there anything else, your honour?

CAESAR. There is. Sit down, and keep me company in a bowl of punch. (*He brings three glasses to the wine table.*)

73

GAISCEEN (*taking his seat in an armchair*). I'm thankful to your honour. You were ever a great warrant to make punch, and it might raise my heart a piece. I'm grieved to think Bartley Dowd is likely to lose his life.

CAESAR (*going to the sideboard*). You may set your mind at ease about that. I have made up my mind to spare him. (*He pours some brandy into the punchbowl.*)

GAISCEEN (*jumping to his feet delightedly*). You have, your honour! What way?

CAESAR. By setting her free, and letting her go with Dowd or young Fenigan, whichever she chooses.

GAISCEEN. Your honour, the blessing of God'll light on you for that; and 'tis a thing I heard ever that 'tisn't lucky for a rich man to put to death a poor man.

(*He resumes his seat agian.* CAESAR *is busy making the punch. Suddenly the baying of the dogs is heard, very fierce, and close.*)

GAISCEEN (*jumping up*). That's him, your honour!

CAESAR (*calmly*). Very likely. You stay in your chair, as if expecting nothing. (*He draws the sword from its scabbard, and places it on the cabinet. He then resumes the mixing and making of the punch. The barking of the mastiffs comes closer and louder, then they are heard howling, as a shillelagh strikes them down.* BARTLEY *jumps in, bloody and fierce looking, shillelagh in hand. He bounds in in such a way that his back is turned to* CAESAR, *who picks up his sword and stands on guard.*)

BARTLEY. Gaisceen, where is she?

GAISCEEN. Happy and safe and sound in the kitchen. Master Caesar forgave her for all, and she can go free.

BARTLEY. Gaisceen, they're tricking you!

GAISCEEN. No, 'tis the truth. She can go free directly with yourself, or anywan she likes. I'll bring her before you.

BARTLEY (*bewildered, and still suspicious*). Where's Caesar?

CAESAR (*stepping forward, hands behind his back, very stern and haughty of eye*). Here; and would horsewhip you for breaking into my house, but that you won my wager for me to-day.

(BARTLEY *turns, and the two stare into each other's faces at fifteen inches' range;* CAESAR *in his sombre fashion interested;* BARTLEY *at first fierce, and as if about to strike, but then restraining himself.*)

BARTLEY (*grimly*). If 'tis the truth you haven't her harmed, and you're giving her leave to go, then I'll say no word.

CAESAR (*peremptorily*). Gaisceen, fetch her in. And let young

Fenigan be brought likewise.

GAISCEEN. Yes, your honour. (*He goes out.* CAESAR *indicates the sofa grimly*).

CAESAR. There while you wait. (*He turns on his heel and goes back to the sideboard.* BARTLEY *sits on the sofa, and watches* CAESAR *warily.* CAESAR *brings the punchbowl and the ladle to the wine table. Then he turns to* BARTLEY).

CAESAR. You're a battered-looking fellow, Dowd, and past your best. Yet you expect these sluts to be faithful to you. You are no better than a fool. (*And, turning on his heel, he walks back to the wine table again.*)

BARTLEY (*eagerly*). On account my youth and looks are lost, your honour, I'll fight the sky and the stars above before I'll lose her. She's my last chance.

CAESAR. Then your last chance is lost. Why do you suppose she waited behind you for young Fenigan?

BARTLEY. No doubt to tell him she was wedding myself in two days, and to cheer him up as best she could.

CAESAR. You will now hear from her own lips what everybody already knows: that from first to last she tricked and betrayed you . . . .

BOORLA (*entering*). Here they are, your honour.
(UNA *enters, looking pale and reluctant.* OWEN *follows, looking bewildered but hopeful. He is dressed in old clothes obviously not made for him.* GAISCEEN *follows in the rear.*)

BARTLEY (*running forward to meet her*). Una, are you safe and sound?

UNA (*in a strangled voice*). I am, Bartley.

BARTLEY (*eagerly*). I bested Kithogue, and won the ten acres; so you'll never see a hungry day again.

CAESAR. Bartley Dowd, return to your place until I tell you to leave it.

BARTLEY (*quietly, but grimly*). Yes, your honour. (*He returns to the sofa, where he sits upright, shillelagh in hand and with half an eye on* BOORLA, *who takes up his stand behind the other end of the sofa.*)

CAESAR. Girl, come here. (*She stands before him*). As I told you, I have made up my mind to let you go, provided you leave my property, and never set foot on it again. You may go now with whichever of these men you wish. I am told you promised marriage to both of them, but as a magistrate, I cannot allow bigamy; and the penalty, as you know, is hanging. So you must

75

do with one of them only. You must go with him directly; and the other must remain here an hour or so until you are well clear of the property. Do both of you men agree to that?

BARTLEY (*delighted*). To be sure, your honour.

OWEN (*bewildered, but confident*). Yes, yes, your honour.

CAESAR. Very well, (*Turning to* UNA.) Which do you choose to go with, and to marry? . . . Answer, woman.

UNA (*at last, tragically*). Owen Fenigan . . . .

OWEN (*quickly, taking her by the arm*). Let us be making our way off now. (*She buries her face in her hands, and turns to go.*)

CAESAR. Well, Dowd, do you believe me now?

BARTLEY. Ye liary ruffians, ye have the truth frightened out of her! (*He springs to her side, swings her away from them and, with his shillelagh at the ready, confronts them fiercely. But, quickly as he has moved, by the time he is in position* CAESAR *has taken his sword from the right wall cabinet, while* BOORLA *takes from his pocket a big horse-pistol.*)

CAESAR (*fiercely*). Can she tell the truth with your shillelagh threatening her head? Stand aside, or I'll run you through. (*He pulls back his sword-arm wristband, and advances.*)

BARTLEY. Hi for Tyrawley, then! (*But, before either can strike,* GAISCEEN *runs between them.*)

GAISCEEN. Master Caesar! – Bartley! – in the honour of God stop, let ye!

CAESAR. He must stand aside, and let her speak her mind.

GAISCEEN. Bartley, 'tis only fair. Let the two of ye stand back from her, and Gaisceen'll ask her fair and easy.

CAESAR. That is all I ask. (*He moves back to the right wall cabinet, and leans against it, sword in hand.*)

BARTLEY. Very well, then. Speak your mind, girl, and have no fear of fair weapons or false. The like were tested before now by Bartley. (*He steps back to the end of the sofa.*)

GAISCEEN. Tell the truth out, girl; which is your choice to marry and to go with now.

(*She looks at* BARTLEY, *and then at* CAESAR *with his sword, and* BOORLA *with his gun.*)

UNA. Owen Fenigan and (*Turning to* OWEN *imploringly.*) let us go, Owen.

BARTLEY. Una girl, have they put spells on you? D'ye forget we were to be wedded in two days?

UNA (*not daring to look at him*). I have my mind changed, Bartley. (*Desperately.*) Owen, let us be off. (*She stumbles towards the door.*)

CAESAR. Come back, woman! You are not to go until you give us the whole of the truth. You did not change your mind. You never intended to marry Dowd at all. Isn't that so, woman?

UNA (*after a pause, helplessly*). 'Tis, your honour.

GAISCEEN (*shocked*). By the elevens!

BARTLEY (*pleadingly*). Una, let you not say you were only mocking me.

CAESAR. And the night of the dance, when you pretended regard and promised marriage to him, it was a trick, so that he'd fight against my men in the kitchen. Wasn't that so?

UNA. 'Twas, your honour.

BARTLEY (*turning away numbly*). Blood and 'ouns! So it was only a trick was in it! And myself full sure 'twas the Chalice time of the Mass. (*He sits down, and buries his face in his hands. His shillelagh rolls across the floor.*)

CAESAR (*to* UNA). Well, you have told the truth at last, and now pack off from French's country, the pair of you before I change my mind. (OWEN *takes her by the arm, and leads her out.*)

CAESAR. Boorla, march them down to the Avenue gate, and off my property.

BOORLA. I'll clear them fast and far, your honour. (BOORLA *follows them out.*)

CAESAR. Gaisceen, serve the punch.

GAISCEEN. Yes, your honour. (*He goes to the wine table, fills the glasses, using the punch ladle.* CAESAR *stalks up and down, looking at his most gloomy and savage. He looks out the window a moment, then turns to* BARTLEY.)

CAESAR. You are a man of mettle, Dowd, and by all accounts the finest shillelagh fighter in this province. You are all that, and you fought seven men for her, yet she throws you over for a smooth-skinned young whipper-snapper of no merit whatsoever. These young sluts are all the same; they are all worthless fools, and the only sensible course is to treat them accordingly. (*He goes back to the window.*)

BARTLEY (*bitterly*). I'd not mind her telling the lie when she was in jeopardy. But when she was saved, she went ahead mocking me for three long days. My curse upon her, and the curse of my people, and the curse of God, moreover.

CAESAR (*with grim satisfaction*). That is spoken more like a man. That is the way to deal with them – curse them into hell, and out of your mind, then drink yourself back into good humour. (*He*

77

rises, takes the plate of gunpowder, and goes out the door back to the library.)

GAISCEEN (*taking his own glass of punch*). Bartley, you have that girl wronged in your mind. The first night she told the lie, 'twas myself put it into her head.

BARTLEY. You did! You reckoned I'd fail a woman, and she in such jeopardy!

GAISCEEN. No, but I reckoned you'd stand no chance against seven men unless you'd fight beyond your best; and her marriage pledge was the likeliest that'd rouse you.

BARTLEY (*somewhat mollified, but still gloomy*). So that was how it all sprung. . . . And she was afeard to tell me after.

GAISCEEN. She was afeard. And then myself sent her word with Rory that Owen was a prisoner, so she gave in to marry you in earnest. Till to-day, when she must hear tell Owen was to escape again.

BARTLEY. So that was the way it was; . . . Well, so long as she wasn't mocking me, I"ll say no more about her. She couldn't help it if God put more love in her heart for him.

CAESAR (*entering with brace of pistols*). Gaisceen, I shall want you at the hunt at Blakemount tomorrow. The Blakes may make trouble over this evening's fight with Blake of Lowberry, so make sure to clean and pack my pistols.

(*Suddenly shouts and screams are heard from the avenue.*)

BARTLEY. What is it? Men fighting? (*He runs to the window.*) Boorla's voice, I'd take my oath. And Una's voice, and she calling for help. And you said you'd let her go free! (*He springs to the sofa, and takes up his shillelagh.*)

CAESAR. Will you make a fool of yourself for her again?

BARTLEY (*fiercely*). I'll not fail her whatever. (*He jumps on to the window sill, and, as he does so,* CAESAR *snatches up his sword, and cries: – "Come back, rascal!" but* BARTLEY *clears the sill and jumps clear.*)

CAESAR. Stand and fight, coward! (*He jumps out the window in hot pursuit.*)

BARTLEY (*outside*). Hi for Bartley! Hi for Tyrawley!

CAESAR (*outside.*) Stand aside, or I'll split you like a Martinmas goose.

GAISCEEN (*running to the window*). Your honour! . . . Bartley! . . . stop, let ye! (*Suddenly a terrible sound is heard as of a skull-crushing blow*). God save us! He's done! He's no more! (*He jumps out of the window. In a moment or two* BIDDY *enters, smoking as usual.*)

BIDDY. Is it ructions ye're having here?

GAISCEEN (*appearing at the window carrying the body of* CAESAR FRENCH.) Biddy, help me.

BIDDY (*dropping her pipe in dismay, and running to the window*). His honour! Is he no more?

GAISCEEN. His skull is beaten in. The poor fellow's sins have him overtaken at last.

BIDDY. God in heaven have mercy on him. (*They carry the body to the sofa.*)

GAISCEEN (*coming in*). At any rate, Our Saviour knows well the poor fellow had the misfortune to have riches and power to do what he liked.

(*Together they lay the body on the sofa, and* GAISCEEN *lays it out.*)

BIDDY (*wringing her hands*). Between fighting and hunting, he was every year in danger, still he wouldn't marry and make an heir for his name. God must be tired of the Frenches of Kilmacreena.

GAISCEEN (*mournfully*). It appears so. . . . Biddy, ready the long table for his laying out. (BIDDY *goes, picking up her pipe.* GAISCEEN *goes on his knees beside the sofa, and solemnly addresses the empty air and the newly-disembodied soul of* CAESAR FRENCH.)

GAISCEEN (*gravely*). Your honour, if you're not left yet, here's Gaisceen's last advice to you. On account of the tallywomen, let you not go stepping boldly in the Gate to St. Peter. Your brightest chance'd be to wait till a big lot'd be going in together, and then maybe you could duck behind them and dodge in that way. But if that plan fails you, and St. Peter draws down about tallywomen, let you have it on the tip of your tongue about how well conducted you were in your youthful days, and swearing all oaths you'd never let tallywomen fool you the same as the fooled your father; till you were reckless with wine a night in Castle Browne, and wan of Browne's tallywomen made a blackguard for life of you. Tell them straight up about that sore misfortune that ruined you.

(RORY *comes in slowly. He is remarkably changed since his last appearance. His eyes are bloodshot and sunken, his shoulders are stooped, his old air of wild arrogance is replaced by one of numb and crazy despair.*)

RORY (*looking at* CAESAR). The curse of the poor on him for losing the life just when I wanted him to shoot me, and relieve me from this world.

GAISCEEN. Rory Commons! (*Noticing the change in him.*) What ails you? Is Cormac well again?

RORY (*dully*). Dead as a mackerel, and brought the gift with him.

GAISCEEN. By the elevens! He didn't leave you his gift!

RORY. I'm no composer. I'm only a man still. (*He wanders back across the room towards the right wall cabinet on which* CAESAR'S *pistol lies.*) 'Twould be great ease to me to be shot. (*He takes down the pistol, and brings it to the table.*)

GAISCEEN. But are you sure, Rory? Did you make any trial of composing?

RORY (*exploring the gun like a sulky schoolboy*). The minute the death took him I set into composing a lament for him, but it failed me to strike two lines together. Then I made off to the cabin of Miser Lally and made a trial of a scolding song, but that failed me, too. (*He turns the muzzle of the gun against his breast.*)

GAISCEEN (*stopping him*). Wait, Rory, till I tell you. You were too grieved and stirred about to be fit for composing that time. 'Twould come easier for you to compose the lament for Master Caesar. 'Twas Cormac composed the laments for Caesar's father and grandfather. (RORY *lowers the gun, and suddenly the old fire comes back into his eyes.*)

RORY (*wildly*). Stand back then, and let me at him! (*He runs to the sofa, goes on his knees beside the sofa. He roars out.*) Cormac, if you refuse me the gift this time, I'll curse you till the divils'll make a mortar of your blood and bones in hell! (*Now burying his face in his hands and rocking to and fro, at another time staring into* CAESAR'S *face crazily, alternatively praying and cursing under his breath, he endeavours frantically to set the gift at work.* GAISCEEN *moves softly about the room in his rear, watching him eagerly.*)

GAISCEEN. Let you not forget his great actions. How he killed Black Bodkin at the pistol, and Colonel Dillon, and George Blake with his sword, and defeated many a gentleman more. How his dark reds won every cock-fighting from the Shannon to the sea. The fine woods he planted, and the many a hundred of young couples he let settle on his land. (BARTLEY *enters through the window quietly and grimly. He looks at* CAESAR *a moment or two, then turns to* GAISCEEN.)

BARTLEY. He's no more?

GAISCEEN (*nodding*). The poor fellow.

BARTLEY. God rest him. . . . I was too much in hurry to weigh my blow. His sword was scraping my ribs. (*He opens his jacket, and briefly indicates some bloodstains in the region of his ribs. He glances at* RORY, *then back to Gaisceen inquiringly.*)

GAISCEEN (*whispering*). Cormac is dead, and Rory is making a trial of the gift. He's composing a lament for Master Caesar.

BARTLEY. I'll wait a spell till we see will it thrive with him. (*He sits on the armchair, and leans forward watching* RORY *closely. His face is grim, the face of a man who realises at last the pattern of life which lies ahead for him.*)

RORY (*jumping up wildly*). Let me in there, Caesar French! (*Suddenly and savagely he drags the body on to the floor behind the couch, and out of sight of the audience. He lies on the couch himself.*)

GAISCEEN (*to* BARTLEY *nodding approvingly*). A wise plan, too. The best way Cormac and Ossian and their like could compose was lying at their ease on a bed. . . . Tell me did you defeat Boorla and his lot?

BARTLEY. I did.

GAISCEEN. Are Una and Owen coming back, or are they making off?

BARTLEY. I didn't ask them. (*He is watching* RORY'S *composing with intense interest, and seems to have no other interest left.*)

GAISCEEN. If you didn't tell them Caesar is no more, she'll be afeard to come back likely.

(BIDDY *and* MAURA *enter, and the latter, seeing* CAESAR, *stops in her tracks, blesses herself, and turns away for a few moments.*)

GAISCEEN. Easy, let ye. Rory is composing.

BIDDY (*coming up to* BARTLEY). The gentry'll hang you for this the same as if you killed Master Caesar for his gold. You must make off for the mountains directly.

BARTLEY (*briefly*). I will. (*His interest remains fixed upon* RORY.)

BIDDY. I'll ready up eatables for your journey.

(BIDDY *goes out.* MAURA *draws slowly over to* BARTLEY, *and looks as if she is trying to pluck up courage.*)

MAURA. Bartley, I'd take my chance with you wherever you're going, and I have thirteen round guineas that'd be great help to you.

BARTLEY (*turning slowly, and with grim incredulity*). Is it wed me, and the hangman already harnessing his cart for me, you might say?

MAURA. I'd take my chance with you, and I'll tell you all honestly and straightforward. I was a tallywoman to Caesar for two years.

BARTLEY (*seizing her arms with sudden excitement*). So misfortune crossed you, too! Maybe so you'd be no worse off if I wed you!

GAISCEEN (*in horror*). Maura Pender, d'ye want to lead him to his downfall? If he's to escape the gentlemen and their horses and bloodhounds he'll want to be wandering fast and free, and not harnessed to a wife.

MAURA (*after a pause*). 'Tis the truth, Bartley. I'd only delay, and ruin you.

(*He releases her, and she goes out. He looks after her a moment, then sets his jaw grimly, and turns his attention to* RORY *again. A moment later,* RORY *rolls over, beating the sofa in anguish and despair.*)

RORY. I'm no composer, I tell ye. I'm only a man still. He brought the gift with him, so here I am betrayed and old and useless for the world. I'll throw myself from the highest tree Caesar has.

(BARTLEY *suddenly crosses, and sits at the head of the sofa, looking down at* RORY.)

BARTLEY (*quietly*). Rory, you have the same mistake made as me. 'Tisn't for good fortune God put our like in the world, but only to do odd jobs for Him. Yourself to give good minding to His composer that was blind, and myself to snatch a girl from the Pressgang, and to keep hunger from my sister-in-law and her orphans. We can no way complain. Himself gave His life for us of a Friday . . . .

GAISCEEN (*as one confirming grave tidings*). It appears all right ye're picked amongst the King of Friday's men. . . . But if ye are itself, He'll reward ye highly when yere life's day is over at last.

RORY (*staggering to his feet*). Bartley Dowd has strength, and can earn his bread, but Rory is too old, and he hasn't the begging prayers off, and there's no road or boreen but has enemies his father scolded. Rory'll not wait for the hunger to melt his flesh in a ditch. From the highest tree he'll toss himself body and bones.

(*He makes for the main hall door, but* BARTLEY *stops him*).

BARTLEY. Rory, you have no occasion to end your days wrong. Come west to the mountains, and while I live you'll not get hunger, and you'll be teaching Cormac's songs and stories to me.

(*He leads* RORY *to the armchair, where he subsides into quietude, his head in his hands.* BIDDY *and* MAURA *enter.*)

BIDDY, Here's a stitch or two left by my own man that's in heaven, or dead at any rate. (*She places a hat and coat on the table.*) And Maura has the eatables for you.

BARTLEY. God reward ye.

(BIDDY *goes out.* MAURA *puts some food and a bottle of wine into the bundle.* BARTLEY *puts on the hat and coat.*)

GAISCEEN. In the run of a couple of years, when the hunt slackens down, maybe ye could settle in some quarter of the mountains; maybe in the Joyce country. The Joyces are very loyal against the English law, and you'd be a great addition to them in their fights against the O'Malleys.

BARTLEY. If I live, we'll draw to the Joyce country at last, so. (*He ties the neck of the bag around one end of his shillelagh.*)

GAISCEEN. Maybe in two years or three, Maura and myself'd meet ye thereabouts at the Gooseberry Fair of Clonbur.

BARTLEY. I'll be there if I'm living, but (*To* MAURA.) Let yourself not wait, but wed a decent lad. Only odd jobs such as minding himself (*Indicating* RORY.) is allotted to me. (*He takes* RORY'S *stick from the floor and puts it into his hands.*)

MAURA (*quietly*). I'll be at the fair whatever.

BIDDY (*appearing at the door, back*). Let ye come this way. I have the front door open for ye.

RORY (*rising, and looking around him with a touch of his old pride*). Any road up, if Rory is only a man itself, no mortal man in the ring of Ireland has all Cormac's songs and stories off the same as him. Rory'll raise the Joyces up to be learned men. So lag no longer, Bartley Dowd.

(RORY *goes out back.* BARTLEY *takes his shillelagh and bundle and puts them on his shoulder.*)

GAISCEEN. Did you see that, Bartley? God never closed wan gap but He opened another. Already you're master of the songs and stories of Tyrawley, and in a few years you'll have off the songs and stories of Cormac and of the Joyce country, too. You'll be a king story-teller from that out till you die.

BARTLEY (*nodding grimly*). Very apt I will be a good story-teller. 'Twill be something. (*He moves towards the door, but halts halfway.*) If ye cross her ever, tell her send to the Joyce country any time she's in jeopardy, and, if Bartley is living, he'll not fail her. (*Matter-of-factly.*) And let ye spare an odd prayer for Rory and myself – for a few days whatever. Misfortune that sticks too long'd wear the rocks. (*In the doorway he halts a moment; squares his shoulders resolutely, frees his shillelagh for action, and goes. And the play ends.*)

CURTAIN

GAISCEEN'S SONG

slán aʒus beannaċt le buaıóneaó an t-saoʒaıl.

(GOOD-BYE AND FAREWELL TO THE TROUBLES OF THE WORLD.)

♩. = 63

Sung by Mr. Martin Burke,
Abbey, Tuam.

1. One morning in June, aʒur mé 'oul, a ṫrairceóıp-eaċt, Carað lıom caıl-ın 'r bað ró-ṫear a ʒnaoı, She was so handsome, oo ċuıt mé ı nʒpáð léıċı, 'S o'fáʒ rí an ap-paınʒ ċpí láp - mo ċpoıóe. I axed her her name, "nó ʒoıo - é an puaıʒ beannuıʒċe, a ċar ınr an áıt ċú a ʒpáð ʒeal mo ċpoıóe? My heart it will break, if you don't come a - long with me, slán aʒur beannaċt le buaıóneaó an t-raoʒaıl."

2. " maıre! caılín beaʒ óʒ mé, ó ċeanntap
na faıpıʒe,
aʒur tóʒaó ʒo cnearca mé ı otorað mo
faoʒaıl,
I being so airy, ó ır é púo bað ċleaċtaċ lıom,
Which made my own parents and me disagree."
"maır', a ċuırle, 'r a rtóıp, aċt a n-éırtá
lıom tamall
I'd tell you a story a b'aıt le oo ċpoıóe,
That I'm a young man that's doughtily in love
with you,
And surely my heart is from roguery free."

3. " Go, you bowld rogue, sure you're wanting
to pláter me,
b'feapp éan ap an láıṁ ná óá éan ap a
'ʒcpaoıb.
I have neither wheat, potatoes, nor anything,
ná fıú an pluıo leabaıċ a béaó ċappaınn
'ran oıóċe."

" Ceannóċaıó mé céı óuıc, 'ʒur ʒléar maıċ
ın aıce pın,
,ʒún' English cotton óe'n fáıpıún atá oaop,
So, powder your hair, love, and come away 'long
with me,
slán aʒur beannaċt le buaıóneaó an tpaoʒaıl."

4. " There's an ale-house near by, aʒur béıómuıo ʒo maıoın ann,
If you are satisfied, a ʒpáð ʒeal mo ċpoıóe,
Early next morning we'll send for a clergyman,
aʒur béıómıo-ne ceanʒaılc' 'nʒan-fıor
oo'n t-raoʒal.
béıómuıo aʒ ól, fao maıpfear an t-aıpʒean,
And then we will take the road home with all
speed.
When the reckoning is paid, who cares for the
landlady?
slán aʒur beannaċt le buaıóneaó an
tpaoʒaıl."

84

The Paddy Pedlar

A PLAY IN ONE ACT

DEDICATION

To the memory of Gerald Molloy who directed the Ballina Players in this play's first production in 1952.

CHARACTERS

OOSHLA, A small farmer.
THADY, A farmer's son.
HONOR, Thady's sweetheart.
SIBBY, A farmer's wife.
MATTHIAS, Another farmer.
THE PADDY PEDLAR.

PRODUCTION NOTE

Don't let any part of the "contents" of the pedlar's sack be seen by the audience; the "contents" are best left entirely to their imagination. The sack itself should never be let stand on its end, or held in any way likely to outline its "contents."

The play is most successful when produced at a good fast pace, and should not take more than 45 to 50 minutes.

The Paddy Pedlar

The scene is the kitchen of a small straw-thatched cottage on the outskirts of a peasant village, in an out-of-the-way hilly part of the Galway-Mayo border country. The time is the autumn of the year 1840 during Ireland's Famine decade

The furniture is rudimentary. There are no chairs, only a few rough home-made wooden stools. There is no table, and the dresser is small and empty save for one wooden mug with a wooden porridge spoon laid across it, one large knife, and a few eggshells arranged in order. On the right hand wall hangs a smoke-blackened cross consisting merely of two sticks nailed together. The dresser stands against the back wall, on the right from the actor's point of view. On the left end of the back wall is the door opening on to the road. In this wall also is the usual small window. Some sheaves of straw stand in a corner. The fireplace is in the right hand wall, and doors in the right hand and left hand walls lead to the two bedrooms.

OOSHLA CLANCY *lies fully dressed on his back on the floor, with one leg across one of the stools, from which he had fallen in drunken slumber. A small whiskey jar stands at his elbow on another stool.*

After the curtain goes up there is stillness for a few moments, then a horseman can be heard riding by and driving a herd of cattle, cracking his whip, and shouting at both cattle and dog as he goes so. "S-go on there! S-go on there!" (Loudly.) "Turn them out, dog! Get before them! Easy there." And so, with much barking from the dog, they move on out of earshot.

But the noise has awakened OOSHLA, *and he shifts uneasily, and finally sits up. He clutches at his head, and groans.*

OOSHLA. Oh, murther! My head is ruined for life and for ever! My curse on the poteen, and the curse of the Seven Ganders that plucked the grass off Solomon's grave! (*He turns over, sees the jar at his elbow, growls in hatred.*) There you are still, and may the Divil fly away with you! (*He hesitates a few moments, weakening at every moment; then with a cry.*) 'Tis kill or cure, and better be dead than the state I'm in. (*He grasps the jar in*

88

both hands and takes a mighty swig. He rises, and sets out for the door, a little shakily at first, but is soon himself again. He is a well built man of fifty with the alert eye and quick speech of the man who has contrived to live for many years on his wits and by roguery. But there is nothing low, or mean looking, about him. On the contrary there is a curious air of the gentleman; and it appears in his seriousness, in his impressive gestures and walk and carriage, in his clear cut speech, and in the way he waxes his moustache ends. His clothes he contrives to wear with an air, although they are old cast-offs. Yet all this seems to proceed not from affections, but from some kind of inner conviction. He unbolts and opens the door, and looks upon the sunset for a few moments. Suddenly he starts, closes the door hastily, puts the poteen jar on the dresser and has just time to stretch on the hearth simulating sleep when THADY *and* HONOR *come in.* HONOR *is about twenty, tall, slow moving and quiet, and good-looking, too, in an unsophisticated country way. She is serious and silent, and her look is abstracted. She seems a kind, sincere type of girl.*)

THADY *is a big, easy-going, good-humoured fellow in the late twenties. His voice is very soft and low for so big a man. Before speaking to, or replying to, anyone, he looks upon him for a moment or two, and then addresses him directly and confidentially as if there was no one else in the room. His shrewd and tolerant eyes look around upon all the world good-humouredly. He wears a hat and he carries a stout blackthorn stick.*)

HONOR. He's sleeping yet. In the daytime he do sleep mostly, on account the dark night is his safest time for stealing.

THADY. And is this all the bed he has?

HONOR. Not it. He has a fine feather bed back in the room. He must be as drunk as a stick, or he'd not fall-off asleep here. (*She sets to work to light the fire.* THADY *espies the jar of poteen on the dresser, and duly sniffs at, and tastes it.*)

THADY. Prime poteen he has. D'ye think did he steal it the same as he steals all his wants of spuds and oatmeal.

HONOR. Ooshla steals only spuds and oatmeal, enough to keep the breath in him. A well-wisher gave him the poteen likely.

THADY (*looking into the bedroom on the right*). 'Tis a fine lump of a house, and as clean as a leaf. We wouldn't call the Queen our Aunt if we were married in here.

HONOR. He's sure and certain to let us live here. He'd never have squandered my fortune only his wife was after dying, and he

THE PADDY PEDLAR

had no family, and he honestly meant to leave me his house and land that'd be worth more than my twenty guineas fortune.

THADY (*crossing to look into the other room*). Your father behaved as silly as a duck to go giving Ooshla your fortune. Didn't he know well that money is tempting?

HONOR. Sure my father was failing fast with the fever himself, so he had to trust it to someone until I grew up. He know my mother was lighthearted, and sure to spend it. (*Pulling a loose stone out of the wall.*) In here Ooshla had the guineas sleeping before the Divil coaxed him to start spending them at last.

THADY. Maybe he hasn't it all spent yet. If I left my thumb on his throat a while, maybe he'd own up to a few guineas saved. (*He kneels beside* OOSHLA, *and begins to push back his sleeves.*)

HONOR. He hasn't a brass farthing left. Once he commenced spending he was a year taking his ease and pleasuring, and then he had to go stealing for a living, for he had the habit of work lost.

THADY. To go robbing a young orphan's fortune was a dirty turn. Rouse up, Ooshla Clancy, till we see will you act manful, and make the loss good. (*He pokes him in the ribs good-humouredly.*)

OOSHLA. Did I hear a stir? (*Sees* HONOR.) Honor, is that yourself? (*Sees* THADY.) And who is the young man? (*He is affable; but serious and gentlemanly as usual.*)

HONOR (*Between whom and* OOSHLA *there seems to be a strong bond of affection*). Thady Durkin my bachelor that I was telling you about. Let ye be talking, and I'll ready your breakfast first, and join in the talk further on.

(*She is busy for some time now. She finds a dozen or so of warm roasted potatoes in the ashes, and places them upon a stool. She puts beside it a mug of water taken from a wooden bucket near the door. She finds a large piece of oaten cake in the dresser, and slices it up with the big knife displayed on the dresser. This also she leaves beside the potatoes. from time to time she pauses and watches the pair, listening in her silent way.*)

OOSHLA (*quickly and anxiously*). Tell me did you win your fight against your young brother?

THADY (*cheerfully*). Not me; I'm no match for him at either the shillelagh, or the thumps. There was more flour in the spuds the year he was born.

OOSHLA (*very disappointed*). Well that's dull news! So your father'll leave him the farm?

90

THADY. He will. Evermore in our family the farm is left to the best fighter. So herself and myself must go foreign in search of a living.

OOSHLA. But did you not tell him, Honor, that ye can marry in here, and have my land.

HONOR. I told him all.

THADY. We're very thankful to you, Ooshla, but the way it is our people bore an honest name evermore, and how then could we go living with a rogue?

OOSHLA (*rising in dignified reproach*). Is it me to be a rogue? Thady Durkin, blow that from your mind. (*He crosses to dresser, and takes up the poteen jar.*) My course of life was that I passed a year one time spending her money, and lost the habit of work, so I had to have the other tenant farmers do the work for me the same as they do for the gentlemen, their landlords. But I couldn't take their crops openly the same as the landlords do. All I could do was take enough to keep me living of spuds and oatmeal in the midnight, when the world is in bed. (*He comes from the dresser with the jar, and two eggshells. He fills one eggshell, and gives it to* THADY. HONOR *takes the turf creel, and goes out the front door.*)

THADY. But, Ooshla, 'tis God's law that all should work, but the gentlemen.

OOSHLA (*quickly and solemnly*). That's it, work for all but the gentlemen, so no work for Ooshla, because God appointed Ooshla to be a gentleman too. (*He sits down, and pours out an eggshellful for himself.*)

THADY (*chuckling*). How could God appoint you for a gentleman when He gave you no riches?

OOSHLA. He overlooked the riches some way or other; still He appointed Ooshla to be a gentleman.

THADY. He did! Give me the ins and outs of that, Ooshla.

OOSHLA. When men that aren't gentlemen get riches, they go ahead with the work, more or less of it; they wouldn't be content unless they were doing something. But from the first minute I had money to spend, I took to idleness as ready and easy as a woman takes to scolding. I didn't care if I never left hand, foot, or toe on a piece of work again.

THADY. At that gait of going every idler in the country was appointed to be a gentleman; every idler and lazy old scratch that does no work only lying across the hearth like a pig that'd be full up. (HONOR *enters with a creel of turf.*)

91

THE PADDY PEDLAR

OOSHLA (*rising indignantly*). Thady Durkin, is every drone in the country the same as me? Can they set their words out on their edges one after another the same as me? (*Taking up an impressive stance.*) Can they stand like gentlemen with their toes out and as straight as whipping posts the same as me? Can they step out like gentlemen the same as me? Steady you sight now. (*He walks up and down the kitchen a couple of times in imposing style.*)

THADY (*admiringly*). No lie, you can show your boot soles as good as any gentleman.

OOSHLA. Wait a minute. You didn't see the half of me yet. (*He goes into the bedroom peeling off his jacket as he goes.*)

THADY. The divil a such a man ever I clapped an eye on! Honor, 'tis time you went outside to see is the sky inclined to fall. In a minute he'll be back with nothing covering him only his spine.

HONOR (*smiling, for she knows Ooshla of old*). When you see him next, he'll surprise you.

(OOSHLA *comes out dressed as before except for the important additions of a top-hat and dress coat, both more or less damaged cast-offs. He swings an ashplant peeled so as to resemble a cane. He crosses the stage, comes back, and confronts* THADY *triumphantly.*)

OOSHLA. Is it any wonder all call me Ooshla, meaning "the Gentleman"! Haven't I the cut of a gentleman every way you take me?

THADY. I give in you have. But still you're not entitled to go taking your needs from the poor people, and give them no return. The landlord gentlemen take a share of their crops, but they give them the use of their land.

OOSHLA (*vigorously*). But amn't I giving my cleverness free to the poor of this country? Here they are lowing with the hunger, and rackrented and robbed and threatened by rogue landlords, and rogue Bailiffs and rogue Attorneys. Whenever a poor man can see no way out, he'll come to me, and say: "Ooshla, I'm an honest man, and no match for these rogues; but you're the cleverest rogue since the Gobawn, and maybe you could save me." So Ooshla makes a little thought, and in a minute has a trick made that'll bring that man safe. Isn't that so, Honor?

HONOR. No lie at all: the poor people are swarming like bees to Ooshla for help. Ooshla has as many tricks as the cat, and one more than him.

THADY. Still and all, Ooshla, if we went living with you, the rogue's

92

brand'd be on all ever we'd have, or spend, or buy. The back-biting lot'd say all, and our daughters' fortunes as well, were saved up out of your rogueries.

HONOR. That's the hobble we're in, Ooshla, so we must go foreign, unless you'll give up the roguery, and earn your living with the spade any more.

OOSHLA. But the digging'd dull my brain again, and I'd not be clever enough to help the poor against the rogue Bailiffs and the rogue landlords. 'Twould be the greatest sin in the world for me to go digging again.

HONOR (*sympathetically*). Never mind so, Ooshla, we'll go foreign to America; and in no time we'll be at the top of Fortune's wheel in it. (*She rises to go.*)

OOSHLA (*genuinely concerned*). But I hear tell there's a bad time out there lately, with a power of Banks failing, the foreign men begging for want of work, and the foreign girls having to earn their daily bread by night.

THADY. Still they reckon the American country is so wide and the people so few, that the dog never barks at a stranger in it. So there'll be land in plenty smiling at us to take it. (*He goes to the door.*)

HONOR. We'll be all right, Ooshla. Thady is coming up now to meet my mother and my brother. (*She goes to the door.*)

OOSHLA. I'll be up to ye the minute I have my supper down; and maybe I'll save ye yet from going foreign.

HONOR. Let you not be troubling your mind about that at all, Ooshla. (*She goes.* THADY *turns in the doorway, and addresses* OOSHLA *cheerfully.*)

THADY. Ooshla, you have yourself believing you're entitled to be a rogue; but you're as soft as a penny book to believe the like of that. You're not entitled to make a living by roguery; 'tis oul' Nick himself is making a fool of you. But we're greatly obliged to you, whatever. (*He goes.* OOSHLA *looks downcast and doubtful for a moment or two; then as if to restore his confidence he rises, and does another superbly gentlemanlike walk around the kitchen. He takes off the tall hat, brushes a speck of dust from it, and goes into the room. He is back in a moment wearing his old jacket and minus the tall hat. He settles down to his breakfast.* SIBBY *comes in, and makes her way up to him. She is haggard and listless with hunger and worry.*)

SIBBY. Sir, aren't you Ooshla Clancy, the rogue of Killeenreevagh?

OOSHLA (*with dignity*). I'm Ooshla Clancy, the friend of the poor!

SIBBY (*sitting down and looking into the fire listlessly*). Last year the spuds failed on us greatly. Seven children we have, and you wouldn't know which of them is the biggest or the smallest with the hunger. Five of them maybe'll be able to stop in our house, but the other two'll be gone to their graves before the new spuds are grown.

OOSHLA. Who is your landlord?

SIBBY. Captain Blake of Lowberry, Sir.

OOSHLA. The Captain is a thorough-bred gentleman, and from the real old stock; still he'll give ye no help.

SIBBY (*unemotionally*). He won't, sir. He has two dogs as big as asses for tearing down poor people that'd come annoying him for help.

OOSHLA. To be sure he has. If a gentleman gave food to one poor person, he'd be swarmed out with people asking. A poor person'll get no help from them unless he'll trick them some way.

SIBBY. All tell me so, and all tell me you're the best hand at tricks on account you're a rogue.

OOSHLA (*impressively in his best professional style*). Sit over there out of my view, while I'm reckoning up a remedy for your hobble.

SIBBY. God spare you the health, sir. God spare you the health. (*She takes up the stool, crosses to the back wall, and sits there watching* OOSHLA *anxiously, blessing herself and praying hard.*)

OOSHLA (*after eating away for a few moments*). Likely the Captain steps out viewing his estate middling often?

SIBBY. Every morning after his breakfast he walks out, but he'll give no hearing to any poor person that'll come looking for help.

OOSHLA. If you ask him for help, your case is lost. Instead, when he's coming the way, let you pass him out, and you driving the ass and baskets with a child in each basket. Let you be looking very wild, and be crying like the Banshee; then he'll halt you and ask you where you're off to. Tell him you're bringing the children to the lake to drown them; that you couldn't be looking at them starving. For that he'll blacken your body with his walking stick; but you'll see he'll put you under keen commands to send the children down to his kitchen door every day till the new spuds are grown.

SIBBY (*jumping to her feet, and wild with relief and excitement*). Ooshla Clancy, you have my lot saved! And, if you're a rogue itself, you're the best friend the poor ever had!

OOSHLA (*confidentially*). Maybe now you could tell me of some well-doing farmer in yere country that has more than his needs of spuds and oatmeal, and that wouldn't suffer if Ooshla fetched away a few hatfuls in the midnight.

SIBBY. Ooshla, I'll give you tidings of where a clever rogue such as you can win riches and valuables.

OOSHLA. You can! Where?

SIBBY. There's a Paddy Pedlar on the roadside below, and several have offered him a night's shelter, but he's refusing them all. So some reckon he must have stolen valuables in his bag, and he's afeard any man'd go looking in the bag, while he'd by sleeping.

OOSHLA. No Paddy Pedlar ever refused a night's shelter before, so he must have more in his bag then the feathers and horsehair and spuds the Paddy Pedlars do be gathering. And, if 'tis stolen valuables he has, they aren't his by right, and isn't Ooshla as much entitled to a share of them?

SIBBY. I have no learning about the right and wrongs of roguery. 'Tis yourself can set the water running clear about that point. (*She moves to the door.*)

OOSHLA. Tell him there's a lone blind man in this house. Then he'll not be afeard that I'd look in the bag. I'll only take what'll buy a strip of land for a young couple that must go foreign without it.

SIBBY. I'll tell him you're blind no matter if it withers my blood. My seven can stop in my house thanks to you ... (*She goes. OOSHLA takes a couple of sheaves of straw from the corner, and makes a bed near the hearth. From the room on the right he brings out a blanket, which he spreads over the straw. He brings his stick from the corner. He sits on the blanket with his back to the door, takes off his jacket, then his shoes. He is thus engaged when MATTHIAS DUGGAN appears. He is a huge powerful fierce-looking man of forty-five or so; and he carries a murderous looking shillelagh. He looks at OOSHLA for a moment, advances upon him silently, takes him by the back of the collar, and throws him full length on the floor.*)

MATTHIAS (*roaring ferociously*). You limb of the divil up from Hell! You robber and thief and murderer!

OOSHLA (*gasping*). Matthias Duggan!

MATTHIAS. Say your last prayers quick before Matthias puts you into eternity. (*He draws back shillelagh for a finishing blow.*)

OOSHLA. Matthias, what did I do on you?

MATTHIAS. Last night you fetched away my spade, and sold it to

Toby Kelly for a jar of his poteen.

OOSHLA (*desperately*). Matthias, I'm as innocent of that as of burning myself in the fire. I never steal anything only enough spuds and oatmeal to keep me living.

MATTHIAS. Didn't my own neighbour see the spade in Kelly's kitchen with my mark upon it, and wasn't he told for true you sold it last night for poteen? My spade that was my only way of living, and now the hunger'll bring my ghost up in no time. You murderer and rogue; you'll rogue and murder no more. Say your last prayers directly; then I'll clout your two temples together, and kill you.

OOSHLA. But, Matthias, if I die without paying you back for your spade, my prayers'll be worth no more than the braying of an ass, and I'll be scorching in Purgatory for maybe ten years. Give me a small while to gather up the costs for a new spade. Then you can thrash my soul out to your heart's content.

MATTHIAS (*suspiciously*). And where would you get the costs for a new spade?

OOSHLA (*quickly*). There's a Paddy Pedlar on the road below, and he's coming lodging here for the night. In his bag he has stolen valuables, and in the midnight when he's asleep, I'll steal enough that'll buy you the finest spade in the Barony.

MATTHIAS. D'ye want to make me as black a rogue as yourself?

OOSHLA. What roguery is in it? They're stolen valuables, so they aren't the pedlar's by right, and we're much entitled to them.

MATTHIAS. But what about the gentleman that owned them?

OOSHLA. Sure he's unknown, and the pedlar'll never tell who he is. And anyway, how do the gentlemen get the costs for their valuables? By rackrenting their poor tenants till they're lowing with the hunger.

MATTHIAS (*in a fury*). They took the last crop I had left in the year of the floods, and the wife and children sickened and died on me. But she didn't die till she cursed the gentlemen with a curse that'll wear them from the earth at last. And now they have the rent raised on me again, so I can afford no pinch of salt with my spuds, nor a sup of milk ever! For every meal of the year I have nothing only potatoes and spits!

OOSHLA. You'll want to go, or he'll be afeard to come in. I sent him word there was a lone blind man in this house, and the like couldn't look in his bag.

MATTHIAS. I'll lie ahiding in the furze until the Paddy Pedlar is sleeping. (*He goes to door.*)

OOSHLA. Tap at the window here after about an hour of the night.
MATTHIAS. Here he's coming with his basket and his bag!
OOSHLA. Creep away in the shadow of the wall.
(MATTHIAS *goes.* OOSHLA *slips back to the straw bed, and is kneeling down smoothing out the straw and the blanket when the* PEDLAR *comes into the doorway. On his left arm the* PEDLAR *carries the long rectangular shallow basket containing pins and needles, combs, brooches, laces, etc., each in its separate department, and separated from its neighbours by a wicker-work partition. In his right hand he carries a home-made walking-stick. On his back he carries the large bag in which the pedlars usually carried the feathers and horsehair and rages with which many country people paid for their purchases. The bag is hung upon his back in the traditional manner. Two potatoes are stuck in the two bottom corners of the bag, and, around the base of the bulges which these potatoes make, two straw ropes are tied, the ropes coming up around the chest and shoulders, where they are tied to the top corners of the bag. A third straw rope tied around the middle of the bag and around his chest keeps the other ropes from slipping off his shoulders. The* PEDLAR *is middle-ages, insignificant looking, and stupefied by extreme physical exhaustion. Dogged devoted will-power keeps him going; but every time he relaxes he seems to crumble up both mentally and physically. He is a sad and lonely-looking figure, and remarkably timid. He peeps in first, and takes stock of* OOSHLA, *and of everything. He works his way stealthily until he is close to* OOSHLA. OOSHLA *is kneeling down facing him, and talking to himself, rubbing his back painfully as he does so.*)
OOSHLA. You had the pains as bad before, still God Almighty picked you up again, and you know well He can do as much for you this time, too. Evermore you're complaining about the pains in your back, and the darkness in your eyes; wouldn't you be a score of times worse off, if you were an unbeliever, or a murderer, or a rogue? And when you see Heaven at last, won't it be twice more wonderful, because you seen nothing at all when you were living in this world? (*After peering into* OOSHLA'S *eyes at close range, the* PEDLAR *seems to be satisfied, so he withdraws a little, and then speaks.*)
PEDLAR (*timidly*). God save you, sir.
OOSHLA (*his gaze falling well wide of the* PEDLAR). God and Mary save you, whoever you are. Your voice is strange to me.

PEDLAR. I'm a pedlar sir.

OOSHLA. A paddy pedlar is it? Draw down to the fire, Paddy, and take your ease.

PEDLAR. I'm thankful to you sir. (*He sits on the stool to the left of* OOSHLA.)

OOSHLA. And very apt, Paddy, you'd like a night's shelter. Between rain and hailstones 'tis nicer weather for looking out than for looking in.

PEDLAR (*anxiously*). But will there be any in the house besides ourselves two, sir?

OOSHLA (*gravely*). No living person, Paddy; but on account I haven't the sight, I couldn't say whether my people that are dead and gone, come back ever in the midnight. They say no word, Paddy, whatever.

PEDLAR. I'll stop so, sir, till morning at the first light, sir; and I'm thankful to you sir. (*He loosens the straw rope tied around his chest.*)

OOSHLA. And, Paddy, have you any wife, or Christian that'd like shelter too?

PEDLAR. I had no wife ever, sir; and I'm thinned out of the last of my friends. All dead and gone, sir.

OOSHLA (*rising with his stick, and tapping his way to the door, which he bolts*). Still you're luckier than myself that is without sight or friends, and as bad as Ossian that was blinded and withered by the first sting of Ireland's ground when he ventured back after three hundred years in the Land of Youth. (*From the dresser he takes the poteen jar and two eggshells.*) The poor fellow – was it any wonder he soaked three towels every day with tears for his lost sight, and for the Land of Youth, and for his Queen Niamh of the Golden Hair?

(*All this talk if to keep the* PEDLAR *from suspecting the fact that* OOSHLA *is watching his movements out of the corner of his eye. For the moment* OOSHLA *moved to the door, the* PEDLAR *pulls himself together, slips off his shoes, and carries the bag stealthily into the room on left, handling it with extraordinary care, as if it contained something very valuable and fragile. He slips back to the stool, and puts on his shoes again.*)

OOSHLA. Fine floury spuds are roasted in the ashes there, Paddy, and let you be making free with them. (*He comes back to his stool with the jar and the eggshells.*)

PEDLAR. 'Tisn't long since I had a good bite, sir; and I don't be inclined for eating in a house, sir, on account I'm eating in the wind evermore.

OOSHLA. Well, you'll down a jorum of poteen. Long travelling'll have you burning for a drink. (*He pours out an eggshellful.*)

PEDLAR (*taking the eggshell*). I'm very thankful to you, sir. (*He drinks it.*)

OOSHLA. Are you a well-doing man at the peddling, Paddy?

PEDLAR. Middling only, sir. I never was able enough, or severe enough at the bargaining; and the times are going worse, too, sir. (*Again and again his gaze returns uneasily to the main subject of his thoughts – the bag in the room.*)

OOSHLA. That's true, Paddy; but did you hear Dan O'Connell is to get a better Act of Parliament passed that'll make everyone well-to-do?

PEDLAR (*sadly*). Every year, sir, that is foretold, and every year Dan has great actions done for Ireland, and great speeches made; but still and all every year the poor are poorer.

OOSHLA. The gentlemen are rackrenting their poor tenants, Paddy.

PEDLAR. The gentlemen are taking more than they're entitled to, sir. (*Again he looks around uneasily in the direction of the bag.*)

OOSHLA. In the olden times Spain and Ireland had the same king; and 'tis foretold that the same will come again. Maybe there will be fair play and plenty for all when that time comes.

PEDLAR. Maybe in God, sir.

OOSHLA (*transferring to straw bed*). Myself must go sleeping now, Paddy, on account the pains kept tickling me every hour of last night. The turf for raking the fire you'll find in the room beyond . . . Do you see where I'm pointing, Paddy?

PEDLAR (*rousing himself*). I do, sir; I'll rake the fire directly, sir. (*He goes into the room on left. He comes out carrying an armful of turf.*)

OOSHLA. Myself must sleep anear the heat of the fire for fear the pains'd come back. You can sleep in my bed in the room there, Paddy. (*Indicating the room on right.*)

PEDLAR (*stopping in his tracks*). Is it sleep in the room beyond, sir? (*He looks towards it, and then back to the room where the bag is, with obvious dismay.*)

OOSHLA. A fine bed you'll have, Paddy. A goose-feather mattress and bolster and all. 'Twould delight you to look at it, not to mind sleeping in it.

PEDLAR (*sorely tempted*). A feather bed, sir! Never in my lifetime did I get sleeping in the like.

OOSHLA. One night's rest in it, Paddy, and you'll be five years a younger man.

PEDLAR. No lie, sir, 'twould do me great good, for too long carrying and trouble, sir, have me made dizzy, like a goose that'd be struck on the back of the head, sir. (*He is still hesitating.*)

OOSHLA. Good night, Paddy. (*He rolls over, and settles down to sleep.*)

PEDLAR. Good night, sir. (*The* PEDLAR *'rakes' the fire by covering some live coals and fresh sods with ashes. Then he comes around, and pears into* OOSHLA'S *face, whispering, "Sir, sir" softly. But there is no reply, and, the* PEDLAR, *satisfied at last that* OOSHLA *is asleep, crosses to the room on left where the bag is, looks in a moment, hesitates again, then comes over to the hearth, and places his pedlar's basket on a stool right beside* OOSHLA, *so that he is bound to feel it the moment he stirs. The he takes the candle, and goes into the bedroom on the right. A few moments after he has gone, closing the door behind him, a tapping is heard at the kitchen window.* OOSHLA *jumps up and runs to the window.*)

OOSHLA. Go easy, you divil, he's hardly in his bed at all yet. (*He hurries to the door, and admits* MATTHIAS.)

MATTHIAS. The bag. Where is it?

OOSHLA. Wait till I light a candle. (*He lights a rush candle at the fire.*)

MATTHIAS. D'ye think he has valuables in the bag?

OOSHLA. From his carry-on I'd take my book oath he has valuables in it. 'Tis in the room beyond. Carry it easy now for fear you'd hurt any of the valuables. (MATTHIAS *goes into the room ahead of him, while* OOSHLA *stands in the doorway holding aloft the candle.*)

OOSHLA. There it is above in the far corner. Go easy with it, man; go easy. (MATTHIAS *comes out, and places the bag on the floor.*)

MATTHIAS. 'Tis as heavy as the Hill of the Heads. He must have half the gentlemen of Ireland robbed, and the Divil mend them. (*He is opening the bag.*)

OOSHLA. Go easy, or you'll rouse him.

(MATTHIAS *opens the bag, and pokes his head into it in his eagerness. Instantly a smothered cry is heard from him, and he pulls out his head as if it had been bitten.*)

MATTHIAS (*in horror putting his hands to his eyes*). Thunder and fire! My sight is scattered! God's Curse has struck me for my league with a rogue!

OOSHLA. Go easy will you! What's in the bag?

MATTHIAS. A fearful thing, or my eyes are false and my friends no more! (*He is screwing his eyes, and blinking, as if testing them.*)

OOSHLA (*incredulous*). 'Tis the truth what they say that you don't be yourself half the time. (*He looks into the sack, and gasps.*) By the kingdom of O'Neill! . . . A woman's body and she killed and cold!

MATTHIAS (*bounding to his feet in a fury*). The blackhearted son of the Earl of Hell! He smothered her life out for her gold!

OOSHLA. She hasn't the looks of money. 'Tis poor clothes that's on her body.

MATTHIAS. Sure isn't it the likes of her that'd have the money. A miser that never let a penny go for clothes, or anything.

OOSHLA (*closing the bag thoughtfully*). Maybe that was it; or maybe 'twas for her body he killed her.

MATTHIAS. For her body, Clancy?

OOSHLA. Yes, to sell it to the doctors. Up the country the high doctors are paying a wonderful great price for bodies for the apprentice doctors to be practising how to cut the insides out of people.

MATTHIAS. One thing is sure, he banished her life someway; and, if we let him go ahead, he'll do the same to many a poor person more. Come in, and we'll take him by the legs, and keep pelting him into the lake until he dies. (*He sets out for the bedroom brandishing his shillelagh.*)

OOSHLA (*urgently*). Matthias, wait a minute.

MATTHIAS (*impatiently*). What's it?

OOSHLA. We'll make a prisoner of him first. Then we'll call in the neighbours to hear his case and judge him. No man should be put to death without a hearing.

MATTHIAS. Very well so. Bring the ropes you.

(*They creep into the bedroom,* MATTHIAS *going first and* OOSHLA *following with the candle, and the two straw ropes. In a moment the smothered cries of the* PEDLAR *are heard, and over all the bull-throated roars of* MATTHIAS: *"Stop quiet, or we'll kill you." "Hold him down." "Tie him to the bedpost." "That's it." "Be saying your last prayers now." "Short till you'll be on trial before your God." They come out,* OOSHLA *carrying the candle.*)

OOSHLA. Let you ring the word out around the village, and bring down a big flock of men to judge him.

MATTHIAS. I will that; and let you stand here in garrison over him; and if he ventures on more villainy, dash his brains against the gable.

101

(MATTHIAS *goes, and* OOSHLA *closes the door. He hauls the bag containing the dead woman back into the room again. He comes out, and considers for a few moments, then he takes a large knife from the dresser, feels the edge and the point of it, takes the candle in his left hand, and goes into the room. He comes out leading the* PEDLAR *by the cut end of the straw rope which had bound him to the bed-post. His hands are still bound with the straw-rope. He does not seem to be frightened or trembling, perhaps he is too tired for that; but he does seem to be downcast and worried.*)

OOSHLA (*motioning him to a stool near the hearth*). Take your ease there till my comrade comes back. (*He swings out the fire-crane, and ties the loose end of the rope to it.*)

PEDLAR (*with humble matter-of-factness*). Is it to cut my neck ye mean, sir?

OOSHLA (*gravely*). My comrade turned very wild and savage ever since the wife and children were starved on him. Wait till I see now ... Tell him he'll be fattening Hell, if he kills you this minute, without first giving you time and chance to get the Holy Sacraments from the priest.

PEDLAR. 'Tis little money I have, sir, but ye're welcome to the lot, sir, if ye'll free me out, and not cut my neck, sir.

OOSHLA (*pouring the last of the poteen into an eggshell*). You'll be wanting extra courage soon, Paddy, so here's what the cobbler gave his wife – the last.

PEDLAR (*taking the eggshell resignedly*). I'm thankful to you, sir.

OOSHLA (*gravely*). Myself is a rogue, too, Paddy. I was stealing enough spuds and oatmeal to keep me living until at last the roguery made its home the same as if it was a maggot in my brain. Then last night I was troubled over the girl going foreign, and the next thing the maggot twisted, and I stole a poor man's spade, and sold it for poteen to banish my trouble. The dirtiest turn ever I done; and was it the same way the roguery kept ever growing till it made a ruffian of you?

PEDLAR. I was no rogue, ever, sir, nor anybody belonging to me.

OOSHLA (*jumping up*). You were no rogue ever! Your impudence is enough to make a dog beat his father. (*He strides into the room, and drags out the bag.*) Didn't you rob this poor old woman of her life? (*On the instance the* PEDLAR *springs to his feet in a state of intense agitation.*)

PEDLAR. Mamma! Mamma! (*He pronounces it M'ma in the western fashion.*) What are you doing to Mamma? (*He runs towards her*

blindly, but is stopped by the rope trying him to the crane.) God
and Mary and Patrick help me! – help me! (*Struggling like a
madman he breaks the rope, and running forward drops on his
knees beside the body.*) Mamma! Mamma! did he bruise you?
He threw you down, and bruised you; and 'twas my fault,
Mamma: for a feather bed I left you. Mamma, Mamma, down
on your back he flung you, and injured you sore.

OOSHLA (*mildly*). Paddy, how could we injure her? She was dead
when we opened the bag?

PEDLAR. Two days she's dead, sir. My heart could never bear to see
her harmed any way at all, sir. (*With feverish haste, and as
skillfully as his bound hands will allow he is laying her out in the
bag. Then he turns to* OOSHLA *in passionate pleading, pointing
to his own throat.*) Let ye cut my neck if ye like, sir, but in the
honour of God, sir, let ye not harm Mamma, sir.

OOSHLA. We'll not harm either of ye, but tell me, Paddy, why have
you her in the bag?

PEDLAR. When she was dying in Clanrickard's country, sir, she
asked me to bury her with my father in the north in Lord
Leitrim's country, sir.

OOSHLA. And we judged 'twas some old woman you robbed and
killed. I'll get the knife and free your hands out.

PEDLAR. Then I'll be able to lay her out nice and decent. God bless
you, sir.

OOSHLA (*taking the knife from the dresser*). She must have a great
wish for your father, Paddy, when she asked you to carry her
that length.

PEDLAR. He cared for whiskey, only, sir. He'd make her go begging
money for whiskey, and, if she wouldn't bring back enough,
he'd give her blood to drink, sir.

OOSHLA (*feeling edge of the knife*). Blood! What blood, Paddy?

PEDLAR. Blood from her lips and teeth, sir, from fisting her down
on the mouth, sir. I had to be ever watching and ever-fighting
him, sir; and that's what has myself left without marriage or a
son that'd lift me out of the dust, or the mud, when the age sets
me tumbling at last, sir. (*Holding up his bound wrists
pleadingly.*) In the honour of God, sir.

OOSHLA (*approaching*). But, Paddy, if he was that cruel to her, why
would she ask to be buried with him?

PEDLAR. She well knew, sir, there wouldn't be one in the world
wide only herself to say a good word for him on the Judgment
Day; so she'd like to rise near him that day. He was good to her

in his younger days before the drink made him ravenous.

OOSHLA. I understand all now, Paddy, and I'll free your hands out.

PEDLAR (*holding up his wrists, his eyes shining with eager joy*). God be good to you, sir. I'll be every day asking God to be good to you, sir. (*The moment the rope joining his wrists is cut, he whips a long bladed knife from some kind of hidden sheath in his belt, and leaps to his feet brandishing it fiercely, while* OOSHLA *backs away in the utmost dismay.*)

PEDLAR. Hullabaloo! Hullabaloo! (*Twice he leaps into the air with that hiss of savage joy; drawing back the knife each time as if about to charge at* OOSHLA. *But instead he leaps again, and cries aloud in triumph.*) Now, Mamma! Timmy has his knife! Timmy has his knife! No one'll dare harm you no more!

OOSHLA. Why should I want to harm her, Paddy? (*But the* PEDLAR *does not hear him. He is standing still, and looking down at his mother, and the life has gone out of him.*)

PEDLAR (*numbly*). She never looked! She heard no word! She'll hear no more till we meet on God's floor. (*He sinks on his knees beside her, and puts the knife back into his belt.*)

OOSHLA. Was she very old, Paddy?

PEDLAR. She wasn't too old, sir. She was young enough and she dying to have sense and reason to talk to God and His Son and the Blessed Virgin.

OOSHLA. You'll be very lonesome after her, Paddy?

PEDLAR. She had the priest in time, sir, and a happy death, so I'm happy since, but lonesome.

OOSHLA. And you're mortal tired too, Paddy?

PEDLAR (*his eyes never leave her face*). Two days I'm walking, sir, every hour that the clock struck. I must have her in her grave soon, before the death alters her, sir.

OOSHLA. Well, if you're only fit to carry her half a mile itself, you should do that, Paddy, for my comrade was never safe since the wife and children were starved on him. He mightn't believe she was your mother, and he might go against your knife, and in the fighting she might take harm.

PEDLAR (*rising quickly*). I'll fetch her away directly, but two of my ropes are spoiled, sir. Have you two idle, sir, that you'd swap for your needs from the basket beyond.

OOSHLA. I have two fine ropes idle in the barn, and you're heartily welcome to them. (*He hurries out. The* PEDLAR *droops a little, and sinks on his knees beside the body again. He murmurs to himself drowsily, and half dazedly.*)

PEDLAR. He's proving a decent man at last, Mamma, still we'll trust no other house till you're safe for ever from the badness of the world. (*Exhaustion seems to overwhelm him for a few moments, but, with a great effort, he pulls himself together, and speaks to her mildly, as if in reply to a comment by her.*) Sure I'm not denying it, Mamma, I am tired. (*Then pressing his hands to his head dazedly.*) My mind is very near off its firmness I'm that tired. I'm not safe carrying you I'm that tired ... (*His eyes wander about a little desperately, and suddenly light up as they see the crude wooden cross on the dresser. He whispers to her excitedly.*) Wait, Mamma. (*He rises, and crosses slowly towards the Cross on the right hand wall. He does not come too near. He speaks with quiet, tired, matter-of-factness.*) They do say Yourself was mortal tired, too, that day, and stumbled greatly while You were carrying it. Just the same way myself is now, my two shoulders cut and scalded with the ropes, and my two feet gripping the ground they're that tired. 'Tis an old saying we have that God is strong, and His Mother is kind, and let the two of Ye help me out this night, so as I won't injure Mamma with stumbles ... I'll be thankful to Ye evermore; and I'll send no complaint over no more against the hunger or the cramp, or the rain every day rotting my clothes, or the snow and hailstones blinding by eyes; or against the want of a son or a daughter that'd keep the rats from my head when I'll be getting death at last. Let ye brace my up till I have Mamma safe in her grave, and after that please Yereselves about me. (*He is on his way back when he turns suddenly.*) And let Ye mind the darkness too. Yereselves will well remember of how awkward the darkness is when the paths are crooked, and rough. (*He comes back to the body, drops on his knees beside it, glances in the direction of the Cross as if to make sure he is not being overheard, and whispers.*) You'll see, Mamma; They'll be with us at every turn and twist.

OOSHLA (*hurrying in with two stout straw ropes*). Here are two good hardy lads that'll carry her till ye come to the mountains whatever.

PEDLAR. Take your needs from the basket here, sir. (*He rolls up the two straw ropes, puts them into the basket.*)

OOSHLA. I'm in want of nothing, Paddy. (*He wanders off to the fireplace thinking hard, makes up his mind, and exclaims aloud.*) Well here! Hit or miss! (*He takes a stool, and sits down at the centre of the kitchen, facing the PEDLAR.*) I'm after making a little thought, Paddy; and I'd reckon I'd be a good man to carry a bag, and a good help at bargaining, too, for I had a quick tongue ever, and it got great practise while I was a gentleman. Maybe 'twould suit you if I went peddling with you through Ireland for evermore.

PEDLAR. Is it to go leaving your home and land, sir?

OOSHLA. I was believing I was entitled to take my needs from the tenants the same as the gentlemen; but it appears now that that was the Divil's notion; for last night the roguery betrayed me all out, and I sold a poor man's spade for poteen, and to-day he found out, so I'm disgraced for life and for ever in this barony; and my life'll be in danger from him too. So 'tis God's Will for me to leave this country, and the roguery.

PEDLAR. But who'll have your house and land, sir?

OOSHLA. That was pledged to a young girl nearby, and 'tis God's Will, too, she to get it, and be saved from going foreign.

PEDLAR (*earnestly looking at corpse*). In three days I'll have no comrade no more, and I'm falling into age, moreover; so 'twould suit me greatly you to come with me. But she was evermore happy when she'd hear good praise of me, and she'd be shamed now when she'd hear I had a rogue for comrade.

OOSHLA (*rising vigorously*). Sure to shake off the roguery is what I want, Paddy; for 'twas commencing to make a mean man of me altogether. With you I'll be in honest company, and you'll help me against the roguery. (*He is getting together the dress coat, top-hat, and cane and some food from the dresser for the journey.*)

PEDLAR (*eagerly*). Maybe I could cure you, sir, the way I cured my father out of hurting Mamma, sir?

OOSHLA (*with enthusiasm*). What way did you cure him, Paddy?

PEDLAR (*taking out knife gravely*). Every time he'd set into lashing her I'd give him a dart of this, sir. I could give you a dart, too, sir, every time you'd commit a roguery.

OOSHLA. Oh, murther! And would it be a deep prod, Paddy?

PEDLAR (*earnestly*). Sure if it wasn't, sir, 'twould do you no good, sir.

OOSHLA (*with a shudder*). But if it was too deep, 'twould do me no good either.

PEDLAR. I'd make sure not to give you a dart in the killing places, sir.

OOSHLA. Oh, murther! Oh, murther! ... Still you'll cure me. The divil a bit of roguery'll stop long more in me. (*They are busy*

106

readying. THADY *and* HONOR *enter.*)

THADY (*excitedly*). Matthias Duggan is up and down telling that you went robbing another rogue for the price of a farm for us.

OOSHLA. Ye're just in time! I'm going peddling for a living with Paddy here, so ye can have this place all to yereselves.

THADY. You're going living in the wind so as you can leave us your place!

HONOR. Ooshla, we'd give ourselves up to the Divil before we'd send you living in the wind – at your age and all!

OOSHLA. But I must leave this country whether or no. Last night I stole a poor man's spade!

HONOR. You did!

THADY. Thunder and turf!

OOSHLA. I did, and by to-morrow all the country'll know. (*He gets his stick from a corner.*)

THADY. 'Tis as well for you to go so before the roguery gets the better of you altogether.

HONOR. Yes, Ooshla, 'tis time for you to go. (*She goes to the hearth, and seems shocked and depressed.*)

OOSHLA (*vigorously*). Never fret, girl. Paddy here has a wonderful great cure for the roguery. Soon he'll have me as honest as a Bishop. (*He turns to* THADY.) Out of your sailing money that you won't need now, give two shillings to Silke the Smith, and he'll sledge out a new spade for Matthias. (*He puts on his dress coat.*)

THADY. I'll not fail you in that, Ooshla.

OOSHLA (*turning to* PEDLAR *who is on his way to the door with bag on his back*). Timmy! Timmy! They do call me Ooshla. I'm fresh. Let me carry the bag for to-night.

PEDLAR (*quickly, the wild look coming back into his eyes*). You will not! You might shake or jolt Mamma! Let you carry the basket. (*He opens the door, and looks out anxiously. He draws his knife, holds it at the ready. He speaks with his humble matter-of-factness, never taking his eyes off the dangerous darkness outside.*) If he crosses me, 'twill be me or him, and if 'tis me, let ye put me down along with Mamma in whatever graveyard is nearby, and we'll be very thankful to ye. (*He goes.*)

HONOR. Did you see the knife! Is he safe at all?

OOSHLA. 'Tis only how he's afeard anything might happen the mother. It appears he was very good to her while she was living, and her dying wish was he to bury her with his father in Lord Leitrim's country.

THADY. Well, when he was that good to the mother, there's no badness in him.

HONOR (*as* OOSHLA *goes to the door*). Ooshla, as soon as you're middling honest at all, draw back to us before the hardship breaks you down.

OOSHLA (*in the best of spirits*). What hardships? Carrying a basket or a bag? What is that only walking? And buying and selling? What is that only talking? Walking and talking isn't that how the gentlemen pass the time? So isn't God good that's after rummaging out a way I can live like a gentleman, and be no rogue? (*At the door he claps the tall hat on his head.*) Ooshla'll be the gentleman-pedlar, keeping only the best, he'll say, and entitled to charge twice more than the rest. When Ooshla comes the way again, he'll be a well-doing man, with a white waistcoat fastened, and a watch chain slinging, and gold guineas sounding and all. Till that day God be good to ye. (*He goes.*)

THADY. Good luck, Ooshla.

HONOR (*at the door waving after him*). God be with you, Ooshla.

THADY (*returning to the fire*). Ooshla'll be all right. He's in lucky company whatever. The Pedlar was very good to his mother while she lived, and the like do be lucky, they reckon. (*He takes out the clay pipe.*)

HONOR (*turning excitedly*). Right enough, Thady: the like do be lucky, all reckon.

THADY (*filling his pipe*). And they say the mother doesn't be slow about sending the luck either.

HONOR (*coming back to fire*). As sure as the day Ooshla himself is the first good luck she sent the Pedlar, for Ooshla should make an able Pedlar, and a hearty comrade for the road! (*She sits beside him.*)

THADY (*taking her hand in his, and smiling wisely*). She sent her son a comrade, and she sent Ooshla an honest way of living, and she sent you and me our own fireside. She has good fortune won for everyone, so she must be well thought of where she is.

CURTAIN

The Wood of the Whispering

DEDICATION

To the memory of Senator John T. O'Farrell and his son Brendan.

Preface

After the Israelites of old escaped from Egypt and long slavery, they wandered in the desert for forty years, never daring to attack the warlike tribes who occupied their Promised Land. But after forty years the old slave-born generation had died, or retired from leadership, and a bold new freeborn generation had taken over. Under new freeborn leaders the new freeborn nation crossed the Jordan, and conquered after many a fierce campaign, their Promised Land.

For forty years Ireland has been free, and for forty years it has wandered in the desert under the leadership of men who freed their nation, but who could never free their own souls and minds from the ill-effects of having been born in slavery. To that slave-born generation it has always seemed inevitable and right that the Anglo-American plutocracies, because they are rich, should be allowed to destroy us because we are poor – destroy us root and branch through mass emigration. So for forty years we have continued to be the only dying free nation on earth, inheriting Turkey's old title of "The Sick Man of Europe." And for forty years our slave-born economic and financial experts have continued to assure our slave-born political leaders that the depopulation is all for the best: that big cattle ranches and big grain ranches are more economic than small farms. But neither cattle nor combine harvesters have ever fought for their country as small farmers have been known to do.

In the last war neutral Norway found itself invaded by both sides on the same day, because its position was strategically important and because its population was too small to defend its big area. And the bitter lesson of the Six Counties and of Partition, and indeed of all history, is that the worst disaster that can befall a nation is not conquest, but colonisation. And depopulation is the thing that invites colonisation and ensures its success. Ourselves and Britain lie like two vast aircraft carriers off the coast of Europe. Every year with the rise of air power our strategic position becomes more important, and every year with the fall in population our defenses become weaker.

While we desert the finest farm-land in Europe, the Jews return from all over the world to the Promised Land from which they were driven nearly two thousand years ago. They set to work to make fertile and to populate land that has been desert for two thousand years, sun-scorched desert where the new grasses have to be watered four times a day. What man has done, man can do; and we could repopulate our deserted farm-lands if only we could find new freeborn leaders with minds and souls not warped or stunted by birth in slavery.

In 1910 the Great Blasket island had one hundred and fifty people and a well-filled school. Forty years later the population was a handful, there was only one child, so they called their island Tir Na Sean, the Land of the Old. There are countless dying villages and townlands in rural Ireland to which the same title could be applied. The death of a village, like the death of an individual, is usually a painful business, and marked by distressing symptoms. But of this fact our suburban depopulation enthusiasts know nothing.

But country people know all about it, and they know the background of this play, the comedy of the eccentric old bachelors, and the tragedy, too. So it was no coincidence that its first amateur performance were by two tiny rural villages: Inchovea in County Clare and Killeedy in County Limerick, which between them won half a dozen drama festivals with it – before their dramatic societies were shattered by emigration. Every activity is hit be a falling population; and every activity is helped by an expanding population.

CHARACTERS

SANBATCH DALY
CON KINSELLA, a woodsman in his middle thirties
PADDY KING, an old farmer
JIMMY KING, his brother
STEPHEN LANIGAN, an old farmer
SHEILA LANIGAN, his daughter
MARK TRISTNAN, a young farmer
HOTHA FLYNN, a farmer in his fifties
KITTY WALLACE, a young girl
SADIE TUBRIDY

THE SCENE: A wood in the West of Ireland.
THE TIME: 1950.

THE WOOD OF THE WHISPERING was first produced at the Abbey
Theatre, Dublin, on 26 January 1953, with the following cast:

SANBATCH DALY	Philip O'Flynn
CON KINSELLA	Ray MacAnally
PADDY KING	Brian O'Higgins
JIMMY KING	Harry Brogan
STEPHEN LANIGAN	Michael J. Dolan
SHEILA LANIGAN	Doreen Madden
MARK TRISTNAN	Joe Lynch
HOTHA FLYNN	Michael O'Briain
KITTY WALLACE	Maire Ni Dhomhnaill

The play was produced by Ria Mooney.

The Wood of the Whispering

ACT ONE

The scene is outside the old Main Entrance to Castle D'Arcy. An early 18th century D'Arcy did the then fashionable Grand Tour of Europe, and returned to his cramped old Norman castle full of ideas for a splendid mansion with demesne, avenues, gates and woods in the best British and Continental style. This was his Main Entrance and he made it an imposing one: a mighty wrought-iron central gate with lofty ornamental pillars and flanked on each side by smaller wooden wicket-gates. But neighbouring landlords, who did the Grand Tour somewhat later, founded new market towns and cut a new main road to join them. This passed on the wrong side of the Castle, so a new avenue was made to open on it, and the old main entrance became a little-used side-entrance and woods were planted within and without. The roof of the gardener's lodge can be seen. [But if an artist is not available, a very simple set would do: a six-foot wall running across the back stage to represent the demesne wall, with a pillar at one end, as if the gates were in the wings. Some branches of trees, bushes, ivy, etc., over the top of the wall would suggest the demesne woods. When a character is supposed to hide behind a tree, he hides in the wings.]

In a little clearing, on the left-hand side of the gate, and well out from the demesne wall, lies the camp of SANBATCH DALY. *There is a fire of turf and sticks, and slanted over the fire is an iron rod with one end deeply embedded in the ground. The other end is S-shaped and from the "S" hangs a kettle with its top half and spout broken off. Behind the fire lies a seven-foot long coffin-shaped box of rough boards, about two feet high and open at the right-hand end. Behind the middle of the box a long sheep-crook is stuck in the ground, and from the crook hangs a print of the famous old Byzantine Madonna, Our Lady of Succour, with its red Greek lettering and bright colouring. On the left of this (from the actor's point of view) stands a dungfork or graipe, and from its handle is hung an Old Moore's Almanac and an old patched-together Rosary Beads. On the other side of the sheep-crook stands a hay-fork, and on this hangs*

SANBATCH's *cap.*
A huge, rusty, three-legged iron pot is on the left of the fire. The lid is on, for this pot is Sanbatch's cupboard and toolshed and would be his wardrobe, too, if he had any clothes besides the rags on his back. A little heap of potatoes lies a yard or so away. An old battered shotgun lies against one end of the long box. An old rusty bucket stands nearby.
SANBATCH, *the lord of all this wealth, is sitting on the long box. He is dressed in trousers, jacket and vest. He is delousing. He picks them out, and drops them into the fire. He is in the middle sixties, lanky, haggard and worn by privation and adversity, but bursting with nervous energy. He is completely unselfconscious and serious, is a little crazy and absurd and wild, but he excites sympathy, too, for it is obvious that he has suffered more than his share. As he liquidates the lice, he chats away, addressing his remarks to someone lying in the long box.*
It is the year 1950, about sunset of a May night.

SANBATCH. 'Tis me that'd be rich, Leggy, if there was any kind of a middling price going for them at all. And to think I hadn't wan in all my life's day till I was over sixty! Still, if we thin them middling often, we'll keep from scratching when the neighbours are around, and they'll never find out that we have them at all. And another thing: according as we're getting more starved in the blood and in the body these divils'll have less to get, till at last they might resign from us altogether ... (*Suddenly the rumble of a distant lorry is heard.*) By the Blessed Iron Book! (*He grabs the gun and jumps to his feet.*) That's the gang! 'Tis surely them. (*He dodges behind a tree, holding the gun at the ready.*) Three warnings I'll give, then if they keep coming, the first of them'll fall. (*The lorry is heard again. Sanbatch is greatly relieved.*) I'm thinking now that isn't them. That's more the sound of a lorry: likely a lorry with barrels for Gowlin's drinkshop. (*He comes back and leaves aside the gun.*) And when they didn't come before this, they'll hardly come at all to-night, so I'll bob asleep for a few hours. (*He takes the kettle off the fire, comes round to the box and starts indignantly.*)
SANBATCH. Well, more bad luck to you, as the goat said to his legs! Dozing asleep you are, and me after squandering many a fine news and tale on you, and wise advices the whole world couldn't buy from me. (*He draws out "Leggy", a philosophical old sheepdog, by his tether, and throws him a leg of a rabbit.*) Leggy, if

you lost your appetite, I wouldn't like I'd get it, because then I'd need a high income ... Now, I'll tie you to your tree, and if any strange mean-looking men come the way, start springing and roaring. (*He leads the dog off, left, is back again in a moment and puts the shotgun into the long box.*) But, maybe, Leggy, they will never trace me, because I promised God, if He'd save my liberty, that I'd never grumble again no matter how poor. (*Feet first he gets into the long box and disappears from view. He pulls in his head.* CON KINSELLA *comes in from the right, carrying a small window frame and boards and a little bag of tools. He is in his middle thirties, with the sturdy build and big facial bones of the work-nurtured farmer's son. He is an intelligent fellow with a quick sense of humour. He takes in the scene for a few moments, then addresses the dog, smilingly.*)

CON. Dog, Where's your master gone? (*Rapping the box.*) 'Tis a fine big kennel he made for you, whatever. You must have a long family. (CON *crosses to the main gate, looks through the main gate, then opens a wicket-gate and goes out. He can be seen standing with his back to the stage, surveying the scene.* SANBATCH *quickly crawls out of the box, gun in hand, and hides behind a tree.* CON *comes back, looks into the long box, then sits on it and lights a cigarette.* SANBATCH *advances stealthily and ferociously.*)

SANBATCH. Put up your hands, or I'll fire. I have you marked as dead as a pointer. (CON *puts up his hands, the cigarette falling out of his mouth with surprise.*) Wan minute is your time to live unless you'll swear to go back to the County Home, yourself and your ambulance, and never come again robbing Sanbatch of his liberty.

CON. I have nothing to do with the County Home. That isn't my trade at all.

SANBATCH. Evermore ye'll deny yeer trade, so as to come at the sleepy side of a poor person. But you won't fool Sanbatch. After my house fell last month, ye sent notice to say ye'd take me to the County Home if I hadn't a house got within a month. But ye'll not trap Sanbatch into the poor-house and disgrace his decent people.

CON. Cutting timber is my trade. Against the tree beyond is the boards for my hut, and on the roadside there aback is my lorry, with saws and engines of many a kind.

SANBATCH. Maybe that was the lorry I heard sounding a few minutes back?

CON. That was it.

(SANBATCH *crosses and examines the boards.*)

SANBATCH. The makings of a hut are in it right enough, so you are a timber-cutter. (*Throwing aside the gun.*) I'll make you a dash of tea now, if we haven't to wait for the summer sun to boil the kettle. (*He hangs the kettle again, fixes fire.*)

CON. 'Tisn't long since I staunched my hunger.

SANBATCH. No matter. Sure the tea is the finest weed that ever grew; though the porter gives a person better courage for working.

CON. I have bread-loaf sandwiches here, plenty and to spare. (*He takes them from his pockets.*)

SANBATCH. Well, stick to them, because you'd want a wonderful great stomach and constitution to thrive on my cakes. (*He goes out left.*) Leggy, I'll not be going sleeping another while, so you might have time to catch a rabbit for youself. God is good, God bless him. (*He returns carrying the tether.*)

CON. How did the house happen to fall on you?

SANBATCH. The way it was, I never was tied by priest or friar, so I had no wan to come after me, and that left me careless, and I had no wan to help me, so once the strength began to leave me both house and farm soon went to rack and ruin. I left the thatch without repairing three years, trusting to God, but He came up last month with a storm, and didn't leave a wisp in it.

(*He takes an empty jam-jar out of the iron pot; rinses it in the bucket. He finds a little packet of tea and a spoon in the pot also.*)

CON (*munching a sandwich*). How was it you could never get a wife?

SANBATCH (*indignantly*). Is it me? I'll have you know I was wan of the best looking men in this country, thank God, with as many curls as a prize bull, and the hardest job ever I got was to keep from getting married. The finest man's daughter I could wink at her, and she'd wink at me, and if I wouldn't put my arms around her, she'd put her arms around me.

CON (*amused*). I'll never meet so lucky a man till I meet yourself again.

SANBATCH. And at a dance that time, when a girl'd want to make you come home with her, she'd steal your cap. All the girls were darting like dogs to steal my cap: some of them girls that were worth hundreds of pounds. But still I never tumbled myself down to marrying any of them.

CON. Why was that?

117

SANBATCH (*solemnly*). The best man is the man that can do without them, and I was as sure as the day I was a man that could do without them.

CON. And you found out since that you couldn't?

SANBATCH (*putting a spoonful of tea in the jam-jar*). The night my house fell I understood at last that I wasn't a man that could do without them. For, if I had a wife, she'd keep me well fed and well scolded, and then I never would let the farm go to waste and the roof drop in. The very minute I'd have each meal finished she'd say to me: "What in the hell are you doing in here? Go out and find some work to do." 'Twas for our good God made them such divils with the tongue.

CON. And now you're too old to get a wife?

SANBATCH. Sure, that's the greatest treachery that's in the world. You won't know whether you can do without them till you're too old to get wan. (*He pours hot tea into the jam-jar.*)

CON. You lost yourself, whatever.

SANBATCH. I did. I was full sure I could do without them. Here's a sup of tea, and the want of milk you must offer up for all that ever died.

CON. Cold water is as good. And thanks for the sup of tea. (*He cools the tea with some cold water from the bucket.*)

SANBATCH. I had a little Kerry cow, and she gave a sweet canful, but when poverty took me by the throat she had to be sold. . . . While you're supping, I'll be filling this vacancy (*a hole in his trousers*) with a piece of blanket. (*Pulling the hayfork out of the ground he pokes in the long box and brings out on the prongs an old dog-eared blanket. With the sheep shears he cuts a piece from this and proceeds to patch his trousers.*)

CON. 'Tis a fine mansion and demesne the D'Arcys had here.

SANBATCH (*proudly*). And my family were chief herds to them so long as they had a bullock or a ewe. But all their lands are sold now except the demesne and all their cattle and sheep are sold, and my sheep-crook is rusty now.

CON. I hear the last of the D'Arcys is a scholar out in Oxford.

SANBATCH (*nodding*). They tell me he was an M.A., but he lost it again through drink.

CON. No doubt 'twas the drink made him sell out the castle and the demesne at last.

SANBATCH. The castle and demesne sold! I wouldn't believe the first or last of that, though 'tis ten years since a Christian lived in them.

CON. Well, it's a truthful tale. Th' other day the castle was sold by young D'Arcy to Kenworthy and he has the woods sold to my boss Markey of the Sawmills.

SANBATCH (*excited and dismayed*). Well, cut my head off if that's so! Markey'll leave only stumps of the last fine woods in this barony, and Kenworthy'll knock the Castle and sell every slate and stick and stone, the same as he did to Browne Hall and Castle Martin.

CON. 'Tis my job to sleep hereabouts in my hut and guard the machinery. Th' other timber men'll come every morning in Markey's lorry.

SANBATCH. Sup up your tea quick. Sadie within must be told about the sale, and she won't appear if anywan is here besides myself.

CON. Why so? What made her nervous?

SANBATCH. The time she was in her bloom th' oul' Depression was on, and no farmer around could afford to marry a girl that had no fortune. So she had to stop with her father and mother till they died, and then she was left alone and the lonesomeness and the darkness and the trees defeated her at last. 'Tis two years now since she spoke to anywan or went out amongst the neighbours. She spends the day and the night within there thinking and ever thinking about how she lost herself.

CON (*rising*). I'll be fetching another batch of boards for my hut.

SANBATCH. She'll be gone when you come back.

(CON *goes out left.* SANBATCH *picks up a stone and bangs loudly on the right-hand wicket gate. Then he opens it, pokes in his head and calls out.*)

SANBATCH. Sadie, I have a news for you. Come on out. The divil a wan is here only oul' Sanbatch.

(*He comes back to the fire and sits on the long box with his back to the gate.* SADIE *appears in the doorway. She is in her late forties, and poorly dressed, but not untidily – there is nothing unkempt or wild-looking about her. A good-looking girl in her day, and her eyes are out of the ordinary still. But all life and interest in life has left her: her expression is one of settled and suffering melancholy. She raises her eye-lids just sufficiently to ascertain that* SANBATCH *is alone, then her eyes return to their endless brooding.* SANBATCH *turns at last.*)

SANBATCH. Sadie, step forward a small piece whatever. Let you not be afeard I'd go mocking you. How could I when myself has a middling share of craziness, too? (*Eventually she comes forward a little, but she does not look in his direction.*) Castle D'Arcy is

119

sold to Kenworthy for tearing down, and he won't leave a stone you could throw at a bird. Whether he'll turn you out of your lodge is unknown yet; if he can he will. (*He wtaches her for a few moments, but there is no reaction.*) If he does turn you out, you'll have to go to the County Home amongst the paupers ... (*Still no reaction.*) ... My reckoning is that'd be the best thing that could happen you now, for in the County Home you'd be swarmed about with paupers all day, and you'd have to alter your habits and start talking again.

(*This takes a few moments to sink in, but it does, and she starts and shudders and turns away.*)

SANBATCH. Why, wouldn't it be nicer and wholesomer to be talking to paupers itself than to be all day and every day lonesome and thinking and ever thinking about how you lost yourself?

(*But she turns away, much agitated, and hurries out. He goes to the gate and calls after her.*)

SANBATCH. Let you not go sleeping another while. I have another news for you that'll be twice better than that wan.

(CON *enters, carrying more boards.*)

SANBATCH. I told her the good and the bad. It'll be something new for her to be thinking about, and the change might improve her.

CON (*sorting out boards and tools*). Myself is after passing a fellow on his way home from the drink-shop. He told me to go ahead – that he was hardly able to bring his legs after hospital and a hard operation.

SANBATCH. That's Stephen Lanigan from the village below. (*Pointing right.*) The highest doctors in Galway searched his insides, and, whatever was in it, they reckon it can't be cured. A long sickness never told a lie yet, so no matter if all Ireland was trusting to him, he'll die.

CON. Sure enough, his colour is beginning to say: "I'm going away."

SANBATCH. He'll have a slow death, too, with leavings of praying-time, and that just suits him.

CON. Why? Was he a rake formerly?

SANBATCH. When he'd have drink in, he was as wicked as a bee for arguing and fighting and tinkering. Many a time we fought and kicked each other.

(STEPHEN LANIGAN *comes in, leaning heavily on a stout stick. He makes his way to a tree stump, and sits down. He is sixty or so, not very grey, but his colour is very bad. A powerfully-built man, and in his day a lively and boisterous man, but illness and the shadow of death have begun to tame and refine him. But some of the old*

120

twinkle is still in his eye, and he is not unduly sorry for himself.)

SANBATCH (*solemnly*). Only last night, Stephen, I was dreaming again about your wife, and how she used to sit on my knee long ago.

STEPHEN (*smiling*). And she had a wish for you evermore, even after I married her.

SANBATCH (*hotly*). 'Tis my wife she'd be, too, only I was so sure I could do without them.

STEPHEN (*indicating* CON). He tells me he was in England, a pick and shovel man, for many a year.

SANBATCH (*eagerly, to* CON). Tell us here, would you be fond if a bit of land and money, and a wife thrown in along with it.

CON (*cynically*). Is she long grey?

SANBATCH. Grey? She's a blossomed flower, a fine looking girl with two big eyes like a lady's and fine features, and she has the promise of the child's breakfast, moreover.

STEPHEN. She's my daughter that lately come from England to mind me for a while after my operation. 'Twould suit me well if some wan'd coax her to marry at home and go no more to England.

SANBATCH. 'Tis a nice farm and house they have with a fine long kitchen for playing pitch-and-toss in on a wet Sunday. If some wan doesn't marry here soon, the village'll be in an awful way with no child swelling up into a man for the days when ourselves'll be without the help of hand or foot. (*Suddenly a car engine is heard.*) Blood and bones! That's the ruffians coming for me, but they'll not catch Sanbatch. (*He grabs the gun and runs out left.*)

STEPHEN. Sanbatch is his nickname evermore since he used be training dogs for oul' Captain Sanbatch. Sanbatch was an able and witty fellow and a lady's man, too, in his young days, but he's gone very odd these late years since he got into such poverty and bad clothes that he couldn't go to Mass or leave the woods at all hardly.

CON. You could tell from his eyes that he got a punishing from the world. (*He is working away, fitting and screwing sections together.*)

STEPHEN. My daughter is finding this village too quiet and lonesome on account all the young crowd are long since gone out of it, all enticed away by the plentifulness of the money in England and America and Dublin. Maybe you'd visit our house middling often, and then she mightn't be in such a hurry racing

121

back to London.

CON. To-morrow night I'll draw to ye.

STEPHEN. Well, God spare you the health! I'd like she'd stop home till my trouble is over.

CON (*cautiously*). Till you're cured again?

STEPHEN. Yes, till my cure is landed: the only cure that never failed – death.

CON. You haven't the looks of that. Did the doctors say so?

STEPHEN. They didn't, but I'm thinking 'tis what Owen Kelly had I have.... They say the two worst times for cancer are the fall of the leaf and the budding of the leaf, so if May doesn't kill me, I might stagger out till October.

CON. 'Tisn't such a thing you have at all. Do the pains be often teasing you?

STEPHEN (*smiling, albeit a little ruefully*). Some days I have a pain that'd burst a sod of turf; other days I feel good but as weak as water.

CON. 'Tisn't a good thing to be living alone when a man has bad sickness.

STEPHEN. 'Tisn't good and 'tisn't safe. The worst time is the long nights when you'd be roused with the pains, wondering would you be able to put up with them always, and wondering would the burning mountain be your sentence when you'd be taken at last. Brehoney below would never hang himself if he had anwan at all to cheer him.... (*Cheerfully.*) Well, we'll have your name in the kettle to-morrow night, and a few rattles of porter on the hob for you. (*He rises.*)

CON. I'll find your house out, even if I have to pull down the moon. (STEPHEN *goes right.* CON *resumes work with vigour. He is down near the footlights when* MARK *runs in from left.* MARK *is carelessly dressed in his work-a-day clothes and wears heavy nailed boots. He is about twenty-eight, is fearfully thin and pale and hollow-eyed and is highly strung and wild to the verge of madness. He runs across the stage, looks into the woods on the right, and gasps with disappointment.*)

MARK. By the living! She's not here yet. (*He turns, sees* CON *and advances on him with frantic urgency.*) Who are you? You must quit this place directly. 'Tis here Stephen's daughter is to meet me. In a small while we'll push ahead to the Tomb Plantation. Then you can come back here. (*Frantically.*) Quick, man, before she comes!

CON. In a jiffy and a half when I have these tidied away. (*He is putting the tools together hurriedly.*)

MARK. Quick, for she'll be here any minute! (*He runs right and peers into the woods again.*) Neither sight nor light of her is to be seen. (*In anguish.*) Maybe she never told the Post Boy she'd meet me here! He brought me false messages from girls before. He's playing that trick on me till he has old shoes made of it.

CON. If he's a joker like that, 'tis likely this girl didn't send for you either.

MARK. Sure, I know well, but what can I do but take my chance?

CON. Well, good luck! But if I was you, I'd cut home first and come back all washed and dressed.

MARK (*dismayed*). You have the truth! Look at my hands from the clay! She'll say I never washed them since I got them. And my hair like the tinker's wife! (*He spits on his palms and tries to make his hair lie down.*) I had right to think of this before; but I amn't able to think of anything with the usage I'm suffering from the wan that's coming into my house. . . . Be going now. I amn't allowed to tell anywan about her.

CON. Well, good luck again.

(*He goes.* MARK *makes another of his frantic dives to the right.*)

MARK (*despairingly*). No sign of her still! She never said she'd come! He fooled me again and that the power of his hands may leave him! (*He sits down on a tree-stump in despair; suddenly lifts his head desperately.*) I will – and I must do it. (*He runs to the left.*) Hi, there! Hi, there! Come back! Come back a minute. . . . Good man! God bless you!

CON. What did you do that she went so quick again?

MARK. She never came at all, and she won't. . . . Tell me first your business and how far your home is?

CON. Timber-cutting, and my home is twenty strong Irish miles from here, just outside the Lake of O'Flynn.

MARK. Good and good and very good. You'll not be long in this country, so maybe I could tell you all. (*He takes the rosary beads from the graipe handle.*) But first swear on the Cross of our Saviour that you'll not tell.

CON (*taking beads.*) I swear I'll not tell till you give me leave.

MARK. First sit over this side for fear Stephen's daughter'd come and hear us.

(CON *sits on the left end of the box. He offers a cigarette to* MARK, *but the latter waves it aside impatiently. He is hopping about behind the long box peering this way and that into the darkness. At no time during this scene does he sit down or calm*

123

down for a moment.)

MARK. 'Twas the darkest night that ever come out of the heavens; and I was within in bed with my first sleep over, and waiting for my second sleep, when, of a sudden, the darkness split up and down, and out glittered the blue elements of the sky. She stepped from the darkness into the light the same as you'd step out from behind a door. Her shawl and clothes were from the old-fashioned times, and before she opened her mouth at all, I knew 'twas Biddy Roche was in it.

CON. And who is she?

MARK. She was a servant girl in our house above a *hundred* years ago, and the people in it betrayed her hiding-place to Major D'Arcy that was landlord then and the worst bastard-maker of all the D'Arcys. She was never seen alive after, and 'twas common report that she ran down to the lake and drowned herself and put a curse on our home.

CON. What did she say to you?

MARK. "You're the last that'll live here," she said, "and the sooner you quit the longer you'll live, and the longer you stop here the sooner you'll die. And," she said, "as soon as you're dead or gone from this house, the rats'll eat it."

CON. What did you say or do?

MARK. This good while back I do stop awake all night sitting between the firelight and the lamplight. Her kind don't like the light at all, and she never come lately only two nights that I dozed off. (CON *rises, come around to where his tools and boards are, and resumes work. He is unimpressed but a little grim.*)

CON. Can a fellow buy bread-loafs in the shop here, or must he bake his own bread?

MARK. There's no bread-loafs selling only an odd day. A fellow must bake his own bread. And 'tis seldom the cakes come out lucky for me. Half the time the dog does refuse them.

CON. Well, there's your ghost for you. Your health got broken down with bad eating, and then you got out of your nerves at last. In this country your case is as common as grass.

MARK (*angrily*). If you say that, you're a fool. I tell you I seen her as plain as I see you now.

CON. You seen nightmares, and you'll see the death if you go ahead eating poison and staying awake all night.

MARK (*wildly*). That's why I must get a wife, no matter what kind she is. With a comrade in the house, I wouldn't be half as afeared of Biddy. ... But if 'twas known I was haunted, no girl'd join me. The sweat'll be out a-through me for fear you'll tell.

CON. Sssh! (*Looking left.*) There's someone stepping our way.

MARK. But that's not the side her house is. (*He looks left and starts.*) Well, the divil scald them! 'Tis Jimmy King and Paddy King, two men I can't put up with at all.

CON. Why so?

MARK. They're two brothers and oul' bachelors living together near the big gate of the Castle, and lately they're gone as silly as geese. They do set me fearing myself'll finish up as silly as them at last. (*He goes right, and sits on a tree-stump with his back turned on the new arrivals.*)

CON. The geese may cackle away, but I can't be losing money and must go ahead with the work.

(*He sets to work, screwing a window into its frame. He is sitting on the long box. The two brothers come meandering in in their usual formation: one six or eight yards behind the other. They are both in their seventies but are hardy and lively. PADDY is the taller and fresher of the two. In his prime he had been a fine-looking man probably, but now he is doting and imagines that he is still as young as he feels. His whole mien is complacent and jaunty; he has no doubt that he is the irresistible lady-killer of this country-side. JIMMY is smaller and much worse preserved. He is somewhat gloomy, and is very simple, and has no opinion of himself at all. PADDY comes in first singing an old ballad.*)

PADDY. "My Judy, she's as fair as the flowers by the Lee,
    She is neat and complete from her neck to her knee."
Mark, did Stephen's daughter come the way?

MARK (*grimly*). No! Why?

PADDY. She sent word with the Postboy that she'd meet me here.

MARK. And he told me 'twas myself she wanted to meet here! He's fooling the two of us, and that he may never be the father of a family! (*He returns to his tree-trunk and to bitter reflections. During this scene he is in torment, and throws black looks at the old men from time to time.*)

PADDY. 'Twas you he was fooling, not me. First she thought I was seventy-seven years, and she said 'twas too long since I was born. But the minute she heard I was only seventy-two years she said she'd wed no wan but myself. (*To* CON.) How are you?

CON. All right, till the doctor sees me.

(*But* PADDY *wastes scarcely a glance upon him. He rummages in*

125

the great pot and brings up a piece of broken mirror. He takes a comb from his breast pocket, and sits down to admire and titivate his bushy grey moustache.)

JIMMY (*who has been taking in the scene*). Is it for trapping rabbits, or for cutting trees, you're setting up a hut?

CON. Cutting trees.

JIMMY. Well, beware of that oak-tree; that's oul' Major D'Arcy's tree. In my grandfather's time some went cutting it, but th' oul' Major's voice was heard from within – "Be off, and leave me alone or your arms'll wither." He's within in it, a prisoner till the Judgment Day, on account he used to set five or six cradles working every year.

PADDY(*hotly*). Silence, there! 'Tis my turn to do the talking first.

JIMMY (*equally hotly*). Who said it wasn't? Say your say quick, because 'tisn't long I'll give you. (*He sits with his back turned to them, and lights his pipe. He seems completely oblivious of the following conversation.*)

PADDY (*complacently*). Wasn't Mark the clown to think she'd prefer a rag and bone dying thing like himself that a double blanket'd smother, to me that's right in the head and strong in the back and that no girl ever got tired of looking at.

CON. How is it the years never caught up on you at all?

PADDY. I never made a day's work this many and many a year. I was the eldest and the house and farm was left to me, so I could do what I liked in it. What I liked to do was no work, and let that lad do it all. Wasn't I clever to think of that?

CON. They say there's no bread for idlers, but it wasn't so with you.

PADDY. Some must work right enough. All can't be clever. Every day I'd leave that lad working harder than any horse with his four bones, and I'd set off rambling; wan day rambling for drink, another day for kisses, and dancing and card-playing and songs and stories. I'd be wedded long ago only too many girls loved me, and my mind was always on the run from wan girl to another. (*He finds the sheep-shears in the great pot, and begins to trim his moustach and side-locks with it.*)

CON. But your mind is made up now to marry this girl and finish with the rest?

PADDY (*nodding*). Yes. She's a good-looking piece of a dark-haired woman and a man should marry in good time before he is past his best.

CON. And you're sure she loves you?

PADDY. That was proved yesterday. I sent her sweets, and she sent them back to me straight away. So she loves me so much that she'd prefer myself to have the eating of them.

CON. When she loves you better than herself she must have a wonderful love for you.

PADDY. That's what everywan is saying.

CON. Your brother'll have to work double any more on account he'll have two of ye to earn for.

PADDY. That's why he's all his life grumbling and growling against me marrying. He'll have to work double then, and she can do her share, too.

CON. 'Twill be hard on him thinking of all the sport you'll be having with her while he's miserable in his cold bed.

PADDY. Let him carry half-a-hundredweight for half-a-mile every night before he goes to bed and that'll warm him. (*Taking out paper bag of sweets.*) Will you have wan of the sweets? (*He takes one himself first.*)

JIMMY (*turning fiercely*). Now 'tis my turn to talk a while.

PADDY (*equally fiercely*). I didn't say it wasn't. (PADDY *turns his back upon them, and concentrates on the sweets and on romantic dreaming.*)

JIMMY. Was he telling you about the clever plan he made: me to do all the work, or he'd give me the high road like the tinker gave his ass?

CON. He said a little about it all right.

JIMMY (*full of admiration*). No lie at all: he's as clever as the giants long ago that had three heads. Still, he doesn't understand the contrariness of the women and how many men have wives that have pains in their heads with them. And he doesn't understand the cost of anything, because 'tis me has to earn the cost of everything. (*He takes a very grubby piece of paper from his pocket.*) I was reckoning up how much she'll cost me, if he marries her. First I must bring her to the town and buy the ring for her. Then another five pounds to the priest for tying them. Then the supper and dance for the neighbours'll cost within a cough of ten pounds.

CON. And she'll cost you many a sum after.

JIMMY. I'm after questioning the drapery shops all over about the cost of cladding a girl each year and, between underclothes and overclothes, I'll have to buy a score of pounds' worth for her. And we have only oul' feather-beds that she'll maybe too swanky for. So I'll have to buy a new mattress, and put it under them. . . . But there's one cost I didn't find out yet: the hair-

127

docking, what they do call the Perm.

CON. That'll be two pounds more in the year on you.

JIMMY. Two pounds for the hair-docking! Two pounds! (*He makes a note of this.*) This I'll tell you: marriage is a kind of byeword, but 'tis a big undertaking.

MARK (*jumping up, wide-eyed*). Ye two crazy oul'l fools. 'Twould give a person weak eyes and a sore heart to see ye. (*He goes out. PADDY and JIMMY smile at CONN, and tap their skulls to indicate that Mark is crazy.*)

CON. And she'll be coaxing your brother with bits of pleasure to make you buy her necklaces and bracelets and ribbons for decorating herself with.

JIMMY (*nodding*). And another thing: the women are never content till they're master in the house, and until the man has no more rights than a servant-girl in it. And if she doesn't get her own way, she'll start fighting and keep fighting. There's tally-ho and Waterloo and tyrannicalism in every house ever they come into.

CON. Still, some say, 'tis better to be fighting than to be lonesome.

JIMMY. Others can't bear the fighting, and I couldn't. Sure I was a very good-looking man long ago, and could be married many a time, but I knew the fighting wouldn't suit me.

MARK (*entering*). Paddy, I'm crossing her at the corner of the Pleasure Ground, and she said she couldn't meet you to-night, that her father is poorly.

PADDY (*rising cheerfully*). Another night'll be time enough so, and I'll go talking to the barmaid to-night.

JIMMY (*Fiercely*). This is my turn to go first. (*He walks past PADDY.*)

PADDY (*hotly*). I didn't say it wasn't. And it's your turn to stand the first drinks.

JIMMY (*shouting back agrily, from the wing*). Did I ever refuse to rap the counter when my turn came?

PADDY. And take notice of this! 'Tis my turn to enjoy the first while talking to the shop-girl. (*He follows JIMMY at the invariable ten yard range, and they recede roaring like bulls.*)

CON (*looking after them*). No lie, you have some comical Irishmen in this village. Did you cross her that time?

MARK. Not me: I only wanted rid of them. They're like wasps in an ass's lung. I couldn't bear to be looking at them. Look at the case they're in though there was two of them in their house! What'll happen to me that has no wan but a bad spirit that's out to banish me?

(*He sits on a tree trunk near the demesne wall with his back to* CON. *The latter looks at him a moment, shakes his head and comes back to his work.* SHEILA LANIGAN *comes in from right. She is tall and good-looking and aged about twenty-eight. Clothes, make-up and accent indicate that she has spent some time in England. She is serious and somewhat discontented looking. She does not see* MARK *at first.*)

SHEILA (*forcing a smile*). Good evening!

CON (*turning*). Good evening to you.

(MARK *jumps up enraptured. But, before attracting her attention, he attempts again to flatten his wild head of hair.*)

SHEILA. My father was telling me you were in England a long while. Would you say he's learning to die?

CON. 'Twouldn't be easy for me to say on account I never saw him before. Your neighbour there'd be a better judge.

MARK (*shyly*). 'Tis you that's looking well, Sheila.

SHEILA (*after a long look – doubtfully*). Are you Mark Tristnan?

MARK. Why wouldn't I?

SHEILA (*shocked at the change in him*). Are you well?

MARK. I'm very well, Sheila. (*Eagerly.*) Why?

SHEILA. You're looking very bad.

MARK. 'Tis only that I'm a little slaved out and in want of a housekeeper. That's why I was so pleased by your message.

SHEILA. What message?

MARK. To meet you here, and that you were set on making your home in Ireland.

SHEILA (*decisively*). That's what I'll never do while my toes are looking down. (*To* CON.) How could you abide this country after England? What's in it but poverty and bad wages and slavery with no cinema within ten miles.

CON (*nodding*). Sure, 'twas all that kept myself from coming home years ago.

(MARK *turns away, and goes back to his tree-trunk despairingly.*)

SHEILA. 'Tisn't as bad here for a man. He can go drinking at night just as good as in England. But what can a girl do, or who can she talk to? There isn't a man keeping a house in this village but is part crazy.

MARK (*jumping up in a fury*). Isn't it you and your likes have made us crazy? Racing off to England and America after plentifulness of money and six nights dancing a week, and leaving us to do a man's work on the farm and a woman's work in the house. How can a man keep evermore working twenty hours a day? Look at

129

how it has myself worn out and thin like a cat that'd been eating crickets. How can a man's mind stand out for ever against misery and the badness of the night?

SHEILA. Mark, I'm very sorry for your trouble, but what can I do? I'm marrying a fellow in England shortly.

MARK (*stunned*). Then I'm done, and she'll worry me and craze me till at last I'll be barking like a dog. (*He goes out left.*)

SHEILA. Jesus, Mary and Joseph!

CON. The poor fellow is neglected and losing his health fast.

SHEILA. We'll talk his case over another time. Myself and a Sligo man are friendly in London, and we're marrying as soon as we can get a flat, or room, in it. What'll I do if my father is six months dying and I'm kept here?

CON. Would he not wait for you?

SHEILA. You know how London is swarmed out with girls. If I stop in this country long, I'll surely lose him. He isn't the kind that could live long without taking out some girl.

CON. Your father'd get good treating in the County Home; but the people see great disgrace in dying there amongst all the beggars and rogues of the country.

SHEILA. If I leave him he'll stay and die at home, no matter how miserable a death he'll get.

CON. They say it isn't lucky to desert your father or mother.

SHEILA. Sadie didn't go foreign, but stopped minding her mother, smiling away there till of a sudden she saw she had lost herself. What luck had she?

CON (*grimly*). She lost herself over a thing that could be managed another way or done without; and that's the Irish mistake. Whatever you do, whether you'll go or stay, don't lose yourself for anywan living. For anywan can get on better without you than you can get on without yourself.

SHEILA (*after a pause*). Come visiting a while to-morrow night, and we'll talk this out when father is gone to bed.

CON. I'll give ye a visit.

SHEILA. Good night now! (*She goes.*)

CON. Good night!

(*He resumes work, but immediately* HOTHA FLYNN *slips in from the left. He is a scraggy, somewhat stooped fellow, between fifty and fifty-five and nature has treated him very shabbily in the matter of looks. Invariably he wears a large battered hat at an outlandish angle, hence his nickname of "Hotha". On each arm he carries an egg-basket containing sundry grocery items. He is very quiet-*

130

spoken, but sad and obstinate and, at times, mysterious.)

HOTHA (*anxiously*). I didn't hear all the words ye had. Did she say Hotha courted Sadie a score of years, then curled his hair and left her and robbed her of the comfort of the world?

CON. She said no word about you, big, little or small.

HOTHA. Some have Sadie's trouble blamed black and white on me; but sure 'twas my father wouldn't allow me to wed her on account she had no fortune. And when my father died at last she was too old to have family. What good was she to me, or me to her, without a son that'd work the farm when ourselves'd be old and weak-handed at last?

CON. Did you get any younger wan since?

HOTHA. Not yet; 'tis mortal hard for a farmer. The few girls in the country are spoiled with working in shops and towns.

CON. I hear Sadie within got a nervous downfall.

HOTHA (*lowering his voice lest she should hear*). She did not. She was swopped.

CON. You mean the fairies took her, and left wan of their own kind in her place?

HOTHA (*nodding*). 'Tisn't Sadie that's in there at all, we're thinking. Sadie's dog was heard barking every night for a week keeping them back from her, but he had to sleep at last, and then they took her, and left this bad sulky thing. . . . But we do all we can for her, just for fear it might be Sadie. (*He leaves one basket at wicket-gate.*) I'll tell you the rest again. (*He goes out right.*)

(CON *resumes work, but in a moment or two* KITTY *runs in from left carrying a couple of newspapers under her arm. She picks up the basket, places it inside the wicket-gate, knocks on the gate, and calls out.*)

KITTY. Sadie, here's yesterday's paper and last week's "Western People" and "Connacht Tribune." Let you be reading them, and stop thinking, for thinking is the worst for you.

(KITTY *comes in, closing the gate. She is a young pretty country girl, but not very conceited or defensive as she might be if she lived in a city, and had to stand an endless siege of admiring glances. Here her consciousness of beauty is just sufficient to increase her native good-humour and light-heartedness and coquettishness. She loves to tease.*)

KITTY. Well, I'm wrong or you're a stranger.

CON (*suddenly cheerful and interested*). You're right and I am a stranger.

131

THE WOOD OF THE WHISPERING – ACT I

KITTY. And how are you?

CON. Faith, I'm doing well – like the people in America. (*He offers her a cigarette which she takes.*)

KITTY. Thanks. Are you going building another storey on Sanbatch's house? (*Pointing to long box.*)

CON. Sanbatch'll lay eyes on his house no more. Did you not meet my mates carrying him to the County Home Ambulance?

KITTY (*her face clouding over*). Poor Sanbatch to the County Home!

CON. He didn't like going first, but then I gave him a crack on the head with this hammer, and after that he didn't mind going.

KITTY. On the head with the hammer! (*Then, detecting a gleam in his eye, she laughs.*) You divil! You're humbugging me! 'Twasn't for Sanbatch you came at all.

CON. 'Tis for cutting down every tree in all these woods, so the devil a bit of shade or shelter ye'll have left for courting.

KITTY (*chuckling*). The Wood of the Whispering they do call this wood on account of all the courting couples that used to be in it some years ago before all the lads and the girls went foreign.

CON. How is it you're not gone foreign yourself?

KITTY. Sure, amn't I? Im escaped from the land and from feeding pigs at any rate. I'm behind the counter in Gowlin's drink-shop.

CON. You're badly paid there and will be for ever. All them country shops are failing fast from the depopulation.

KITTY (*cheerfully*). Ours is a middling strong shop still. The people around here have great belief in an old saying that tis unlucky to pass Gowlin's without going in for a drink.

CON. Still, you'll have to go foreign at last. And the younger you go foreign, the easier you'll settle down foreign.

KITTY. Likely enough. You have great sense in you.

CON (*grimly*). Like all the Irish, I got great sense at last – when 'twas too late to do me any good.

KITTY. How is that?

CON. I couldn't bring myself to settle down in England I was so lonesome for Ireland, and I couldn't bring myself to leave England and face again the poverty and bad wages of Ireland. So English landladies got my earnings and I remained a tramp navvy. Any road I go, I'm going home, because I have no home.

KITTY. Sure, you're a young fellow yet!

CON. I am not! And with the wages a man gets in this country I'll be as old as the sea and as white as bog-cotton before I'll have the price of a home.

KITTY (*not disposed to worry about this or about anything*). At night-time I can easy get leave from the shop on account Gowlin is always in it himself at night-time. I'll come down often and we'll have the sport of the world with Sanbatch.

CON (*eagerly*). Do! . . . but stick to your own fellow, whoever he is. For my years for young good-looking girls are over. Any more I must be looking out for a girl with a house and land and no matter at all about what kind or age herself is.

(SANBATCH *comes in whistling and calling "Leggy!" He carries the gun and, seeing* KITTY, *is immediately in great humour.*)

SANBATCH. Now, Kitty, didn't God tell me here in the night there was a fine fellow coming for you and he having a stone-weight of money after England.

(*He throws aside the gun and comes round to the fire.* MARK *comes in, following* SANBATCH.)

KITTY. He's giving me strong advice to go foreign and not waste my time here.

SANBATCH (*jumping up in a fury*). He's sending you foreign! The last bright little face that's left in our country? (*He runs for the gun.*)

MARK (*grappling with him*). Stop, man! Have sense, man!

SANBATCH. Out of the way till I send his heart's blood flying out of him.

KITTY (*grabbing hold of the gun*). Sanbatch, I'm not leaving this country, but I'll have to if there's a murder over me.

SANBATCH (*to Mark*). Will he swear to leave this little girl alone, and not send her from us?

CON. I promise, Sanbatch! Sure, why would I want her to leave this place where I'll be staying myself?

SANBATCH (*grimly*). Very well, then. (*Relinquishes gun to* MARK.) Kitty, leave us a while. I have words for this fellow that you shouldn't hear.

KITTY. Don't go too hard on him. (*Mischievously.*) He was only trying to talk sense to me. He's fully believing he's sensible. Good-night to ye. (*She runs out left.*)

MARK AND CON. Good night!

SANBATCH (*furious again*). D'ye hear what she said? He was talking sense to her! The rottenest action in the world wide that a man could do.

CON. What kind is she then that 'tis wrong to talk sense to her?

SANBATCH. The minute she gets sense she'll give up working for a couple of pounds a week and go to England where she'll have eight pounds a week. And if she doesn't go itself, the minute she gets sense and sees the world is hard and bad, she'll turn serious, and the last bright smile in this country'll be quenched for evermore.

CON. And d'ye think so little of her that you'd like to see her waste her time here and lose herself, the same as we're all after losing ourselves?

SANBATCH. How do you know, but 'tis God's will her to brighten up this country a while more, and save more of us from doing what Brehoney did when he soaped a rope and hung himself? How do you know what God's will is, and, when you don't, how dare you interfere?

MARK. Don't be too hard on him! He hadn't time yet to survey this country right and understand how it is now.

SANBATCH. That is so too. So I'll help you with your hut in the run of a few minutes when I have Leggy flocked in. Hi, Leggy! – you have me going around like the bad luck! (*He goes left.*)

CON. Tell me, have you a spare bed in your house?

MARK. To be sure! My mother's bed is alive yet.

CON. I have sheets and blankets myself, but tell me honest, have you any fleas in your house?

MARK. Not yet! Sure my house is without a woman for only three years.

CON. Then I'll stop in your house to-night, and finish the hut again. (*He collects some of his things.*)

MARK. Stop in my house for your term here, and God'll bless you. I won't be half as much afeared of Biddy when there's a living person in the next room to me.

CON. A lorry'll be bringing the timbermen from the town every day and they'll bring bread-loafs for you, so soon you'll coax your health back again.

(*They go.* SANBATCH *comes in, goes to wicket gate, bangs upon it and calls out.*)

SANBATCH. Sadie, come out a while. The timberman is gone sleeping at Mark's and myself only is here.

(*He finds a little bag of lime in the iron pot, and takes a sheepskin down from a tree-branch. He sits on the long box sprinkling lime on the inside of the sheepskin.* SADIE *comes out, makes sure there is no one around, and comes in a little way.*)

SANBATCH. Sadie, I'm as well to camp here any more on account my house is down, and every day we can be having many a fine talk unknownt to the world. Anything is better for you than to

134

be in there thinking always about how you lost yourself. Sit over there at your ease on my house. Don't be shy or shamed for I haven't time to look at you coming at all. (*He turns his back upon her.*) The plush of my blankets is getting very bare, so to season this sheepskin I'm putting lime tickling it.

(SADIE *draws nearer, watching him fearfully out of the corner of that tragic eye, as if she was doing something criminal.*)

SANBATCH. I'll keep the talk going. Sure Leggy isn't able to speak either, still we enjoy many a fine talk together.

(*She comes right up to the long box. Suddenly his eye falls upon his shotgun and he forgets her in his grief.*)

SANBATCH. Look at my poor oul' fowling gun that I must sell at last, for I'm safe no more! To-night I very near shot a fellow that went sending away the last little bright face that was helping us to bear the world.

(*She sits at the opposite end of the long box. His mind is on another track now, and he has forgotten his promise not to look towards her.*)

SANBATCH. Oftentimes, I do be thinking poor Brehoney never would hang himself if she come to the drink-shop two months sooner. For then he'd go drinking a while every day and she'd cheer him. . . . God sent me to Behoney's that day, and there he was with a rope threw over the crossbeam and he soaping the rope. "'Tis a great sin," I ses. "As for sins," he ses, "there's bad women coming in my dreams every night at the midnight hour, and they'll not leave any night till I commit sin with them. So 'tis better for God, too, me to commit wan last sin and have done with it." 'Twas just the week before that the sinew in my arm parted from its fellow in my shoulder, so I was very little worth that day and no match for him at all. So I made a plan, and said, "Timmy," I ses, "This is the first day ever in Ireland that you hung yourself, so we'll have wan last drink to your success and happiness. I'll bring down a heel of whiskey I have in the house." "That'd be very lucky and very nice and decent," he ses. But when I got help and come back he was hanging and well hung. The young priest was talking to me about it and about the unsane. "A lot are in the asylum from leading a bad life," he said. "Father," I ses, "there's more in the asylum from the want of married life." 'Tis easy for the priests and nuns to live straightforward; they have God every morning. But we can't go to Mass on a Sunday itself, we're gone so old, some of us, and more of us are so starved and raggedy. If only we had good learning! The finest thing in the world is to be a little crazy, and to have great learning. D'you remember oul' Jack the Papers and the poems he made:

> "Down I came for want of pence,
>   It grieved me sore;
> Down I stayed for want of sense,
>   It grieved me more."

(*Putting aside pipe and tobacco.*) Still there's some of the gifts of God we didn't lose yet. I'll diddle a tune for you now that'll put the two of us in great humour.

(*He folds his arms, crosses his legs, closes his eyes and lilts a lively Irish dance tune using the usual diddling words – "Doodledum dandy, dum daree," etc. He sings with spirit, beating time with his head and toe. But there is no change in her expression throughout this scene.*)

SANBATCH. I haven't the breath for diddling now, but wan time I could keep a score of couples dancing half a night. (*Suddenly grave again.*) And about the night: the greatest remark of all I'm coming to now. Always before midnight, no matter if your teeth are cracking with the fear itself, leave the fire, and creep away to your bed and quench the candle. For the oul' people had a saying: *"Leig an oidche leis fein" ("Leave the night to itself")*; and 'tis true – the night never likes any wan to interfere with it. Look at young Mark Tristnan below; he's sleeping in the day and stopping up all night with the lamp lit, and look at how the night is wasting him away and maddening him! But let you have no fear of leprechauns or fairies at all. 'Twas only last week that myself asked oul' Mickil Doogan and oul' Jimmy Walsh was there fairies out these times, and they said there was nothing out now except man. And they're two men that'd be bound to know, because they're dead thirty years. . . . But even the dead themselves aren't half or quarter as plentiful as they used to be in the midnight. 'Tis very near a week now since a gang of ghosts stretched their fingers at me. They were a crowd that died without christening. Now I'll diddle another tune Piper Rainey left me:

(*He folds his arms, closes his eyes solemnly as before. Suddenly a short bark is heard from nearby. SANBATCH jumps up roaring.*)

SANBATCH. Hi, Leggy! Come back here you vagabone!

136

(*He runs out. Her reactions are slow, and seconds pass before she realises that he is gone. She thinks about that a little, and then sinks back into her melancholy once more. The fire is burning low now, and the darkness closes in upon her. Suddenly she realises this, and grows frightened. She bends her head over the fire, putting her hands to her eyes in blinkers fashion to shut out the darkness. Finally she takes a rosary from her apron pocket, and blesses herself with it several times, her lips moving, her eyes full of fear. She presses the beads to her lips and to her heart, but still her fear grows. Suddenly she puts her hands over her eyes, so that she cannot see the shadows. She rises, feels her way around the end of the long box and over to the demesne wall. She misses the wicket-gate but, with one arm covering her eyes, she gropes until she finds it. With a sob she pulls it open, runs out and into her house. The door bangs shut, and there is a silence until* SANBATCH *suddenly appears in the firelight with Leggy. He stands grave and erect for a moment. Then he sits on the long box and begins to tether Leggy.*)

SANBATCH. You drew me away, Leggy, before I could tell her the best news: that there were prospects of a marriage in the village again. If there was only wan child in the village itself, he'd keep us smiling half a score of year more, and then he'd be hardy enough to run for the priest when we'd be suffering death. (*Suddenly gleeful and triumphant.*) For we won't be always miserable, Leggy. We'll die at last. (*Chuckling cheerfully.*) That much is sure. God never refused Death to any wan!

CURTAIN

ACT TWO

The scene is the same, and the time is after nightfall at the end of September. SANBATCH's *camp is as before, and the fire is burning low.* CON *comes in carrying a folded Ordnance Survey Map of Connaught. He calls out: "Sanbatch!" a couple of times, but there is no reply. He stirs up the fire, sits on the long box, opens the map and studies it by the light of the fire, marking and ticking off various points with his pencil.* KITTY *trips in from the left. She is as youthfully lighthearted and playful as ever, but underlying this there is deep affection between herself and* CON.

KITTY. God save all here, except the dog!

CON. Did you hear to-day's news?

KITTY. What's the cause ye're going away so soon when ye haven't cut this wood yet, or the Tomb Plantation, or the Park of the Challenge?

CON. The Forestry Department sent word we can't cut the rest of these woods yet. No doubt some other timbermen'll get the cutting of them after a couple of years.

KITTY. And ye're off to the Castlebrowne Woods on Monday?

CON. Fifteen strong Irish miles away! Will you miss me sore, or will you miss me at all?

KITTY (*mischievous*). If I can't get another fellow, I'll miss you; but if I can, I won't!

CON (*knowing her*). Fair enough! Now, crush over here near me. I have big things to tell you to-night. But first I must humour you, or you won't listen to me right. (*He is about to kiss her.*)

KITTY. Not to-night! Look! Angels are passing! (*She looks left.*)

CON. Are they? (*Looks around.*) The way it is, lads, if I don't throw her an odd crumb, she won't visit me at all, and then she'd have no wan to learn sense to her . . . (*Listens for a moment.*) And good luck to ye!

138

KITTY. They're gone up! Quick, while we're safe! (*They kiss.*)

CON. I'm as serious as a ghost all hours of the day, but the minute you come I'm as hearty as a drunken fiddler. But, if we were married, would you keep light-hearted long?

KITTY (*slyly*). As long as you wouldn't trouble me.

CON. Faith, that wouldn't be long . . . And now, look at the green patches in this map! They're the woodlands of Connacht and while they last, my job with the timbermen is safe.

KITTY. 'Tis a job for years, so! The counties are greatly sprinkled with them.

CON. There was hardly a parish, or half-parish, without its woods when this map was made forty years ago. But now they're all cut down very near, and not wan in thirty of them was ever replanted. The timbermen say the last of the woods'll keep us going for maybe three years more; after that we'll get high road. So, before we could wed, we'd spend three years waiting for a dwellingplace in some Connacht town where there'd be a thousand people too many already. Then the woods and my job'd run out, and we'd spend another three years waiting for a house in London where there's a million people too many already.

KITTY. But wouldn't we keep for that five or six years – if we salted ourselves well?

CON. You would, because you could paint yourself well. But these are my last few good years, and at the finish we might be no nearer a home, and sick and tired of each other moreover.

KITTY (*cheerfully incredulous*). So you'd reckon we should finish up now?

CON (*rising*). I'm sure of it, but I haven't the sense to do it. (*He crosses stage gloomily.*) I came from England vowing I'd overlook ye young good-looking wans any more, and search the country for wan like Sheila that'd have land and a home. Instead of that I'm after squandering another five months with you! So, after thirty no man can alter his habits or improve himself any more.

KITTY. Listen! (*She looks out.*) 'Tis Sanbatch coming by himself, and talking his head off the same as always.

(SANBATCH *comes in left carrying some groceries in an old tattered sack, and on his left shoulder a great load of straw which prevents him from seeing the pair. He throws the straw backstage and opens the bag.*)

SANBATCH. Another thing, Leggy, that ruined me; wance a man

139

gets a bad name 'tis very hard to wash it away again. Wan year I went to a circus and a rotten liar of a circus pony picked me out as a man that was fond of kissing another man's wife. I was crying my character many a month after that. . . . (*Seeing them.*) Ye're here! (*Running left.*) Mark! Mark! Come back! She's here! (*Coming over to the pair.*) I know well ye two are true lovers, but 'tis no good for ye when ye have no money or a home.

CON. I drank before you there, Sanbatch. Many a time I have that told to her.

SANBATCH (*pulling the hayfork out of the ground*). Mark is the man for you, Kitty, on account he has a fine farm and home. And he's a wholehearted man and the finest ever you heard at saying the Rosary. You could know well he means it.

KITTY (*cheerfully*). Sure I know well he'd be all right for any wan that'd like him good enough.

SANBATCH. Well, if he hasn't a heated love for you, my name is Tadhg.

(MARK *enters, carrying a shopping-bag. He is still a very serious-minded fellow, but in health and nerves he is now completely back to normal.*)

SANBATCH. Tell the truth, Mark, wouldn't you bear snowballing with cowdung for her?

MARK. I'd bear it as long as any man in our country.

KITTY (*parrying this*). Sanbatch, how does a person know whether they have true love or not?

SANBATCH (*with the fork, raking the blankets and straw out of the long box*). There's two sure signs! When you're really in love the bit you're eating doesn't be doing you much good, and you don't be learning anything new at your trade.

MARK. I'll tell you no lie at all, Kitty, I can conquer any fair meal that's put before me; and I'm up as early and as keen for the work as ever I was in my days.

SANBATCH. So you see he's back to his full health and nerves again ever since Con started sleeping at his house, and cold fear was no longer waking him and shaking him in the dead hour of night.

MARK. But Conn'll be gone away again after Tuesday, and the double work and the darkness'll walk away with my health and nerves again. And the timbermen'll be coming no more that were bringing me breadloaves from the town, so I'll be poisoned with my own cakes again. So, if you're to wed me at all, you must wed me now.

KITTY. Myself mightn't be wan degree a better warrant to make a cake. But isn't it for Sheila your wish is?

(CON *carries the fresh straw over to* SANBACH.)

MARK. That book is shut on me now. Her fellow in England is after writing to her again. (*Producing letter.*)

CON. His first in two months!

SANBATCH (*bitterly*). 'Twould put a false face on a monkey to see it.

KITTY. Show me the letter, Mark.

MARK. Bring it to Sheila yourself. (*Hands letter.*)

KITTY. That isn't his handwriting.

MARK (*suddenly elated*). Are you sure?

KITTY. That's from a comrade girl in London that used to write to her.

MARK. Well, if that's so, let ye tell her I'm going courting her all out to-night. And then if she won't have me, I'll ask yourself, Kitty. (*He snatches up shopping bag, and is running off excitedly.*)

SANBATCH. Wait, Mark! 'Tis Kitty you should ask and let Con marry into Sheila's farm. Then ye'll have two young families rising up in the village.

MARK. Sanbatch, if a man is to sleep forty years with a woman, the first wan he should ask is the wan he likes best. (*He goes.*)

CON (*grimly*). Sheila won't marry him! Like myself and like all the born old maids and old bachelors, she wants to marry only some wan she can't marry, or some wan that doesn't want to marry her.

SANBATCH. If you stick to that, ye'll lose yourselves the same as our generation lost themselves.

CON. We know that well, but we can't save ourselves. The same curse is on our generation. (*He looks at his wristwatch.*)

KITTY (*tossing his hair*). D'ye hear him, Sanbatch? He thinks he knows the depths of everything because he was in England and can tell the time by the back of his hand. Sanbatch can tell the time by the sun.

SANBATCH (*merrily*). I can and by the daughter.

CON (*rising*). And time flies, as the cobbler said when he threw the clock at his wife. (*To Kitty.*) We'll be bringing her letter to Sheila. (*They set out.*)

SANBATCH (*wistfully*). Kitty, will you leave this district when himself and the timbermen go away next week?

KITTY (*smiling sympathetically*). Why, Sanbatch?

SANBATCH. There's many a why, but I'll tell you only wan. To be

141

old is to be bad, and in any village where there's no young
person, there's no pleasure in the times, and even the brightest
summer sunshine is lonesome and sad.

KITTY. Sure, where would I go? To England where the smoke and
fogs gives an Irish girl T.B., or to America where wan summer
leaves her as withered as a burnt leaf on a dead tree?

SANBATCH. This evening I was so afeard ye'd soon go that I went
spending wild, hoping that'd cheer me. Look at all I bought!
(*He empties the bag out on the ground.*) A brace of socks, a bit
of a decent oul' cow that saved the butcher the trouble of killing
her, a glass of whiskey, an ounce of tobaccy and yesterday's
paper – he said it had a lot more newses than to-day's. All that
spending'll leave me with more dinner-times than dinners for a
fortnight.

CON. But what'll you do soon at the height of winter? In that oul'
coffin you'll be getting wet skin and cold every hour, and soon
you'll be full of coughs and spits and diseases.

SANBATCH (*with hayfork, tossing fresh straw into his house*). If a
man'll keep himself very tidy, and dress his bed very tasty
wance a fortnight, that'll keep him hardy and wholesome.

KITTY. But your farm is all lapsed back into rushes and water and
bog. A snipe couldn't live on it unless he had leggings. How will
you earn enough to keep life in you anymore?

SANBATCH (*running to the upper roots of a tree*). In here I have hid
the first makings of a secret invention and, if I can finish it right,
it'll make us all as rich as factory masters, and you'll have no
more need to go foreign in search of a house or good pay. So,
till the invention is made, let ye not go foreign.

CON (*sceptical*). We won't; but now we must go over the path to
Sheila's.

KITTY. 'Tis easier than going under it. We'll be back soon.

SANBATCH. Do, and God'll bless ye!

(*They go. He sorts out a small parcel of meat, gets a knife and
cuts it in two. He talks to the dog tethered onstage or off.*)

SANBATCH. 'Tis noways fair, Leggy, you to be rambling evermore
and leaving me without wan to talk to when fear is on me that
the young people'll go foreign before I get time to finish the
invention that'd set them up rich and happy in this village for
life. (*He sits down.*) This was for myself, but I'm dividing
between us now in equal parts, the same as the wren divides the
worm. (*He is cutting the meat.*) Some curse, Leggy, is scattering
the youth from our country for evermore. Some reckon 'tis

142

because they won't obey the Missioners, and go walking any more with their own sisters, and give up walking with other fellows' sisters. There'll never be sport again like long ago. A lot used to be drowned and murdered that time, and the finest of songs used to be composed about them all. Myself has to make a lump of cake for the breakfast.

(*He leads the dog off-stage and returns himself in a moment. He finds flour and soda in paper bags in the iron pot; also a big glass jam-jar. He fills the jar one-third with water, pours flour and soda on top of it, and mixes with a knife. This done he scrapes the lot into the pan, and mixes another jam-jar full. When enough has been made he sets the pan on the long box and pounds the dough with his fists and elbow. This work continues in fits and starts during the next scenes. He talks away as usual.*)

SANBATCH. I wouldn't miss you, Leggy, or be lonesome at all, if I was a good Christian, and could pass the time thinking ever-more about the Sacred Mysteries up there. But I'm as greedy for the world as ever I was. 'Tis only last night I was thinking of a girl I was with at Tim Crowley's wake long ago.

(STEPHEN *and* HOTHA *come in from the right,* STEPHEN *leaning heavily upon his stick and upon Hotha. He is very stooped and thin and sharp-featured with the strained expression of a man who has suffered much. But at the moment he is enjoying an easy spell, and the relief is so great that he is in good humour.* HOTHA *helps him to a seat on a tree-stump.*)

SANBATCH. Are ye tripping far?

HOTHA. Stephen is making the last journey to Gowlin's drink-shop so he wants you to come, too.

SANBATCH. The last journey! What, man, you'll make many a trip yet, and down many a sweet glassful.

STEPHEN (*smiling*). The way it is, after each bad spell the legs are less inclined to carry me. After the next, the bed'll hold me. (*He is lighting pipe.*)

SANBATCH. You're wise to go to-night, so! 'Twould be the saddest thing in the world you to go up without making the last journey. (*Washing his hands in the bucket and wiping them on blanket.*) Were you vexed with me, Stephen, because I put the Blessed Candle in your hand the last night you were bad? The way it was we were full sure 'twas the death last night.

STEPHEN. I thought 'twas the death myself.

SANBATCH. You aren't vexed with me, so? I was afraid you might think we were in a hurry with you.

143

STEPHEN (*puffing resignedly*). 'Tis no loss at all to be leaving Ireland now. Anymore 'twill be a miserable bare country with all its fine mansions and woods destroyed.

SANBATCH. The springtime of the year'll lift our hearts no more. In the spring when the trees put their jackets on, they were like strangers and like giants.

(HOTHA *has been setting out some papers and a pen and ink beside* STEPHEN.)

HOTHA. Here you are! Sign here! Be watching this, Sanbatch.

SANBATCH. I'm watching; and Stephen watch not to drink too much to-night. You know yourself how it makes you a rotten blackguard for fighting and the tinkers' litany and English army talk.

STEPHEN. I'll be as quiet as a stick any more.

(STEPHEN *and* HOTHA *have signed.* SANBATCH *is reading the will over their shoulders, and he starts indignantly.*)

SANBATCH. This will is the lowest and the saddest ever I seen. If you're leaving Sheila your house and farm you shouldn't give her power to sell them. Because she'll sell them directly you're gone, and give herself and the money away to that wastrel in London.

STEPHEN. 'Tis what she'll do, I'm afraid.

SANBATCH. Put a clause in that'll forbid her to sell it; then we might convert her to stand loyal to her own village. Which is worse, that she should have to live in her own village, and marry a farmer like her mother before her, or that us, your oul' neighbours that drank with you forty years, should be left to die on the ground, like dogs? I'll not witness such a will. (*He walks away.*)

STEPHEN. If we try to tie her here, we'll only vex her, and then she'd be sure to go.

HOTHA. That's the truth. We'll put our hands in the fire altogether if we go thwarting her.

SANBATCH. All right, so! I'll sign, but St. Peter'll be pulling your ears over this before you're well inside his door. (*He signs.*)

HOTHA. There's as good men for her in Ireland as ever went to England. (*He pockets papers, etc., again.*)

SANBATCH. You're all the year singing that tune to us. Why don't you drink half a pint of whiskey, and ask herself straight out will she marry you?

HOTHA. To-night I'm going telling herself and Kitty about the £700 I have in the bank and my two thousand pounds' worth of land

and stock. They have heads like feet if they don't understand such a man'd be better for them than young fellows that have nothing but the clothes on their backs.

SANBATCH. And when they refuse you, will you agree then to wed Sadie? 'Twould encourage the young people to see marriage stealing back into fashion again. 'Tis so long out of fashion here, the people are fearing it more than death.

HOTHA. Isn't half the country saying she never lost her mind like that so sudden: that the fairies stole Sadie and left this thing in her place, a bad thing that'd betray me to them? Didn't the village hear her dog barking at them every night for a week till he had to sleep at last, and then they took her.

SANBATCH. The same dog wouldn't be alive if he wasn't barking at some wan. Still I give in she should be challenged before 'twould be safe for anywan to marry her.

STEPHEN (*rising*). Are you coming to the drink-shop?

SANBATCH. In the run of a few minutes, I'll be after ye.

HOTHA. Don't delay. He won't be fit to drink long.

(*Both help Stephen out left.* SANBATCH *comes back and sits on the long box looking very troubled.*)

SANBATCH. Leggy, 'tis long since I had five pounds, if I had five pounds again, I'd sit up all night looking at it. Still I'd be better pleased than five pounds not to have to do what I have to do now – challenge poor Sadie that never took a bite out of any wan. But 'tis a thing must be done, because Hotha is the only wan that can mind and save her any more, on account that secret invention'll keep myself working far away and night and day from the Wood of the Whispering. And if I can contrive to get herself and Hotha wedded, they'd be using only wan of their two houses anymore, and then, maybe in God, Kitty and Con could marry into the idle house and bring back children to the village once more.

(*He takes his rosary off the graipe handle and hangs its around his neck, under his shirt. He takes the Madonna off the sheep-crook and leaves it on the long box. The sheep-crook he places against a tree near the wicket-gate, putting it there, not to have it out of the way, but as part of his general strategy. He hangs the Madonna and Child on the graipe handle. As he does so, he addresses Them matter-of-factly and gravely.*)

SANBATCH. Ye know th' oul' proverb: "Every fool is dangerous," so let Ye stand between me and her to-night for fear I'd go too savage. I must go middling savage, or the challenge'd be no

145

good and unfair to Hotha. (*He opens the wicket-gate and calls out.*) SADIE, SANBATCH!

(*He comes back, takes off his old torn pair of socks and puts on the new ones.* SADIE *comes in the gate, looks around to make sure* SANBATCH *is alone, then comes quietly down and sits on the long box. She looks in front of her as silently as ever. Yet she seems much improved. Her reactions are quicker and more marked; she is also less fearful and ill-at-ease. He places the old torn pair of socks in front of her.*)

SANBATCH. There's a needle and thread with them. If you'd sew them up for me, I'd be strongly obliged to you. (*Lacing his boots.*) I bought a new brace of socks hoping they'd cheer me. The minute I heard the timbermen were leaving, God struck me that Kitty and Sheila'd soon leave this country now. If Kitty goes, the strings of my heart'll break . . . (*Wildly.*) . . . God of Heaven, I can't stand that at all. I must do it! (*He runs to the iron pot, finds there a little brown paper packet.*) Here is the last few raisins I had left since last Christmas and was keeping for this Christmas. But now I must put them in this cake, hoping they'll cheer me.

(*He takes a nailing hammer from the pot, empties the raisins over the cake, and drives them in with taps of the hammer, continuing to lament the while. For the moment he has forgotten* SADIE, *who picks up the socks, and examines the holes professionally.*)

SANBATCH. She's the nicest little branch that ever got her picture taken; she stirs up sport and glee wherever she goes, and her smile'd bring back the summer on Christmas Day. Just as the little children used to do when they were still in this village, she'd make you forget the world was so big and so old and so hard to understand. She's just the same as you were when you were white and rosy in your youthful days. Only your laugh had three hops. . . . (*Suddenly he pauses. He remembers the work on hand. His face darkens gradually until finally he leaps to his feet and stands over her with blazing eyes, hammer in hand.*)

SANBATCH. What did ye do with our Sadie? Where did ye put her? Bring back our Sadie this minute, or I'll kill you against the ground.

(*She rises in terror, thinking he has gone mad, but he runs past her to the wicket-gate, and closes it. He takes the sheep-crook, and stands between her and the demesne wall.*)

SANBATCH. And never think you can rise in the air and fly over the wall. The sheep-crook goes with Christ, and can bring you down if ye were as high as the clouds. 'Tis only a fairy stronger than God can save you now.

(*He is advancing upon her slowly and relentlessly whilst she keeps retreating around the long box and the fire.*)

SANBATCH. 'Tis no good at all for you to be looking so innocent. Let ye not think at all that we didn't hear ye that night crossing the lawns with a noise like a lot of fillies that'd have no shoes, and her dog barking at the butt of her door till he bobbed asleep at last, and ye filled in and swept her with ye. . . . You're not our Sadie at all! I know for positive because there was witchery in my people, and my grandfather could put himself in the power of the divil and make thieves appear and tell me where the stolen things be. He did worse things and fearful things till at last he did what ruined Ireland, he went out into a field and cursed the weather. So here! The Earl of Hell was my god-father, and if you don't bring back our Sadie I'll open up the ground here – (*He stoops and pretends to do so.*) – and in two minutes he'll be running through the streets of Hell with you in his mouth. . . . You won't? Very well then. (*Raps the ground.*) Open up there, and send up the worst divil ye have with horns five miles long. (*Listens.*) What's delaying ye? No matter whether ye're eating or sleeping, ye're to come up this minute, or I'll set God after ye again. . . . (*He listens with ear to ground: is suddenly elated.*) 'Tis shaking. 'Tis shaking and breaking, so they're coming. (*To* SADIE.) Bring back our Sadie this minute and I can still save you. . . . (*Jumping up.*) So ye don't care for God, man or the divil! Well, there's wan thing left that none of ye can stand, and 'tis here! (*He pulls a brand out of the fire.*) Bring back our Sadie, or I'll fry the two eyes in your head!

(*He darts at her and she, sinking upon the long box with a gasp, pulls the Madonna picture from the graipe and squeezes it against her eyes. Immediately* SANBATCH *smiles happily.*)

SANBATCH. Sadie, 'tis yourself is in it for certain! If you were wan of them you wouldn't trust Our Saviour or His Mother. (*He tosses the brand back into the fire, and mops his brow.*) For you and for me that was a hard hill to climb. But there's a cause for everything, and the cause of the challenge was – Hotha'd be afeard to wed you without it. (*He puts the sheep-crook back in its place, and hangs the Madonna upon it. He takes off rosary beads and hangs it on the graipe handle.*) 'Tis Hotha must mind you and save you any more, and you're very near improved enough for marriage now, too. You mended greatly all the

147

summer on account the nights were short, and, in place of thinking all day, you had many a thing to be watching: the saws cutting and the trees falling, the lorries dragging and the gangs shouting. And you had myself here spreading newses before you all hours of the day. But soon myself'll be gone, and the timbermen'll be gone, and the lonesomeness and the long winter darkness and the trees'll destroy you again. (*Coming back to her.*) Will I bring Hotha and yourself together wan of the days? . . . Nod your head so. . . . There isn't wan to see you do it only oul' Sanbatch. . . . When you'd be wedded a while the talk'd come back to you again and, if it doesn't itself, what matter? The two of ye are old enough to know what ye should do without more instructions. So let ye be hard at it, gathering up courage and sense and longing for the marriage. Stephen is gone making his last journey and I pledged my word to him. Wait till some wan comes the way for fear the cake'd burn.

(*He hurries out left. Out of the corner of her eye she watches him go. Then she is pensive and troubled for a few moments, but shakes it off and sets to work on the socks. Suddenly she hears someone approaching from the right. She runs out through the wicket-gate bringing the socks with her.* KITTY *and* SHEILA *run in from the right.*)

KITTY (*full of mischief*). Which of them will I propose to?

SHEILA. Either of them will do.

KITTY. Poor oul' Jimmy, so, that no girl ever proposed to before.

SHEILA. That'll halt Paddy from pestering the life out of me. He has a red track worn to my house.

KITTY. That's very inconvenient for you now, when your father is so bad. Hide, quick!

(*They dodge behind the gate.* KITTY *climbs the gate.* JIMMY *comes in, followed by* PADDY.)

JIMMY (*fiercely*). Have you the costs for a few pints?

PADDY. No.

JIMMY. You big bloater, you have all our money spent up, buying sweets for every rap in the country.

PADDY (*fiercely*). Have you any money yourself?

JIMMY. No.

PADDY. You bloody Daniel, we'd be heavy loaded with money if only I could make you work a hard day.

(KITTY *whistles at, or calls to* JIMMY. *He looks up at her.*)

JIMMY (*gloomily*). Hello, there!

KITTY. Jimmy, my aunt was out working in a field, and she left the gate open and caught a cold and is now dying. She's leaving me her public house in Curraghmore. 'Twould suit me greatly to have yourself for a husband and master over the apprentices. You wouldn't have a stroke to do only sitting on a barrel behind the counter drinking all you have room for of porter and whiskey and beer and rum and wine. So will you marry me?

JIMMY (*enraptured by the list of his privileges*). I will . . . But no! 'Tis Paddy's turn to do the talking first.

(*She turns to* PADDY, *who has listened to the proposal with indulgent contempt.*)

KITTY. Paddy, d'ye mind if I deprive you of Jimmy, and wed him?

PADDY (*serenely*). Sure, how could he wed you? He has to stop on my farm and do all work for me.

JIMMY (*angrily*). I can wed her if I like. Any more I'll have a house of my own, and I care no more about you than the cat cares about his father.

PADDY. You hanging blackguard! How can I wed Sheila if you won't stay and work the farm for us? I don't know how to put wan stone over another to make a wall.

JIMMY. Well, 'tis time you shook hands with work, and 'tis too long I'm digging deep and splitting worms.

PADDY. So you're out to desert me! Well, take notice of this! You belong to the seventies, and you're slaved out and soon you'll be getting the invitation up or down. 'Tis a bit of a wrong age for you to be turning dishonest, but you must do it now. On account of the depopulation no shopkeeper can keep alive unless he waters the drink and sells short weight and robs both rich and poor.

JIMMY (*overwhelmed*). You have the truth! Girl, I can't wed you! I lived honest all my lifetime, and so long as I burned the candle down to the inch, I'm as well to finish it.

KITTY. Jimmy, we'll have no need for roguery. She's leaving me three thousand paper pounds as well.

JIMMY. Three thousand pounds! Then you're a fine plentiful girl and I will marry you.

PADDY. Take notice of this! They're all nice and sweet and wholesome till they get you bound under them, then they aren't happy any day unless they spend a while tongue-lashing and fighting. And you're a man fighting doesn't suit.

JIMMY (*the incorrigible old bachelor in him reasserting itself*). 'Tis the truth, girl! I was evermore a very respectable man that fighting with women wouldn't suit, so I can't wed you.

149

KITTY. But, sure, if you aren't fighting with me in our house, you'll have to be fighting with his wife in his house.

JIMMY. That's the truth, too! And Stephen's daughter should be wan of the worst divils for fighting in the four red corners of Ireland.

PADDY (*spitting on his palm like a jobber at a fair*). Well, here! No woman'll ever hang up her coat in my house, if you'll come back and do all work for me the same as before.

JIMMY (*spitting into his palm*). 'Tis a bargain! (*They shake on it.*)

KITTY. Stephen is gone making the last journey, so he'll stand ye black lashings of porter.

PADDY and JIMMY (*solemnly*). The last journey!

PADDY. 'Tis my turn to go first. (*He runs out left.*)

JIMMY. Run, you divil! (*Mournfully.*) Poor Stephen! As decent a man as ever got hold of a shilling. But sure the death is only the brother of sleep. (*He goes left.*)

SHEILA (*emerging*). Good, yourself! That'll keep Paddy away from me for a few days.

MARK (*running in, urgently*). Kitty, could you be taking your legs out of here?

KITTY. I could, and will as soon as I ask Sheila wan question – what was the best news in the letter from your comrade girl in London.

SHEILA. She sees him here and there with different girls.

KITTY. He's only a rag on every bush at that rate.

SHEILA. I well know he was the kind that'd have to have some girl to take out. But when he's going with different wans, he's only passing the time with them.

MARK. Sure, isn't it plain he was only passing the time with you, too?

SHEILA. He was not! He'd wed me that time, only I had to come home.

KITTY. Still, he never wrote to you for very near three months, and that's as blue a look-out as any clear evening.

MARK (*almost fiercely*). Kitty, are you going at all?

KITTY (*cheerfully*). This minute, and as fast as a dog can trot. (*She runs out left.*)

MARK (*urgently*). Sheila, Con and the timber lorry will be leaving us on Tuesday and soon my health and nerves might fail again from bad bread in the day and fear in the night. So if you won't marry me, I'm selling out both house and farm and going foreign directly.

SHEILA. 'Tis a housekeeper you want, Mark, and I'd prefer a man that'd want me.

MARK (*eagerly*). To be sure! You want a husband that'd have a true wish for you.

SHEILA. Marriage isn't an easy life, they say, and without true love, 'tis miserable. (*Lights a cigarette.*) You're all right, Mark. You're as good as my fellow, and maybe a sight better. Still, I amn't able to alter my mind and have more wish for you.

MARK (*vigorously*). How can you alter your mind when you won't give me chance to court you the same as you gave him? Sure, ye should give every man a fair trial.

SHEILA. If we did that, we wouldn't get time to eat or sleep.

MARK (*drawing near her, urgently*). Sheila, if you'll let me court you for a while, I'll prove I can court a girl as good as him ... A few years back wasn't I as wild as any and as funny and fond of sport?

SHEILA (*smiling*). That time you weren't behind the door at all at courting.

MARK. I'm able still, and easy pleased. After five years any girl at all'd be Heaven to me, but your fellow'd be hard pleased: He's after skimming the cream off the finest girls in England.

KITTY (*entering with* CON). Are ye settled up yet?

MARK (*jumping up*). Con, her fellow is going with other girls as fast as he's coming up to them, and he never wrote to her in three months. But still she has every excuse for him.

CON. The reason for that is, she's a born old maid the same as I'm a born old bachelor. Unknown to ourselves, Sheila, we're afeard of marriage, and that fear won't let us want to marry any wan that could, or would, marry us.

SHEILA. That isn't so! I was well willing to marry him at a time when he was hot and warm to marry me.

CON. You thought so, but before the marriage day'd come you'd find too many faults in him, too. But what'll you do now?

SHEILA. I'll wait another while, whatever.

MARK. Well, Kitty, what will you do?

KITTY. I'll wait another while, too.

CON. "Wait another while!" – the old maids' and old bachelors' litany. That's what Sadie used to say and Hotha and Sanbatch, when well-wishers advised them in their youthful days.

KITTY (*slyly*). And what'll you do yourself?

CON. I'll wait another while, too. There's no use in talking sense to us, Mark. We're fools and cowards and that's what we'll remain.

151

Trip to England where you'll get plenty that aren't born old maids.

MARK (*jumping up bitterly*). To-morrow I'm going to O'Connell the Grazier, and selling him my farm. He'll turn horses into my mother's kitchen and cattle into my father's garden. I'll blame you two women for all and I'll not wed ye after that if ye came to me on yeer two knees and ye hanging with diamonds. ... Here's Stephen! We'll say no more and not go troubling his last journey. Make room for them there!

(HOTHA *comes in pushing a wheelbarrow containing* STEPHEN. *He is followed by* PADDY *and* JIMMY, *and by* SANBATCH *carrying a bottle of whiskey.*)

PADDY. The time Stephen and Sanbatch were playing – that was the best team of football men that ever kicked in this quarter of the country.

JIMMY. They weren't the best at football, but they were the best at kicking.

CON. Did they win all before them?

PADDY. No, mostly they were beat, but any team they played'd never be much good after. Half of them'd die the next year.

(SANBATCH *gets two jampots, and gives whiskey to* CON *and* MARK.)

SANBATCH. That time the country was full of young, powerful men, all hair up to their throats and as wild as cross bulls. You could make many a pair of shoes out of Stephen, his hide is so tough with all the blows and kicks he got.

MARK (*rising*). Here's to you good health, Stephen. I'm low spirited and I must go.

SANBATCH. Did you ask the girls?

MARK. They turned me down worse than a bad shilling.

SANBATCH. And what'll you do now?

MARK. I'm skelping off to England.

SANBATCH (*stunned*). Well, I don't know whether I'm sitting or standing! Sheila is deserting us, and the other two must go sooner or later! If you go, who'll give us a drink of water when we're dying in a few years?

MARK. If I stay, who'll give myself a sup of water when I'm dying in forty years? I'll not stop in any village where I'll be the last to die. (*He goes.*)

SANBATCH (*to the girls*). Girls, ye'll decay like snow on the mountains. Ye'll never have a day's luck for letting Mark go, that's our last chance.

152

HOTHA (*rising in anger*). Sanbatch, you know as much about marriage as my coachman that never cracked a whip, and you're after giving them girls advice that'd ruin them. They're good-looking and Mark and Con are good-looking, and 'tis the wrongest and the unluckiest thing in the world for wan good-looking person to marry another good-looking person. Ye should marry plain-looking persons such as me, and give our children their fair chance to be good-looking.

SHEILA. No. Hotha, we'll wed our choice, and 'tis as well for you to know it first as last.

KITTY. We'll chance our luck, and wed the first middling good-looking fellow we see.

HOTHA. All right! Marry them, and when ye die at last ye'll have more to go through than just shake hands with God Almighty!

PADDY (*rising gravely*). Sheila, I know the good-looking fellow you're thinking about, and I have bad tidings for you. I can't see my way to marrying you no more.

JIMMY (*in terror*). Tell her why, quick, man! D'ye want her to sue you, and put her brand on every sheep you have?

PADDY. Right enough! Sheila and Stephen, it isn't at all that yeer blood isn't good enough. 'Tis how this lad of mine is failing fast, and he reckons he couldn't do double work and keep the two of us well fed and happy.

HOTHA (*angrily*). Sit down, you oul' load! She'd marry an ass before she'd marry you.

PADDY. D'ye think I'm a world's pity the same as yourself? In all your life's day you never ruined any girl but Sadie. How many girls did I send to their graves and to convents and hospitals and lunatic asylums and America?

HOTHA. That's as true as the man could hear the grass growing! Every sickness and misfortune that overtook any girl within ten miles was all over you letting her down!

PADDY. Isn't my house full of letters from them, each cursing me for destroying her?

HOTHA. How is it all the letters are in the same handwriting?

PADDY. Well, I won't curse you or damn you, but that the Lord may shorten your life!

HOTHA. The Lord wouldn't kill a flea for your prayers.

(*They struggle and the wheelbarrow is turned over, throwing out* STEPHEN. *The young people run to his rescue.*)

SANBATCH. A burning pain to each of ye, with an oak wedge in it to keep it open for ever. Don't be disturbing his last journey.

STEPHEN. Let the lot of ye go ahead, except Hotha and Sanbatch. I must leave farewell to Sadie.

(*They all set out, right.*)

JIMMY. Tell her we wish her well. (*Goes out right.*)

PADDY. In or about a score lost themselves over me. But sure if I was the greatest man since Diarmuid of the Women, I couldn't please all that loved me. (*Goes right.*)

SANBATCH (*quickly*). Hotha, 'tis Sadie is in it for certain.

HOTHA (*startled*). How do you know? Did you challenge her?

SANBATCH. I brought God against her, and the divil, and fire at last. Then she ran for help to Our Saviour and the Blessed Virgin.

HOTHA. 'Tis Sadie is in it, so. I'll hide in the laurel bushes and see is she improved much. (*He goes right.*)

STEPHEN. D'ye remember the last night when ye thought I was gone?

SANBATCH. No lie, we were full sure that was your last puff.

STEPHEN. Maybe I was dead and gone, but they kicked me back again. Maybe I won't be taken till I get Sadie's pardon for the way I used be humbugging her long ago.

SANBATCH. That could be so, and I'll tell her so. You'll want to hide first, or she won't appear.

(SANBATCH *pushes the wheelbarrow into a dark corner at the back where she won't see it. He calls* SADIE, *and comes back to the fire, and looks at the cake.*)

SANBATCH. 'Tis burned again, but no matter. The hunger'll eat anything. (*She comes out and takes her usual seat.*) Soon Stephen'll be on his road home, and I must tell you about him. The poor fellow is suffering death greatly, and still not getting it, so there must be something else he has to do before he'll be taken. He's doubting 'tis that he must bid you farewell first. So give him a chance to speak to you, or you might keep him a long time sick, sore and sorry on this earth. . . . I must fetch a sup of water for the breakfast.

(*He takes the bucket, goes backstage. He wheels the wheelbarrow forward until it is between* SADIE *and the wicket-gate. Hearing something she rises in alarm.*)

SANBATCH. Never run, girl. Give him his chance to bid you farewell and die easy.

STEPHEN (*holding out his hand*). Sadie . . .

SANBATCH. Sadie won't fail you, Stephen. Look at that. (*He retreats to the end of the long-box.*)

STEPHEN (*earnestly*). Some years ago I was slinging many a joke

154

and mock at you about Hotha and yourself, and that you'd be left at last and finish as you began, weak, small and miserable in your mother's house. If any of them jests injured your mind, I'm as sorry for it as ever a man was sorry for anything. I'd never have dealt with you in such a way if it crossed my mind at all that you might ever lose yourself.

SANBATCH. Sure now she's as good as ever again, only still a little heartbroken.

STEPHEN. And, Sadie, you know how I passed my life: a bondsman to fighting and temper and drink. Be saying an odd prayer for me and 'twill cut a while off my sentence in Purgatory.

(*She takes the rosary beads from her apron pocket, and inclines her head a little.*)

STEPHEN. And I'll pray for a quick and a good ending to your own trouble.

SANBATCH. And now, Sadie, you may be going. You aren't well enough for much yet.

(*She goes quietly, and* SANBATCH *closes the wicket-gate behind her.* HOTHA *runs in excitedly.*)

HOTHA. Sanbatch, she's on the mending hand surely, and very near improved enough for marriage. But maybe she hates the living sight of me on account I let her down?

SANBATCH. The minute you have Stephen left at home, bring up your fiddle as far as Major D'Arcy's tree, and play a batch of jigs and reels for her.

HOTHA. How would music search out her view of me?

SANBATCH. That's for me to know and for you to find out!

HOTHA. Well, right! I'll run like a lamplighter. (*Runs out right.*)

SHEILA (*entering right.*) Father, come home to your bed. You're too long on the ground.

STEPHEN. I must be. I'm commencing to get dizzy again.

SANBATCH (*helping him out*). Faith you're heavy and hardy in your bones still.

(SANBATCH *wheels* STEPHEN *offstage,* SHEILA *following.* SANBATCH *returns quickly.*)

SANBATCH. Sadie, he's gone, and I have another news for you.

(SANBATCH *rummages in his long box, and brings out a length of copper piping suitably curved for poteen or whiskey distilling.* SADIE *appears.*)

SANBATCH. I up and told Hotha about the challenge, so he isn't doubting any more that 'tis yourself is in it. And d'ye know what he said in the minute? He said he'd take the fiddle down and play for you! (*She rises in alarm but he holds her.*) He said he won't come into your presence till you're better improved. He'll play out there under the Major's tree. (*She sits down again.*) Himself and his music is all the company you'll have soon on account myself'll be away in a secret place making an invention that'll bring back riches and young marriages and children to the village. (*Showing the piping.*) These are the first accoutrements of it. But, if the invention fails, a marriage between yourself and Hotha is the last chance to save the village. Wan of yeer two houses'd be idle then for Kitty and Con to wed into; and wan marriage encourages another.

(HOTHA *is heard tuning his fiddle. She starts but settles down again.*)

SANBATCH. 'Tis in his own interest the cat does be purring, and 'tis in his own interest Hotha is playing. He wants to make public and sure that he's sorry for leaving you and that you're again the only four bones he wants out of all the women in the world. If you don't wed him, the bad things of the long winter darkness and the thinking all day'll run down your courage and your mind again.

(HOTHA *plays a lively Irish dance tune, and* SANBATCH *watches her stealing furtive side-glances in the direction of the music. The music changes to a slow lullaby melody, and this gives him an idea.*)

SANBATCH. The whiskey made me drowsy, so I'll nod asleep for a while. Let you be listening away.

(*He slips on to the ground, settles down to sleep with his back to the long box. But his head is turned a little in her direction so that he can watch her between nearly closed eyelids. After some time she steals a side-glance and, finding him asleep, she becomes excited. Soon she turns round and strains her eyes long and wistfully in the direction of the music. Two or three times she looks back at* SANBATCH *fearfully, as if what she was doing was the most terrible thing in the world. But on each occasion he closes his eyes just in time. So she returns to her eager gazing until suddenly the music stops. She is startled, and turns away as if fearful that* HOTHA *might come in now at any moment. But he does not, and she is sad. Suddenly her face lights up again as the music starts again. This is an exhilaratingly lively tune, and it takes her right out of herself. She smiles and with head and hands keeps time with the music. Again she peers eagerly in the direction of the music, and* SANBATCH *leans forward so as to watch her expression. Suddenly she turns, and catches him red-handed. She shrinks in confusion, and buries her face in her hands.*)

SANBATCH (*gravely*). Let you not be shy or shamed at all. Let you be thanking God that you're coming back to yourself, and you only two years strange. Plenty never come back to themselves at all. Will I bring him in? . . . I will! Hotha, come in! She wants to see you! Quick, man!

(*She jumps up looking scared and confused. Finally she runs out through the wicket-gate.*)

SANBATCH. Go ahead, girl, I'll send him in to you.

HOTHA (*entering with violin and case*). Did she ask for me surely and truly?

SANBATCH. No, but your music touched her. She was evermore twisting and turning to catch sight of you, just the same as long ago in yeer courting days when she'd be expecting you to come.

HOTHA. Good and good and very good. But she said no word good or bad?

SANBATCH. If we could only get her to say her first word! After that she'd talk the head off a minister . . . I have it! Go in, and put your two arms around her, and squeeze her till she says "Oh!"

HOTHA. To-night, is it? I will not!

SANBATCH (*angrily*). Well, if you won't, I will! (*He sets out.*)

HOTHA (*pulling him back equally hotly*). Sanbatch, you won't! She's mine now and you'll not go within a fist of her.

SANBATCH. D'you want to wait till the long winter darkness breaks the strings of her heart again?

HOTHA. I'll wait only wan week or two, and I'll play every night for her, and coax her by degrees like the lawyer goes to Heaven.

SANBATCH. Well, by the virtue of my oath and conscience you could be right in that . . . (*He puts the pieces of piping back in their hiding place.*)

HOTHA. What are them for?

SANBATCH. For a secret invention that'll make many a sum for me, if it comes out right.

HOTHA. Good inventions are very hard and very costly.

SANBATCH. This invention'll drink my last shilling and, if it fails, that'll be the end of my battle against the world.

HOTHA. Keep your hands off it altogether so, and wait till we see what the next election'll do.

SANBATCH (*fiercely*). Isn't that what we're doing all our lives, and each gang we elected turned out to be worse than the last? Sure,

157

they don't know how we're living at all and how could they? Wance in every five years they come down to draw our votes, halting their cars at the crossroads for five minutes, with big detectives all around them, for fear they'd see or hear us.

HOTHA. Please yourself about the invention, so; and come down to Stephen's now quick before our share of the whiskey is all drank, or spilled in the arguing and fighting.

SANBATCH. The next one that spills my glass, I'll spill his blood. (*Goes to wicket-gate.*) Sadie, keeps an eye to the fire for me. We're going down to Stephen's where there's an awful drink for us, a splendid drink. (*He sets out.*)

HOTHA (*looking skywards as they go*). D'ye think will the night keep civil?

SANBATCH. 'Twill get enough to do. (*They go.*)

(SADIE *comes in, sits on long box, and turns towards tethering-tree. She begins to speak anxiously and almost desperately.*)

SADIE. Leggy . . . Leggy . . . Listen a while . . . I . . . must . . . learn . . . conversation again.

CURTAIN

ACT THREE

The scene is the same and the time is three weeks later. The only change is that the great iron pot is missing, and its contents are scattered around.

The wicket-gate is open and HOTHA *is seated in the gateway playing some Irish traditional airs.* PADDY *enters from the right, wearing an overcoat. He looks at* HOTHA *briefly, then hurries on to Sanbatch's camp where he finds the broken mirror and settles down to make minor adjustments.*

JIMMY *comes in after the usual interval. He listens to the music for a few moments, then he sits at the fire. He is wearing an old overcoat also.*

It is a sunny autumn evening.

JIMMY (*after deep thought*). Well, I will sanction you to wed Kitty instead of me – if you'll sign over your farm to me.

PADDY. I'll do that. Why would I go dirtying my dear and fancy shoes with land when I'll have her aunt's shop and three thousand pounds?

JIMMY. I wonder who converted her to thinking you'd be better than me for her shop?

PADDY. Myself did. I ses to her: "When your customers see behind the counter a fine, smart-looking fellow, well-fed and as honest as an egg, they'll say 'This must be a well-doing, honest, up-to-date shop. Only the best'd be sold here.' But 'tis the opposite they'd say if they saw behind the counter a starved-looking, mean-looking, thievish-looking fellow such as you. Sure you're like something you'd get in a penny packet. . . .

JIMMY (*impressed*). Right enough, I didn't think of that at all. . . . (*He crosses to* HOTHA.) Had yourself and Sadie any word yet?

HOTHA. She spoke no word yet to any wan, and my good sense is telling me to wait till she has a little more improvement made. (*He rises and comes in.*)

159

JIMMY. Let you not hurry her. Wait till she's full sure you won't desert her this time: then she'll follow you through fire and water.

HOTHA (*closing the gate and coming in*). But how can she keep improving when Sanbatch is for the last two days neglecting her and telling her no newses?

JIMMY. Lately he's busy as a bee in a bottle and he's still below in the Tomb Plantation with a great blazer of a fire, and he'll let no wan come near him, for fear we'd discover the invention before himself does.

HOTHA. He has the pigs' pot with him, so maybe he's seeking the invention for making beer from heather that the Danes had in Brian Boru's time.

PADDY. Did you hear of the great seam of luck I struck? Kitty and her aunt's shop and money!

HOTHA. Kitty has a handsome head right enough, but when Sadie was her age, if a sixpenny bit was left on her face when she'd be going to sleep, 'twould be a half-sovereign in the morning.

(SANBATCH *runs in from the right, holding aloft a black bottle.*)

SANBATCH. Hi for Sanbatch! that has the first blow struck against the misery of the times and the want of money and young marriages and children! Hi for Sanbatch, that has invented the only thing in the world that's before love or gold! . . . I'm after succeeding in the invention for drink!

HOTHA. Is it the heather beer the ancient Danes were making long ago?

SANBATCH. Not it! 'Tis the finest of poteen whiskey. And all I want now is wan of ye to sup a share of it to make sure 'tis safe and made right. Here, Jimmy!

JIMMY. And did you not sup it yourself yet?

SANBATCH. Is it me to go supping it first? And if it wasn't altogether right and it killed me, no wan else in the village could remedy the invention. Here, Paddy, you have your fingers on eighty, so, whether this poisons you or no, we'll soon be throwing clay on you.

PADDY (*indignantly*). Be aware of this! I'm wedding Kitty in a few days, and d'ye want to make a widow of her before she enjoyed even wan night with me?

SANBATCH. 'Twould be a mortal sin for the priest that'd marry ye. Putting funeral expenses on the girl he'd be. Here, Hotha, sup it, you!

HOTHA (*sniffing contents*). Who learned you the invention for drink?

SANBATCH. Wan year that I was harvesting in Lincolnshire over

160

against the North Sea, some Connemara men were working for the masters around, and they gave me an account of the invention, but I made it better than their way. I put everything in that suited my own taste and fancy.

HOTHA (*handing back the bottle decisively*). Well, if you did, 'twould give us more than a red nose.

SANBATCH (*indignantly*). The next time you fall drunk, may it be amongst thorn bushes! Here, Jimmy, you're drinking since the olden times when whiskey was so good it wasn't a penny too dear. Smell that, and look at how clear it is!

JIMMY. It has a nice scent and 'tis as clear as spring water. If I don't sup much 'twill do no more than sicken me, and to have the invention for drink in the village'd be worth many a day's suffering. (*He puts bottle to his mouth.*)

HOTHA (*running forward and stopping him*). Jimmy, don't even wet your lips with it. Stephen sent a bad message over since he died.

JIMMY (*blessing himself*). The Lord save us!

SANBATCH (*hotly*). And when we asked you before, you said he sent none!

HOTHA. The message was so bad that I didn't like telling ye; but now I must.

SANBATCH. How slow was his corpse in stiffening?

HOTHA. When he was a few hours dead and well cooled, I handled and tested him, but there was no stiffness in him at all. I handled him every hour after that, and he didn't begin stiffening till the black of the morning.

SANBATCH. You had no right to keep your tongue under your belt about that! When Stephen was that slow in stiffening, he must be fearful lonesome where he is, and when he's that lonesome he's sure to bring two or three of us soon from the village to keep him company. (*Taking the mirror from Paddy.*) Give me a look at my oul' withered jaws till I see am I making clay.

HOTHA. 'Twas myself handled Crawley Comm after he died, and he wasn't as lonesome as Stephen; still he brought three from his village within a year.

JIMMY. With Stephen so lonesome, 'twould be safer to resign from this. (*He puts the bottle on the ground.*)

SANBATCH. Look at me! I'm like a gutted herring! If I met a strange priest, he'd anoint me.

JIMMY (*feeling himself*). I'm afeard there's a damage in myself somewhere too. Any walking I do puts me out of puff in no time.

161

PADDY (*strolling about complacently*). 'Tis through the want of wives Stephen'll bring ye. The winter frost and ye having no wan to thaw out yeer oul' bones.

HOTHA (*feeling himself also*). No, 'tis some disease, or Sanbatch's whiskey.

SANBATCH (*rising vigorously*). 'Tis not my whiskey; 'tis the winter'll perish us. Last winter we kept ourselves all muffled up in clothes like the tinker's wife, and still we were half the time shivering and shaking worse than a miser when he'd be paying his men. (*Taking "Old Moore's Almanac" from the graipe handle.*) Old Moore has foretold that this winter's frost'll have the waterfalls tied. But if we had fine mugfulls of my whiskey every day 'twould warm us and keep our courage high till the south winds'd blow again.

JIMMY. Sanbatch, you have no word of a lie! We're in twice worse danger without your whiskey than with it.

SANBATCH. Come up, Jimmy, till I show you the invention, and you'll see 'tis as safe as the dearest Parliament whiskey that ever was. (*He sets out.*)

JIMMY (*carried away*). Sanbatch, I'll go, and I'll sup it, too. You never were wrong yet, except a little in the head lately. (*They go.*)

HOTHA (*calling after them*). Jimmy, if you sup that stuff you'll rue it. Remember Stephen's message!

PADDY. Sure, what harm if he's soon called up! Sure, he's not worth the water the eggs were boiled in!

HOTHA. Isn't it him that's doing all the work on your farm? And keeping you alive?

PADDY. I'm wedding Kitty, and the shop and three thousand her aunt is to leave her'll keep us going, so 'tis equal a damn about Jimmy and the farm any more.

HOTHA. Many a niece was promised shops and money, and didn't get them after. And if she doesn't and you're without Jimmy, we'll be measuring yourself for a wooden suit before St. Patrick's Day.

PADDY (*suddenly uneasy*). Maybe so, 'twould be safer to keep him alive another while. (*Setting out left.*) I'll bring the police, and they'll arrest the invention for drink.

HOTHA. Don't do such a thing! That plan'd ruin more than 'twould cure. I'll follow them and let Jimmy sup only a thimbleful that'll not be able to sicken him bad. (*He goes out right.*)

PADDY. Jimmy won't be said or led by you. He'll drink his fills of it, if 'tis any blood-cousin to whiskey at all. (*To himself gravely.*) The police only can save him.

(*He picks up and pockets his pipe and tobacco and matches, and is about to set off, when* CON *comes in, left, with* KITTY. *She immediately skips out of sight behind a tree.*)

CON. Well, Paddy, how are you?

PADDY (*turning and immediately bridling up at him*). I'm none the better for seeing you! What brought you back to this district?

CON. The fellow that bought Mark's farm sold the timber on it to my boss, so for a few days we'll be back here slashing it down.

PADDY. Well, take notice of this! Your girl is my girl anymore and I'm a very jealous-minded man, so don't let me catch you talking to her.

CON. Well, what's allotted can't be blotted, so if I do go talking to her anymore, 'twill be only about the news of the country and the twists of the world.

PADDY (*sternly*). Make sure you won't be guilty of praising her looks, or her figure. I'm a saint of a man only not to vex me. Wance I'm vexed I'd clear a racecourse leaving nothing but corpses lying and horses flying. If any man tried to take a girl off me, I'd bring him up to the river and jump on him.

CON. I'd be wasting my tongue and my time if I went saying more than I ought to say to her. Sure there was no man ever could coax a girl away from you.

PADDY (*completely mollified by this*). Since you say that, you're an honest fellow and not a moocher like some. Tell me: is there any police in the drink shop?

CON. There is a couple of them improving their health in it.

PADDY. I must be off so. I'll give you all the facts about the wedding again.

(*He goes left.* CON *sits down, unrolls his pack containing some blankets, shaving kit, drinking mug and various food parcels.* KITTY *comes from behind the tree. She wears a topcoat also, and she is as cheerful as ever.*)

KITTY. Wasn't I very lonesome after you and sorely in need of cheering when I had to go teasing Paddy?

CON (*sorting out things*). That's as much as to say you didn't go teasing any wan younger than Paddy.

KITTY. I didn't yet. . . . Did you?

CON. Not yet either.

KITTY. In Castlebrowne is there any girls with land and houses and money?

163

CON. A few, but wan isn't as good-looking as you; and another isn't as hearty and as funny as you, and another doesn't smile and draw near the same as you. So I couldn't bring myself to bother with any of them.

KITTY. At that gait of going, you're what you said you were: a born old bachelor.

CON. I'm half a year back in this country now, and 'tis the best country in the world for learning and seeing that an oul' bachelor is seldom a good thing to be. But what about yourself?

KITTY. This place'd be too lonesome with yourself and Mark and Sheila gone; and even in the drink shop the sport is dying away and leaving . . . . Sheila is to search out a job for me in London.

CON. For the first while London'll seem so lonesome and sad and cruel, you'll reckon 'tis wan town God deserted and gave away to the divil. . . . Everywan so stern and serious and sad. After a few weeks you'll get used to that and if you reckon you could settle down in it, let me know and maybe I'll be able to cure myself out of oul' bachelor at last.

KITTY. But would you ever forgive me for parting you from the only country you ever felt contented in?

CON. I would – if you made me a very good wife. And would you be able to forgive me for dragging you down to a back-street backroom with nothing in it, or around it, but dust and darkness and noise and poverty and petrol smoke?

KITTY. I would – if you made me a very good husband.

CON. The two of us'll want to be very good, for we're giving up too much, maybe, and that's dangerous.

KITTY. I'm in hopes you'll bring me great luck. The divil's children do have luck, they say.

CON. And they say God likes best of all a poor person that's cheerful, so I'm in hopes you'll bring me better luck, that'll promote us out of that back-room before it withers or kills us.

MARK (*entering with a little bag of potatoes*). How are you, Con?

CON. As you see! Here's a few loaves I brought you.

MARK. I'm very thankful to you and tell me this? You weren't in this district since the night you came back to regret the death. Would you see much change in me since?

CON. Maybe a pinch thinner. . .

MARK. My own cakes are fast poisoning me again, so 'tis a good thing I'll be in England in a good lodging house in a few days when the lawyers have all signed up. (*He is adding potatoes to a little heap near the fire.*)

164

KITTY. Don't put many out, or Sanbatch'll notice, and he'll be insulted.

CON. Did you get a fat price?

MARK (*gloomily*). Two thousand three hundred for the land and house and seven hundred pounds for the stock.

CON. That makes you the master of three thousand pounds, and with that much you can surely get some Irish girl that has a farm, and that isn't spoiled with cities and shops like Sheila and Kitty.

MARK (*fiercely*). Irish women could have saved my farm and home, but they wouldn't. The last breed I want to meet is an Irishwoman. I wouldn't marry one if they were hanging over each other in hundreds.

(*He crosses to the wicket-gate, and empties the remainder of the potatoes on the ground inside it.* SHEILA *enters right. She is dressed in black, and is serious-looking as usual.*)

SHEILA. How is yourself?

CON. Still tearing away at the world . . . I saw your farm for sale in the papers.

KITTY. She has wan offer of £2500 got already.

CON. So between farm and stock you'll top the three thousand, too! Did you tell your fellow in London?

SHEILA. I wrote and told him all, the day after the funeral, and when he didn't answer before now he can save his ink. All is over between us.

CON. Let Mark and yourself go to the same quarter of London, and ye'll be company for each other.

SHEILA. We're two neighbour's children, and 'tis what we should do.

MARK (*in the wicket-gate*). Who turned me down and lost me my home and farm?

CON. 'Twas this country she turned down and the want of cinemas and baths and high wages. When you taste a good thing you want a good thing, and she couldn't help that.

MARK (*impressed*). Well, fair play is bonny sport, and maybe she couldn't help taking a craze for England and the towns.

KITTY. Let ye tell Mark and myself about England. Is it true the English eat a boiled egg with a spoon instead of a knife?

CON. 'Tis true, but that isn't the biggest difference ye'll find. Around here the people don't think enough about this world: in England they don't think at all about the next world.

(SANBATCH *runs in with the black bottle, followed by* JIMMY

165

who looks happy but a little unsteady, and by HOTHA *who is still very anxious.*)

SANBATCH. Sanbatch is top dog of this country any more and master of the invention for drink. Jimmy supped it well, and look at how he's still living!

JIMMY. The more I was supping the livelier I was getting and the happier. Give me another sup, and I'll show them.

SANBATCH. Give these lads a chance first. (*Offering bottle to* CON.) If you drank a pint of this and, if you had a propellor, 'twould bring you as far as England.

HOTHA. Don't taste it yet till we give Jimmy another while for dying. (*He is bending over* JIMMY *who is slumped against a tree.*)

CON. A taste of anything never killed anybody. (*Tastes.*) By the book! 'Tis equal to the best Connemara poteen. What would you say, Mark? (*Gives him bottle.*)

SANBATCH (*to the girls*). Let ye cast out of yeer heads every notion of going foreign. Around here any more we'll be shovelling the gold the same as the D'Arcy's were long ago. Con can be selling poteen in the county above, and Mark in the county below and Hotha in the county over.

KITTY. And have you any jobs for Sheila and myself?

SANBATCH. I'll give you a queen's dowry, so you'll be able to wed your choice of the men in Ireland. And if the pair of ye'll wed two lads that whiskey puts in good humour, I'll have them as drunk as mops every day, so ye'll be the two happiest married couples in Ireland.

MARK. 'Tis dang good poteen whiskey, but more like Mayo poteen I'd say.

SANBATCH (*taking the bottle and setting out for the wicket-gate*). Hotha, this is the invention that'll make man and wife of yourself and Sadie. Half-a-pint of this and you'll have courage to face her, and half-a-pint in her'll loosen her tongue. Clear out, the lot of ye, for a small while.

(PADDY, *looking very grave, has suddenly appeared in their midst.*)

PADDY. Take notice of this! Two Civic Guards are making fast for the Tomb Plantation.

SANBATCH. Have they shotguns? Is it poaching pheasants they are?

PADDY. 'Tisn't poaching anything. I was in the drink shop and I heard wan say: "Why are we spending good money here, when the finest of whiskey poteen is waiting for us at the Tomb Plantation?" Ses th' other blackguard: "If we go now we might catch and arrest the gang that made it – whoever they are!" And with that, off they set at a good hand trot for the Tomb Plantation.

(SANBATCH *smashes the bottle against a tree in fury and despair, and runs out right.*)

PADDY (*shouting after him*). They'll be there before you, and you'll get yourself arrested. (*He runs after him.*)

KITTY. Sanbatch, wait! Run, Con! (CON *runs after* SANBATCH.)

HOTHA (*Following*). Take body-grips on him, let ye.

JIMMY (*hauling the gun out of the long box*). I'll fire shots over the police and scatter them like crows. (*He is half-drunk and falls, and the gun goes off.*)

MARK (*putting the gun away*). D'ye want to send us to Heaven without our suppers?

JIMMY. We must try some endeavour. Hard work is the only thing that can overcome misfortune.

MARK. If they lodge him in jail for the winter, wouldn't it save his life now, when he has no right fireside, and the last of his money is gone?

JIMMY. Jail'd shame his mother and all belonging to him that are at God's right hand. We'll save him some ways besides jail. (*He runs out right after the others.*)

SHEILA. That's the end of Sanbatch's poteen. The Guards'll be watching out twice as keen any more.

KITTY. What'll Sanbatch do now when he has no money and is too proud to take charity?

MARK. He won't surrender to the County Home either . . . Maybe he'll break a window the same as Dowdall did and wan or two more?

SHEILA. 'Tis a pity he doesn't know where his sisters in America are living, or whether they're living.

(SANBATCH *enters, followed by* CON *and* JIMMY *and* PADDY *and* HOTHA. SANBATCH *sits on the long box staring in front of him. He is deadly pale.*)

CON. The Guards are making off with the invention for drink and all the poteen.

SANBATCH. I lately got a warning that some trouble was boiling for me. I dreamt of the mother, and a mother always comes with a warning.

JIMMY. Cheer up, Sanbatch! There's wan great blessing out of this. That much poteen'll keep the Guards going for two weeks, so they won't need to be cadging drinks off us for that while.

167

PADDY. And the Guards can't prove who made the poteen on account 'twas found on the land of young D'Arcy that's drinking beyond in Oxford. Come down to my house, Sanbatch, for the winter.

SANBATCH. (*rising grimly, tongs in hand*). The last of my money went on the invention, so now I must break a window. Jimmy, go for the guards and tell them to jail me.

(*There is a general consternation.*)

HOTHA. Sanbatch, don't do it!

SHEILA. Don't, Sanbatch! 'Tis a bad place!

(*But he is gone through the wicket-gate.*)

CON. To jail he wants to go, is it?

MARK. Not it! The mental hospital at Ballinasloe. He'd prefer the asylum to the disgrace of the poorhouse.

(*A smashing of glass is heard.*)

PADDY (*in admiration*). The same as Dowdall did. And Linehan. A clever plan, and how was it I didn't think of it?

JIMMY. I'll be hailing the Guards whatever. (*He sets out.*)

CON (*stopping him*). Come back, Jimmy. We'll not stand for this. 'Tis crazy!

JIMMY. Why would it? For dinner every day in the asylum they get soup and fourteen wheelbarrowfulls of spuds.

(SANBATCH *crosses to the fire, throws down the tongs, and loosens the tether-rope from its hook.*)

SANBATCH. Mark, your farm and work is gone, and 'tis better to be knotting grass than to be idle. Sell all I have, and put in a new window for her, and buy anything else she's wanting in. (*He brings rope to a tree.*) Hotha, tie me to this tree. (*Hotly.*) Jimmy, may no child be at your death! What's the reason you aren't gone for the Guards yet?

CON. My hand and arm – and because this plan is crazy. Why can't you take the loan of a few pounds from each of us all round that'll set you up again, and you can pay us in a few years when you're enjoying the Old Age Pension.

SANBATCH (*tying rope around his waist*). Stephen sent me a clear message to-night, and the Old Age Pension I'll never live to see. And 'tis as well. All that I drank with are dead.

MARK. Sanbatch, money is made round to go around. I have £3000, and I'll never miss a half-score out of that.

SHEILA. I'll soon have £3000 too, and I should pay you a score of pounds for all the nights you stayed up minding father.

SANBATCH (*hotly*). Ye're talking like I was a man of no account.

My people were Chief Herds for the D'Arcys of Castle D'Arcy, and were every day mixing with the oldest blood in Ireland when the D'Arcys wouldn't have yeer people as dog-boys. (*He puts his back against the tree, and gives the rope to* HOTHA.)

JIMMY. Don't let them fret you, Sanbatch. I'll have the Guards for you in the run of a few minutes. (*He goes out right.*)

HOTHA. (*tying* SANBATCH*'s arms and then tying the rose around the tree.*) Whatever else you'll do never trust the lunatics. Never turn your back on wan of them at all, or he'll set into killing you.

SANBATCH. I'll watch well and give them no chance, no matter how innocent they look.

PADDY. The minute wan of them goes smiling at you the same as a miser'd go smiling at money, that's a sure sign he's getting ready to split you.

KITTY (*coming over earnestly*). But, Sanbatch, what'll we do without you? Sure, isn't it you that was keeping us all going?

SANBATCH. Leave this country, Kitty, before you lose yourself too. Soon the crows'll be flying between every two rafters in this village; then the drink-shop'll fall like a rotten egg, and you'll be flung out without a trade or riches on the waves of the world.

MARK. What'll we do with Leggy? 'Tisn't good for a dog to be too much by himself.

SANBATCH. Give him away to Tim Cawley, or to any other man that's cruel to the wife. The like do be very kind to animals.

HOTHA (*warmly*). Never mind the dog. What about Sadie, that you're depriving of the only wan of us she was trusting in? How can she keep improving in her reason and her memory?

SHEILA. Sanbatch, you're pleasing neither God nor man when you go deserting Sadie.

SANBATCH (*after brief reflection*). Hotha, free me out again!

KITTY (*clapping her hands*). He's going to stay.

MARK (*grimly*). Hi for Sanbatch!

HOTHA (*untying rope hastily*). Twelve men with white shirts will carry your coffin if you stay.

SANBATCH. Stop! Don't free my arms. (*Stepping towards the wicket-gate.*) Let all of ye, except Hotha, scatter east and west till I give my last good advice to Sadie. Bring me fast warning when the Guards are drawing near. Hurry, let ye! (*Bangs loudly on wicket-gate. The others drift away except* HOTHA.) Sadie, come out quick! I have news so big 'twould keep an oul' woman going for a week. (*Coming back to the tree.*) Tie me to the tree

169

again, quick! Then hide behind Major D'Arcy's tree.

HOTHA. If you see any chance at all, bring us together before they take you.

(*He ties rope around tree, and hides behind the other tree. She comes in looking quite normal, but still shy and timid. She advances towards the fire as usual, not even looking to make sure* SANBATCH *is there.*)

SANBATCH. Sadie, 'tisn't at my fireside I am this time. I have promotion got to here!

(*She sees him, is frightened, and blesses herself.*)

SANBATCH. Take a last look at oul' Sanbatch. . . . The invention for drink got arrested, and my last shilling was gone, and I couldn't disgrace my decent people by going to the poorhouse. That's why I made pieces of your window, and in a few minutes when the Guards come, I'll behave foaming mad, and they'll despatch me to the asylum . . .

(*She turns away in consternation, and buries her face in her hands.*)

SANBATCH. 'Tis no harm. I'll be as fed as a butcher in it, and there's a fine Christmas goose coming for you, too. Mark is to sell all I have and repair your window and buy a lot for you. But don't let him sell the Blessed Virgin's picture that was hung at my mother's head and my father's when they were dying. (*Suddenly alarmed.*) By the Blessed Iron Book! I was nearly forgetting my rosary beads. Sadie, take it from the graipe handle and put it here in my pocket. Sadie! Stir up, you divil! Wance the Guards come I'll be roaring mad, and I couldn't ask for it then, Sadie!

(*She rises, takes the rosary beads from the graipe handle, puts it into his pocket.*)

SANBATCH. God spare you health, girl. And may you be dead six months before the divil hears you were sick. . . . The beads'll be my sheep-crook and spade any more.

(*As she puts the beads in his pocket, she whispers something with averted face.*)

SANBATCH. What's that? But, sure, Sadie, *I must go!* Misfortune has defeated me the same as it can defeat any wan . . . (*Listens again.*) . . . No, I will not lose myself in it, but you'll lose yourself soon again if you don't join Hotha. Hotha! Step forward manful and face her!

(HOTHA *steps out from behind his tree. She does not turn around.*)

SANBATCH. Listen, now, with the ear of your heart to what Hotha has to say.

170

HOTHA. The way it is, Sadie, the young people are going foreign; Sanbatch is going, and this winter Stephen'll bring Jimmy and Paddy. Only ourselves two'll be left in the village and, if we don't join each other now, the lonesomeness'll destroy us both.

SANBATCH (*to* SADIE). Thirty years you might live yet, and 'tis a fearful length to be by yourself in there between the trees. Take a last look at him, and quick! before the Guards come in. Sadie, in the honour of God . . .

(*She turns around at last, and faces* HOTHA, *but she is too shy and upset to meet his gaze fully.*)

HOTHA (*after a pause*). You didn't change greatly at all, Sadie. You're a fresh-looking woman still.

SANBATCH (*impatiently*). What matter if ye have skins like corduroy so long as ye're company for each other. Hotha, tell her the great wish you have for her. Wouldn't you sleep on a harrow with her?

HOTHA. Sadie, I'd carry you in my two hands, I'd be that proud of you.

SANBATCH. Now, Sadie, 'tisn't two minutes since you proved there was no briar or stumbling block in your throat when you spoke to me then. Why don't you speak now to Hotha that gave you every hug you got for twenty years?

(*She turns around, and approaches* SANBATCH'*s ear again. She seems distressed.*)

SANBATCH (*almost despairingly*). Sadie, never mind how I'll fare, and give his answer to the only man that'll be left to pull you out of the fire in twenty years time when the age starts making you dizzy. If you saw the awful strange bad-looking smoke that was coming from oul' Mickel Kelly's the day he got roasted. I'm telling you 'tis a bad death to get roasted.

PADDY (*hurrying in from right*). Sanbatch, start raving! They're coming!

SANBATCH (*roaring out, right*). Let me out, I tell ye! Let me out till I wound ye to death with shots and fists and kicks and stones.

(SADIE *runs through the wicket-gate.*)

HOTHA. She has turned me down!

SANBATCH. After her quick, before she loses herself again.

HOTHA. Is it break into her house!

SANBATCH. Don't lose her now, no matter if you have to make dust of every window and door.

HOTHA. Well . . . hit or miss . . . I will! (*He runs out through the wicket-gate.*)

171

SANBATCH (*roaring*). Let me out, or I'll curse you, and my curses don't fall on stones. That you may choke with asthma and work into convulsions and your face turn into a monkey's backside before morning!

PADDY (*delighted*). Well done, Sanbatch; you're a born lunatic!

SANBATCH. My curse on Kilclooney of the night walkers and the day sleepers!

(CON *and* KITTY *enter.*)

CON. 'Tis too soon for you to go bawling yet!

SANBATCH. Why? Did the Guards come back again?

KITTY. Sure, they're the far side of the Tomb Plantation yet, and loaded down with poteen cans.

SANBATCH (*hotly*). Paddy, you're a man that'd want a great slash of a stick. Why did you tell me that they were near?

PADDY (*equally hotly*). Wasn't it a needful thing for you to spend a while practising?

SANBATCH. Too many months and years I'll have for practising. . . . Let me out now till I have a last look at the Pleasure Ground of the D'Arcys.

CON (*untying rope from tree*). We'll watch out for them here, and give you warning.

SANBATCH. Come with me, Paddy, holding wan end of the rope, and ye can say 'tis to break away I did.

(*They go out through the other wicket-gate, and turn left.*)

KITTY (*gravely coming down to fire*). Can you think of any shift at all that might save him?

CON (*hanging kettle on fire and getting some sandwiches and tea out of his bundle*). By hard work, in my spare time, I could make land out of Sanbatch's farm again, if he'd let us marry into it and look after him. But what can we do when there's no house or stick of furniture, or the price of either?

HOTHA (*running out through wicket-gate*). Sanbatch, she has more words said! Where is he?

KITTY. Taking a last look at the Pleasure Ground.

HOTHA. She declares she'll wed me, if I save Sanbatch from going to the mental hospital. I must tell him. (*He runs to the other wicket-gate.*)

CON (*springing up*). Wait a minute! Kitty and myself are the only two that can save Sanbatch, but we can do it only with your help.

HOTHA. What way?

CON. If you wed Sadie, ye'll have two houses and ye'll want only wan. Let us wed into the other house, and we'll look after

Sanbatch and his land. There'll be no charity or disgrace for him in that. He can leave us the land when he is dying.

HOTHA. Ye're welcome to my house and all that's in it, if ye can save him from going. But that plan is no good; he'd smell a charity and disgrace in it. (*He runs after* SANBATCH.)

KITTY (*happily*). Now, haven't we friends in Heaven? There's a furnished house for us in the turn of a hand!

CON (*seriously*). 'Tis our first, and likely our last chance of marrying in our own country. Wance Sanbatch's land is reclaimed from the rushes and water, we'll never suffer hunger, but 'twill be the plainest of food we'll have on our table, and maybe shabby clothes on our bodies, and plenty looking down on us because we're poor. Could you be contented with that, d'ye think?

KITTY. The tinkers are raggedy and poor, too; still there's no class so happy as them.

CON. They were never worse off than they are now; but we'll be worse off than we are now, and to come down in the world is hard.

KITTY (*smiling*). To let Sanbatch go'd be harder still.

CON (*coming to her*). When you say that, you're saving Sanbatch and saving me and saving yourself, too. Like Sheila and the most of the Irish girls in England you'd soon turn English and too stern and serious and sad, and then you wouldn't be Kitty any more.

KITTY. They say a wife grows very like her husband, if she loves him greatly; so, if you'll live lighthearted, I will too . . .

SHEILA (*entering with* MARK). Where's Sanbatch?

KITTY. Taking a last look at the Pleasure Ground, but wait till ye hear! Sadie is agreeing to wed Hotha, if he can save Sanbatch from going, and we're wedding into Hotha's house and looking after Sanbatch and his land, if we can coax him from going.

CON. And ye two can help us greatly in that!

SHEILA. I'd give my right eye to save Sanbatch.

KITTY. Give Mark your ring finger, and you'll save Sanbatch. Wance he sees two young couples here and the village coming to life again, Con's lorry and ropes won't be strong enough to drag him from it.

MARK. You might be right there – but Sanbatch is so contrary . . .

CON. Let ye marry here for if ye marry foreign, your children will be foreign. If ye want your children to be Irish and of the same mind and knowledge and taste as yourselves, ye must marry in Ireland, and on the land of Ireland.

173

(PADDY *comes in, breathing slaughter, and peeling off his jacket, topcoat and waistcoat.*)

PADDY (*to* CON). I hear Hotha say you're out to marry my girl! I told you before the kind of man I am – a saint, only not to vex me; and now you have me vexed enough to stick an awl in a landlord.

(*He folds his jacket quickly; places it on the ground. He takes off waistcoat, folds it and leaves it on top of the jacket. He peels up his sleeves.*)

PADDY. In wan minute, when I have stacked my drapery, I'll make bits of your bones.

KITTY. But, Paddy, I got awful bad news since. My aunt isn't dying after all. Soon she'll be as good as ever and she wants to marry you herself now. She's only thirty-two years.

PADDY (*furious*). Thirty-two years! I'd burn my house before I'd take such an aged woman into it!

KITTY. Please yourself about her; but she's not leaving me the shop or a penny piece now.

PADDY (*thoughtfully*). I see . . . (*To* CON, *magnanimously.*) Well, seeing as you're a man that finds it hard to get girls, I'll give her away to you. I have another girl in Tuam that's promised a butcher's shop in Chicago.

(SANBATCH *comes in, followed by* HOTHA. *He goes to the tree: stands with his back to it as before.*)

SANBATCH. Here, Paddy! Tie me to the tree, you!

KITTY. Sanbatch, will you not agree?

SANBATCH. My farm is only a moor of a place now. Ye couldn't live on it unless ye were fish and could live on weeds and water.

(PADDY *ties rope ends around the tree.*)

CON. But my job and pay'll keep us going a few years till we have land made of it again.

SANBATCH. A shorn sheep is little good to any wan, and I'd be no help to ye at all. I'd be living on your charity, and that was never the custom of my people.

KITTY (*coming to him*). Sure, Sanbatch, 'tis Con and myself that are asking a charity from you. We're asking you to take us in and adopt us, on account our own people have no place for us.

HOTHA. Look at that! You have a son and daughter of your own at last, and that's more than I'll ever have.

(SANBATCH'*s grim face suddenly begins to smile a little.*)

KITTY. Your heart's wish was to save the village, and at last 'tis in your power to do it. If you'll adopt us, we can wed, and Sadie

174

can wed Hotha, and Mark and Sheila can marry.

SANBATCH. Mark, is that so?

MARK. Well, if every wan else is marrying, I'm willing to have a run at it too.

SANBATCH. Are you willing, Sheila?

SHEILA (*smiling*). If you'll agree to what Kitty and Con are asking you.

SANBATCH. Two young couples in the village again! Paddy, untie the rope!

HOTHA. I'll tell Sadie. (*He runs out through the wicket-gate.*)

PADDY (*indignantly*). I'm after making the finest double knot that ever was known, and what sense or reason is in changing your mind again?

CON (*whipping out knife, gaily*). 'Tis your throat, or your knot, Paddy; and I couldn't say at all which is most valuable. (*He cuts rope.*)

MARK (*running right*). I'll tell the Guards you were only shamming mad and fooling us. (*He stops, and takes out some pound notes.*) Girls, bring these to the drink-shop, and put a fire in the snug for us, and chairs and porter and whiskey and lemonade and biscuits and red-meat and the loaves there, and we'll have a night till morning. (*He runs out right.*)

KITTY (*counting money*). Sanbatch, tell Hotha to bring his fiddle, and we'll dance the eyes out of our heads.

SHEILA. The loaves are here. (*She is putting them together.*)

CON. I'll carry them. I had a great dinner to-day, and it made me as strong as an elephant.

SHEILA. Let ye not be long, Sanbatch.

(*The three run out left.* PADDY *lights his pipe.* SANBATCH *makes his way wearily as far as the fire. A reaction has set in.*)

SANBATCH. This minute I'm as weak as water. When I saw I'd have to go to the mental hospital it frightened the wind in me. Linehan broke a window, too, and he didn't live two months after he went amongst them; and Keenan didn't last any length either. (*He sits on long box.*)

PADDY. These are decent fellows, and they'll give us three great weddings with lashings of roast goose and cold porter.

SANBATCH. Too much roast goose and cold porter killed oul' fellows at weddings before now.

PADDY. Them fellows were so done up they could hardly look against the sun. They weren't the same as me: sound and hardy as a goat's horn.

MARK (*running in with* JIMMY). We turned back the Guards. Come on to the drink-shop, let ye. (*He runs out left.*)

JIMMY. Three great weddings and three great days at roast goose and porter! (*Hotly, to* PADDY, *who is moving off.*) Stand back there! 'Tis my turn to go first! (*He runs out past him.*)

PADDY (*hotly, after him*). Take notice of this! Four great weddings, and four great days! To-morrow I'm off to Tuam to settle up with my girl! (*He goes off left.*)

HOTHA (*coming out*). Sanbatch, we have all settled. . . . Where's the lot?

SANBATCH. Gone for a night's singing and jollying at the drink-shop. Will ye go?

HOTHA. She'd be too shy to go amongst so many yet. Wait till I bring down a batch of eatables and drinkables, and we'll have a party for ourselves and her. (*Runs to gate.*) Sadie, Sanbatch only is here. (*He runs out right, and she comes in back, looking very shy and happy.*)

SADIE (*earnestly*). Is it the truth, that you'll never go to the asylum if I wed Hotha?

SANBATCH (*vehemently*). If there's wan word of a lie in that, you can bury me upside down, so that when I think I'll be scratching up, I'll be scratching down. (*He imitates a man clawing his way out of the grave.*)

SADIE. If I wed him, will he desert me again?

SANBATCH. Not him! Soon you'll be going out again happy amongst the neighbours, and he'll be every bit as proud of you as he used to be long ago.

SADIE. But will he be evermore fretting and blaming about our want of children?

SANBATCH. The want of a son isn't stinging him much at all any more, because myself is every day telling him that's a pure Godsend, on account himself and all his breed were so stubborn and contrary. So let ye do what ye should do as well as ye can do, and ye'll be company for each other, and so happy that ye'll think every day Christmas Day. You'll wed him?

SADIE (*smiling*). . . . I will. (*She sits beside him.*)

SANBATCH. In the English Army as soon as wan man is killed they enlist another; and that's God's plan, too: for each person that dies, a child to be sent into the world. But around here we reckoned we were men of brains, as good as God, and we reckoned we could do without ye, and God never said wan word only let us go ahead and ruin ourselves: and then Himself

176

scattered all women and girls away from us to the ends of the world. . . . But maybe now He thinks we have enough good sense got again, and maybe soon He'll bestow children on the village again. If He does, we'll have nothing more to want or to do, only wait for the death, and then die happy because we will be leaving room for more.

CURTAIN

Daughter from Over the Water

A COMEDY IN THREE ACTS

DEDICATION

To Tom McNeice from Queen Maeve's country, that enchanted land of giants' finger stones and many a Fairy Tree; where in mighty array the Coolaney mountains stand, like an eternal Guard of Honour, facing her cloud-capped cairn tomb on Knocknarea across the Bay.

Preface

The old adage that great minds think alike is not always or often true of literary men. Shaw and Yeats, both Nobel Prize winners, and both practising dramatists for nearly half a century, held very different views on didactic drama. Shaw maintained that all great drama is didactic; and he pointed out that didactic dramatists usually achieve a large output of plays in their zeal for the various subjects or causes they wish to teach or preach about. But dramatists who have not got this teaching – preaching urge soon weary of the pains and labour of playwriting. As examples of this Shaw named two brilliant dramatists, Sheridan and Congreve, who both retired from playwriting at thirty.

Against this Yeats pointed out the dangers of too didactic a tendency in drama: it led to truth being sacrificed to propaganda, as in war films where the enemy are all unrelieved villains and the patriots all angels incarnate and neither are credible human beings. The result is an unconvincing play which is neither god drama nor effective propaganda. Honesty is the best policy in playwriting. As Yeats said, "truth and beauty are the essentials and they must not be distorted or deserted for any cause no matter how worthy." Or as his most famous disciple Synge put it, "The drama like the symphony does not teach or prove anything. Analysts with their problems, and teachers with their systems are soon as old-fashioned as the pharmacopeia of Galen – look at Ibsen and the Germans!" Synge wrote this pretty accurate forecast less than a year after Ibsen's death in 1906.

But while many didactic and propagandist plays have had their hour of fame or notoriety and then faded, probably for ever, Shaw's didactic plays have conquered the world and show little sign of fading. So which was right, Shaw or Yeats? The truth probably lies midway between their two extreme points of view. Most plays, including Synge's, do tend to show, or prove, or criticise, something; but that is all to the good, provided that characterisation, or plot, or the style of the play are not sacrificed to propaganda.

The classic example of this was Ibsen. He started off with poetic problem plays like *Brand* and *Peer Gynt* which are as fresh today as they were a hundred years ago, because they had style – the great preservative of drama and literature. But then, turning his back on this traditional poetic drama, he launched the new starkly realistic contemporary problem drama: completely unrelieved by beauty or eloquence of style. Like most revolutionaries he went too far. The realistic unadorned dialogue in these later plays is quite effective theatrically; but once the plays' problems became out of date they had no beauty of style to keep them alive.

Shaw's first play *Widower's House* is as grim and unadorned as anything by his first master, Ibsen; but just then and very fortunately for Shaw a new master arose, and achieved a brilliant success in the great Anglo-Irish tradition of classic comedy. This was Oscar Wilde, who after showing Shaw his true road to success and greatness, further obliged by dying and leaving Shaw without a serious rival. Shaw grafted the new Ibsen drama of ideas into the traditional Anglo-Irish classic comedy; and went of indefatigably to become the most famous dramatist since Moliere.

But it may tell against Shaw in the long run that his didactic tendencies made him sacrifice truth and reality so often to propaganda. (This is especially evident in his plays on religious problems.) He disliked all branches of Christianity, and his plays religious laymen or clerics are usually presented as either fanatics or cynical hypocrites. Thus in *St. Joan* he presents as a fake miracle the historical incident of Joan picking out and identifying, at their first meeting, the Dauphin, as he hides poorly dressed and incognito amongst his courtiers; and the leading ecclesiastic present is made to defend fake miracles as if they were standard Church practice. Perhaps Shaw thought they were and are, because in his young days relations between Catholics and Protestants were in a most unChristian state.

But religious problem plays in general suffer all too often from propagandist distortion for or against religion, and this distortion weakens them as plays and as propaganda. Tragedy or comedy are the dramatist's two safest roads for bypassing the propagandist death-trap. *Maurice Harte* is probably the greatest Irish religious problem play; and it is the greatest because it avoids propaganda by being a true tragedy, which the author allows to develop naturally, he himself taking no sides. But in truth any dramatist is free only in choosing his characters and their initial predicament; out of which they must struggle to extricate themselves in accordance with their characters and ideas. The dramatist who makes them act contrary to these in order to fit in with his propaganda does so at his own artistic peril. In this religious problem play my characters led me an unexpected dance; but I dared not interfere. And anyway why should the devil have all the comedies, as well as all the good tunes?

MICHAEL MOLLOY

DAUGHTER FROM OVER THE WATER

A comedy in three acts

by

M. J. Molloy

DAUGHTER FROM OVER THE WATER was first produced by Castlerea Macra Na Feirme Dramatic Society at the Castle Cinema, Castlerea, on December 16th, 1962, with the following cast:

'TUL' HIGGINS	Michael O'Flynn
KIT HIGGINS	Mrs. Mollie Keegan
RITA HIGGINS	Stephanie Hanmore
PETE HIGGINS	Kevin Rogers
'TUPPENY' HAYES	Michael Dolan
SIBBY HAYES	Mrs. E. Quinn
NICHOLAS BURKE	Patrick Kennedy
LARRY BURKE	Patrick J. Kennedy
NELLIE FLOOD	Geraldine Curran
'RAM' ROONEY	Paddy Concannon
ALAN PAGE	Brendan Gaynor

The production was by Michael O'Flynn.
Setting by Own Ridge and James Quinn.

Daughter from Over the Water

ACT ONE

The scene is the kitchen of a new farmhouse of the usual bungalow type, with large windows, and doors leading from the kitchen into the bedrooms and sitting room. The fireplace is in the right hand wall (from the actor's point of view) and the dresser, which is of the new cabinet factory made type, is against the left hand wall. A radio stands on a small table against the right hand wall. Two wooden armchairs face each other on opposite sides of the fire. They and the other chairs are painted cream; and the table is covered with a brightly patterned oil cloth. The kitchen has electric light, and a little electrically-lit cross glows before a picture of the Sacred Heart. The Byzantine picture Our Lady of Perpetual Succour *hangs on the wall. The walls are brightly distempered, or papered, and the general picture is one of modest prosperity.*

But the room contains two unusual features which leave one in no doubt that the inhabitants of this house are out of the ordinary. One is a rather fantastically stocked and placed 'library', consisting of a couple of homemade bookshelves attached to the back wall in a dominating position near the door. Its books include many old and new copies of Old Moore's Almanac, a battered dictionary, a few old battered poetry books and novels, together with, for bulk's sake, many old out-of-date Latin theology books bought by the bundle for a song at the late Parish Priest's auction.

The other unusual feature is a considerable number of small cheap picture frames hanging on the walls, and containing not pictures, but printed poems torn from Old Moore's Almanac, Ireland's Own *and similar periodicals. For the owner of this house is a poet, and a famous one – in his own opinion.*

It is the morning of a sunny June day. The door opens and the woman of the house comes in. She is a sturdily built woman in her middle fifties; is remarkably alive and vigorous, her mobile expressive face changing in a flash from fun to seriousness or even tragedy. But in general, she is a very pleasant, witty and humourous woman and so

185

is still best known by her Christian name of 'KIT' as so often happens in the country when a married woman is a 'character'.

She wears the usual housekeeping dress and apron, and strong rubber boots. She carries a white milkpail, which seems to be empty. She comes in hastily, and is dismayed to find no one in the kitchen:

KIT. Tul, you vexer! Are you not left the bed yet? And your breakfast ready this half-an-hour! I'll have to wet fresh tea for you now. (*She empties out teapot, wets fresh tea.*) I'm after searching all over for our cattle and sheep, but there isn't a hoof left on our land. All gone trespassing on the neighbour's! Get up and drive home your stock and repair your fences. That'll pay you better than lying in bed composing poems for Old Moore's Almanac. The glory of the poets is dying away in Ireland: football is all the people are interested in now.

(*She goes to bedroom door.*)

KIT (*she goes to table, slices bread*). Like myself you're melting with age and bone weary after the bog yesterday, still we must struggle on and keep the farm alive until either Peter or Rita come home and settle on it.

(TUL *comes out in his shirtsleeves, with his jacket slung across his arm, and his waistcoat and shoes open. He carries an open school notebook and a pencil. He is a tall, impressive-looking man in his late fifties, lively, intelligent, vigorous and humourous. When engaged in composition, however, he is oblivious of all things else. With his rather long hair in disarray, and his reading glasses at an unorthodox angle, he looks a poet and a character.*)

TUL. Every night I'm worrying when I should be sleeping, over Rita not writing home lately. So last night, to cheer myself, I composed this little love song and enigma for the Almanac.

(*He makes some small corrections with his pencil.*)

KIT. 'Tisn't often a love song makes a good enigma. Recite it for me.

TUL. I will, but it isn't perfected yet.

In the parlour one evening, were sitting till late,
A young man and maiden so fair,
I'm sure they were lovers, and some people say
That they did not use more than one chair.

KIT. Close enough!

TUL. *Be that as it may, they were happy and gay,*
As they chatted away at their ease,
And they talked of the weather, the prospects, and love,

186

And each other still seemed to please.
"Do you think I'm improving in courtship?" he cried,
As his arms encircled her zone.
With a smile and a blush the young maiden replied:
"I think you are holding your own!"
KIT. "His arms encircled her zone." Are the younger generation too ignorant to know that "zone" is the poet's word for waist?
TUL. If they are, so much the worse for them. I'll not give up writing my best for the sake of ignoramuses.
KIT. 'Tis a nice little enigma. What is the solution?
TUL. Holding you own! He was doing that in two ways: holding his own at the courting, as she said, and holding his own sweetheart in his arms as well.
KIT. You should send it off as it stands. It's good enough for the Almanac.
TUL. But is it good enough for me? Should I leave it short and plain, or adorn it with a few nice similitudes about the beauty of the maiden? And should I touch on a couple of more emotions? (*He walks about, notebook and pencil in hand.*)
KIT. When our stock are found trespassing on the neighbour's that'll touch on a power of emotions.
TUL. What signifies a bit of grass in July when every farm has too much of it? Tomorrow is the last entry day for this year's Almanac, so I'm as tied down as a bootlace till I have this poem perfected.
KIT. You have to uphold the name and fame of the parish in the Almanac, so the neighbours have more time for fencing than you have.
TUL. And composing is harder work than theirs and worse paid, except for Tom Moore who fitted his poems to old Irish airs that were going about like spirits without bodies. (*Jealously.*) I'd be every bit as good a poet as Tom Moore, if I knew as much grammer.
TUL. But our broken-down fences are calling, and our meadow fields and bog are calling.
TUL. Soon I'll be able to reach them all – after this poem is perfected.
KIT (*resignedly*). Well, let it be so. I'll have another scout around after the stock. Join me as soon as you can. (*She goes to door.*)
TUL. I will – in a few minutes. Sure, if we worked every hour that God sent us, we'd still be only poor small farmers, so let us not neglect our one glory: the only poet in Ireland, England or

America to have poems printed in the Almanac every year for thirty years.

(KIT *opens door, closes it quickly again, bolts it.*)

KIT. Dear to-night! Here's Tuppeny slashing in to us over trespass!

TUL. Give him no answer! Let him think we're out, or in bed still.

(*With the speed of long practice, the two take up positions against the back wall, so that they cannot be seen through the window. An angry knocking and kicking is heard at the door.*)

TUPPENY (*outside*). Open, ye lazy good-for-nothing drones! Open, or I'll knock the flying house on top of ye!

(TUPPENY *rains blows and curses on the door.*)

KIT (*blessing herself in horror*). D'ye hear him? His language 'd break stones!

(*But* TUL, *copybook and pencil in hand, works away at his poem, and is too devoted to his art, or to accustomed to such assaults, to pay them the slightest attention. Soon* TUPPENY HAYES *appears at the window on which he taps with his stick. He is in his late fifties and rather resembles a stork with his long legs, long neck, long nose, small blinking eyes, and intense seriousness. Usually he walks with a stoop, his nose leading the way, but when he looks at, or addresses a person, the head goes back, the eyes almost close, and he peers along his nose in a shortsighted way. He is, except when excited, rather slow and shambling of movement and speech, illustrating his points with his index finger. His clothes and hat are green with age.*)

TUPPENY. Let me in, don't you know, and hell sweat the drop of blood I'll leave in ye! Your stock have eaten me out of house and home and this morning your dirty mongrel of a ram killed my fine pedigree ram that cost me thirty pound! Thirty pound you'll have to pay me and law cost as well.

(*He leaves window goes back to door, hammers on it again.*)

KIT. Dear to-night! His prize ram killed!

TUL (*wrapped up in his poem*). So our five pound ram was stronger then his!

KIT. Will you wake up, Tul? Thirty pounds out of our pockets.

TUL (*dismayed*). Thirty pounds! And we haven't ships on the ocean!

(TUPPENY *returns to the window.*)

TUPPENY. Will ye leave the bed, ye lazy oul' sleekers! There was never a poet yet but was a scoundrel, and you're the worst since Bobby Burns that had two girls in trouble the day he got married!

(*Suddenly another, much milder, knocking is heard on the door.*)
KIT. That's the postman's knock!
TUPPENY (*facing towards door*). They're in bed yet, G.P.O. They'd
sleep a thousand years ... Is there an English stamp on their
letter? Good! Had it the feel of money? ... Good, G.P.O.!
(*Turning to window again.*) There's an English letter put under
your door, and it has the feel of money. I'll want thirty pounds
out of that.
(*He leaves window and resumes hammering on door.*)
KIT (*approaching door cautiously*). Pete and Rita are two months
without sending us a cheque! If there's none this time, they're
surely saving up to marry beyond!
TUL (*looking up, with sudden sharp anxiety*). Is that letter from
Rita?
KIT. Without my glasses, I can't make out the writing.
TUPPENY (*re-appearing at window*). 'Twould be fitter for your son
and daughter to come home and repair your fences in place of
buying arm-chairs and radios that are only making yourselves
and work worse enemies than ever. Have my thirty pound for
me within the hour, or I'll kill you with this stick, and put your
lazy rap of a widow through the law. (*He goes.*)
TUL (*bitterly*). So he wants thirty pound and no less, for his worn-
out ram! That's his thanks to me for composing the longest
elegy ever printed in Old Moore in sad and loving memory of
his old blackguard of a father.
KIT (*having opened the letter*). Dear to-night! There's no cheque in
this letter either.
TUL. They're surely saving up to get wed beyond. Six weeks without
a cheque!
(KIT *takes her spectacles from the mantelpiece – puts them on.*)
KIT. And, if they marry townspeople, the like'll never consent to
come home here and wear a guano-bag apron and big yard
boots and go milking cows.
TUL. If they settle down beyond, we'll finish up lonesome, and
bitter poor, with nothing to look forward to but the Old Age
Pension – the ticket to the grave!
KIT. This letter isn't in either Pete's or Rita's handwriting. (*She
starts reading.*)
TUL. It isn't! Well, 'tis a true saying that the hardest time of life is
when they're grown up and gone, and you're every day
expecting a letter and getting none. When they're children,
they'd make you laugh!

189

KIT. Dear to-night!

(*She blesses herself in dismay.*)

TUL. What's amiss, Kit? Is any of them sick or hurt?

KIT. Worse! Ten times worse!

TUL. Is it dying then? . . . Or dead?

KIT (*moaning*). Worse! Worse! Ten times worse!

(*She half-collapses into a chair, puts her hand to her head.*)

TUL (*putting an arm around her*). Courage, Kit, courage! Tell me quietly. What could be worse than death?

KIT. To be damned is worse than death. And damned is what Rita is, our only daughter!

TUL. Damned? Never! We know 'tis nothing new for an Irish girl in England to get careless about her religion for a while. . . .

KIT. She has given up all belief, and next Friday in a Registry office she's marrying an out-and-out unbeliever – an atheist!

TUL. A Registry Office marriage! What the Church condemns as no marriage at all!

KIT. So she'll be only living in sin with him!

TUL. And cut off from all the sacraments of her religion! (*Snatching letter.*) Who says it? It's dirty lies! (*He reads.*)

KIT. I wish to God it was. But it's from Rita's pal and our own neighbour, Nellie Flood, a pious decent girl, who wouldn't enjoy seeing us in trouble.

TUL (*reading*). And she says Rita is so crazy about him that she has shut her eyes and ears on Nellie and on Pete and on all Catholics. (*Dropping the letter and his precious poem on the floor.*) Rita! Rita! And there wasn't a better-living girl on this earth!

KIT. When she was going, I warned her that the English 'd make a smart girl out of her, or a fool.

TUL (*going around like a man half demented*). We know there does be a fog around the good-looking girls, still who'd ever think this'd be her end?

KIT. And we had the rosary ringing in the house every night when they were young!

TUL. We could have been better Christians, we know; still we were no worse than the neighbours.

KIT. Where was her Guardian Angel?

TUL. They say they don't be as good for some as for others.

KIT. She wasn't educated enough to argue religion with that atheist fellow, so she had to listen to him.

TUL. The time she was dying of diphtheria, I stopped up without

190

sleep six nights until I near lost my mind ... If she died that time she was sure of Heaven, but any more death will make an evil spirit of her. (*He is going around distractedly.*)

KIT (*bitterly*). Why did God entrust the money-bags of the world to the unbelievers of America and England? The money king can do what he likes and wed who he likes. ....

TUL. Talk is no good. We must plan some way to save her. (*He is reading through the letter again.*)

KIT. We have only four days left for pulling the divil's veil off her eyes. Friday is her registry office marriage day.

TUL. Nellie says our only chance is to coax her away from that athiest fellow before the wedding and back to Ireland, if only for a few days. She says Rita won't find it so easy to despise her faith when she's back in Ireland.

KIT. How can we coax her away from him when Nellie and Pete have preached her black and blue, and failed?

TUL (*going around, letter in hand, thinking hard*). D'ye remember the trick Bernadette Duffy's parents played on her the time she was to wed the Mahommedan black man in Liverpool?

KIT. They drew her home with a false telegram that her mother was dying.

TUL. That's our last and our only chance, so we're duty bound to take it without delay. (*He tears a page out of his poetry notebook, sits at the table, begins to write.*) Fetch me Pete's and Rita's addresses quick.

KIT. Why Pete's?

TUL. Pete will have to be telegramed home, too, or she'd guess we were only tricking her.

KIT. Yes, telegram the two home. Then we might with God's help convert her and rekindle the old love match between herself and Larry Burke. (*She takes a large bundle of letters from the dresser drawer, gives two to* TUL, *and he writes down the address.*)

TUL (*grimly*). But Larry's father 'll forbid their marriage as he did before, unless Rita his a big dowry. And we have nothing to give her only this farm.

KIT. If we give her this, we'll be disinheriting our only son! Then poor Pete would have to put down his nest in England for ever!

TUL. Still we should bear with that and with everything to save Rita. The world will come to an end at last; but her soul won't. (*He returns to writing the telegrams.*)

KIT. But when Bernadette Duffy was tricked home by telegram and

191

found her mother wasn't sick at all, she blazed up and sailed like a fireball back to England and her tawny Mahommedan.

TUL. There's only one sure way to hold Rita here for a spell; you to take to your bed and sham dying. That'd give us time to convert her, and rekindle the old love match between herself and Larry Burke.

KIT. Me sham dying! But the neighbours know I amn't dying, and they'd guess we were trying to save her from some disgrace. Then none of them 'd marry her.

TUL. We'll have to deceive the neighbours, too. I'll tell them you got a heart attack last night between darkness and day; and I invited out the priest and doctor to see you.

KIT. But at least two of the neighbours seen me out seeking our stock this morning.

TUL. Then 'tis me will have to sham dying, and that means I'll have to rewrite these telegrams.

KIT. You're an able captain; still even you wouldn't be able to fool them.

TUL. That's what they think, too; and they'll never believe we'd have the nerve to try. That'll make it easier to fool them.

KIT (*looking out window*). Here's Larry Burke coming against us with a look that's worse than a summons!

TUL More trespass! Hide quick!

(*They take up their accustomed positions on each side of the window. Angry knocking is heard.*)

LARRY (*at door*). Get up and open up, ye bone-lazy good-for-nothings!

KIT. 'Tis a pity, just when we need to kindle up the old love match between himself and Rita.

TUL. Once word came that she wasn't taking her holidays in Ireland they year, Larry guessed well that she had him let down for good.

(LARRY *comes to the window. He is in his late twenties, a good-looking fellow and intelligent. Generally he looks rather gloomy and browbeaten but at the moment he is very angry indeed. He wears a battered straw hat and no collar or tie or jacket.*)

LARRY. Well, the divil take ye soon and sudden! Your cattle are battering the face of our oats crop and eating it ... We'll put ye through the law without mercy this time, and twenty pound won't clear ye between compensation and law costs. Leave the bed, ye drones and day-sleepers!

(*He goes back to door: lashes it with his stick.*)

KIT. Two lawsuits along with Rita's downfall!

TUL. We mustn't answer Larry or vex him now, no matter what he says or does.

KIT. Yes, marriage to him is our best chance to save Rita.

(LARRY *returns to the window.*)

LARRY. Father is on his way here with the longest stick he has, and he won't leave a white spot on you with beating. After that you'll repair your fences instead of writing oul' rubbishy poems that'd sicken a dog!

(LARRY *goes.*)

TUL (*beside himself with rage*). "Oul' rubbishy poems!" The badly-cultured idiot! Where is my stick? Get me a stick!

(*He is searching over the dresser.*)

KIT. Leave him so, Tul! He didn't mean a word of it. He was only mad vexed.

TUL (*finding stick and making a couple of practice swings with it*). Rubbishy poems! And all Ireland dwelling on them for thirty years! Out of the way, woman!

KIT. Don't Tul, or he'll know you aren't sick.

TUL. Out of the way!

KIT. Remember . . . Rita!

TUL (*pausing, as he opens door*). Yes, Rita! Only for her, and only for he's gone, there'd be blood like you'd spill water! (*He throws stick into corner.*) And only for my poems the idiot 'd never be born at all. Only for all the love poems I composed for his father, and the scoundrel telling the poor girl that he composed them himself!

TUL (*pointing to the several letters hanging in picture frames on the wall*). And he all his life reading these letters from editors classing me with Robert Burns and Tom Moore and Goldsmith!

(KIT *takes up the telegrams again. He is beginning to calm down a little.*)

KIT. Still, Larry has a fine new house like a Yankee house, and a fine big farm, not like this, and a fine car for carrying her around. . . . He'd be better for her than this atheist fellow, wouldn't he?

TUL (*grudgingly*). Well, I suppose the idiot would. In bad times a person has to take anything.

(*He returns to re-writing the telegrams.*)

KIT. If Larry's father finds out why we telegrammed her home, he'd never let Larry wed a girl that forsook her religion.

TUL. All about her atheist-fellow, we must keep in darkness. Set

193

out the blessed candles and the crucifix for a happy death.

KIT. They're here!

(*She takes them from the dresser. She puts the candles into the candlestick.*)

TUL (*having finished telegrams*). I fair hate having to lie in bed all day and the sun splitting the bushes . . . So we'll say I'm stricken with a kind of heartfailure that makes it hard for me to breathe lying down. (*He moves one of the big armchairs out from near the fire.*) Then I can sit here all day with a rug lapped around me.

KIT. I'll fetch a rug and your night shirt.

(*She hurries into bedroom. He takes off his jacket and waistcoat and unlaces his shoes. She comes out with his nightshirt, a rug and a pillow or two. She arranges these on the armchair.* TUL *puts on the nightshirt.*)

KIT (*uneasy*). But, Tul, mocking is catching, they say, and now we're mocking the most dangerous man out – the death!

TUL (*grimly*). I know! The death is the most dangerous man out, and one of these mornings you and me may be found stone cold and twisted across each other in the bed.

KIT. But 'tis only out to save our daughter we are, so maybe God'll save us from the death.

TUL. 'Tis our only hope that God will.

KIT. I'll fetch a pillow for you. (*She goes into bedroom.*)

TUL. No doubt a poet should die with some of his poems clasped to his breast. (*He goes to his library and rummages through the pile of Almanacs.*) I'll pick the copies with the elegies printed in sad and loving memory of Nicholas's wife and of Tuppeny's scoundrel of a father. That'll touch Tuppeny and Nicholas and Larry and it'll temper the edge of their vengeance over the trespass.

(*He brings three copies of Old Moore back to his armchair bed.* KIT *comes out with a small bottle containing water and with a quill sticking up out of it. She also carries a home-made four-legged child's stool.*)

KIT. Here's Rita's little stool to rest your feet on.

(*She puts the stool under his feet and the bottle of holy water on the small table at his elbow. He is making himself comfortable in the armchair, wrapping the rug around him.*)

TUL. Tell them the Doctor did his best for me but his best has failed. Say he sees no hope at all for me. That news 'll anchor them at home for a while. (*He arranges Almanac copies on his breast.*)

194

KIT (*bringing bottle of Aspirins from dresser*). We'll say these aspirins are heart pills the Doctor gave you. (*She scrapes off label.*)

TUL. Tell Nicholas I'm willing my farm to Rita.

KIT. Yes. Then she'd be a moneyed girl and Nicholas 'd allow Larry to marry her.

TUL. But you'll have to do all the talking for the first while. For a start it will look better if I'm entranced and speechless.

KIT (*alarmed*). Me do all the talking? No. Tul, you'd be twice better and quicker at the lies on account you're a poet.

TUL. Sure, the greatest poet that ever lived wasn't as quick a liar as a woman.

KIT. No, Tul; without your help I'll never be a match for them.

TUL. The less you say the better, and they'll think 'tis the sickness of grief that's on you. And every time you get stuck for lies, start shedding down tears.

KIT (*brightening up*). You're right! Every tear'll be worth a hundred words. A big handkerchief is what I need, so!
(*She hurries into bedroom.*)

TUL (*after her*). A fool is born every minute and two are born to catch him. They'll inhale your story the same as if it was the sweetest fag that ever came out of a factory.
(KIT *comes out of bedroom, carrying a big handkerchief and her rosary beads.*)

KIT. I'd want to send someone with those telegrams. (*She opens door; closes it hastily again.*) Here's Sibby making in!

TUL. Start fanning the poor and broken dying man!

KIT. That the Lord may brighten me now and make me a match for them all! (*Starts fanning him with handkerchief, standing between him and the view from the street door.*)

TUL. Courage now, Kit! Courage! Sure lately Sibby and Tuppeny have gone silly enough to believe anything.

KIT. Well they must be when they're stopping the clock one day a week to keep it from wearing out.

TUL. Their oul' skinflint of a father fairly ruined them: refusing them land and money the time they were marriageable.
(*The door latch is rattled a couple of times.* TUL *settles back and closes his eyes. At last the door is pushed open slowly and* SIBBY *can be seen. Like her stork-like brother,* TUPPENY, *there is something bird-like and innocent about* SIBBY, *but she is small and plump and more like a thrush. Her clothes, like* TUPPENY'S, *are well-patched and green with age and, as she has worn the*

195

same clothes winter and summer for so many years, they are now a skin-fit as if specially designed and made for her by some Parisian fashion-house. The hat is a helmet-shaped affair which gives very little view of her hair. An old topcoat which has shrunken up to her knees and an old skirt reaching half-way to her ankles are other main items. Below that, woollen stockings and a pair of broken, heavy men's boots for farmyard work.

Yet all this is due to carelessness and oddity rather than to the fanatical parsimony of the miser. There is something very childlike and innocent about her big soft eyes and unfailing smile, and her soft voice and easy-going ways. All emergencies, past, present and future, she meets with the same childlike smile.

Her face is very sun-tanned and her age anything from fifty to sixty. She stands in the doorway raising her face and hands to the sun.)

SIBBY. Isn't it great weather? This'll be a great year for big spuds and small sods of turf. All I came about was the thirty pound for our ram that ye killed. Half of that belongs to me on account father died without making a will. And if ye gave the lot to Tuppeny, it might tempt him to bring in a wife before myself was wed and out of her way ... (*Coming in cheerfully, and peering down at the breakfast on the table.*) It isn't a young man, or an old man, that'd suit me, but a man between young and old. (*Raising her head, she sees* TUL.)

SIBBY. Lord bless us and save us! Is it dying he is, or only funning me?

KIT. He took a pain and a fluttering in his heart at the break of day, so I frightened up and cycled for the priest and doctor.

SIBBY. And they did their best for him.

KIT. They did, but their best has failed.

SIBBY. He's as white as a pig sure enough, so he's going somewhere. Poor Tul of the Songs! – the sweetest singer since the Italian Robinson Crusoe.

KIT (*sobbing*). What'll I do without him at all?

SIBBY. 'Tis no wonder you to be crying like a calf after your bed pal. Still the Widow's Pension is a fine cheque to be getting every week. The widows now make out they have more money without them. When they had them they never had a copper. Isn't it great weather?

(*She takes a cigarette butt from her pocket, and lights it at the fire.*)

KIT (*dabbing her eyes*). And he a powerful man that could quench the fire with a spit!

SIBBY. Sure the best horse that ever ran is beaten at last. But did ye get any token of a death to come?

KIT. Friday night last, in a dream, the dead bell was booming in my ears.

SIBBY. The dead bell! A sure token! And a Friday night dream is one that always comes true ... But, Kit, did he think of me at all, or leave me anything?

KIT. He said that as soon as the clay was over him, you were to be given his American watch.

SIBBY. That great time-piece! I'm glad now that no matter how often he trespassed on us, I never insulted him by telling him what he was.

KIT. St. Peter, they say, is the nicest man out, if your ticket is the right colour.

SIBBY. Tul's ticket will be the right colour. Sure he never was a moneyed man, and drunk or sober, his only curse was, "May the devil do this and that to you!"

KIT. He was the nicest husband in Ireland, even if he had a backbone like the coulter of a plough.

(*Taking advantage of the fact that* SIBBY *is relighting her cigarette at the fire,* TUL *opens his eyes in mock protest at this speech, but* KIT *shoves his head back onto the pillow again.*)

SIBBY (*suddenly excited*). But maybe he'd come all right if you gave him a sup of tea?

KIT. No; the doctor said he's a case without a cure.

SIBBY. But doctors do make mistakes in people, and 'tis hard to beat the sup of tea. (*She sets out for the fire and the kettle.*) And, sure, if it doesn't do him good itself, it'll do us good.

(*She wets tea. The door is flung open and* TUPPENY *appears in doorway, stick in hand.*)

TUPPENY. Will ye come out, ye two lazy oul' dodgers and take yeer trespassers off my land? Ye're living here like two oul' buck cats, walking in and walking out and sleeping.

SIBBY (*turning to him mildly*). Keep your tongue in your pocket and your stick on the ground. Tul has the death!

TUPPENY. You can believe that, don't you know, but all the flies on me died long ago. (*He comes in, stops suddenly and stares suspiciously.*) What tricks is he up to this time?

SIBBY. No trick at all! At break of day he had the priest and the doctor, and the doctor has the worst opinion of his chances.

TUPPENY. If he's mocking the death, the death 'll give him the most suffering end since poor Robert Emmet.

KIT. Tuppeny, here's money and would you send these telegrams to Pete and Rita telling them the doctor said he can't live passing a couple of days.

TUPPENY (*blinking at the telegram*). So he really is done!

KIT. He has the worst breed of heart failure. He can't breathe in a bed with it.

TUPPENY. Tul of the Songs! And I thought he had a heart as strong as an eagle. A couple of times he came in the way of my stick, still it didn't kill him.

(SIBBY *puts out cups and saucers for herself and* KIT.)

KIT. 'Tis a pity to put so gifted a head down into the clay.

TUPPENY. True. True. And the decentest man that ever broke bread, don't you know?

SIBBY. And look at what's nearest to his heart: the Almanac of the year they printed his elegy in sad and loving memory of father!

TUPPENY. The finest and the saddest elegy he ever composed. Every house that was recited in the cat'd go out he'd be so ashamed when he couldn't cry.

SIBBY. They say it isn't safe to cry too much until after the corpse is washed and laid overboard. It might draw his ghost back around the place.

TUPPENY. There's no fear of Tul having to walk the world. He'll find peace in the grave like a decent man.

SIBBY. Kit, where do ye buy your coffins?

KIT. I forgot to ask Tul that! This is the first coffin that was wanted since I joined the Higginses.

SIBBY. Sure, Tul is easy-going and he won't care what kind of a coffin he has, so long as he has a good grave.

TUPPENY. True! . . . So, Kit, you should buy the cheapest coffin out. The compensation to us for the ram and the trespass won't leave you enough money to baptise a fairy.

SIBBY (*cheerfully, readying tea*). Half the compensation money belongs to me, on account father died without making a will.

TUPPENY (*sadly*). And we were married long since only for the way he left us tied together and in each other's way.

SIBBY. Now is your chance to get out of my way! Marry into Kit's house and farm. She'll need someone.

TUPPENY (*gravely*). True. True . . . These late years since father died I'm on the look-out for a fairly good wife. Kit, d'ye think would you be industrious enough for me?

KIT. I might! but first hurry off with these telegrams.

TUPPENY. True! (*Goes to door, turns.*) But tell me? Did he say anything about my right of way?

KIT. His very last words were that his ghost 'd pester and plague any that interfered with your right of way.

TUPPENY (*blinking and sniffing emotionally*). That has touched me don't you know?

KIT. And he said Tuppeny was to get his English pipe and his clothes.

TUPPENY. He did! Well, speak fair: he was the decentest and the best neighbour that ever the village had, don't you know?

(*But at this moment, the door is kicked open, and* NICHOLAS *appears outside. He is a farmer in his late fifties or early sixties, of middle height and very square set, with a bulldog jaw and a rolling and fanatical eye. He wears his work-a-day clothes and a battered hat, and he brandishes a stout stick. Sometimes he roars, but more often he spits his words between his teeth. He looks and is the kind of man who is always ready to explode if his wishes are thwarted in the slightest degree.*)

NICHOLAS. Mister-my-good-man, you hound at any rate and loafer! You public pest and married to a worse pest, will ye come out and take your trespass out of my land?

TUPPENY. He's disabled, Nicholas.

NICHOLAS. Too lazy to put on his clothes you mean! (*Coming in.*) He wants to drive us all crazy so as we'll be locked up. Then he'll have all belonging to us. (*Coming up to the death-bed scene.*) What trickery and treachery is he up to now?

SIBBY (*pleasantly*). His heart is clocking off, Nicholas, and isn't it great weather?

NICHOLAS. How could he be dying without being sick?

TUPPENY. Read these telegrams to his son and daughter to come home quick. (*Gives him telegrams.*)

NICHOLAS. I can't read without my glasses. Where are Tul's glasses?

KIT. On the dresser there, Nicholas.

SIBBY. The doctor says he's an uncurable.

TUPPENY. And all the doctors in Ireland can't cure an uncurable.

KIT. But the doctor said his blood isn't high enough to put him to death to-day.

TUPPENY. You'll see the attacks 'll go on for three times, and the third attack is the one that kills.

NICHOLAS (*trying to read telegrams*). These are cheap bad oul' glasses with a queer squint in them. They're not straight-forward like mine.

199

TUPPENY. Death never comes to the village but he sends us a token. Th' other night we heard a step passing our door, a queer step, giving every second blow.

SIBBY. And Garrytim's fairy bush was humming in the wind like an airoplane!

NICHOLAS. Poor Tul of the Songs! And isn't it hard how God 'll let us suffer on when we're struggling to rear our families, but when that's done and we can rest at last – that's when He'll knock the breath out of us!

KIT. Nicholas, his last words were that the bushes on our mearing fence belonged by right to you.

NICHOLAS. So God converted him at last!

KIT. And he left his shotgun to yourself and Larry.

NICHOLAS. Tul of the Songs! Sure he was as generous as the Pope. The best neighbour the village ever had.

KIT. How will I live without him at all?

NICHOLAS. The lonesomeness 'll punish you sore. For a long time after I buried my own woman, I couldn't bear to hear a woman's voice or step.

SIBBY. She'll need help to run the farm, so she should marry again. (*Gives* KIT *cup of tea.*)

TUPPENY. And why not? The horse that ran before, she'll run again.

KIT. I'll need a man to run the farm for me whatever. (*Drinks tea.*)

NICHOLAS. A fine farm, too! ... D'ye know what I'm going to tell you, Kit?

KIT. I know it won't be a lie.

NICHOLAS. The best man for the army is a soldier, and the best man for marriage is the trained man, the man that was married before.

TUPPENY (*jealously*). But many a good soldier never fought, don't you know, and she isn't going to throw herself away on any oul' second hand fiddle.

SIBBY (*pleasantly*). Sure, the older the fiddle the sweeter the tune.

NICHOLAS (*ferociously*). Mister-my-good-man, did you call me an oul' secondhand fiddle?

TUPPENY. What else are you, don't you know?

NICHOLAS. D'ye want a few smashes of this stick?

TUPPENY. You may thank you're an old dying cat, or I'd crown you with this.

NICHOLAS. Come on and fight! I'm still in my best days and fear no man.

(*They brandish their sticks bloodthirstily, but take care to keep the table, or a safe distance, between them.*)

SIBBY (*sipping tea*). 'Tis hard to beat the sup of tea.

KIT. If ye fight, it'll be the death of Tul his heart is gone so weak and tender.

TUPPENY. You won't frighten me to death the same as you did your poor wife.

NICHOLAS (*turning to* KIT). Kit, I never did. She went to hospital with the drinking diabetes, and they let her die of the drouth, and the cold curse of God on them!

TUPPENY. Talking of getting wed, and the one tooth he has left dancing a jig in his head.

NICHOLAS. Kit, I buy a car and everything good, according as I want it, not like these misers.

TUPPENY. You old pawn office of a second hand car is outside your door, and hunger is inside you door.

(*The door is flung open, and* LARRY *appears, in his shirtsleeves and carrying a stick.*)

LARRY. Come out and take your trespass out of our land. Anyone that's neighbour to ye is living seven miles below hell!

NICHOLAS (*attacking* LARRY). You common blackguard, what d'ye mean, insulting the best friends and neighbours we ever had?

LARRY. An oul' drone so lazy, that if you shifted him he'd stay where you left him!

SIBBY. He'll be God's neighbour any more.

TUPPENY. Yes, whatever Tul was or wasn't, don't you know?

LARRY (*approaching* TUL). He's tricking ye!

NICHOLAS. How could he trick the priest and the doctor that were here half the night?

LARRY. Well, he wasn't there at all when I was at the window before.

TUPPENY (*suddenly*). True, Larry, don't you know?

KIT (*emerging from the big handkerchief*). He couldn't breathe well lying in the bed, so I carried him out to here.

SIBBY (*cheerfully*). He's a case without a cure, Larry, and isn't it great weather?

LARRY. Was it heart failure or a stroke that dropped him?

TUPPENY. The heart! He must have a white heart, a tender heart.

NICHOLAS. But he didn't forget me and you, Larry. He left us his shot-gun.

LARRY. He did! Tul of the Songs! He'll be an awful loss to us. God send him the light and the glory of Heaven!

201

KIT. Tuppeny, maybe Larry 'd be quicker with the telegrams to Pete and Rita!

LARRY. Why wouldn't I, with a car that can go like a bird? (*He takes telegrams from* TUPPENY – *excitedly.*) And maybe Rita and Pete 'd stay at home this time and go no more to England!

SIBBY. Sure, even if she was counting gold beyond, she'd come home if you'd marry her.

NICHOLAS. No girl without £600 is coming into the farm I worked and suffered for fifty years!

LARRY (*bitterly*). If you let us wed three years ago, Tul 'd be a sound man to-day. It was her going that wounded his heart first. (*He goes out.*)

NICHOLAS (*going to door – calling after him*). Buy a bottle of whiskey to dull the pain of death for the poor fellow.

TUPPENY. True! The dying man's blood does be colder than frost. I'll fetch a sup of whiskey from my house. (*Hurries out.*)

KIT. God 'll reward ye!

NICHOLAS. Didn't his printed elegies make us families of great fame in Ireland. (*He takes billhook from behind dresser.*)

SIBBY (*taking up basket*). Kit, I'll gather the eggs and do all that's to be done. (*She goes out.*)

NICHOLAS. And I'll cut bushes for your fences now and drive home your trespass.

KIT. I'm in a kind of a tremor, and not fit for much work just now.

NICHOLAS. We'll be hand and foot to ye; and everything will be done twice better than when he was able himself.

KIT. Poor Tul! We all know where we are; but we don't know where we're going.

NICHOLAS. God'll forgive Tul after a while for his laziness and his trespassing. Look at how St. Paul was forgiven for shooting the Catholics in the desert! But who'll look after your farm and yourself? Pete?

KIT. Sure Pete has refused time and again to come home and give up his big wages in England.

NICHOLAS. If Tul 'd will this farm to Rita, she'd have as good a dowry as what's going; and I'd be very greedy to wed Larry and herself. This farm 'd make a fine addition to our farm. (*He looks out window.*)

KIT. I'll get Tul to will the farm to Rita, if he wakens up to take a last look at the world. (*She goes to dresser drawer, takes out a writing pad and pen and ink.*)

NICHOLAS. He will. They generally always do.

KIT. Maybe you'd draw up the will for me. You're ranked amongst the smartest hob lawyers in Ireland. (*She puts writing pad and pen and ink on the table.*)

NICHOLAS (*grimly*). But you and me have seen many a good parent starved out or plagued out of their homes by bad sons-in-law, or bad daughters-in-law. When our two farms are one you'll be at the mercy of a son-in-law, and I'll be at the mercy of a daughter-in-law.

KIT. Maybe a man of brains such as you could think of some clause that'd protect us.

NICHOLAS. This will 'll make us safer than if we were in a glass case. (*He is writing with expert speed.*) It leaves the farm and all to Rita, but you're to have it for the balance of your days, and your new husband for the balance of his. All me and you have to do then is wed in here independent of both son-in-law and daughter-in-law.

KIT. If you do wed me, Tul's last words were a true prophecy. "You'll wed Nicholas now," he said, "because" he said, Nicholas is the best patent of a husband in Ireland."

NICHOLAS (*writing away*). Once Tul signs this, I'll sign over my farm to Larry; then Larry 'll be able to give her a good living. And as for you and me on this farm, I could earn a pound where Tul couldn't earn a shilling.

KIT. If I was wedded to Tuppeny, my eyes wouldn't be able to open with the hunger.

NICHOLAS. All of a woman he wants is her image on a pound note. (*Handing her the will in an envelope.*) Put this into your bosom for fear Tuppeny, or his slob of a sister, 'd come across it, and burn it.

KIT. Tul 'll sign it when he wakens up for his last look at the world.

NICHOLAS (*walking around grimly*). But a woman must obey her husband always, because it was a woman that committed the first sin. So, if you wouldn't make a quiet and obedient wife, you should wed any easy-going part fool such as you wed before.

KIT. Sure Tul can tell you I'm as quiet as a donkey, and as obedient as a prize sheep dog.

NICHOLAS. And I'll want a good dinner and a clean dinner. Near a pound of bacon and spuds and cabbage accordingly. I don't like this modern stuff: this jelly and custard. So no modern stuff. (*Fiercely.*) D'ye hear me?

KIT. No modern stuff and no waste. That just suits me.

SIBBY (*Entering with a basket of eggs*). The road 'd hold you with the way the tar is melting. 'Tis God help Tul if he brings this weather with him.

NICHOLAS (*setting out for the door with the billhook*). Kit, all that was agreed between us, keep it in darkness for another while. And if Tul gets time and chance, he should compose an elegy in sad and loving memory of himself, and we'll send it to the Almanac.

KIT. I won't forget that either.

(NICHOLAS *goes.* SIBBY *is taking eggs out of the basket, and putting them into the bowl on the dresser.*)

KIT. That fire 'll say good-bye if we don't attend it. (*She puts turf on the fire.*)

SIBBY (*smiling*). Nicholas 'd like well to wed your farm and yourself; but sure the fear wouldn't let you.

KIT. Sure Nicholas 'd rather be fighting than not.

SIBBY. But Tuppeny and yourself could live together like two saints: never a row! And then I'd have the house to myself and could wed Ram.

KIT. D'ye remember the day long ago the gypsy took down her crystal, and told you there was a man for you?

SIBBY (*smiling*). Pelting bits of turf at each other across the hearth was the way we used to be courting in this village long ago. Some way I could never hit the one I wanted to hit.

KIT. If Tuppeny was wed in here, Ram 'd wed you in your house. His own house is too racked and fit to fall down.

SIBBY. 'Tis only the want of a wife and housekeeper is driving Ram to the pubs. Ram and myself 'll be a real love-match. He has a rubber neck from watching me these twenty years.

(TUPPENY *comes in, nose in the air, and blinking as usual. He carries a half empty bottle of whiskey. He wags a reproachful finger at* SIBBY.)

TUPPENY. You should be going about your business don't you know. A lot of jobs are calling.

SIBBY (*taking bucket*). I'll milk your cows now, Kit; and I'll milk them clean.

KIT. Ye'll reap an awful reward in Heaven.

SIBBY (*in the doorway*). They say the people of the next world are a very dark-haired race of people: no fair-haireds amongst them. (*She goes.*)

TUPPENY (*uncorking whiskey bottle*). About this match between us: did Tul make his will yet leaving the farm to you?

KIT. Not yet! He said he'd let his last hour be the hardest.

TUPPENY. Then we must keep him alive until he has that will made. Hold the bottle till I part his jaws. (*Using a farmyard rather than a sick-room technique, he pulls* TUL'S *jaws wide apart.*)

KIT. Go easy or you'll kill him.

TUPPENY. Not me! Sure I'm bottling sick cows and calves all my life don't you know? (*He grabs the bottle, and shoves the neck into* TUL'S *mouth.* TUL *soon coughs, and struggles.*)

KIT. Hold on there. You'll smother him.

TUPPENY. After all ever he drank who'd think he'd have such a small swallow?

KIT. Give it to him nice and gradual! That's better.

TUPPENY. He's taking it very greedy now. Isn't it wonderful how his throat knows 'tis whiskey, even when his brains are asleep.

KIT. His colour is improving already.

TUPPENY. I'll buy a full bottle of whiskey to-night, and never be tired of keeping him alive – until he has his will made, don't you know?

KIT. Yes, until he has his will made . . .

TUPPENY. If he dies then, it'll be a good change for you. If I was master of this farm, I'd soon double every penny you have.

KIT. The doctor cautioned hard against giving him too much at a time.

TUPPENY. That much 'll do him so! . . . (*He tries to pull out bottle.*) By crimers, Kit! His jaws have the bottle trapped! He wants more!

KIT. He has enough. Let you pull open his jaws, and I'll pull out the bottle.

TUPPENY. So best!

(*He wrenches apart* TUL'S *jaws and the bottle is extracted successfully.* TUL'S *jaws remain wide apart, and* TUPPENY *closes them with some difficulty.*)

TUPPENY. Composing must be thirsty work. There was never a poet yet but liked his bottle.

KIT. His last words to me were to wed a good farmer. But an oul' secondhand such as me! What man 'd want to put his shoes under my bed?

TUPPENY (*solemnly*). Plenty would, but I'm a special man, don't you know?

KIT. You're a great farmer and a great man every way.

TUPPENY (*solemnly*). Well, I am somehow. And the question is: are you industrious enough for me? If you aren't, I couldn't love you good enough, don't you know?

205

KIT. Sure if I had an industrious husband such as you, I'd be out working at the first light.

TUPPENY (*shaking his head dubiously*). But every time Tul and me were to do a morning's work on our mearing fences, he'd come late; and evermore his excuse 'd be that he couldn't get up because you were asleep on the tail of his shirt.

KIT. Well, that won't happen you, if we trim and shorten the tails of your shirts.

TUPPENY (*gravely*). True, don't you know. I didn't think of that. You'll trim my shirt tails first, then we can wed any time. And, please God, plenty of hard work will soon make you as lively as a wasp again.

KIT. Tul used to say I was built more for comfort than speed; but it was his own lazy ways I fell into.

TUPPENY. Give no heed to Nicholas's lies that I'd starve you, I'd never grudge enough to any woman that'd work a hard day. My motto is enough, but no extravagance – such as putting on jam and butter at the same time. So it'll have to be one or th' other: jam or butter.

KIT. Yes, one or th' other, jam or butter.

TUPPENY. Waste not, want not, as God said. (*Goes to door.*)

KIT. Don't tell anyone yet that we're engaged.

TUPPENY (*opening door*). I will not, because they might say we dosed Tul to hurry him ... Engaged! A thing I never was before; but I know this much: 'tis a time kisses should be swapped. (*Closing door again.*) So come on, Kit, and me and you will do a line for a few minutes.

KIT. No, no. Tul might wake up, and put the dying man's curse on us.

TUPPENY. No fear of that. The whiskey has him brained even if the death hasn't. So come on, and give me just one don't you know?

KIT (*retreating around* TUL). And he not dead yet! That'd be sinful.

TUPPENY (*stepping across* TUL'S *legs*). Sure isn't he as good as dead? And aren't we engaged? And amn't I giving up the finest girls in Ireland for you?

KIT. But just now I'm too heartbroken for courting.

TUPPENY. A fine long hug from a good-looking man, there's no better cure for heartbreak. Stand you divil!

(*He is shambling after her around the table.* TUL *comes to her rescue by stirring and moaning.*)

KIT. D'ye hear him? He's stirring and waking!

TUPPENY. Listen!

(TUL *moans again.*)

TUPPENY. Have no worry about that noise at all. That's only his death rattle, don't you know?

KIT. If he catches us, he won't leave me his farm.

(TUL *groans loudly.*)

KIT. He's dying! (*Running to him.*) What is it, Tul?

TUL (*feebly, eyes closed*). A heart-pill!

KIT. A heart-pill! Yes, Tul. (*She takes an aspirin from the bottle.*) How are you feeling?

TUPPENY (*setting out for door*). Look after him so. Don't let him die until he has his will made. Tonight you and me will stop up minding him, and that'll give us our chance to do another great line tonight.

(*He goes, closing door.* KIT *hurries over and bolts it.* TUL *sits up laughing at her.*)

KIT (*mopping her brow*). Another great line tonight! Tul, in pulling your daughter out of the river, you have shoved your wife into the lake.

TUL. Kit, you fooled them powerful ... And any more when Tuppeny is here, I'll stay as wide awake as the midday sun. (*He comes over, takes* TUPPENY'S *whiskey bottle off the table.*) And now we'll drink the miser's health in his own whiskey.

KIT (*bringing two glasses from the dresser*). When Rita finds that Larry is free to wed her at last, she'll give the dog's knock to that athiest fellow.

TUL. Yes, please God, we'll save her yet. And look at how God is rewarding us already for battling to save her!

KIT. Yes, fee whiskey, and all our work done for us!

TUL. Well, here's to yourself and Tuppeny!

KIT (*chuckling*). To our great line tonight!

(*They drink.*)

TUL. Who'd ever believe that to be living is good; but to be dying is better?

CURTAIN

ACT TWO

Scene One

The scene is the same, and the time is a few days later. TUL *attired in a night-shirt below which his trouser ends appear is walking up and down with his poetry notebook and his pencil. He is composing, and chuckling to himself from time to time.*

TUL (*reciting*).
   "Old Moore still comes to cheer us in December,
   Just as he did a hundred years ago;
   But the greatest bard Old Moore can e'er remember
   Higgins of Ireland is lying dead and low."

TUL. That'll leave them in no doubt that I'll soon be growing shamrocks instead of toenails.
   (*He comes to the window, looks out at the sunny scene a little wistfully, puts the notebook and pencil down on the sill, does some arm stretching and exercises like a man who is growing a little weary of confinement. He resumes his peripatetic composing. Suddenly the latch of the door rattles.* TUL *tiptoes swiftly to his bedside.*)

TUL (*calling in a weak voice*). Who's there? Kit! Is there anyone with you? No! Good.
   (*He goes to the door unbolts it, and* KIT *comes in smiling. She is dressed in her workaday clothes, and wears a white handkerchief on her head to protect it from the sun. She carries a five naggin bottle.*)

KIT. Pete wants another bottle of tea. He's working like a Dublin ragman.

TUL. If he hadn't gone to England that time, this 'd be a good farm still.
   (KIT *takes the kettle off the fire, and wets tea. She takes milk and sugar from the dresser. Tul pours some whiskey into a glass.*)

KIT (*smiling*). Have you finished the elegy for the Almanac in sad and loving memory of yourself?

TUL. I have; but it isn't perfected yet, and Nicholas and Tuppeny, in spite of their greed to wed you, don't want me to die until I have my elegy finished. (*He sips whiskey.*)

KIT (*smiling*). Between smoking and whiskey you'll have yourself embalmed before you die.

TUL. It was like a miracle how quick Rita consented to wed Larry.

KIT. And if you hadn't taken a chance, and mocked the death for her, she was a lost bird.

TUL (*walking about glass in hand*). But if Nellie Flood hadn't sent us that letter about her from England, we could never have saved her.

KIT. And now Nellie is spending as much of her holidays as she can spare with Rita, trying to talk her back into her religion.

TUL. Rita must be converted already, or she wouldn't have consented to wed Larry, and forget the athiest fellow.

KIT. But 'tis a pity that Nicholas is so greedy, demanding this farm as Rita's dowry before he'll let Larry wed her. Because it appears that Pete and Nellie are within two courts of getting married, and they'd settle down here, if we had this farm to give them.

TUL (*looking out the window*). Here are Rita and Nellie coming at last from the town!

(TUL *quickly unbolts the door, leaves his glass on the table, takes his poetry notebook, and hops into his armchair.* KIT *has put milk and sugar into a jug, pours the tea into that, stirs it thoroughly, then pours the tea into the five naggin bottle.* TUL *wraps his rugs around him.*)

KIT. That letter from England Rita got today upset her so much that she didn't know whether it was night or morning.

TUL. That must be from her athiest fellow throwing tar on her for letting him down.

KIT. Or maybe coaxing her back to him?

TUL. Tell Rita and Nellie I'm dead asleep after hearing every stroke of the clock last night. And go back to the hay you, leaving them alone here, then they might kick up talk about that letter.

KIT. Yes, that way we might glean what was in it. Sleep now. (*Looking out window.*) They'll be in a hop.

(KIT *runs back to her work at the table.* TUL *settles down to feign sleep, with a rug half across his face. The door opens and* NELLIE *and* RITA *come in.* RITA *is in her early twenties, is very pretty*

209

and very well dressed in light summer clothes. Like her mother she is lively and volatile, changing in a flash from a brilliant smile to a most serious look: she has no half moods.

NELLIE FLOOD *is about the same age; and is well dressed likewise. She is a sturdier, less sparkling but more balanced type. She has the easy poise and smile of the experienced Legion of Mary member who is used to tenacious interviewing of all kinds of characters.* RITA *carries a well filled shopping bag, and a bunch of flowers.* NELLIE *carries some magazines.*)

RITA (*eagerly*). How is daddy? (*She throws her parcels on the table, and runs over to her father.*)

KIT. You could hardly waken him with a hayfork after his bad night.

RITA (*adjusting his rugs*). The sleep 'll do him good.

NELLIE. He's looking well enough. (*She leaves the magazines on the table beside him.*)

KIT (*with a sigh*). If he is, 'tis just like you'd paint an old door.

RITA (*anxiously*). Mother, did anyone call since?

KIT. No. Were you expecting anyone?

RITA (*hastily*). No-no. I just thought that maybe Larry or Nicholas. (*She is taking parcels out of shopping bag.*)

KIT. When Nicholas calls tell him about your father's bad night. Then Nicholas 'll know for sure that this farm will soon be yours by will, and he'll delay no longer about letting Larry wed you. And now I must give Pete a hand at the hay. (*She moves to the door with her bottle of tea.*)

NELLIE. Tell Pete we'll give ye a hand in a few minutes.

KIT. God spare ye the health! This weather won't last. The moon was too bulky when it was young. (*She goes.*)

RITA (*taking flowers out of the shopping bag. Urgently*). Nellie, I am expecting a visitor. Would you arrange these in the vases? (RITA *runs into bedroom.*)

NELLIE (*smiling*). Flowers! It must be Larry!
(NELLIE *takes vases from the window sill and mantelpiece and arranges the flowers in them.*)

RITA (*coming out with a new tablecloth*). It isn't Larry, and I must tell you who it is, because you're the only one I can trust ... Alan!

NELLIE. Your English fiance! Inviting him here where he might meet Larry! You're crazy!

RITA (*ruefully*). Invite him! I sent an express telegram and a letter to stop him, but 'tis nearly certain that the telegram passed him

210

out as he was in the air on his way to Dublin.
(*She puts new tablecloth on the kitchen table, dusts and tidies the kitchen.*)

NELLIE. Is he afraid they'll coax, or bully, you into marrying Larry?

RITA. He is, though I told him I hadn't a notion of wedding Larry. Alan has to take his holidays now anyway, so he said he'd make some excuse to call here as an English friend on his way to the lakes.

NELLIE. But maybe Pete saw him with you in England and knows him by sight?

RITA. That's the awful danger, so the first chance you see, ask Pete does he know Alan by sight.

NELLIE. Out at the haymaking I'll ask him that at the first chance. Pete thinks it was all Alan's fault that you lost your religion.

RITA. It was more Ireland's and England's fault than Alan's fault; still Pete and Larry might attack Alan, and kick him out through that door.

NELLIE (*going to door*). If Alan hired a car in Dublin, he could land here any minute!

RITA. Any minute at all!

NELLIE. This may be your last chance to see the priest before Alan comes. Come on to him and you'll see he'll soon knock the bottom out of Alan's arguments.

RITA. No, I won't meet a priest, because he'd tell my parents about me, and the shock 'd kill daddy, and break mother's heart as well.

NELLIE. If you settled down in Ireland, your faith would be nearly sure to come back. It's a pity you can't bring yourself to wed Larry. And long ago the time his father stopped ye, you were all on fire to wed him.

RITA. I'm still very fond of Larry; and maybe I could wed him, if I wasn't so crazy about Alan . . .

NELLIE. Maybe that's just infatuation, a thing you'd get over, if you stayed away from Alan long enough.

RITA (*smiling*). Whether it's true love, or infatuation, I don't want to get over it. It has turned England into Heaven for me; and before it was more like Hell.

NELLIE. Yes, we get so lonely and homesick over there that we think anyone who is nice to us is Prince Charming. Especially when he's an educated man, an engineer like Alan.

RITA. Larry could have come to England when his father refused us, but he wouldn't give up his farm.

211

NELLIE. It wasn't easy for him to give up such a fine farm and house; and go into bad digs and navvying in England.

RITA. I amn't blaming Larry; and now I'm doing him the best turn anybody ever did for him: our fake engagement is tricking Nicholas into signing his farm over to Larry.

NELLIE. Once Larry has his farm in his own name he'll easy get another girl, if that'll satisfy him!

RITA. It'll have to. (*She renews her make-up before the mirror.*) (TUL *moans and wakes up.*)

RITA (*running to him*). Daddy, how are you?

TUL. I was in an awful mist of sleep . . . (*Opening his eyes.*) Rita! . . . Nellie!

NELLIE. You're looking great, Tul.

TUL (*excitedly*). Nellie, did you ever read or hear that the soul takes the shape of the body after death?

NELLIE (*smiling*). I never did, Tul.

TUL. Well, 'tis true, because I'm just after seeing my father as he was in life!

RITA. You only dreamed it, daddy. (*She gives him a glass of whiskey.*)

TUL (*taking glass in his hand – excitedly*). It was a true vision, I tell ye, and a death-token that runs in our family.

NELLIE. It's bad to be exciting yourself.

TUL. Grandfather appeared in a dream of the night to my father just before the death made cold meat of him. So my last day has come, and let ye run down to Larry and Nicholas and tell them we must all go in to the lawyer and sign up everything to day.

RITA. Is it leave the bed in the state you're in?

NELLIE. Why not bring the lawyer out here?

TUL. We ever heard that death and marriage must be kept far apart. So my deathbed is no fit place for signing Rita's marriage settlements.

RITA. That's only superstition.

TUL (*sitting up*). It is not, and if ye won't go for Larry's car, I'll go myself. (*Struggling to get out of chair.*)

RITA. Father! For Heaven's sake!

TUL. Let me out! If I had only one leg, I'll go.

RITA. Father, I'll go! Watch over him, Nellie!

NELLIE. Right! Take it easy, Tul!

(RITA *runs out and* TUL *immediately calms down.*)

TUL (*anxiously*). Well, have her brains still no spare room for religion?

212

NELLIE. Once you lose all belief in religion it's very hard to get it back. It's a pity she didn't join one of the Catholic parish societies like the Legion of Mary. In England you're an apostle or an apostate: there's no halfway like here.

TUL (*gloomily*). Kit and myself have tried every prayer and every plan to convert her; but our best has failed.

NELLIE. If you could get her to make a pilgrimage to Lourdes . . .

TUL. To Lourdes a thousand miles away! When we can't get her to even meet a priest!

NELLIE. Still she won't like to refuse your last request. So make her promise to make a pilgrimage to Lourdes, and she might have the good fortune to see a miraculous cure there.

TUL. A miraculous cure . . . ! Of a case without a cure! Of someone condemned by the doctors, like myself! (*A gleam of excitement appears in his eye.*) You think that'd convert her?

NELLIE. It should, unless she's one of the people Our Lord talked about, that wouldn't believe even if someone came back from the dead.

TUL. Well, I'll seek her pledge to go to Lourdes. But first I must bring Nicholas in to the lawyer. Run and tell Kit I want my clothes.

NELLIE. She's in the meadow field. (*She runs out.*)

TUL (*flinging off his rugs excitedly*). A miraculous cure! And surely God 'd forgive me when He knows 'tis our last chance of converting and saving her!

(*He runs into the bedroom, and can be heard moving about. The door opens, and* KIT *enters. She bolts the door quickly.*)

KIT. Tul, what's the reason that you're going in to the lawyer? Did you overhear anything?

TUL (*coming out carrying new shirt, collar and tie and new shoes*). It turned me white all I overheard. She hasn't a dog's notion of marrying Larry; and her athiest fellow is to call here any hour or minute. (*He is putting on the shirt, collar and tie, etc.*)

KIT. Coming in here! A black athiest that believes in nothing but his own needs! He'll steal all he can lay hands on! (*She takes an old fashioned purse from the dresser, puts it into her pocket.*)

TUL. I must get Nicholas to sign over to Larry before her Englishman shows up and shows her up!

KIT. Sure what good is Larry's farm to her if she won't marry him?

TUL. If she's converted, she would give up this athiest fellow and wed Larry; and at last God is after enlightening me about how to convert her. I'm going to work a miracle.

213

KIT (*cynically*). Which miracle? Is it laziness or whiskey you're giving up?

TUL. Neither, nor poetry ... Watch now. (*He empties a small aspirin bottle, and fills it with water from the bucket.*) Tomorrow morning we'll tell them this came by post from my cousin the nun, water from some holy well out foreign; and that it has cured many people condemned by doctors. Then when the time comes, and I'm at my last gasp, you'll throw this water and a prayer on me; and I'll rise up as cured as Lazarus.

KIT (*dismayed*). Fake a miracle! But, Tul, that'd be very sinful.

TUL. We aren't doing it for gain or glory; we're doing it only because 'tis the last chance of converting and saving our only daughter. She has refused again to meet a priest.

KIT. A fake miracle! Who ever heard of such a thing! I don't like it, Tul, by no means.

TUL (*grimly*). Neither do I; but 'tis better than to have the divil toasting her and turning her like you'd be turning a herring on the tongs. And no Christian, except me and you, will ever hear or find out it was anything but a true miracle.

KIT (*glancing out window*). Here's Sibby coming, and she like a Christmas postman, she has so many parcels. Wedding clothes as sure as there's a tail on the cat!

TUL. And maybe Nicholas and Tuppeny have wedding clothes bought for their wedding with you!

KIT. And if you fail to die, none of them can get wed. They'll all be ruined according to themselves.

TUL (*grimly*). All my life I thought I was a valuable man that the world could hardly get on without; but my dying has shown me that I'm only in everyone's way. (*He gets back into his armchair, pulls the rugs around him.*)

(*A knock is heard at the door.*)

KIT. Come in if you're good-looking!

(KIT *goes into bedroom, and* SIBBY *comes in, cheerful as ever, dressed as in the last act, and carrying two large parcels.*)

SIBBY (*excitedly*). Tul, last night I dreamed of a runaway horse, and a runaway horse means a speedy news.

TUL. That means ye'll soon have news of God sending for me!

SIBBY. That's it, Tul, and we'll all cry our fills after you; but I'm in hopes that I'll be less lonesome after myself and Ram are wed. (*She puts the parcels on table, proceeds to open them, showing a new pair of lady's boots and new clothes.*)

214

TUL. Yes, the double bed is the best medicine out for the lonesomeness.

SIBBY. I'll put on my wedding clothes now. I'd like Kit to judge them.

TUL. Why did you go buying them so soon?

SIBBY. So as to give you a fine stylish funeral. Sure only for you dying, none of us 'd be able to get wed at all.

TUL. But, if I heal out of this sickness, you might want to return them clothes.

SIBBY (*cheerfully*). No, you're looking very ghostly, Tul, so you'll die away fast the same as the doctor foretold.

TUL. Isn't it wonderful the way the best doctors do be boozers?

(KIT *comes out of the bedroom, having changed into her Sunday clothes, and carrying her Sunday hat and jacket.*)

SIBBY (*showing her some underwear*). Are these nice, Kit?

KIT. Very nice, Sibby. Tul, you will have a fine stylish funeral.

TUL. The man with a bad wife always gets – out of pity – a big funeral!

KIT. But, Sibby, does Ram really mean to wed you? Maybe he's only out to wheedle money out of you to buy enough drink to weigh him down.

SIBBY (*taking off her topcoat and putting on new skirt and blouse over her old clothes*). Sure Ram and myself 'd be wedded and bedded a basketful of years since, only for his father wouldn't let him wed; and at last Ram lost heart and started going for feeds of drink.

TUL. Still, if Ram is now a bondsman to drink, he could talk love, and want only to sup your land and money.

SIBBY. If that was his mind, why did he urge me ever so hard to spare no expense in buying new clothes from the skin out? And he urged me to go to the hairdressers and get my hair warped and my face improved – well, as much as they could.

(*She takes off her topcoat, but not her old hat, and puts on new skirt.*)

KIT. Maybe he has a true regard for her!

SIBBY. He has that! And he's a shocking fine man: as big as a scoundrel!

(KIT, *having brushed her hair before the mirror, gives* TUL'S *a brush. Having brushed his shoes, she puts them on him.* SIBBY *has put on the new skirt over her old clothes, by this time.*)

SIBBY. Is this nice?

TUL. You're as dressed a woman as ever I seen.

215

KIT. Ram is the luckiest man of his name.

SIBBY. I had great taste evermore, thank God! My last suit was so nice that I couldn't bear to buy anything new these ten years. (*She starts putting on the new jumper. Suddenly there is a loud knock on the door.*)

KIT. Who's there?

RAM (*rough voice*). Ram!

SIBBY. Ram! Let him in! (*She runs to door eagerly.*)

KIT (*stopping her*). No! No! Hide back in the room till you're dressed right.

TUL. Take off your old clothes and dress right.

SIBBY. Don't let him go till he sees me.

KIT. We won't!

(SIBBY *and per parcels are bundled into the bedroom by* KIT *and the door is closed.*)

KIT. I'm coming, Ram!

(*She opens the door and* RAM *comes in. He is a big, powerfully-built man in his early fifties, still vigorous and loud-voiced and wild-looking with the complexion of a hard drinker. His look is often wild, often gloomy, sometimes wildly joyous and occasionally quite tender and sad. His face is marked by some fresh and some old scars and he wears a bloodstained bandage around his head. His battered hat hangs on the back of his head. His shirt neck is open and so is his jacket, and his clothes are untidy and torn and old. He wears a leather belt around his waist and its brass buckle is made even more formidable by an ass's shoe tied to it. He carries a long, dangerous looking ash-plant and a porter bottle sticks up out of his jacket pocket.*)

KIT. How are you, Ram?

RAM (*gloomy and wild and little drunk*). Rough, Kit, rough: dog-rough and boozed to dull my troubles. (*He comes over to* TUL, *stick in hand.*) If it isn't too busy a question, Tul, d'ye think are you far from the timber?

TUL (*smiling*). Near enough to suit everyone, except maybe myself.

RAM. We'll be awful lost for you, and we'd like you'd live a hundred years. But I don't want to spend my rates penny on wedding clothes I can't use if you fail to die.

TUL. Pay your rates first, Ram. You can wed any time.

RAM. If marriage or something doesn't change my ways soon I'll die in drink or fighting, then I'll be sent to the burning mountain. (*He pours a drink of whiskey for himself, feverishly.*)

KIT. Did the Guards trace yet the cyclist that knocked you down?

216

RAM. Cyclist! That was only an excuse I gave to fool the Guards.

TUL. You were fighting again, so?

RAM. With the cursed tinkers over a tinker's wife that found me as drunk as a fiddler, and came home with me and robbed me of the money for my marriage and wedding clothes. (*Lifting bandage.*) A doubled hoop of a barrel burst my head like a knife.

KIT. 'Tis time a fresh bandage was put on that. (*She goes into bedroom.*)

TUL. Did you fail to recapture your marriage money?

RAM (*wildly, producing an old battered purse*). There it is, barring a couple of pounds they had drank. Single hands, with only this belt and stick, I recaptured my wedding costs and, after shedding my best blood for it, I'll be tempted to take your life away, Tul, if you fail to die. (*He stands over* TUL *shaking his stick at him threateningly.*)

TUL. I'll make sure to die, Ram, and save an old friend's neck from the rope.

TUL. A middling cross woman with a chisel in her tongue – that'd be the best wife to convert you out of the drink.

RAM. No – that kind 'd hide the pounder behind her back to give me a blow. I'd cuff her for that, and then the police 'd be sent for.

(KIT *comes out of the room with a bandage.*)

RAM (*sitting down*). God spare you the health, Kit. (*She rebandages his wound.*)

TUL. But Sibby is too easy-going – she'll let you drink ahead.

RAM (*gravely*). Sibby is very gentle and an innocent kind of a being, and that way she may soften me out and shame me out of the boozing and the fighting.

KIT. She has a fine, warm, dry house, what you need now that your own roof is fit to fall in.

RAM (*gloomily*). The way it is with the thatched roof: when the weather is good, you don't need to go repairing it; and when the weather is bad, you can't.

TUL. Your house and land need Sibby's money; and when a woman puts her bit of money along with a man's bit of land and money, that's all love is.

RAM (*gloomily*). But one thing is sure: if I marry her for her money, I'll drink all her money.

KIT. D'ye think you can love her good enough to spare her money?

RAM. I could if she'd dress more up-to-date, and not have her clothes hitting the ground. I begged and craved her to dress more up-to-date, and to spare no expense at the hairdressers and beautifiers, but she'll do nothing. She'll stay as old-fashioned as the hills of Connemara: then I won't be able to love her good enough. (*Jumping up wildly.*) D'ye know what I'm going to tell ye? I wish to God I was a bush!

TUL. You shouldn't be saying that, Ram!

KIT. It isn't right!

RAM (*rampaging about wildly*). Right or wrong, 'tis true. If I was a bush, I could be cut down, or I could die, but when I died I couldn't be changed into an evil spirit the same as now.

KIT. Your father wasn't for your good, and wouldn't sign over his farm and let you wed when you were young and honourable.

SIBBY (*coming out of room smiling*). Ram, I dreamed of a runaway horse, and that means a speedy news.

(RAM *is standing with his back to her, and he stiffens angrily.*)

RAM (*fiercely to* TUL). Blood and bones! Ye had her at the keyhole set so as to trap me in words!

KIT. No, Ram, she was only trying on her wedding clothes.

(RAM *turns fiercely, then his expression changes, first to astonishment, and then to delight.*)

RAM. Sibby! You look as nice as an American apple. (*Wildly.*) Thank God, I amn't a bush.

SIBBY (*smiling*). Thank God you aren't, Ram.

RAM (*Coming over to her*). Sibby, since Lot's wife there never was a woman so changed and so promoted. We'll wed as soon as Tuppeny and Kit are wed in here.

SIBBY. Yes, and the sooner the better, Ram; but not wishing Tul any harm.

TUL. I know that well; and I wish ye both the angel's happiness and the Devil's luck.

(*The door opens, and* TUPPENY *enters carrying a large parcel. He is displeased to see* RAM *and* SIBBY *together.*)

TUPPENY (*angrily*). What's going on here, don't you know?

KIT. What's going on evermore since the first night long ago that Adam left Eve home.

TUPPENY. If you wed Ram, he'll give you a hundred acres. That's the amount of land covered by the road from here to the poorhouse. (*He opens his parcel on the table.*)

RAM. I will not starve her. Anymore the sun will be shining for me; and I'll be working so fast that ye won't be able to see me.

TUPPENY. She'll be like the woman long ago that hadn't a rag on her back when she got wed, but when she was a while wed she was all rags.

TUL. Talk a little less blunt, Tuppeny. 'Tis often a person's mouth broke his nose.

RAM (*laughing wildly*). Blood and bones! Never fear, Tul, I'm so happy now that he couldn't vex me even if he spat in my eye. Come on, Sibby, till we admire his wedding clothes. (*They examine clothes.*)

TUPPENY (*taking off his jacket and waistcoat*). A fine worsted suit! You wouldn't get a finer from here to Dublin and back.

KIT. 'Tis me that'll be proud and happy coming down the aisle along with that.

TUPPENY. Tul, myself and Kit won't wed until you're well cold; but I bought my wedding clothes now to let you see how proud and happy I'll make her.

TUL. Good. But don't make her too proud to gain Heaven.

RAM (*coming over*). Tul, I'd like greatly to read your elegy in sad and loving memory of yourself.

TUL (*giving the poetry notebook*). Here it is, and tell me if I'm writing the truth in saying ye were all so sorrowful after me.

RAM. Sibby, we'll tell him the truth about that, be it sweet or sour.

(RAM *and* SIBBY *sit at the table reading the elegy.*)

TUPPENY. But, Tul, there's one very deep question: if a woman marries twice which is her husband in Heaven.

TUL. The old people used to say her first husband is the one she must go with in Heaven.

KIT. If that's so, I'll be very sorry to lose you, Tuppeny. The finest image of a man since Jack Dempsey!

TUL. The way it is, I intend to lead a very quiet and pious life in Heaven and a wife makes it impossible for a man to be quiet, and very hard for him to be pious. So in the next world, Tuppeny, she's yours. I resign her to you altogether.

TUPPENY (*shaking* TUL'S *hand warmly*). A thousand thanks, Tul, don't you know? and the measure you gave is the measure you'll get. As soon as your grave settles down I'll put a fine headstone up with your name picked out in letters so deep that they'll defy time.

KIT. But ye needn't leave room for my name on it, because I'll will myself to be buried with Tuppeny. (KIT *goes into bedroom.*)

SIBBY. Ram, I'll never desert your grave like that, even if I do marry secondly.

RAM. Kit is turning mean and queer like Tuppeny himself.

(TUPPENY *takes two naggin bottles of whiskey out of his pockets*

219

and shoves them under TUL'S *blanket.*)

TUPPENY. Here, Tul, but don't tell Kit on account of the doctor saying too much whiskey was bad.

TUL. Thanks, Tuppeny. My blood is gone cold and needs warming no matter what the doctor says.

RAM. Tuppeny, are you spending for Tul's good, or just to make sure of his widow?

(*The door opens and* NICHOLAS *comes in, dressed for town in his best suit and hat.*)

NICHOLAS (*grimly*). Tul, I hear you want me before the lawyer today to sign over my farm to Larry, and let him wed Rita without delay.

TUL. Yes, Nicholas, I want to see her happily settled before ye hearse me off to the bony acre.

NICHOLAS. I know you have willed your own farm to her as a dowry, but if you fail to die, she'll have no dowry; so I'll not let Larry wed her until I see a surer sign of death in you.

TUL. Last night I got the surest death token yet. An awful lamentable crying was knocking about outside the house all night.

(KIT *comes back from bedroom.*)

SIBBY. The banshee!

NICHOLAS. No, it was only cats.

KIT. No, it was ghosts. You couldn't fool us with cats.

TUPPENY. And did ye try to see what ye could hear, don't you know?

KIT. Several times I opened the door, and stroked a match; but could see nothing.

NICHOLAS (*impressed*). Well, everyone that's going to die gets some kind of a notice; but we never heard of any man to get as much notice as Tul.

KIT. Tul, go into the doctor while you're in town today; and if the doctor says what he said before, that you're dead only to wash you, Nicholas 'll sign over his farm to Larry today; and let him wed Rita.

NICHOLAS. Well, right, I will; but after that, if you pull out of this sickness, and deprive us of your farm and your widow, I'll put you through the wickedest and the worst lawyers in Ireland.

TUL. That I may die a sinner if I don't take to the Heavens after Rita's match is made.

TUPPENY. Nicholas, do you think Kit 'd wed you, a contrary oul' geezer of the Burkes, one of the three dirty drops the divil let

220

fall while he was running.

NICHOLAS. Judas starved himself to make money the same as you; but Judas had enough shame to hang himself. (*Raising his stick.*) That's it. Run as fast as your long crooked legs can carry you. (TUPPENY *runs to the fire, takes up the tongs and turns.*)

TUPPENY. Come on now, and I'll give you some of this iron on the head!

TUL (*weakly*). Ructions 'll stop my heart like a clock.

KIT. Ram, part them quick!

NICHOLAS (*keeping far away from the tongs*). One tip of this and he won't get his breath for hours.

(*But already* RAM *is between them.*)

RAM. Sure ye should live the two best pals in the world, because ye're the world's two most ignorant men.

NICHOLAS (*turning to* RAM). When we want advice we'll ask a man. We won't ask an old boozy make-mischief who isn't a drop's blood to a man.

RAM. Thank God I amn't a drop's blood to either of ye. I'd sooner be a bush with the four winds tormenting me.

TUPPENY (*to* NICHOLAS *plaintively*). And my fool of a sister is as fond of that fellow as ever a cow was fond of a head of cabbage. (*A car horn is heard, and* RITA *runs in.*)

RITA. Larry's car is here. Are ye ready?

TUL. We're ready. Help me out let ye.

KIT. Let ye not hurry him, or ye'll put him to death. (RITA *runs out. All help* TUL *to his feet.*)

RAM. Lean well on us.

TUPPENY. For a man who's a week without eating anything you're weighty enough yet, don't you know?

TUL. If I'm heavy, 'tis with the weight of sins. (RAM *and* TUPPENY *help* TUL *out.* KIT *gets a rug and a bottle of whiskey.* RITA *runs out.*)

NICHOLAS. Kit, a dying man does often turn jealous, so we'll want to watch out, or Tul might slip in a clause forbidding you to wed.

KIT. You'll be my state councillor defeating every wrong clause in his will.

SIBBY. I'll see ye off, and then mind the house for ye. (NICHOLAS, KIT *and* SIBBY *go out. Immediately* RITA *and* NELLIE *run in.*)

RITA (*anxiously*). What did Pete say? Does he know Alan by sight?

NELLIE. Lately as his gang were passing in their lorry, he saw

221

yourself and a fellow coming out of a cinema.

RITA. Hell! It was Alan, of course! So he'll surely recognise him.

NELLIE. What'll we do now?

RITA. They're making me come in with them to the lawyer. Will you mind the house here and, if Alan calls, bring him up to your house until I get back?

NELLIE. Right! I'll do that.

RITA (*going to door*). And now I'll have to spin lies the length of your arm to stop Larry from buying an engagement ring for me.

NELLIE. It's a pity you can't tell him that your engagement is a fake to trick Nicholas into signing his farm over to Larry.

RITA. Larry 'd be too much afraid of his father to go through with it if he knew it was a trick. Then he'd maybe never get his farm, or liberty to wed. (*She takes ring from her handbag, puts it on her finger.*)

LARRY (*running in eagerly*). Rita, are you ready?

NELLIE (*laughing*). She is ready and willing. I'll give Pete your message. (*She goes out.*)

LARRY (*exulting*). Rita, isn't it hard to believe it! In half an hour father's farm will be in my own name at last, then I can wed my own choice.

RITA (*smiling*). Any more, you'll have to be kicking girls away from you.

LARRY. You're the only girl I ever wanted to marry or ever will. (*Putting arms around her.*) We'll go straight to the jewellers, and I'll buy you an engagement ring that'll outshine the sun.

RITA. I'd like to save you and me that much money, Larry, and it so happens that I can. Wouldn't this do?

(*Showing him* ALAN'S *engagement ring.*)

LARRY. 'Tis winking nicely, but I'm more of a judge of jobber calves.

RITA. Ask your jeweller and he'll tell you it's a true and a costly engagement ring.

(LARRY'S *face clouds over suddenly. He releases her and walks away.*)

RITA (*following him*). Larry, what's wrong?

LARRY. A rumour crossed the water that you were engaged to an Englishman. This was his ring, and now I know why you stopped writing to me.

RITA (*trying to laugh this off*). Not at all, Larry! If I was engaged to an Englishman, why would I get engaged to you now?

LARRY. Maybe to deceive your father, so as he'll will this farm to you.

RITA. I'll tell you who gave me this ring. An Irish fellow I saved from a trap in England.

LARRY. What trap?

RITA. He was going marrying a girl, and never knew until I told him that she was married already and that her husband, a crazy ex-soldier, was roaming all London with a gun to shoot her. The Irish lad reckoned I had saved his life, so he gave me her engagement ring.

LARRY (*suspiciously*). And how is it that it fits you so exact?

RITA. Sure, it doesn't! (*Moving it on her fingers.*) It's too loose on me.

LARRY (*shamefaced*). Rita, forgive me for doubting you!

RITA (*smiling*). Sure an engagement ring 'd make any man doubt. I was nearly afraid to show it to you at all.

LARRY. But it wouldn't be right or lucky for us to get engaged with another man's ring. So today in town I'll buy you a new ring; and you can sell that one.

RITA. But a jeweller wouldn't give us half the value of this; and he'd charge us twice as much for a ring not half as good.

LARRY. What harm? After waiting half my life for you I'm not looking into fifty pounds.

RITA. But I cherish this ring as your own after keeping it two years for you.

LARRY. No matter; we'll buy a new one today, and then go in to the priest about our wedding day.

RAM (*entering*). Will you hurry on, and don't have your father dying on the road.

RITA. Run, Larry. (*She runs out.*)

LARRY. I'll knock grit out of the road I'll drive so fast.

(*He runs out. RAM sits at the table, and takes up TUL'S poetry notebook.*)

RAM (*gravely*). "Elegy in sad and loving memory of the late Tul Higgins, Poet and Patriot. Composed by his dearest and best friend." Best friend is right – himself!

(SIBBY *comes in, smiling as usual.*)

SIBBY. You're by yourself, Ram?

RAM. "Sibby and I, and nobody by,
On the rocks of Carrigabawna!"

SIBBY. You have nice ditties of songs.

(*She rummages under TUL'S rugs until she finds one of TUPPENY'S small bottles of whiskey.*)

223

RAM. Songs is nearly all I have, Sibby but, if I was strong enough in money, I'd give you a thousand pounds every day.

SIBBY (*uncorking whiskey bottle and placing it on table in front of him*). We'll be happy, even though we'll have no help.

(TUPPENY *enters.* SIBBY *goes to fire and lights a cigarette butt.*)

TUPPENY. Ram, sound Tul's elegy till we see has the poor fellow slipped into any lies in it, don't you know? (*He sits near table.*)

RAM. Yes that he asked us to do. (*He reads.*)

"Our homes are lonely, our hearts are broken,
While we those tears of sorrow shed.
Our friend is gone, ne'er to return,
Alas, he rests now among the dead."

Will your heart be broken, Tuppeny?

TUPPENY. The truth is, we'll be lonesome after him for a while, don't you know? but not heartbroken. We'd be twice as heartbroken if he fails to die. (*He starts filling his pipe.*)

SIBBY. Poor Tul of the Songs. We'll all be ruined if he fails to die.

RAM. Yes, he's in our way. We're all in someone's way. And when our own end comes, the breed belonging to us will be kneeling beside us with their hearts crying, "What'll we do without him?" and their brains crying, "What'll we do if he fails to die?"

TUPPENY (*filling his pipe*). Sure wasn't that the truest proverb of Ireland: the grave often brings plenty to those who need it badly?

SIBBY (*cheerfully*). We let the world slip by us. That's why nothing can save us now but Tul's grave.

TUPPENY (*angrily*). And how can Tul die soon, don't you know? when Ram is drinking the whiskey I bought for Tul with my own sweat-earned money?

RAM (*refilling his glass*). Whiskey or no, he'll die soon; and I'm saving you from the sin of murder.

TUPPENY (*jumping up*). What murder? My whiskey is only shortening and sweetening his dying.

RAM (*grimly*). Buy more for him then. I need this whiskey more than you need money. (*He drinks.*)

TUPPENY. Well, it serves you right if Tul staggers out for a score of years, don't you know?

CURTAIN

ACT TWO

Scene Two

The scene is the same, and it is an hour or two later. NELLIE *is reading a magazine when the door opens and* PETE *enters. He is twenty-seven, a sturdy country man smartened up in clothes and in manner by two years in England. He seems a more energetic and serious type than his father, and at that moment he looks a little depressed. He wears a straw hat, no jacket, and carries a hay-rake with a couple of teeth missing.*

PETE. They're not back yet from the lawyer?

NELLIE (*jumping up*). Not yet, Pete; but it's time I started readying their tea. (*She lays the table for tea.*)

PETE. By now everything is signed and sealed, and you and me are done out of this farm that was to be our home. This world is a queer auction. You and me kept our religion in England, and now we have to give up our future home to save the one who threw away her religion. (*He takes a couple of spare rake teeth off the mantelpiece, and rams them into the rake.*)

NELLIE (*smiling*). Well, they say anything you give away God gives it back to you.

PETE. And just when we had enough money saved in England to buy an addition of land that'd make this farm big enough to marry on.

NELLIE. Our savings will pay the deposit on a house in England; and when we have a house of our own we can wed in comfort any time.

PETE (*staring*). What are the fancy table cloth and the flowers for? Is she expecting someone?

NELLIE. When there's a sick person in the house people are always expecting someone.

PETE. But she got an English stamped letter today; and I'd say it was from her Englishman, because it stunned her. If only I

225

could find that letter. (*He searches the dresser drawers and shelves.*) Their honeymoon holidays were to begin yesterday, so maybe he'll fly over, and try to coax her to give up Larry, and sell this farm and buy a home for themselves in England with the money. His flat landlady won't allow children.

NELLIE. Are you sure that you'd know him if you saw him again?

PETE. I glimpsed him with her only once from our passing lorry; but I took the full of my eyes of him as good as I could. And if he comes in that door, he'll go out again fast with a bigger swelled head than he came in with.

NELLIE. But if he was a bigot and a bully she'd hardly fall in love with him. Maybe she never asked him for a church wedding. The registry office marriage is very handy and cheap.

PETE. Some girls will marry anything to get out of a lonesome flat, or a bad digs, or a tough job.

NELLIE. The car! They're back (*runs to window*) and Nicholas is with them still!

PETE. That means this farm is now willed to Rita.

RITA (*running in anxiously*). How are things? Any visitors?

NELLIE. All well, and no visitors.

PETE (*suspiciously*). Why? Are you expecting anyone?

RITA. No one in particular; but some English friends are touring Ireland these days.

LARRY (*entering in great humour*). Rita, see if this engagement ring isn't nicer and a better fit for you than that Irishman's. (*Opens ring box.*)

RITA (*dismayed*). Larry, I told you not to.

LARRY. Sure that's why I bought it when you thought I was going for a drink. But here's father coming in, and never let him know it cost sixty pounds.

(*He helps* NICHOLAS *and* KIT *to bring in* TUL, *who seems very weak indeed. They lower him into his armchair.*)

KIT. That journey was too much for him.

PETE. Ye all deserve free lodgings in jail for letting him go.

TUL. A heart-pill.

RITA. Here, Daddy. (*She puts an aspirin in his mouth.*)

KIT. Drown it down with this. (*She gives him some whiskey.*)

LARRY. He was as bad many a time.

NICHOLAS. They'll be no next time. The doctor said this round 'd finish him.

(RITA *carries* TUL'S *topcoat and hat into the bedroom.* NELLIE *resumes readying the tea.*)

226

NICHOLAS (*turning on Larry*). What does she want two rings for when your mother did with one? I'll bet that engagement ring cost up against twenty pound.

LARRY (*smiling*). Sure we can sell it again, if bad times come.

NICHOLAS. Two rings for these young women, and a man 'd need the nerve of a ghost to eat anything they'd cook or bake.

(*There is a knock at the door.*)

LARRY. Someone is cracking the door.

NICHOLAS. Someone is. I heard a rat-tat-tat. (*He opens door, and then respectfully.*) Good day, sir!

ALAN (*off*). Does Miss Rita Higgins live here?

NICHOLAS. She do, but she's soon marrying out of here to my son.

KIT (*dismayed*). Good tonight! Ask him in Nicholas.

NELLIE (*running into bedroom*). Rita, you're wanted!

NICHOLAS. That's a fine car you had under you, sir. Come in.

ALAN. Thanks very much. I will.

(ALAN *come in, a good-looking refined looking, pleasant and cheerful looking young English city man. He carries a fishing rod in its bag, and wears an anglers suit and hat. As he comes in,* RITA *and* NELLIE *come out of the bedroom.*)

ALAN (*smiling*). Which of you is Miss Rita Higgins?

RITA. I am, sir!

ALAN. An Irish friend of yours in our office gave me this for you. (*He hands* RITA *a letter.*)

RITA (*looking at address*). Maureen's handwriting! Many thanks, sir.

ALAN. She said your people might be able to put me on to some good fishing around here.

RITA. They might, sir! Won't you sit down, sir! (*She opens the letter and reads it.*)

ALAN. Yes, thanks – for a few moments.

LARRY (*cheerfully*). Here, sir! Take the weight of your socks, sir.

(LARRY *takes a chair from the kitchen table, sets it out at the centre stage for* ALAN. LARRY *sits on another chair himself.* RITA *is beside him standing and reaching the letter with frequent anxious glances at* PETE *who is standing up beside* TUL *and staring at the newcomer suspiciously.*)

TUL (*to* PETE). Give him a drink, Pete, to help him on his way. (*But* PETE *stands staring darkly at* ALAN.)

KIT (*Marking this*). Look sharp, Pete. Give them all a round, quick!

ALAN. I'm getting it!

(PETE *goes inside* TUL *to the little table, takes the bottle of*

227

whiskey and uncorks it slowly. NELLIE *runs to the dresser for glasses. In the meantime conversation is proceeding.*)

ALAN. Don't bother, please!

NICHOLAS. Why wouldn't we? Isn't it England that's keeping us all going?

ALAN (*laughing*). Is it? I thought it was the Irish who kept England going!

LARRY (*in great humour*). Any work they do, they're well paid for it, and they find the Englishman as honest as the stars.

NICHOLAS. No mater how much the Englishman pays, his hand doesn't be lonesome after it.

(NELLIE *holds the glasses on a tray for* PETE *to fill.*)

KIT. You'll wait and have tea with us, sir?

ALAN. Please don't bother! I've only another few miles to go to my hotel.

NICHOLAS. You're tired travelling, but the whiskey and the tea will make you as lively as a hound again.

LARRY. About the fishing, sir. Lord Duneagle has some fine fishing but he has a very mean scoundrel of a water-bailiff. No man can bribe him.

ALAN. No matter! Loughs Corrib and Mask and Carra will keep me going.

NICHOLAS. There you'll have forty miles of the finest free fishing in Europe.

(PETE, *taking the tray of glasses from* NELLIE *gives glasses to* LARRY *and* NICHOLAS *and his father, then comes with the last glass to* ALAN. *As he approaches,* ALAN *lowers his eyes a little.*)

PETE. Take a swallow, sir.

ALAN. Thanks very much. You're very kind.

(ALAN *takes the glass smilingly, but still does not look* PETE *in the eye.*)

PETE. Make yourself at home, sir. Take off your hat, sir.

(*Reaching out suddenly he takes of* ALAN'S *hat, and drops it into his lap.*)

ALAN (*smiling uneasily*). Thanks!

PETE (*fiercely*). Hell's fire! 'Tis him! Without the hat I'm as sure as there's a hand on my body! Buy your own whiskey!

(*He hits* ALAN'S *hand, spilling the whiskey into his eyes and blinding him for the next couple of minutes.*)

RITA (*running between them*). Pete, are you gone mad?

PETE. I didn't give up this farm for you to sell it and give the price to this scoundrel.

228

KIT. Pete, you're talking wild.

RITA (*to* ALAN). Are you blinded badly?

ALAN. I'll be all right in a moment or two.

LARRY (*rising in wrath and dismay*). As sure as ever I was called Larry, this is the boyo that bought her the engagement ring!

PETE. He is, and a bigoted athiest that tried to bully her out of all religion. (*Going to door, he flings it open.*) Here, get out you blackguard, before I beat a blast on you and tumble you.

ALAN (*rising quietly*). I'm going!

RITA. Alan, don't heed him! It's my house as much as his.

TUL (*sharply*). Pete! Cancel your orders!

KIT. Or she may go with him!

LARRY (*throwing* ALAN'S *fishing rod out the door*). Here, out, Englishman!

ALAN (*handkerchief to his eyes*). I'm going!

RITA. If ye hit him, we'll bring ye before the court!

PETE (*shoving* ALAN *out*). Snow to your heels, and never again come within an atom bomb's range of this place.

LARRY. If you do, it'll take three men to take my thumb off your throat. (*He flings* ALAN'S *hat out after him.*)

RITA. Two of ye are well fit to bully a lone man, but ye'll not bully me. I'll follow him through the world and leave ye to drink out your old farms. Alan, wait for me! (*She runs out despondently.*)

TUL (*moaning loudly*). I'm dying! Tell her my last hour has come!

KIT. She'll knock a long run out of us now. (*She goes out despondently.*)

LARRY (*at door – Calling*). Rita, don't desert me and us going together since the year of one! (*He goes out.*)

TUL. Pete! Larry! Save her! The worst pain of this world loses its edge after a while, but if she dies with him she'll be an evil spirit for ever!

NELLIE. Our only chance now is to keep Alan, too! (*She goes to door.*)

TUL. Quick! Tell him before he starts the car!

(NELLIE *hurries out.*)

NICHOLAS (*In a fury*). So this is the damsel I gave up my farm for? Marrying an athiest and a conjurer and an artist born at the hour of scandal!

PETE (*bitterly*). Yes, bell that all over the country now.

(PETE *pours out some whiskey, and offers it to his father.*)

NICHOLAS. We won't marry her at all now.

TUL (*refusing whiskey*). Fetch her quick! I'm dying.

229

NICHOLAS (*fiercely*). May the divil die along with you! Tricking me out of my farm and home for such a wench!

PETE. Father, make a new will quick while you're able. If you don't, Rita will sell the farm, and mother will have to live with that atheist in England, and he won't allow a priest to her deathbed.

TUL (*Moaning*). Bring the two back quick before I'm gone.

PETE. But she'll only hinder you from making a new will.

TUL. Don't refuse your father's dying request.

PETE. All right! I'll tell them, but you're sentencing your home to the auctioneer's hammer and your wife to an exile sky.

(PETE *goes out.* LARRY *comes in.*)

LARRY (*despairingly*). No hope! He's starting the car. And my heart craving for her in the world's worst way!

NICHOLAS. Don't be sorry for anything but your sins. I'll put you through the high court for defrauding me out of my farm. Five years you'll get, and that you may die under it!

LARRY. Wasn't it she and her father tricked me, and made me a public fool and a byeword?

TUL. Farewell, Nicholas. I'm going fast.

NICHOLAS. Not half fast enough; but you have more lives than the cat. While we're worn out working for you, you're going up one sleeve and down the other, and we don't know which.

RITA (*running in*). Father, forgive me, forgive me!

NICHOLAS. Tul, if you don't forgive before you die, you're lost. Hurry up, you scoundrel, forgive the bitch!

LARRY. Father, if you don't stop that tinker's litany, I'll put you out, and am able to do.

NICHOLAS. Mister-my-good-man, do you know who you're talking to?

LARRY. Do you? I'm the leal owner of your farm now, so you can't boss me any more, or give me the road.

KIT (*running in*). Tul, Tul, don't die on me!

NELLIE (*entering*). Here's Alan!

ALAN (*entering*). How is he? I'm very sorry.

NICHOLAS. Too late you're sorry. Why didn't you wed an English collier's daughter, or a cotton-dodger, or a typewriter. And millions of them beyond, and all jumping out of their skins to marry anything!

RITA (*giving* ALAN *a chair*). It wasn't marriage chances he was looking for; it was marriage choices; and he has made his choice now for once and for all.

TUL (*faintly*). Kit?

KIT. Yes, Tul?

TUL. I heard a kind of a heavenly voice. If it wasn't Nicholas, it was an angel.

KIT. Sure maybe you heard both. But Nicholas was shouting, and angels do be singing.

TUL (*tempted*). I hear lovely music and singing . . .

NICHOLAS (*disgusted*). Well, d'ye see this pair of hands? (*Holds up his own.*) They'll never work a hard day again. To think of him after forty year's laziness getting played and sung straight into Heaven!

CURTAIN

ACT THREE

The scene is the same and the time is a few days later, in the afternoon. TUL *is in his armchair sleeping soundly. A half empty whiskey bottle and a glass stand on the little table within reach, also the bottle of aspirin 'heart tablets' and the little bottle of 'miracle working' water.* TUL'S *poetry notebook and another book lie on the rug as if they had dropped from his hands.*

A motor car is heard pulling up outside; the door opens and RITA *enters followed by* ALAN. RITA *looks serious enough, but* ALAN *is in his usual cheerful mood. She carries her shopping bag, and he carries his fishing bag.*

RITA. Daddy! . . . I hope it's only asleep he is, and not as full as the moon with drink! Wake him and tell him the priest is on his way here. (*Hurriedly she empties her shopping bag onto the table.*)

ALAN (*holding up* TUL'S *whiskey bottle*). Not bad going! – unless he got help!

RITA. His excuse always is that the nicest whiskey in the world is the miser's whiskey. Poor Tuppeny!

ALAN. Before I wake him: this is our first chance of taking his pulse. (*He takes* TUL *by the wrist, and looks at his watch.*)

RITA. He'd always refuse saying, "Too many doctors is worse than none at all."

ALAN. He wasn't far wrong there; but I know this much: the normal rate is around seventy two.

(*While he takes* TUL'S *pulse,* RITA *unparcels some groceries and puts them into the dresser. Then she unparcels some drapery items, and leaves them on the table.*)

RITA. I'm sorry now I told Pete about me going back to England with you tomorrow. That's why he told the Parish Priest about me today. Their last chance to save my sinful soul! I wish they'd mind their own business, like you English, and let every man go to hell in his own way. (*She goes into the bedroom, comes out immediately with a suitcase; and proceeds to pack the new clothes into it.*) As soon as mother, or Pete, come back you and me will drive off to the mountains for the day, and so dodge the priest.

ALAN. His pulse rate seems normal enough to me. But maybe sleep slows it down to normal.

RITA. Maybe it was some other doctor he had. But Doctor Kelly was always our doctor.

ALAN. Maybe Doctor Kelly wasn't available and they got another. (*He is examining the 'heart-pill' bottle.*)

RITA. Maybe; but I thought it was Dr. Kelly they said.

ALAN. Maybe you just took it for granted it was Dr. Kelly; and at last came to think they told you.

RITA. Maybe; we'll know sooner or later.

ALAN. There's one way we'll know the truth for certain: if he's cured by this alleged miracle working water. (*He examines the miraculous water bottle.*)

RITA. There's a surer way then that of knowing.

ALAN. What is it?

RITA. If he isn't cured by the miracle working water!

ALAN (*smiling*). So heads we win and tails he loses. (*He puts the cork back on 'miraculous water' bottle, and replaces it on the table.*)

RITA. When they see me packing for England they'll delay no longer about trying the miracle working water.

ALAN. Don't let them stop you from coming with me. If you do, they'll finally wear you down with their Catholic brainwashing.

RITA. I'm going this time; and fifty miracles won't stop me; but Alan, we'll have to give up our plans for marrying in the registry office. Because Pete or Nellie, or whoever informed on us before, would inform on us again. And I can't break their hearts just to save the expense of a Church wedding.

ALAN. Any Church you like. A church wedding has more style about it anyway ... But your parents won't be satisfied unless you give me up and marry a Catholic.

RITA. I owe them everything; and I'll do everything else for them, but I won't give up you.

ALAN. Every younger generation has to break free from the out of date ideas of the older generation. If they didn't, people would still be burning witches and hanging children for stealing a handkerchief.

RITA (*busy packing*). Well, it's just as well that I amn't staying any longer in Ireland.

ALAN (*smiling*). Is Nellie beginning to convert you with her

233

arguments?

RITA. Apart from Nellie, it's hard, somehow, not to believe in Ireland. Religion is in the air in Ireland ... But now with the priest on his way here it's time to waken up father.

(*She shakes* TUL'S *shoulder gently; but at that moment the door is flung open, and* LARRY *appears, hatless and angry.*)

LARRY. Will ye take your thieving cattle out of my land, or I'll have ye before the bench!

RITA (*dismayed*). Are they in again, Larry? The gadfly is driving them all over again today.

LARRY. The fly! Ye have a handy excuse for everything.

RITA. I'll tell Pete in a few minutes, Larry. The priest is on his way here.

LARRY. 'Tis high time the priest came and cursed ye out of Ireland the same as St. Patrick cursed out the snakes. Because snakes is all ye are for treachery and lies!

RITA. Sure, Larry, I won you your farm the only way I could. If I told you at the time that I was tricking your father into signing over to you, you'd back out of the plan afraid of your father.

LARRY (*bitterly*). Tell that to a blind horse, and he'll kick you. (*He goes to the door.*)

RITA. Now you have your farm in your own name, and you can marry any man's sister.

LARRY. The more a man knows about women, the less he likes them and the less he wants them. Any more I hate the sight of them.

(LARRY *goes banging door.* TUL *moans and opens his eyes.*)

TUL. Put on the light, Kit.

RITA. Put on the light, and the sun the height of a man out of the ground!

TUL. Well, if it is, the death is dogging my sight. The room is as dark as the inside of a bag.

RITA. Father, don't say the fog of death is coming on your eyes!

TUL. I'm afraid so. The doctor foretold that'd come just before the end. Kit, have the miraculous water ready. (*He looks around unseeingly.*)

RITA. Mother isn't here.

TUL. Run for her quick, let ye. Only she knows the special prayer that goes with his water.

RITA. I'll try the neighbours' houses and the fields.

ALAN. I'll mind your father.

RITA. Do. (*She runs out.*)

ALAN. Would you like a heartpill, or anything?

TUL. A pill first anyway.

ALAN. Here you are, and wash it down with this.

(*He gives* TUL *a pill and a little whiskey.* TUL *gropes for* ALAN'S *hand as if he cannot see it.*)

TUL. Alan, will you promise to be a good husband to Rita?

ALAN. I'll do my best. Have no fear about that.

TUL. And don't cause her to lose her religion. If she does, she'll suffer trouble of the mind evermore.

ALAN. Unless I feel I can make her happy, I won't marry her at all.

TUL. God bless you! Each of ye might be better off to marry your own kind.

(KIT *comes in carrying eggs in her apron, and unaware that anything is wrong.*)

KIT. Isn't it master weather? That sun 'd crack the hair on your head.

ALAN. He's had a little set-back, ma'am.

KIT. Don't say it! God save us!

TUL. Run, Alan, and tell them Kit is here.

ALAN. Right!

TUL. And tell them all to come and pray for the miracle.

ALAN. Yes, as many as I can find.

(ALAN *runs out.*)

KIT (*closing door after him*). What happened that you're chancing the miracle so soon?

TUL. I was asleep till Larry wakened me with shouts like he was getting stabbed with a hayfork. Soon I heard mention that the priest is on his way here.

KIT (*dismayed*). The priest! He'll want to give you the Sacrament for the dying; and you can't take it when you aren't sick!

TUL (*grimly*). Then I'd have to confess that we were only mocking the death; and for the next Sunday he'd rock the windows with his sermon against us.

KIT. And after that the lads around 'd marry an ass before they'd marry Rita.

TUL. And the priest 'd never allow this miracle that's our best chance of converting Rita. So we must have the miracle over before the priest pulls in here ... I wonder what's bringing the priest.

KIT. He has heard about Rita, or about you dying.

TUL. We'll soon know which.

KIT. Who'd ever believe that an atheist could be such a nice decent

235

fellow as Alan is?

TUL. Still when he has no religion, in time that 'd wear away her religion. So don't pour the water on me till after I have stopped breathing. Then I can say I was dead for a few seconds, and got a little vision of the consuming fire.

KIT. Yes, if you could kindle even that much faith in Alan, he'd marry her in church, and he'd be afraid to divorce her when her youth and looks 'd be gone.

(KIT *is tidying herself and tidying the kitchen.*)

TUL. I'll not be sorry to be going back to work. Even a poet grows tired of living like a daisy.

(KIT *looks out window.*)

KIT. Here are Tuppeny and Sibby pulling in to us! Now when you're cured their plans are ruined, and they'll give us queer dogging and a big spatter of law.

TUL. The best of friends must part as the tramp said when he lost one of his shoes. But I hope the priest doesn't come in at the height of the uproar.

KIT. And I hope the priest doesn't hear about this miracle.

(*The door opens, and* SIBBY *runs in followed by* TUPPENY. TUL *closes his eyes.*)

SIBBY. We hear poor Tul is sickening for the death again.

KIT (*dabbing her eyes*). He is, God help him.

TUPPENY (*gloomily*). Sure he'll get over this bad turn the same as he got over the rest.

KIT. This time the sight left his eyes first and the doctor foretold that 'd be the end.

TUPPENY (*brightening up a little*). Is that so? True: he's looking very bad, like an old woman that'd be after losing someone she was very fond of.

SIBBY. Please God this water from the holy well in Italy will cure him.

KIT. His cousin the nun said it can do the world and all.

SIBBY. There used be holy wells in Ireland long ago; but we never heard that they used to cure anyone.

TUPPENY. Tul, you have to die sometime, don't you know? So it might be as well for you to die now when you have most of the pains of death over you.

TUL. I know Heaven is a better place than this earth; still the lark that was reared in the bog doesn't like to leave it.

SIBBY. You'll be very happy in Heaven, Tul, if it isn't too religious for you.

236

TUL. I'm afraid it will be.

(*The door opens, and* RAM *enters looking a little drunk and with a bottle sticking out of his pocket.*)

RAM. I hear Tul is due for dying again.

KIT. He's sinking fast, Ram.

TUL. My legs are colder than two sticks.

(*They tuck the rugs more tightly around him.*)

TUPPENY. He's getting broken in the voice, too.

SIBBY. Spill it on him, Kit, before he's gone too far.

KIT. No, this miraculous water will cure only when a person is drawing his very last breath.

RAM. I hope it cures you, Tul, though if it does, I'll die kicking – of booze – and all alone, with plenty of room to kick.

TUPPENY. Live or die, Tul, we hope we'll have the pleasure of seeing you again.

TUL. Good luck to ye all for ever; and may the money of the world come to rest in this village.

(*The door is flung open, and* NICHOLAS *storms in with a big stick.*)

NICHOLAS. Your trespass and yourselves should be staked to the ground!

RAM (*angrily*). Behave yourself! You have no more sense than a cat that'd be after getting struck on the head with a mug.

NICHOLAS. Mister-my-good-man, why don't you obey the eleventh commandment: to mind your own business.

RAM. You're the greatest piebald for shouting and fighting, and, if you don't stop now, I'll dumb you.

SIBBY. Quiet let ye, poor Tul is as near as a pin to being dead.

KIT. His last chance is this water from the holy well.

NICHOLAS. Then what's the reason ye aren't backing up the water with prayers?

KIT. Ye'll have to pray silent. I want to hear the change of breathing that comes just before death.

SIBBY. That's to be your signal?

KIT. It doesn't cure any sooner.

(TUL *takes his cue from this, and his breathing now becomes very laboured. His eyes are closed. The door opens and* RITA *and* PETE *run in, looking very distressed and anxious.* ALAN *and* NELLIE *follow looking suitably grave.*)

RITA. Mother! How is he?

TUPPENY. His breathing is changing, Kit!

RITA. Try the water quick!

237

PETE. Give it its chance anyway!

NICHOLAS. He's drawing his last!

RITA. Mother, quick!

PETE. Mother!

(KIT *gives the bottle a vaguely ritualistic shake and twist; then she spills the water on his forehead; and thrusts her hand into* TUL'S *hand.*)

TUPPENY. Too late, don't you know?

SIBBY. He's gone up!

KIT (*hand under rug*). Tul, if there's life in you squeeze my hand . . . Tul! His pulse is stopped! He's no more!

RITA (*throwing herself on her knees weeping*). Goodbye, daddy, for ever and ever!

NICHOLAS. Not for ever. Can't ye meet in heaven, if you live right?

PETE. Too late. Goodbye, dad!

SIBBY. God rest you, Tul of the Songs!

RAM. The only landmark we had! The only man fit to take the middle of the floor in any company.

TUPPENY (*blinking tearfully*). I'd sooner lose twenty pounds don't you know?

KIT. Nicholas! (*she hands him a folded white cloth.*)

NICHOLAS. Right, ma'am, I'll tie his chin up, and look after everything for you.

TUPPENY (*jealously*). You will not, don't you know? He said I was to dig him a good grave and I will.

(NICHOLAS *puts his hand under* TUL'S *chin, raises his head. Immediately* TUL *opens his eyes, the eyes of a man who has just seen strange and terrible things.* NICHOLAS *jumps back startled.*)

NICHOLAS. Hell and the divil! He's living!

RITA (*jumping up*). Who? Daddy?

PETE (*jumping up off his knees likewise*). He's not dead!

KIT. Then the miracle has worked!

RITA. Thank God!

PETE. Thank God!

TUPPENY. Well, he has more lives than nine cats, don't you know?

RAM. It was only a fainting spell.

SIBBY. That's all it was.

TUL (*sitting up, horrorstruck*). Did ye not see them?

KIT. See who?

SIBBY (*eagerly*). Did you see heaven, or any of the heavenly staff?

TUL. No, I'm near sure it was the other fellows I saw. They had eyes like cut-glass; and you couldn't see a ha'porth else white of

238

them only their teeth.

NICHOLAS. Maybe that was only a dream of sickness.

RITA. You doubt he wasn't dead?

RAM. After all the times we seen him dying! Ye're as green as grass if ye believe he was dead.

KIT. The true test is: Tul, are the pains gone?

TUL. What pains? (*Puts hand to his heart.*) Gone! Altogether gone! The heart pangs that had me torn asunder! I'm cured I tell ye. (*He flings off the rugs and jumps out.*)

RITA. Take it easy, daddy.

PETE. Till the doctor examines you.

TUL. While I was sick I couldn't eat a meal's meat for a fortnight; but now I could eat a soldier and his belt. Kit, put down a pot of spuds, and ye won't be able to see me behind the pile of potato skins.

KIT. Thank God you can eat again. (*Running to fire.*) Pete, Rita, help me.

PETE. I'll get the spuds and water. (*He takes up two buckets and runs out.*)

NELLIE. I'll help you. (*she runs out after him.*)

SIBBY. He's as cured as plug tobaccy, once his appetite is back.

(*She folds up his rugs, and carries the rugs and pillows into the bedroom.* RAM *is applying himself gloomily to the whiskey bottle.* NICHOLAS *and* TUPPENY *seem equally gloomy and reluctant to believe.* TUL *is walking around the room, bracing his muscles.*)

NICHOLAS. Maybe his belief in the miraculous water has deceived his appetite.

TUPPENY. And put his heart pangs to sleep for a while. Maybe he isn't cured at all.

TUL (*laughing and bracing his muscles*). Not cured! The heaviest man in the world I could carry around like a scythestone.

RITA. Alan, take his pulse you. That's the doctor's test: the true test.

TUL (*coming over to* ALAN *and offering him his wrist*). Alan, can you time a pulse?

ALAN. Certainly. That's easy.

TUL. Well, time mine now, and see whether 'tis set fast or slow for the graveyard.

NICHOLAS. The pulse tells no lies they say.

(ALAN *proceeds to take* TUL'S *pulse.* RAM *comes up to* TUL *with a glass of whiskey in his hand.*)

239

RAM (*gloomily*). Tul, if by any chance you are cured, I'll die drunk or fighting, so tell me the worst about all you saw of my eternal home. Sup this if you have a horrible statement to make. (*He gives* TUL *the glass.*)

TUL (*gravely*). I have . . . Death and nightmare are near akin, blood cousins; and whichever of them it was, I saw this raging sea of fire, and it black with poor sinners swimming in it. And as I looked, it came to me as a kind of 'flos', or knowledge, that the sinners in it were mostly fellows that divorced or deserted their wives for younger women. (*This with a side-glance at* ALAN.)

TUPPENY. If that's so, they'd be mostly all Americans, don't you know?

NICHOLAS. Yes, they do say the Americans are worn to shadows from stealing each others wives.

RAM (*drunkenly*). A sea of fire; and I never learned how to swim! I wish to God I was a bush. (*He returns to the whiskey bottle.*)

ALAN. Amazing! Perfectly normal!

TUL. Now hasn't the miracle recovered me?

KIT. Thank God! His heart is renewed!

SIBBY (*emerging from bedroom*). Now, Alan, doesn't that miracle show that God isn't an atheist?

RITA. Alan, what do you think? Wasn't that a true miracle?

ALAN. A real miracle and nothing less. Marvellous!

RITA. And now, Alan, doesn't that prove that ours is the true religion?

ALAN. There isn't the slightest doubt about it; and I intend to join the Catholic Church when I get back home.

TUL (*happily*). Thank God!

KIT. Thank God!

RITA. We'll get wed in a Catholic Church; and we'll send ye your fares to come over to the wedding.

ALAN. Yes, we'll be very disappointed if both of you can't come.

TUL. We'll we there, even if we have to swim the Irish Sea. And now I must dress myself decent before the priest docks here. (*He hurries into the bedroom.*)

KIT. I'll get your clothes. (*She goes into bedroom.*)

RITA. Alan, come out for a few minutes stroll, and we'll talk over all you have to do to become a Catholic. (*She goes to the door.*)

ALAN. Yes, that's what I want to know. (*He follows her to the door.*)

RITA. We'll be back soon, Pete.

(*This to* PETE *whom they meet coming in with two buckets.*)

PETE. The priest is due any minutes. Don't go far.

ALAN. We won't.

(ALAN *and* RITA *go out.* PETE *brings the buckets to the hearth.* NELLIE *appears in the doorway.*)

NICHOLAS (*ferociously*). Mister-my-good-man, take your dirty greedy rogues of cattle out of our aftergrass!

PETE. This minute, Nicholas, and I'll make sure they won't break in again. (*He takes a stick from the corner.*)

NELLIE (*to the others*). If ye'll take my advice, ye'll not tell the priest about this miracle. If ye do, Tul and us all may have a lot of testing and cross-questioning to go through.

PETE. And our house will be damned out with people calling, so let ye tell no one.

NICHOLAS. Put out your thieving blackguards of cattle!

PETE. Come on, Nellie, and we'll spur them out, and maybe skelp a little honesty into them on the way.

(PETE *and* NELLIE *go out.*)

SIBBY. The priest should be told about this, the greatest miracle around here since the druids raised up magic fogs to blind St. Patrick.

NICHOLAS. The priest might be promoted to be a canon over such a miracle honouring his parish.

TUPPENY (*gloomily*). But what about us? Now we'll never get any colour of a woman.

RAM (*grimly*). Yes, now we'll die lone fellows; and as oul' Doherty said; "Tis a terrible thing to be living alone and to waken up in the morning and find yourself dead." (*He sits at table, fills himself another glass of whiskey.*)

NICHOLAS. The poorhouse will be my fate. As soon as a divil of a daughter-in-law gets her heels stuck into my heartstone, she'll starve me out and plague me out.

SIBBY (*cheerfully, smoking cigarette butt*). I cracked two twenty pound notes for wedding clothes and blankets; but now they're no use to me.

RAM. And I spent my rates penny on wedding clothes, and now my last cow will be seized to pay the rates. I wish to God I was a bush.

TUPPENY. And I wasted on wedding clothes for myself and whiskey for Tul three ten pounds notes I worked hard for.

NICHOLAS. And I'm tricked out of this farm the same as I was tricked out of my own.

241

SIBBY (*cheerfully*). Still 'tis a lovely world, a splendid world. Even the poorest has a suit of clothes, and a bit to eat. And if we're single itself, we're used to living single, and use makes master.

RAM. You can go to bed when you like anyway. You'll have no husband to stop you, or to hurry you.

SIBBY. Ram, I can put one pound note after another from here to Dublin very near. So never be lame or lazy about coming to me for any money you need.

TUPPENY. D'ye want that noted ruffian to drink out all we have?

RAM (*hotly*). I wouldn't come to her for booze money even if my tongue was out a yard. (*Offering her glass.*) Take a toothful.

SIBBY. No, Ram, drink it yourself sweetly.

(TUL *comes out carrying full whiskey bottle.*)

TUL. Now, to honour my cure, we'll all have a few snips of whiskey and a revelling day entirely.

TUPPENY (*hotly*). Give me back my whiskey, don't you know. Too long you're drinking bottles to any number and me paying for them!

TUL. This isn't your bottle. Rita bought this for me.

NICHOLAS. You promised us the world and all, and tricked us out of everything at the finish!

TUL. Sure, when I promised, I didn't know this miraculous water was in the world.

SIBBY. Sure we couldn't expect Tul to suicide himself just to oblige us.

TUPPENY. Hand me out thirty pounds for my murdered ram.

TUL. Next month when I sell my lambs and can pay you, we'll get someone to give a close judgement on the value of your ram.

NICHOLAS. And hand me over the twenty pound you owe me for trespass.

TUPPENY. And the ten pound you owe me for trespass!

TUL. I owe ye for trespass; but not that much. (*He is pouring glasses of whiskey, gives one to* RAM.)

NICHOLAS. A couple of pound to a lawyer 'll find out how much.

TUL. If ye do, I'll hire a smart hardy lawyer to stand fair play for me.

TUPPENY. And the bench 'll make you pay for all the work we did for you.

NICHOLAS. And for all the whiskey we bought for you!

TUPPENY. And for all the wedding clothes that's no good to us, don't you know.

TUPPENY (*supping a glass of whiskey coolly*). That's strong talk out of weak bellies.

NICHOLAS. Mister-my-good-man, how are we weak?

TUL. If ye put law on me, the police 'll soon be tapping yourselves on the jackets for conspiracy and attempted murder.

TUPPENY. The divil shoot you! What murder?

TUL. Weren't ye bringing me whiskey galore against the doctor's orders so as to murder me, and wed my widow and my land?

RAM (*hitting table*). Tul, I witnessed that; and I'll swear for you, and we'll hang them without their breakfasts.

SIBBY (*shocked*). No, Ram. Not without their breakfasts!

TUPPENY (*blinking*). So this is our thanks, don't you know?

NICHOLAS. Ram, you're drunk and vicious again!

TUL. If ye leave the law idle, I'll leave the law idle.

NICHOLAS. We won't leave the law idle, and besides the law we'll curse you in your marrow and your bones.

TUPPENY. May you never please God or man, don't you know!

TUL. Cursing me – when it was my dying opened all your eyes, and roused ye up out of a dream of years ye were all decaying away in!

NICHOLAS. We were working like horses while you were moping over old poems.

(KIT *comes out of the bedroom, puts the potatoes and water into the pot, hangs it on the fire.*)

TUL (*vigorously*). Ye were working so hard that ye never took time off to think. Tuppeny and Sibby kept dreaming that money in the bank was worth more than a decent suit of clothes. But no one 'd wed them, because each of them looked like the image of Poverty riding on Hunger!

NICHOLAS. We know they're brainless old misers; but I'm no flat tyre.

TUL. You are all that. You thought no daughter-in-law at all ever was better than one without six hundred pounds.

RAM. And now Larry is going for feeds of drink over losing Rita, and vowing that he'll never join any woman.

TUL. And Ram kept putting off marriage until he'd be less poor, but for want of a wife's work and help he crept a mile nearer to the poorhouse every year.

RAM (*gloomily*). No lie, Tul, no lie. I got four bones and brains from God, but I let them down.

KIT. Sibby has plenty of good clean money that God gave her. Let her money repair Ram's house and restock his land. Then ye can live together as happy as two bees.

243

SIBBY (*happily*). Ram, I will! I'll furnish you out with everything. I never thought of that before.

TUPPENY. Hold on there, don't you know. You're not going to steal away my housekeeper!

TUL. Sure, when Ram does take her out of your house and way, that's when yourself 'll get a fine woman not a year over the two pounds.

TUPPENY (*bitterly*). 'Tis the blessing of God I didn't get your widow, a lazy greedy rap that'd eat me down to the crumb.

NICHOLAS. And Tul himself is only a rotten traitor and ever was. No one knows who he votes for.

(*The door opens and* NELLIE *appears.*)

NELLIE. The priest's car is coming! Don't tell him about the miracle, or we'll all find ourselves in trouble.

TUL (*urgently*). Yes, leave the miracle in darkness from both priest and parishioners.

NICHOLAS. Sure I must tell the priest so as he'll sanction you to tell whether my missus is in the sea of fire.

TUPPENY. Sure when Tul can't tell you she isn't, she must be roasting, don't you know.

TUL. Nicholas, your wife wasn't in the sea of fire at all, at least not in my views of it.

NELLIE. If ye tell the priest, he'll be bound by Church law to investigate the miracle, and get sworn statements from all us witnesses, and from Tul's doctor, and from the nun who sent the water.

KIT (*dismayed*). Sworn statements!

TUL. Call on my doctor! Nellie, are you sure?

NELLIE. Certain. No priest can let his parishioners go around claiming miracles without proof.

TUL (*to* KIT). If he calls on the doctor, he'll find out the lot!

RAM. The priest must be told, because I must find out how the likes of me that can't swim will fare out in the sea of fire.

SIBBY. And God might never harbour us, if we denied His great miracle.

KIT. We must tell them the whole truth and quickly.

TUL. 'Tis the only way to stop them from boasting to the priest and to everybody about the miracle.

NELLIE. It'd be safer for me to tell them, wouldn't it?

KIT. What could you know to tell them?

NELLIE. Everything. Rita was in to your doctor about you today, and finding out one thing she guessed the rest.

KIT. She did! Dear tonight!

TUL. They know the lot!

NELLIE. Rita and Alan do; but they preferred ye to think they didn't know.

(TUL *turns as if to fly into the bedroom; but* TUPPENY *grabs him by the arm, and raises his stick.*)

TUPPENY. What's it about, don't you know?

TUL. 'Tis about this: Nellie got a rub of Convent education, so I'll tell her all I saw, and let her be the judge and jury on how much ye should be told. If we tell the priest, we won't get time to save our harvest with all the cross-questionings we'll have to go through, and journey's to bishops and to the Pope maybe. Let ye go outside and I'll tell Nellie all.

NICHOLAS. Be quick about it before the priest goes. Because if she won't sanction ye to tell, the priest might.

TUPPENY. True, don't you know. The women are contrarier than any priest.

SIBBY. Find out if they gave Tul any knowledge of when we're going to die.

RAM. And find out whether 'tis lies, or a truthful tale, that the devil spends every night baptising with fire the behinds of the boozers.

NELLIE (*laughing*). I will.

(RAM, NICHOLAS, TUPPENY *and* SIBBY *go out.*)

KIT. Now Nellie, we have a clear coast.

NELLIE. Today Rita called in to your doctor to ask if any hospital treatment could save Tul. He told her he hadn't been called on to attend Tul at all. At once she remembered the trick played on Bernadette Duffy, and she guessed that Tul wasn't sick at all.

TUL. She did!

KIT. Dear tonight!

NELLIE. She told Alan and Pete and me just before your fake miracle.

TUL. So they were only fooling us, pretending to be converted by the miracle.

NELLIE. Not to fool ye, but to make ye happy they're pretending to be converted.

TUL. But is she certain sure that I wasn't sick or dead?

NELLIE. Once we suspected you at all it was easy to see you were shamming sick.

KIT (*looking through window*). The priest is talking to them. D'ye think there's any chance that he will convert her?

245

NELLIE. It'll take more than one talk with a priest to convert her. But Tul's dying taught her one thing: that she can't give up her religion without causing a lot of heartbreak to herself and others. As the poet says,
"He who lives more lives than one,
More deaths than one must die."

TUL. The fake miracle was out best chance to convert her.

NELLIE. That's where you were altogether wrong. The priests say only the Grace of God can convert anyone, so they say a sinful lying fake miracle couldn't win God's grace and convert anyone. And it would bring disgrace on the Church.

KIT. If they tell the priest about it, all the wells that are feeding the rivers won't wash us free.

TUL (*at window*). We're betrayed! They're calling the priest away from Alan and Rita, and the priest is going over to them!

NELLIE. I was thinking they couldn't keep such a big thing a secret.

KIT. And they shouldn't tell even his little finger.

TUL (*retreating towards the bedroom*). Now we're back to the luck that's plentiful: the bad luck! Tell the priest I amn't rightly sensible ever since I got sunstruck in June. And we'll let him find me in bed and badly.

(*But before he goes into the bedroom* RITA *and* ALAN *enter both looking cheerful enough.*)

KIT. Did they call the priest to tell him about the miracle?

RITA. We don't know why they called him. I had told the priest that I was converted already by a fortnight in Ireland and by Nellie's arguments.

TUL. And wasn't that only more lies to put him off, and to cheer us?

RITA. It was not. Before we went to England we heard no arguments against God, or answers to them. Nellie asked English priests, and they said nothing can come out of nothing, so the world had to be made by an infinite God.

NELLIE (*smiling*). And they said St. Augustine said, "Heretics were given to us that we might not remain in infancy."

ALAN. I'll never interfere with her religion, and we'll have a Church wedding.

RITA. To prove that we're inviting ye over to our wedding and paying your fares.

TUL (*to* KIT). Well, converted or no, she's getting wed in Church anyway.

KIT. If the clergy ever again allow any belonging to us into a church, after they hear of the fake miracle! (*She goes to door.*) They're

246

still telling the priest!

TUL. And Nicholas and Tuppeny very near drew my blood because I was cured by miracle. What'll they do when they hear I was all along as healthy a man as ever a doctor sounded? (*He pours himself a drink of whiskey worriedly.*)

ALAN (*at window*). Here they come!

RITA. Nicholas and Tuppeny!

KIT. And what'll the priest say? I'm more afraid than an eel that'd be after coming out of the sea. (*She goes to the safe side of the table.*)

(NICHOLAS *and* TUPPENY *come in.*)

NICHOLAS (*grimly*). Mister-my-good-man, are you going to tell us all they dying and the dead see ahead of them?

TUPPENY. If you don't the priest might curse you in Latin, the worst curse of all, don't you know.

TUL (*bitterly*). I don't know what kind ye are if ye aren't fools. We told ye to keep your tongues in your pockets about the miracle.

NICHOLAS. And sure we never did let that cat out of the bag.

TUPPENY. We can swear blind to that. We never told him about the miracle, or about you seeing the two worlds this day.

KIT. For what else did ye call him away from Rita and Alan?

NICHOLAS. Ram called him to settle about his wedding with Sibby.

TUPPENY. He did the scoundrel, and he having an eye like a duck in trespass. The priest should refuse him marriage and let him stiffen and starve.

(RAM *comes in followed by* SIBBY.)

RAM (*triumphantly*). Before I hadn't a home, but only an address, like all the bachelors. But soon I'll have a home, and we'll live poor but pleasant like the old stonemasons.

SIBBY. Having no one to talk to was driving him out to the pubs; but any more he'll hear every day enough talk to train a filly.

TUL (*anxiously*). I hope ye didn't give the priest any glimpse of the miracle.

RAM. About that we kept as dumb as a snowman.

SIBBY. And the priest is gone ahead on a sick call to old Keaveney.

TUPPENY (*to* NICHOLAS). Then we can halt him on his road home don't you know?

NICHOLAS. We can, and we will do, if Nellie won't sanction you to tell all the next world is.

TUL. Nellie herself will tell ye all I saw and heard and smelt – brimstone and all! (*He pinches his nose with a grimace.*) And while she's telling ye Kit and me will be putting on our frock

coats, and readying up to go with this great miracle news to the
Bishop. You'll drive us, Alan?

ALAN. With pleasure.

KIT. We'll want to hurry, or we'll be late for tea with the Bishop.

ALAN. Tea with a bishop! That'll be something!

RITA. We'll be starting the car! Come on, Alan.

(RITA *and* ALAN *go out.*)

SIBBY. Ye'll want to be of great manners at tea with a bishop.

TUPPENY. Let ye not be grabbing things, or slugging your tea.

KIT. Yes, Tul, you'll want to behave less greedy.

TUL. That isn't easy, for a very hardworking man.

(TUL *and* KIT *go into bedroom.*)

RAM. Cough up the truth, Nellie, be it sweet, or sour.

NELLIE. I'll tell ye everything in one word, not two. There was no
vision and there was no miracle, because Tul was never sick at
all.

NICHOLAS (*angrily*). Mister-my-good-woman, what trickery and lies
are you up to now?

TUPPENY. Not sick! A man that had the priest and the doctor!

NELLIE. He had neither priest nor doctor, as you'll find out, if you
ask them. To stop his daughter from a wrong marriage in
England he sent her a telegram that he was dying, and today, to
convert her, he pretended to be cured by miracle.

RAM. Tul of the Songs! Tul of the Lies!

SIBBY (*smiling*). You wouldn't know whether 'tis silly or wise he is.

TUPPENY. Tricking us out of free whiskey and free work till we're
worth nothing and fit for nothing!

NICHOLAS. The devil was never played with us until now!

NELLIE. He was only out to save his daughter, and he had to
deceive us all in order to deceive her.

TUPPENY. While he lives no honest man can flourish away. Come
on till we break his bones.

NICHOLAS. You wouldn't give a worse blow to an ass than what I'll
give him.

(*They are trying to pull open and shoulder open the bedroom
door.* NELLIE *goes to the street door, looks out.*)

NELLIE. Stop let ye. The priest will be coming soon.

TUPPENY. His death will be a godsend to priests, parsons and press.
Come out to your downfall!

NICHOLAS. We'll kill you and bury you, and 'tis a bad grass that'll
grow out of you. A goat out of Connemara wouldn't eat it.

(RAM *comes over, and pulls* NICHOLAS *back from the door.*)

RAM. If ye beat a man in his own house, the law will jail ye, and rob ye with fines and medical expenses. Sue him, instead, and ye can make him pay for all your whiskey and work.

TUPPENY. Nicholas, maybe Ram's principles and wisdoms about the law are right, don't you know?

NICHOLAS. Are you afraid of a few calendar months in jail?

TUPPENY. I am not; but I'm reckoning now 'tis fitter for us to rob and jail Tul through the law than to beat him, and give him the chance to rob and jail us through the law.

NICHOLAS. Come on then to a devil of a lawyer who'll rob him and jail him for ever.

TUPPENY. McNabb is the wickedest lawyer, I'd say, from the whites of his eyes. (*They set out for the door.*)

NICHOLAS. If he gets out of jail after McNabb, I'll give up talking. Out of the way woman! (*He pulls* NELLIE *out of the doorway.*)

NELLIE (*urgently*). If ye tell the priest about the fake miracle, he'll condemn ye, too, for believing in the fake miracle.

TUPPENY. We'll tell the priest, no matter if he never allows a cross over our graves. (*He runs out.*)

NICHOLAS. No radio ever made will talk as fast as us. (*He goes.*)
   (TUL *and* KIT *come out of the room.*)

TUL (*cheerful enough*). By the time they reach the lawyers their tempers my be cooled down, thinking of how the lawyers will pluck themselves, not leaving them as much as a tail feather.

NELLIE. Now the two are arguing, like as if they're falling out.

KIT. One or the other is beginning to fear the priest might preach against themselves.

NELLIE. They're not waiting for the priest. They're going!

SIBBY. And they're not cripples going!

KIT. Glory and thanks be to God!

RAM. No match should be finished without a good drink. Come here the lot of ye and drink luck to Sibby and myself. (*He pours out drinks.*)

NELLIE. I'll call in Alan and Rita. (*She runs out.*)

TUL (*taking up his glass in great humour*). Well, Kit, Rita is getting wed in church, and Ram and Sibby are getting wed, so I didn't die in vain.

KIT. And Pete is after telling me he's wedding Nellie in here, so any more we'll have good help and good fences. And good fences make good neighbours.

TUL. And with Pete working the farm I can spend all day composing. So I'll soon be the finest poet since the first poet

249

ever: the Greek Homer, a man like myself, a small farmer, but gifted.

RAM (*putting an arm around* SIBBY). Wasn't I the lucky man not to be born a bush?

SIBBY. Tul, sound the marriage toast to us!

RITA (*running in followed by* ALAN, NELLIE *and* PETE). And to us!

PETE & NELLIE. Yes, to us!

TUL. May your farms be lands of plenty, and may your homes be houses of peace and as neat as matches in a box. May ye find marriage a good college that'll train ye to defeat the devil. And may ye be so happy that ye'll think the longest day or night is too short.

ALL. Here, here! (*They touch glasses and drink.*)

RAM (*rising*). Many a girl I walked with and talked with; but (*Turning to* SIBBY.) you have to wait for the right one.

CURTAIN

Petticoat Loose

DEDICATION

To Siobhan McKenna. Ireland's greatest actress of this or any generation.

Preface

Country folk have always been slow to abandon their religious beliefs and superstitions. The word "pagan" comes from the Latin word "paganus", which originally meant country dweller. Long after the cities and towns of the Roman Empire had become Christian, its country folk remained faithful to the old Roman Gods and Goddesses. So the townspeople began to call non-Christians "pagani", likening them to the still heathen country folk. When the word "pagan" finally entered the English language, it was in its new meaning of heathen, or non-believer.

The Celtic peoples of Ireland, Scotland, Wales, Brittany, Cornwall and the Isle of Man found it equally difficult to discard their old Fairy Religion after they became Christian. So they gave their old beliefs new Christian interpretations. The Fairies were no longer prayed to as Gods, but they were feared and honoured as Fallen Angels who could do good or evil to people or farm animals. To placate them, they were called "The Good People", or "The Noble People", it being understood that they heard everything people said. Mannanawn Mac Lir, God of the Sea, and the Goddess Maeve, etc, became Fairy Kings and Queens. The pagan holy well was now called the holy well of the ancient Christian saint. The pagan sacred tree had its holiness attributed to the fact that it had grown from the saint's staff stuck in the ground. The pagan cursing stone became the saint's cursing stone. And the Druids of the old Fairy Faith were succeeded by half-pagan, half-Christian priestesses and priests called Fairy Doctors. These survived into the present century, and the poet W.B. Yeats and his Abbey Theatre co-founder Lady Gregory interviewed several of them about their visions and beliefs, and wrote about them. Many years before the brilliant parents of Oscar Wilde had written about them, as had Sir Walter Fitzgerald, and other Irish writers. They figure prominently in Ireland's folk traditions and folktales. So what were the Fairy doctors? Like all primitive peoples, the Celts believed that most illnesses and ailments in people and farm animals were caused by the actions of evil spirits, devils and fairies, or by evil spells, the Evil Eye and curses. The Fairy Doctors were women or men who

253

claimed to be able to cure these ills by counter-spells and charms, which enlisted, or resisted, the powers of the Fairies. They also cured with herbal remedies which they prepared themselves. They practised as fortune tellers, and they supplied love charms and love potions which were called coaxiorums. For a fee many of them would lay a curse on your enemy, calculated to ruin him or drive him mad. In fact, they practised many of the arts of the African Witch Doctor. Yet they were baptised Christians who claimed to be Christians, and to have no truck with the Devil. They claimed to have got their healing and prophetic powers from the Fairies. Many of them told how they had been carried off by the Fairies to the Fairy Forts, and had lived there for months or years and learned the Fairy skills and powers.

During the long centuries when medical science was scarce and primitive, and when veterinary science was non-existent, the Fairy Doctors were kept busy and prosperous. Folk traditions and written accounts tell of many remarkable cures worked by them. But even if all their herbs and spells were useless, it would not be easy to perceive or prove this. Present-day medical experts have calculated that most illnesses and ailments are cured by time, no matter what the treatment. But if the Fairy Doctors had treated these illnesses, they would believe, and their patients would believe, that the cures had been effected through their treatments. And their belief in the existence and the power of the Fairies would be confirmed.

The inevitable enemies of the Fairy Doctors were the priests and schoolmasters. But when England became Protestant in 1534, all Ireland's rural churches and monastic schools and bardic schools were destroyed, and the priests and schoolmasters and bards became hunted fugitives banned by the Penal Laws. These Penal Laws remained in force for nearly three hundred years, but were quite unaware of the existence of the Fairy Doctors. So the latter were free to develop their influence and their theology and their rituals during all that time. The priests were too persecuted themselves to be able any longer to oppose the Fairy Doctors. By the end of this three hundred year period, the Fairy Doctors had become very numerous and powerful. Within a radius of about seven miles, at least three of them were operating at the same time, including Biddy the Tosser, the Fairy Doctor in this play.

The Fairy Doctors converted the peasantry to their belief that most babies and young middle-aged people who died and were buried were, nevertheless, "not dead all out". Instead, their

254

spiritual selves had been stolen by the Fairies, and that is why they had seemed to die. But, in fact, they were living with the Fairies in the Fairy Forts. The Fairies might allow them to go back home after seven years, or longer. But if a Fairy Doctor was hired to work certain spells, the dead might be allowed back and for good very quickly. When the spells failed, the Fairy Doctor's excuse was that nobody could be "spelled back" from the Fairy Forts, if he, or she, had been stolen by the Queen of a Fort, or the Fool of a Fort. Presumably the Fairy Doctors made a lot of money out of this belief. During centuries of rack-rented poverty, when the death rate was appalling, the belief that the lost loved ones might return from the fairy forts may have softened death's blow for a lot of people. The Fairy Doctors and the peasantry believed in Fairy Changelings. Babies, or young or fairly young adults, who looked or behaved strangely, or who became suddenly stricken with a mysterious illness, were suspected of being Fairy Changelings. The original baby or adult had been secretly stolen by the fairies, and an ancient worn-out fairy had been left in its place, looking like the stolen baby or adult, but behaving oddly, or seeming to be very ill. The Fairy Doctors were hired to discover whether the suspected changeling was that, or simply the original person being genuinely ill, physically or mentally. Some Fairy Doctors recommended dangerous and cruel tests which sometimes caused death to babies and adults. In 1895, in South Tipperary, Mrs Brigid Cleary, a 26 year old woman, died of fire tests applied to find out if she was, as suspected, a fairy changeling. Yeat's first play "Land of Heart's Desire" about the stealing of a young married woman by the Fairies, had its first production in London the previous year.

The Penal Laws against priests and schoolmasters were repealed by the beginning of the nineteenth century. This meant that the priests were free again to oppose this rival and pagan priesthood, which the Fairy Doctors had become. A religious war, as depicted in the play, now began. Like all religious wars, it was marked by the destruction of rival places or worship – holy wells, holy trees, cursing stones, and art treasures like the thousand year old crozier of St. Grellan. These acts of destruction were reported to the Government by the great archaeologist John O'Donovan a few years later. But the spread of education and of medical and veterinary service was destroying the people's faith in, and their need for, the Fairy Doctors. Today the Fairy Doctors are as extinct as their predecessors, the Druids. Few country people now confess to a belief in the Fairies, but many still fear to break the old Fairy

255

PREFACE

taboos. They have seen death or misfortune strike people who destroyed Fairy Forts or Fairy Trees. Fifteen years ago three young men from the town of Ballyshannon went out into the country and contemptuously cut down a famous Fairy Tree. All three were dead within a year.

The great mediaeval theologian and philosopher St. Thomas Aquinas wrote, "There had to be a revealed religion because the ordinary man has not time to argue". And we know that the ordinary man was illiterate up to modern times, and, even when he was not illiterate, he preferred stories and poetry to philosophy or theology or science. So the old religions were revealed, or taught, through allegorical stories and parables and poetry. The Celts lost vast treasures of stories and poetry when their Fairy Religion became a creed outworn. They still throng to their Isle of Man, but no longer hoping to see their God, King Mannanawn Mac Lir, rising in majesty from the depths of his Kingdom of the Sea.

In history and in this play, the chief rival and opponent of the Fairy Doctor was the suspended priest, who earned a living by giving "gospels" for the cure of the sick. What the peasantry called "a gospel" was a text from St. John's Gospel written on a piece of paper by the priest. This was sewn into a piece of cloth, and worn around the patient's neck, and both the priest and the patient were to pray for a cure. Folk traditions held that these "gospels" could be very good for curing the patient, but dangerous for the messenger who went for the "gospel", some great misfortune often befell himself or his property. So it happened sometimes that a family would be afraid to go for a "gospel" for a very ill parent. And the parents would bribe a neighbour by offering him his two best bullocks. The custom of asking and giving "gospels" died out when the Fairy Doctors died out. So the clergy may have begun the practice of giving "Gospels" long ago in order to wean their flocks away from the pagan magic spells and rituals of the Fairy Doctors. Or suspended priests may have begun it, because they had no other means of livelihood. Papal dispensations to priests allowing them to leave the priesthood and marry were unknown in those days. Even suspended, unfrocked priests continued to be bound until death by their ordination oaths of celibacy and chastity.

A century and a half before 1822, the period of this play, Moliere's last play, "The Hypocondriac" had attacked the medical doctors for bleeding their patients for every illness, bleeding them repeatedly until they died from loss of blood rather then from the illness. "Bleedet et killat" was their motto, according to Moliere's

English translator. In 1815 they were still at it. An English captain bleeding from six wounds was carried from the battlefield of Waterloo into the field hospital behind the lines. The surgeons immediately proceeded to bleed him. The Fairy Doctor and the "Gospel" giving priests were much less likely to kill their patients, and they were also much less expensive. The treatment of suspected changelings by the Fairy Doctors was sometimes cruel and dangerous, but fatal results seem to have been rare.

History tells of a severe famine in the west of Ireland in 1822, caused by bad weather destroying corps and by overcropping and over population. It was one of the warning forerunners of the Great Famine of 1845–49.

Concerning the existence of ghosts, the Church's view was, "De occultis Ecclesia non judicat". Which left everybody free to believe or disbelieve. The Church's view of the Celtic fairies may have been equally non-committal and neutral. But no Church could ignore the maltreatment of suspected fairy changelings resulting from the advice of the Fairy Doctors.

M. J. Molloy

CHARACTERS

PETTICOAT LOOSE, A country-style semi-whore.
*SHAWN LALLY, A big free-hold farmer and a 'half-sir'.
HONOR, His wife.
MULLEE, One of his farm-hands.
BIDDY THE TOSSER, A fairy doctor.
FR. TARPEY, A suspended priest.
PEG ABOVE ALL, A famine refugee.
MICKLE DONEGAN, A weaver.
HARKAWAY WALSH, A journeyman tailor.

(*"Half-Sir" – Descended from Irish chiefs who lost most of their estates during the English Conquest.)

TIME: The winter of the year 1822.

PLACE
Act I, The kitchen of Shawn Lally's farmhouse in Co. Galway, about noon.
Act II, Scene 1, The combined bedroom and kitchen of Fr. Tarpey's one-roomed cabin on the edge of a bog. Nine o'clock a few nights later.
Act II, Scene 2, Scene the same, a few hours later.
Act III, The Holy Well, holy tree, cursing stone and other remains of St. Bannon's ancient church, or monastery, and its surrounding graveyard. Moonrise, a few nights later.

The play includes some lines for a couple of additional characters in the Confrontation scene of Act III. But these characters are not essential, and the play can be produced with a cast of nine.

The first performance of Petticoat Loose was given at the Abbey Theatre, Dublin on 16th May 1979. It was directed by Tomas McAnna; and the settings were by Wendy Shea. The lighting was by Tony Wakefield. The cast was as follows:

PETTICOAT LOOSE	Maire Ni Ghrainne
SHAWN LALLY	Micheal O hAonghusa
HONOR	Eileen Colgan
MULLEE	Emmet Bergin
BIDDY THE TOSSER	Maureen Toal
FR. TARPEY	Patrick Laffan
PEG ABOVE ALL	Martina Stanley
MICKLE DONEGAN	Peadar Lamb
HARKAWAY WALSH	Mick Lally

Crowd in graveyard. Brid Ni Neachtain, Sharon O'Doherty, Rosemary Henderson, Brendan Conroy, Sean Lawlor, Marcus O'Higgins.

(The play can be performed by its cast of nine, and without any additional actors for the graveyard scene. Author's note.)

259

Petticoat Loose

ACT ONE

*The scene is the big kitchen of a gentleman farmer's house in the
northern marshes of Co. Galway. The time is nearing midday during
the famine winter of 1822. The house, a long thatched building,
contains several rooms. The portrait of an ancestor occupies a place
of honour. A print of Raphael's Madonna of the Chair hangs on the
back wall. An old fowling piece hangs over the fireplace. On the
mantelpiece there is a Bible, and a Penal Days crucifix with the
characteristic short arms which made concealment easier up a sleeve.
The table, chairs and dresser have been strongly made by country
carpenters. The street door is in the back wall. On its left – from the
actors point of view – is a fairly big window, divided into several
small panes. In both side walls doors lead into bedrooms.*

*The fireplace is in the right-hand wall. It is equipped with the old
time iron crane and pot-hooks and pots and kettles. A wooden
armchair containing a cushion stands near the fire. The dresser is
against the left hand wall. Between it and the footlights, a bag of meal
stands against that wall. The table is on the left-hand side of the
kitchen, near the dresser. Chairs are drawn up to both sides of it.*

*A knocking is heard at the door, but there is no-one present to
answer. Finally the door-latch is lifted and* PETTICOAT LOOSE
*enters. She is in her middle twenties and is merry and attractive and
coquettish in dress and manner, though her clothes show sings of
hardship and poverty endured. She wears a coloured blouse and a
red petticoat, and around her shoulders a coloured shawl. From her
waist in front hangs a short apron. She is full of reckless vitality.*

PETTICOAT LOOSE. Are ye sleeping it out? Or stolen by the fairies?
(*She takes a quick look into each bedroom closes the street door,
runs to the dresser.*) Every mug should be full of money. (*She
looks into jugs and mugs, at last stops at one.*) Three pennies! If
I steal more than one, they'll miss it. (*She pockets penny, begins
to steal meal out of the bag. A man passes the window, she closes*

the bag, door opens and MULLEE *enters, a burly farm worker in his late twenties.*)

MULLEE. Petticoat Loose! Have you come for goodness, or for badness?

PETTICOAT LOOSE (*grinning*). For my own good, and not for your badness. Where are the oldest blood in Ireland? The follys?

MULLEE. The missus is in the yard foddering calves, and the master is still poaching for bargains at the fair. (*He takes a jug of milk from the dresser, pours some into a mug.*)

PETTICOAT LOOSE. You have a great head of sweat on you.

MULLEE. I'm thrashing oats since the second round of cockcrow. (*He is at the dresser, pouring milk into a mug.*)

PETTICOAT LOOSE. Mullee, have you anything good in your heart for me? You never paid me yet for your last night's fun.

MULLEE. I have a small bag of meal hid in their barns, but I didn't get chance to fetch it away yet.

PETTICOAT LOOSE (*merry*). If you loved me right, love'd make you bold. The hunger will kill me before I'm ready to die.
(*She takes the mug out of his hand, begins to drink out of it. He opens the dresser, takes out a bottle, uncorks it, pours a little whiskey from it into her mug, then raises the bottle to his lips.*)

MULLEE. Here's to the bird that flew the highest,
And never lost a feather!
That you and I may never die,
Till we sleep one night together!

PETTICOAT LOOSE. Two words before a priest, and we can sleep every night together.

MULLEE. Mother will put her widow's curse on me, if I wed a girl nick-named after Petticoat Loose – the wickedest and worst ghost that ever was in Ireland.

PETTICOAT LOOSE. That Petticoat Loose was damned because she murdered her unbaptised children. I have racked my body and soul to keep alive my children of the moon.

MULLEE. Our potato ridges are no good to us now that the spuds are rotting. Your children will die unless you wed a farmer with enough land for a grain crop and a cow.

PETTICOAT LOOSE. The farmer that'd wed a petticoat loose isn't born yet, and his mother is dead. (*She is searching tins and boxes on the mantelpiece.*)

MULLEE. The wars of Bonaparte earned a man's weight in gold for this two hundred acres of freehold. And they'll never have a child to spend it on.

261

PETTICOAT LOOSE. I'll rummage in their bedroom. If you hear them coming, cough in to me.

(*She runs into the bedroom. He goes to window, drinking and watching out.*)

MULLEE. Maybe their gold is buried out in the headlands, for fear of robber men. And if the missus seen you coming, she'll be in to inquire about your baby that was stolen by the fairies.

PETTICOAT LOOSE (*coming out sadly*). Sure, 'tis over that baby I have such a want of gold. Unless I cross Biddy the Tosser's hand with gold, she can't pull the only two herbs that can win my baby back from the fairies.

MULLEE. Biddy says them are the two herbs that brought Our Lord back from the dead.

PETTICOAT LOOSE. Mullee, on my holy oath, this baby sprang between me and you, so lend me a gold sovereign, and Biddy will win our baby back from the fairy forts.

MULLEE. If I had a sovereign, you wouldn't need to ask. But with eight pence a day here, and paying high rent for four ridges of rotting spuds!

PETTICOAT LOOSE. Maybe Honor Lally would rather have my prayers than a sovereign. (*She returns to stealing meal.*)

MULLEE. She might to save a baby. When she could never make a baby herself.

PETTICOAT LOOSE. I must leave a share of meal at the fairy fort for my baby. If it doesn't eat the fairy food for the first week, they might bring it back to me.

MULLEE. Tonight I'll fetch away that bag of meal I have hidden for you. Be waiting under the eye of the bridge.

PETTICOAT LOOSE (*happy*). I will, Mullee, though 'tis cold weather for having a poor girl half stripped. We should get wed and have a bit of heat and comfort.

MULLEE. No, the stolen bit is the sweetest bit.

(*A rattle of buckets is heard.*)

MULLEE. The missus!

(PETTICOAT LOOSE *closes the mealbag, and runs to the fire.* MULLEE *hurries to the door and opens it.*)

MULLEE. I was as thirsty as a fish, mam.

(*He goes out and* HONOR LALLY *comes in carrying a pail or two. She is a good looking woman in her late thirties, but rather sad looking. Her blouse, skirt and apron are workaday, but of good quality.*)

HONOR. Petticoat Loose, how is the fairy baby the fairies left in

262

place of your own baby?

PETTICOAT LOOSE. It looks just like my own baby; but it has a blush on its face and it's sickly and crying.

HONOR. Then maybe it is your own baby and it's teething.

PETTICOAT LOOSE. Biddy the Tosser passed her hands over it and found its heart was ticking like an old person's heart, and no longer like a baby's heart.

HONOR. Then it's some old person the fairies stole when young, and now they have swapped him for your baby, after turning him into the likeness of you baby.

PETTICOAT LOOSE. So Biddy says. And after she turned her three rods, they showed the fairies stole my baby a day I was out digging spuds.

HONOR. Did your mother see them?

PETTICOAT LOOSE. No, but she felt a shadow come in, and baby took a fit of screaming in its sleep; and the cat arched its back and made for the door.

HONOR. Surely and truly, it was then they swapped your baby for its likeness, their fairy baby.

PETTICOAT LOOSE. Maybe we vexed the fairies by not calling them the good people.

(HONOR *has taken a torn garment and a needle and thread from the dresser drawer, and puts them on the table in front of* PETTICOAT LOOSE.)

HONOR. Finish that bit of sewing for me, and it'll earn a share of meal for your family.

PETTICOAT LOOSE (*sitting at table*). God bless your two hands, mam Biddy the Tosser told me to leave a share of meal at the fairy fort of Lissatava for my baby.

HONOR. Then I'll fill a small bag for you now, for fear my man will come home drunk and fighting from the fair.

(HONOR *takes a small cloth bag from a drawer, and begins to fill it with meal.*)

PETTICOAT LOOSE. May you have a long life and a funny wake.

HONOR. Is Biddy still advising ye to tie the fairy baby to the head of a shovel and leave it out all night?

PETTICOAT LOOSE. She is. And it cries with cold, or fear all night. Sleep doesn't be on our eyes five minutes together.

HONOR. Biddy's plan is that when the Good People see their baby suffering, they'll take it away, and give back your own baby.

PETTICOAT LOOSE. But if the fairy baby is my own baby, and the frost kills it, it'll be buried down dead until the end of the world.

263

HONOR. Biddy should know a fairy baby, a fairy latchiko, after living with the fairies seven years till her share of red blood was gone.

PETTICOAT LOOSE. I hope the fairies don't steal my baby's blood, and fill it with their own white blood.

HONOR. But if they do that, they'll gift it with magic powers and prophecy the same as they gifted Biddy.

(*There is a loud sinister treble knock on the door.*)

PETTICOAT LOOSE. Biddy's knock!

(HONOR *hurries to the door and opens it.* BIDDY THE TOSSER *is standing on the doorstep. She advances to the table, ignoring the two women. A clothing bag shaped rather like a school bag is hung by a strap from her shoulders. She carries three rods of unequal length and shape under her other arm. She is a commanding and a sinister figure, deadly pale, with a black patch over one eye, middle aged but vigorous, though at times she can look sad and lonely looking. She wears a dark shawl and blouse and a red petticoat. When she addresses people she often looks past them, or away from them, as if she can see invisible beings in high fairy places. She takes a bottle from her bag, sniffs at it, shakes it.* HONOR *has closed the door, and the two women are now watching* BIDDY.)

BIDDY. How is your sick mare, Honor Lally?

HONOR. Thanks to your last bottle, Biddy, she can stand at her dead ease again.

BIDDY. Today we'll annoint her heart with this bottle. Every herb in it can heal seven diseases.

(*She hands the bottle to* HONOR, *who leaves it on the dresser. She takes a coin from the dresser, gives it to* BIDDY, *who pockets it.*)

HONOR. Still, Biddy, if that mare has any milk, she keeps it to herself.

BIDDY. The Good People are stealing her away every night to give milk to a fairy foal.

HONOR. Even though we're doing what you told us. We're putting three deep spits on the mare every day.

BIDDY. A stranger's spits are double as good as a friend's spits. So let ye recruit any stranger ye see passing the way. (*She opens the street door wide.*)

HONOR. The mountainy people are passing all day, running east from the hunger.

BIDDY. Petticoat Loose, did you put out your fairy baby last night?

PETTICOAT LOOSE. I did, Biddy, and this morning it was as cold as a frog and near death maybe.

BIDDY. The latchiko baby was only pretending to be that way,

They're as cunning as Christian sinners. (*She is spacing and viewing her rods.*)

PETTICOAT LOOSE. Biddy, here's a penny I worked hard for. Toss and ask the Good People should I get a gospel from Fr. Tarpey to recover my baby. (BIDDY *pockets the coin, and takes two or three coins from a secret pocket. She balances them on her palm, intones, "Curra pee and Crabs Alley!". She tosses them, catches them coming down, consults them gravely.*)

BIDDY. The Good People say, "No." It does no good, but harm to have priests take notice of people that are fairy struck. (*She hides her coins again.*)

PETTICOAT LOOSE. But maybe the Good People say that because Fr. Tarpey says there's no longer such things as fairies.

BIDDY (*fiercely*). How was that fool every priested? That doesn't know how God created the angels by dipping his bright hands into the Well of Divinity; and every drop that fell from his hands turned into an angel. But when Lucifer warred against God in Heaven, some angels were afeard to fight for either side, so God condemned them to dwell for ever on earth as fairies.

HONOR. And to this day the fairies hate to be seen but ghosts and spirits love to be seen.

BIDDY (*again taking observations through her rods*). St. Patrick of the Bells said, "If we're neighbourly and friendly with the Good People, they'll be neighbourly and friendly with us."

PETTICOAT LOOSE. But Fr. Tarpey denies that St. Patrick ever said the like.

BIDDY. Who'd believe a disgraced priesteen without a bell? Put out for drink. And making a living selling gospels that kill instead of cure. And with silence between himself and the priests that have bells!

(HONOR *comes from the dresser with a glass.*)

HONOR. Biddy, you'll drain this sup of whiskey.

BIDDY (*accepting it*). For fear ye'd think I have anything against ye. (*She tastes, then proceeds to drink it expertly.*)

PETTICOAT LOOSE (*merry*). Biddy, you have the right twist in your elbow for it!

BIDDY. A spur in the head is worth two in the heel.

HONOR. Petticoat Loose wants you to pull the only two herbs that can bring her baby back from the fairy forts.

PETTICOAT LOOSE. The herbs that brought Our Lord back from the dead.

BIDDY (*sadly*). If I pulled them before my hand was crossed with

gold, I'd fade away into nothing like snow in the sun.
(MULLEE *comes in smiling.*)

MULLEE. Biddy, I seen you dawning over the hill ... The whites of our sick mare's eyes were out with the fear again today.

BIDDY. Then an evil spirit has gone into her stomach. Honor, bucket a few coals there.

HONOR (*putting a few coals into the bucket*). Maybe in God the fire'll fence evil spirits away from her.

MULLEE. But she's coming back to her strength again.

BIDDY. We'll pass the coals over and under her body.
(HONOR *hands the bucket and the tongs to* MULLEE. MULLEE *goes out, followed by* BIDDY *with her bundle and her rods.*)

HONOR. Why did you vex Biddy with your talk of priests. If Biddy strips her evil eye, she'll put that priest where he'll never see daylight.

PETTICOAT LOOSE (*also worried*). Unless I get a chance call to Dick the Cock's bed, where'll I earn a gold sovereign to cross Biddy's hand with?

HONOR. If my man comes home from the fair with a light heart and a heavy purse, I'll ask him to part a sovereign to you.

PETTICOAT LOOSE (*smiling*). Remind him of that sure proverb: "When the hand stops scattering, the heart stops praying."
(*A man appears in the doorway, dressed in dark and rather shabby clothes of the period. He is in his middle or late thirties, and looks pale and sad and strained. But he is not lacking in vitality or intelligence. His accent and speech is homely and vigorous, typical of the farm-reared country priest of that time and later. Under his arm he carries a canvas bag.*)

PRIEST (*smiling*). The glory of the morning on ye!

HONOR. Come in, father, and take an air of the fire.
(*She smooths an armchair cushion for him; but he goes to the table, takes bottles out of his bag.*)

PRIEST. Honor, would ye swop these narrow-shouldered bottles of whiskey and poteen for a share of meal and spuds?

HONOR. To be sure, father. We'll send Mullee over with the meal and spuds.

PRIEST (*urgently*). But not till after dark. And don't let man, or mortal, know that I didn't drink every drop of that. (*He throws himself wearily into the armchair, and* HONOR *hides the bottles in the bottom shelves of the dresser.*)

PETTICOAT LOOSE (*smiling*). But, father, what everyone says must be true; and all say your gospels don't cure unless you drink the whiskey and poteen your customers bring you.

PRIEST (*ruefully*). I well know 'tis what they say; but it's the biggest lie that ever came out of a mouth. It's saying that the Creator of the Universe can't cure an illness unless I'm too drunk to keep a leg under me.

HONOR. Sure the priests are entitled to the drink. (*She pours whiskey into a glass.*)

PRIEST. We are, but we're entitled to save our lives from it, too.

HONOR (*coming over with glass*). This drop of red whiskey will warm you.

PRIEST. No, thanks, Honor. I'm two days without a drink now, and never again, though 'tis shaking me. (*He displays his shaking hands.*)

HONOR. But, father, to give it up too sudden could put you to death.

PRIEST. Let it kill. I'd rather die of the drouth than go before my God drunk.

PETTICOAT LOOSE. Father, Biddy the Tosser has a sure cure for the shakes. Herbs from the hill.

(HONOR *leaves the glass of whiskey on the table.*)

PRIEST. I wouldn't trust the choking of a rat to Biddy the Tosser. Petticoat Loose, is she urging you to leave your baby out all night on a shovel?

PETTICOAT LOOSE. Yes, I do put out the fairy latchiko to make the fairies take it back.

PRIEST. There is no such thing as a fairy latchiko. It's your own true baby.

PETTICOAT LOOSE. It's my baby's spit and image, but Biddy proved it's a fairy baby.

PRIEST. It's your own baby, and the frost may kill it.

PETTICOAT LOOSE. I do have it wrapped in half blankets like an onion.

PRIEST. Still the frost can pinch the nose off it and kill it.

(BIDDY *appears in the doorway. The priest does not see her.*)

PRIEST. Biddy the Tosser and Biddy Nawpla are tricksters of women from God knows where. They failed to win husbands or farms, so they took to the black arts instead. By telling ye lies, they're making more money than robbers or coiners.

BIDDY (*handing the tongs to* HONOR *and coming forward*). Tell us another lie while your mouth is warm, you disgraced priesteen from the Divil knows where. (*She puts her bag and rods on the table.*)

PRIEST. You're turning people back to the pagan druid's religion.

BIDDY. Anciently Ossian and the Fenians defeated giants so big that they could see the whole world between the giants' legs. Yet the Fenians were pagans who never said a prayer. So it wasn't God made them mighty It was the fairies and the druids.

PRIEST. There were no giants. And if there were fairies, time wore them out long ago.

BIDDY. Because of your insults the Good People have put the weather and the crops under a penalty. They're taking the goodness out of the spuds, and leaving the people to starve. Soon the people will come in their numbers, and gather stones to kill you.

PRIEST. During last night were your cocks crowing for a death?

BIDDY. Not them. They never crow out of time.

PRIEST. They should crow out of time when their owner commits two murders.

BIDDY (*contemptuous*). Lies and a noisy windpipe! ... that's all you're good for.

PRIEST. You told the journeyman tailor Harkaway Walsh and his wife that their only child was fairy struck and stolen, and a fairy likeness left in its place.

BIDDY. A fairy laitchiko it is. All my life I seen them, and enough of them.

PRIEST. You bade them tie it out on a shovel all night. This morning they found it as cold as a plough and dead.

PETTICOAT LOOSE. By the seven blessed candles!

HONOR. God comfort them!

BIDDY (*quickly regaining composure*). They didn't call me in time to that baby. It was already in the forts, and what died was an old spent person who'd die soon anyway.

PRIEST. Their child was out of sorts, and you made them put it out all night in the bleak of winter.

BIDDY. I warned her – not a blackfrost night; or a night the wind had teeth in it.

PRIEST. You can say that now, because you know she's no longer alive to deny it.

BIDDY (*really taken aback*). Maura Harkaway dead! Is that truth or lies in the name of Mary Mother and the Good Angels?

PRIEST. Harkaway is after calling on me, sick of his life, and seeking a gospel that'd save him from joining his wife in the lake. When he was gone seeing to their child's grave, she drowned herself. (*The three women bless themselves.*)

HONOR. The dear blessing of God on her!

PETTICOAT LOOSE. Poor Maura! But the fish swims dead or alive, and so does the soul.

BIDDY. The will of God must be ... And madness drops true to breed sooner or later.

PRIEST. It would never drop, if you didn't make her kill her only child.

BIDDY. I well know who brought on these deaths. It was Johnny Eat-A-Bit. He called in to Harkaways for a crust a few days ago. Johnny Eat-A-Bit has the evil eye, but he doesn't know he has it.

PETTICOAT LOOSE. True for you, Biddy. Because Johnny Eat-A-Bit called into our house that day, too.

BIDDY. My rods told me that's why your baby got fairy struck.

(*The* PRIEST *suddenly switches from all out attack on* BIDDY *to leading her into a trap by seeming to flatter her for the moment.*)

PRIEST. Biddy, your followers claim for you wonderful cures and prophecies. If these were worked through the black arts, you'll have to pay for them some day.

BIDDY (*calmly*). I have paid for them already.

PRIEST. Is it by your seven years in the fairy forts?

BIDDY. Yes. Where else could I learn how to stretch out a hand to help people?

PRIEST. And in the forts you learned that the fairies have to sacrifice a baby to the Devil every seven years to pay him for the power and knowledge he gives them?

BIDDY (*suspiciously*). I hadn't to go to the forts to learn that. Women, didn't ye hear that at your mothers' knees?

HONOR. We did.

PETTICOAT LOOSE. Yes. Truth is truth.

PRIEST (*rising, and returning to the offensive*). Then why can't ye see that Biddy is sacrificing your babies to the fairies, or the Devil, to pay them for the power and knowledge they're giving her?

BIDDY. Because they don't shut their eyes like you do. They see its fairy laitchikoes that die, while the real babies live on in the forts, if they aren't charmed back.

PRIEST. Petticoat Loose, you must rouse your soul against Biddy's plots against the life of your baby.

BIDDY (*furiously*). Plots! You bloodsucker! The earth is heavy with you!

PRIEST. From now on I won't stop walking and talking against your murders until the people band together and run you to the edge of the sea! (*He is moving towards the door.*)

BIDDY. The curse of the hungry is on you! And my heavy hatred likewise.

PRIEST. The back of my hand and the sole of my foot to you! (*He goes.*)

BIDDY (*following him to the door*). I'll soon end your trade of writing crooked gospels that wouldn't cure a cat's sneeze! (*She comes back to the table, takes observations with her rods.*)

HONOR (*uneasy*). Biddy, his gospels must be holy, because they won't burn.

BIDDY. Because people are afeard to burn them. There was never a fool, but he had bigger fools to admire him.

PETTICOAT LOOSE (*anxious*). Biddy, did we call you in time to my baby?

BIDDY (*sternly*). If ye called me in time, it wouldn't be in the forts.

PETTICOAT LOOSE. Even if it's frost and snow, should I put out the fairy latchiko again tonight?

BIDDY. Do not. If too much cold puts lumps on your fairy latchiko, the Good People may give your baby the Dead Man's pinch.

HONOR. Biddy, we could carry you to the wake at Harkaways tonight. He'd like you to join in the three keens of sorrow over them.

PETTICOAT LOOSE. Harkaway can afford a fine plentiful wake. We'll be fed and drunk for a week after it!

BIDDY. Tell Harkaway I'm heartsore that I can't honour his wake. I have people to save from the fairy sickness and the fairy forts. (*She has taken out her secret coins.*) Curra Pee and Crabs Alley! (*She tosses and consults her coins.*) Tell Tailor Harkaway his wife and child aren't dead all out. The Good People have them in their forts. So tell him to leave the nails loose in their coffins.

PETTICOAT LOOSE. So if Harkaway crosses your hand with gold, you can charm them back from the forts.

BIDDY. I can. If they weren't fairy struck by the Queen of a fort, or the Fool of a Fort.

PETTICOAT LOOSE. If they were, can nothing bring them back, or my baby?

BIDDY. Nothing over the earth or under the sky. (*With her bundle and her rods she is moving to the door.*) Honor, your man is home at last from the fair!

HONOR (*matter-of-fact*). Is he walking, or rolling?

BIDDY. He has a black eye, and there's a cut in the black-ness. I have a bottle that'd cure him. (*She comes back to the table, rummages in her bag.*)

HONOR (*looking out door*). Shawn is in the heartsblood of every fight in the country.

PETTICOAT LOOSE (*laughing*). He has no regard at all for his four bones.

(SHAWN LALLY *comes in pulling off his fight damaged hat, which he flings into one corner. His blood-stained stick, or shillelagh, he casts into another corner. He is a vigorous man of forty or more, head-strong and proud and wild, but not mean or evil looking. His watch and chain indicate prosperity, and his clothes are the good strong kind a well-to-do farmer would wear at a fair. He has a swelling cut over one eye, and a worse cut on his right temple. He is in a rage, and goes straight for the whiskey bottle on the dresser.*)

SHAWN. I'm dry with rage. (*he pours some into a mug.*) Biddy, have you your herbs for a split skull?

BIDDY. On a fair day I wouldn't go on my rounds without them. (*She is shaking a bottle.*)

HONOR (*matter-of-fact*). Was it a pedigree row, or a faction fight?

SHAWN. Neither . . . Dick the Cock got as drunk as a whore, and set into clearing the fair with his loaded whip handle. Mostly they left his way until he came to me, and I sent him running like a dog without a tail.

HONOR. Dick the Cock! A landlord and a magistrate!

BIDDY. The next Bench day Dick could throw you into the body of the jail.

(SHAWN *comes over to the armchair and sits down mug in hand.* BIDDY *begins to dab at his wounds with liquid from her bottle.* HONOR *is tearing a strip for bandage at the dresser drawer.*)

SHAWN (*bitterly*). I hadn't my faction with me, and he had a hundred tenants. After our ructions, his tenants began casting up the old prophecy standing against us Lallys: that we'd die out at last for want of a manchild.

HONOR. Please God and His Mother we'll make babies yet. (*She looks up at the Madonna.*) Last night again I dreamed very hard that we would.

PETTICOAT LOOSE. And there's great virtue in dreams.

SHAWN (*bitterly*). For years she's dreaming that dream until she has old shoes made of it . . . Then his tenants jeered that I was too cowardly to make a chance child, and too miserly to part a little money to one of the poor girls around who's falling out of their

271

standing with the hunger.

HONOR. If you do that, you'll be joining the bull's religion.

SHAWN. A chance-child 'd keep the grass from growing up to our doors when we're old and weakhanded at last.

HONOR. The Good People told Biddy we didn't breed, because some enemy tied a knot against us, while we were being wed. But that old spell against us should be worn out soon.

SHAWN. Every year you're saying that. But my mind is made up at long and at last. I'll make a chance child while this famine has all the poor girls out in the open. Amn't I right, Biddy.

BIDDY (*bandaging his head*). If you betray your wife, you'll vex her brother Shawn the Widowman, seven foot high, and his sons nearly as lofty.

SHAWN (*bitterly*). And they're like dogs, fighting and slashing at every fair.

BIDDY. If you vex the Big Joyces of Connemara, they'll put you out to grass, with a daisy quilt over you.

SHAWN. I know they can three me and four me; but I have my Queen Anne gun, and I'll make it speak up.

BIDDY. If you do, you'll get a short trial and a long rope from Dick the Cock.

HONOR. And, Shawn, while you'd be enjoying your whore, what about the woman that owns you?

SHAWN. Too long I'm the prisoner of a childless marriage, and too long you're going around with a lip as sorrowful as a foalless mare. It's a cold fireside without a baby.

HONOR. Before you sin your soul and shame our name, I'll cross Biddy's hand with silver. (*She rummages in a dresser drawer, comes back with a coin.*) Ask the Good People is the black spell against us worn out yet?

SHAWN. Ask them are we fated ever to breed a man-child?

(BIDDY *pockets* HONOR'S *coin, and produces her tossing coins from a secret pocket.*)

BIDDY. God doesn't tell the Good People everything. And they don't tell me all they know. But they don't tell me no lie. Curra pee and Crab's Alley! (*She tosses, and consults.*) The Good People declare ye'll make a man-child when Honor is wearing the shift of a priest's wife.

SHAWN. The only priests with wives are the ones who turned Protestant for the lucre of thirty sovereigns a year from King George's Government.

BIDDY. The shifts of their wives wouldn't break the spell that's binding ye. Because such men are no longer priests, or Catholics.

PETTICOAT LOOSE. But no priest can wed right.

BIDDY. The Good People don't value sacraments. If a girl sleeps one night with a priest, they'll bestow a spell on the shift she wore that night.

HONOR. But where could we get tale, trace, or tidings of such a shift?

BIDDY. If ye part enough money to a starving girl, she'll do your bidding, like the stones came long ago at the bidding of the druids.

SHAWN. But where can we find a starving priest?

BIDDY. That disgraced priesteen'd sleep with a girl.

PETTICOAT LOOSE. But, Biddy, he has made it public and sure that no woman is to call at his cabin after dark.

BIDDY. He has to behave a blessed man with the local women, because he couldn't silence their mouths.

SHAWN. And he knows no woman can keep a secret, because she has no apple in her throat.

BIDDY. The Good People have made me the wiser of how he's whoring with stranger girls that came for Gospels from the mountains and the sea.

HONOR. Stranger girls wouldn't know he forbids women to call after dark.

BIDDY. But they'd know that, if they told people about whoring with a priest, they wouldn't get much of a man, or any man.

SHAWN (*enthusiastic*). Then if he's a whoremaster of old – Petticoat Loose, if you'll lie a night with him, I'll pay you what'll bring your children through this famine and the next.

PETTICOAT LOOSE (*scared*). But if I lie with him, I'll be cursed into the pit. And they say the hand of a priest's whore grows up out of her grave.

HONOR (*also scared*). The grave could refuse her altogether, and refuse us who bribed her.

BIDDY. It could, if the priest was a good-living priest; and a priest with a bell. (*She takes out her tossing coins.*) I'll ask the Good People how sinful it'd be for a girl to lie a night with a whoremaster and disgraced priesteen. Curra Pee and Crab's Alley! (*She tosses and consults.*) They declare it would be no worse a sin than if she lied a night with Dick the Cock.

PETTICOAT LOOSE (*chuckling*). What myself done, and will need to do soon again.

SHAWN. No, Petticoat Loose, my money will save you from ever again dirtying your blood with Dick the Cock. If you'll lie a night with this priest.

(*A girl is seen stumbling past the window.* PETTICOAT LOOSE *springs to her feet.*)

PETTICOAT LOOSE. A stranger passing! Three spits for your mare! (*Putting down her sewing, she sets out for the door.*)

HONOR. Tell him he'll get a bellyful for a mouthful.

(*A young and pretty girl staggers in, and falls on her face. She wears a coloured shawl and blouse and a red petticoat.* HONOR *and* PETTICOAT LOOSE *run to her aid.*)

PETTICOAT LOOSE. She's in a fainting spell!

HONOR. God grant it isn't from the famine fever!

SHAWN. She could have fever enough to kill a thousand! Turn her out quick!

BIDDY. Wait till I handle her. (*She feels* PEG'S *forehead.*) She has no fever. She's too long past her last meal. Lift her into the armchair, and give her milk with a small dash of red whiskey through it. (*As* HONOR *and* PETTICOAT LOOSE *carry out her instructions, she goes over to* SHAWN.)

BIDDY. Shawn, that priesteen will say to himself, "I'm a gone man if I trust a petticoat loose for silence, or for anything else".

SHAWN. Then we'll wait for a mountainy girl running from the hunger.

HONOR (*pointing to* PEG ABOVE ALL). That shawl is from the mountains, but her shoes are from the islands of the sea.

(PETTICOAT LOOSE *keeps her hand on the girl's shoulder to keep her from falling out of the armchair.* HONOR *is preparing the drink.*)

PETTICOAT LOOSE. She ran from the hunger in good time. There's still good flesh on her bones.

SHAWN. Maybe she walked on the hungry grass, where a corpse fell, or was left down long ago.

(BIDDY *is helping the girl to drink from the mug.*)

HONOR. Her face puts me in mind of Barbara of the Children who tramped Connemara, and slept many a night in my mother's bed for the poor.

PETTICOAT LOOSE. Barbara of the Children! Was she a petticoat loose, too?

HONOR. She never was wed, and every child had a different father; but she reared them as good as she could, or gave them away to farmers.

BIDDY (*to girl*). Was Barbara of the Children the mother of your body?

PEG ABOVE ALL. She was, but she died out last winter.

HONOR. God rest her soul! Were you there to shut her eyes?

PEG ABOVE ALL. No, mam. I was a kitchen slut to McEgan's wife.

SHAWN. How do they name you?

PEG ABOVE ALL. Peg Above All.

BIDDY. What John the Baptist put the name on you?

PEG ABOVE ALL (*sadly*). The lads around, making out that I was the best looking. And when the landlord's son heard that he came to McEgan demanding the best of me. Himself and McEgan let on he came buying oats, and he went out to the barn judging the oats.

SHAWN. Buying oats! An old landlord's trick! They never lost it.

PEG ABOVE ALL. McEgan sent me out to the barn with empty sacks for the oats. The minute I went in McEgan bolted the door and left me at the landlord's son.

PETTICOAT LOOSE. And the next day did McEgan give you the high road?

PEG ABOVE ALL. No, not until my baby was born and hardy enough for the road.

BIDDY. Where is you baby? Did you give it away?

PEG ABOVE ALL (*revolted by the idea*). No, no — I never will! It's where we slept last night in the deserted cabin by the bridge.

BIDDY (*taking command*). Honor, give her thing to eat. And, Petticoat Loose, come outside you. I have new tidings of your baby.

PETTICOAT LOOSE (*thrilled*). Is it in the fairy fort of Lissatava, where I was leaving the meal?

BIDDY. You'll hear that and you'll hear more. (*She goes out.*)

PETTICOAT LOOSE. Shawn, mind would she fall out.

(SHAWN *stands beside* PEG ABOVE ALL, *and keeps a hand on her shoulder,* PETTICOAT LOOSE *runs out door.* HONOR *is readying a slice of bread and butter at the dresser.*)

SHAWN. You're tramping the long dark roads east to Leinster where the spuds didn't fail?

PEG ABOVE ALL. Yes, you honour. Unless you'd have a run of work for me. I can take a hook and cut the harvest.

SHAWN. So can a thousand big men around here, but they can't even buy a day's work. The long roads to Leinster are dangerous.

PEG ABOVE ALL (*sadly*). Yes, your honour. You'd meet a score of

275

tramps every mile of the road.

HONOR (*giving bread to* PEG ABOVE ALL). Take this. An empty stomach is a heavy load.

PEG ABOVE ALL. Glory and thanks be to ye all. (*She eats,* BIDDY *enters followed by* PETTICOAT LOOSE.)

BIDDY. Shawn, what time is it by your watch and chain?

SHAWN. The two hands are courting for noon.

BIDDY. And noon is one of the fairy times of day, so we'll anoint your mare's heart now. Shawn, we'll need you to hold her, and, Honor, you to hold the bottle. Petticoat Loose, give Peg Above All her fill, so as she'll be able to put three good spits on the mare.

PETTICOAT LOOSE. I'll make her as fat as a fool.

(BIDDY *sweeps her bundle and her rods off the table, and goes out.* HONOR *takes the bottle from the dresser, and follows her. As* SHAWN *is following her out, he turns in the doorway.*)

SHAWN. Let ye warm yourselves with a good bumper of whiskey. (*Points to dresser.*) Today's there's a step-mother's breath in the air. (*He goes.* PETTICOAT LOOSE *runs to the dresser, pours whiskey into two mugs, brings them over.*)

PETTICOAT LOOSE. The Lallys keep whiskey so good that you'd give it to your mother and take it off her again. We'll drink to our inclinations – soon and sudden! (*Tips* PEG ABOVE ALL'S *mug with her own.*) Put it at the back of your soul!

(*The drink, and* PEG ABOVE ALL *coughs a little.*)

PETTICOAT LOOSE. And now we'll drink to the safety of my baby in the forts and to your baby in a cabin that was deserted after a swan was seen perched on it.

(*The drink again.*)

PEG ABOVE ALL (*agitated*). The hungry eye sees far, and I see the greybacked crow picking out my eyes and my baby's eyes when we're dying of hunger in a ditch.

PETTICOAT LOOSE. The same as the greybacked crow picks the eyes out of dying sheep.

PEG ABOVE ALL. And the same as he picked out my mother's eyes when she was dying alone against a rock.

PETTICOAT LOOSE. You could save your baby, if a childless couple would take it.

PEG ABOVE ALL. If I have to do that, I'll cry enough to wash myself. My baby is all I have to live for now.

PETTICOAT LOOSE (*smiling*). God is always making wheels, and the spokes that are down today will be up tomorrow. Our spokes are down since the first day the carpenter made us, but our spokes will be up if we act as bold as rams now.

PEG ABOVE ALL. I'll venture anything to save my baby. It isn't able to save itself.

PETTICOAT LOOSE. Biddy of the hidden eye belongs to another nation – the Good People; and Biddy foretells that the childless couple in this house will make a man-child, if they can find the shift a girl wore a night she slept with a priest.

PEG ABOVE ALL. I heard by the fireside about the shift of a priest's wife. But that's only lies and daftness. What priest would let a woman lay her skin on his skin?

PETTICOAT LOOSE. A cockshout from here a disgraced priest lives lonesome on the brink of the bog. You and me can quit poverty for ever, if we win the shift of a priest's wife off that priest, and sell it to the childless couple in this house. (*She crosses to the dresser, uncorks the whiskey bottle.*)

PEG ABOVE ALL. To take his vow against women off a priest would be the wrongest act since Judas betrayed Our Lord.

PETTICOAT LOOSE. Judas was greedy for riches. We're only trying to keep alive the children we carried in our bodies for three quarters of a year.

PEG ABOVE ALL. If we do it, no man will ever marry us.

PETTICOAT LOOSE. No man will ever know. There's fifty gold sovereigns for me if I set this priest drunk, and fifty gold sovereigns for you if you creep into his bed while he's well drunk and asleep.

PEG ABOVE ALL. Fifty gold sovereigns'd buy the lease of a farm and stock it.

PETTICOAT LOOSE. And when we're masters of stocked farms we'll get our choice of husbands. But if you won't sleep a night with this priest, another starving girl will be hired to do it. Then yourself and your baby will be left to the greybacked crow and death. (*With her finger she demonstrates the swoop at* PEG'S *eye.*)

PEG ABOVE ALL. The fox throws its cubs to the hunters to save itself. Have we to throw ourselves to the hunters to save our babies?

PETTICOAT LOOSE (*smiling*). Yes, like your mother Barbara of the Children. The life of a petticoat loose is to have to breed more to keep alive what we have already. Until they're up to our shoulders. Then we'll turn saints like Mary Magdalene.

PEG ABOVE ALL. Every mortal is against us fallen women. No one is for us.

PETTICOAT LOOSE (*smiling*). The Mother of God is on our behalf. She knows it isn't good times we're having; but the height of hardship.

PEG ABOVE ALL. But if I rouse the love of women in this priest, he'll join the clergy of the woman – the Protestant ministers!

PETTICOAT LOOSE. No; the minute the shift of a priest's wife is won, Biddy is to set spells and charms that'll turn him against you and against all women for ever.

PEG ABOVE ALL (*relieved*). Thank God for that! But when the priest wakens and finds me in his bed, he may corpse me with blows and with the worst curses of all: curses in Latin!

PETTICOAT LOOSE (*gravely*). It could happen so. And even if it doesn't, every time two make one the woman is gambling her life. So make the people of this house swear to rear your baby, if their plan takes away your life. Here they come!

(SHAWN *enters followed by* HONOR *carrying the bottle.*)

SHAWN. Petticoat Loose, show her the mare now, if she can pull foot after her again.

PETTICOAT LOOSE. Faith she can. And they say a stranger's spit is as good as to say, "God bless it!". (*She hurries out, and can be seen outside the window, talking to* BIDDY.)

HONOR. Our herd's children are gone to fetch your baby here. And there's a fine bed and room for ye in there.

PEG ABOVE ALL (*radiant*). May God send ye the Heavens! And I'm well able to humour the spinning wheel. Isn't it for that ye want me? (*But they turn away, and do not answer, and she realises that they want her for a very different service. She shrinks and turns towards the door, and meets* BIDDY *coming in.*)

BIDDY. Peg Above All, three deep spits from under your small tongue. (PEG ABOVE ALL *hurries out, and* BIDDY *comes forward.*)

BIDDY. Petticoat Loose has asked her, but Peg thinks she'd be buying gold too dear.

SHAWN (*grim*). Like Owen the Coward she won't be allowed into Heaven for fear the saints'd take the same disease.

HONOR. Maybe if we shoved on more money?

BIDDY. Yes, bribery can split a stone. (*She is rummaging in her bag.*) And then, Honor, you'll need to collect a share of her sweat and a little dust from her navel for a love charm and coaxiorum we'll put into that priesteen's whiskey.

HONOR. I'll ask her.

BIDDY. And, Shawn, I'll need a corpse's hand to stir the coaxiorum.

And for the greatest of all coaxiorums, the spancel of death, I'll
need a strip of skin from a corpse's head down to its heel.
SHAWN (*proudly*). Biddy, the blood cousin of Count Lally De
Tolendal isn't going digging up dead men and butchering them.
BIDDY. Give me a shake of gold for Teig of the Tomb. Teig of the
Tombs will dig up and shape all our needs.
SHAWN (*giving her money*). Don't tell Teig of the Tombs this
money and command are from me.
BIDDY (*proudly*). Teig of the Tombs is my true friend and a very
discreet man. He has to be with his way of living.
PETTICOAT LOOSE (*entering*). She has put on three spits big enough
to trip you. But I doubt she won't venture her soul.
SHAWN. So the cowardice of the women follows Peg Above All!
Now she'll suffer a worse fate from the tramps on the road!
(PEG ABOVE ALL *appears in the doorway, but avoiding their
eyes and looking up the road eagerly.*)
BIDDY (*sternly*). What is your word, Peg Above All? Yes or no?
PEG ABOVE ALL. They should be soon here with my baby.
BIDDY. Peg Above All, we can work out of everything except the
grave. Isn't everything and anything better than black
starvation?
PEG ABOVE ALL. My poor mother's fate! Alone against a rock with
her eyes picked out and snow for a coat of thatch. With no
priest to read over her, and no keeners to cry over her! The
hunger is like the fox: its last bite is bad. (*She comes forward to
the table, and drops into a chair heavily.*)
BIDDY. The same end is for yourself and your baby, if you let the
price of a stocked farm go to another girl.
PEG ABOVE ALL (*sadly*). I came from badness, and a cup-tosser
foretold that Hell would be my last home and my first home . . .
Still I might be good enough for God to take me.
BIDDY. Forgiveness for this sin is easy got from the Three Saints at
the South Pole.
PEG ABOVE ALL (*relieved*). Is it? Then I will do your bidding. (*She
turns to* SHAWN.) If your Honour, will swear to rear my baby, if
this priest makes a dead woman of me. Ye won't be sorry.
(*Pleading.*) It's a lovely darling baby.
(SHAWN *takes down the Bible, kisses it.*)
SHAWN. I swear to that on God's blessed book. (*He hands the book
to* HONOR.)
HONOR (*kissing book*). And I swear.
PEG ABOVE ALL (*radiant with relief*). The King of the Graces will

279

reward ye! And it's a darling baby! (*She looks out.*) And it's here! (*She flies to meet her baby.*)

HONOR. Will God ever pardon our souls?

SHAWN. Sure we're only trying to make another soul for his Heaven! (BIDDY *in triumphant mood, sweeps her rods and her bundle off the table, and sets out for the door. Near the door she turns.*)

BIDDY. Honor, without no delay, Peg Above All's sweat and dust from her navel. Myself is going straightaway down to a true friend and a gifted man Teig of the Tombs, who sleeps by day, and – like the hare – with one eye open! (BIDDY *goes. Suddenly* HONOR *panics.*)

HONOR. But, Shawn, if Biddy calls on the name of Devils, we could spawn a Devil's child. I'll shout Biddy back, and wait another year. (*She hurries to the door.*)

SHAWN. If you wait much longer, your first baby may put you to death.

PETTICOAT LOOSE. Too long ye're spell bound, and the world is slipping by.

HONOR (*sadly, coming back from the door*). My years are passing by at a full gallop . . . The next crossroads will be the end of hope.

SHAWN. Then whatever Biddy is to say and do, let it be said and done. (*He strides into the bedroom.*)

PETTICOAT LOOSE. Praying with the priests and pleasing the Good People will rescue our souls again.

(PETTICOAT LOOSE *hands* HONOR *the repaired apron, and* HONOR *gives her the little bag of meal in return.*)

HONOR (*smiling*). Yes, that way, please God, we'll end as blessed as another.

PETTICOAT LOOSE. And with children of your own to close your eyes.

(PETTICOAT LOOSE *goes out.* HONOR *turns to the picture of the Madonna. She blesses herself, and prays to the picture silently, with imploring and misty eyes.*)

CURTAIN

ACT TWO

Scene One

The time is a few nights later, and the scene is the priest's one-roomed cabin on the edge of a bog. The only door is in the middle of the back wall, and it has a latch and a wooden bolt. The only small window is on its left, from the actor's point of view. So the bed can be seen through this window, as the head of the bed is near the left hand wall. The bed runs parallel to the footlights, and is nearer to them than to the back wall. The small table is near the right-hand wall, with a chair drawn up to it. The table holds some weighty volumes, and a lighted candle and a wooden Penal Days crucifix. The fire is at the footlights, about the middle of this missing "fourth wall". A small iron pot and kettle stand beside it, and a pile of turf sods. A wooden stool faces it, and on its left the room's second chair. Bottles, some corked and some empty, stand around the walls, and on the wall shelves which do duty as dresser and as bookshelves. On pegs stuck into walls hang a couple of cloaks and hats. The priest is walking up and down, reading his breviary.

PRIEST. Allelulia, alleluia. Tu es sacerdos in aeternum, secundum ordinem Melchisedech. Alleluia (*He goes on his knees beside the table, and resumes his reading.*)
(*Somebody rattles the door-latch and, finding the door bolted, begins to knock thunderously. The priest is disturbed for a moment but resumes his praying. Soon the door is lashed with a stick.*)
PRIEST. Per Christum Dominum nostrum, Amen. (*Making sign of the cross.*) In nomine Patris et Filii et Spiritui Sancti. Amen. (*He rises, closing breviary.*) That's hard knocking! In the name of St. Patrick, who's there?
VOICE. (*fiercely*). Mickle Donegan! (*Again lashes the door.*)
PRIEST (*to himself*). Mickle, a word and a blow was ever your way!
You'd get cranky on cold water. (*He unbolts the door quietly,*

returns to his table and call out.) Come in, Mickle!
(*The door is flung open, and a middle-aged frantic looking man runs in brandishing a lethal looking shillelagh. He points at the crucifix.*)

MICKLE. There he is! The worst God since Crom Dubh that rose storms and fogs against Saint Patrick!

(MICKLE *lashes with full force at the crucifix, but the priest snatches it away just in time, and carries it to the opposite side of the room.*)

PRIEST. Mickle, that's sacrilege and blasphemy!

MICKLE. There's no good in Him! He's after losing my young lad to the world! The only child I ever had, or ever will now!

PRIEST. Is Timmy dead? I'm very sorry for your trouble, Mickle.

MICKLE. Here's your gospel that didn't cure him. It only put him astray. (*He throws on the table a small packet sewn into a red cloth.*)

PRIEST. You didn't come to me in time. And by the time you came to me that fool of a doctor had bled and leeched the lifeblood out of Timmy.

MICKLE. Maybe God wouldn't cut off Timmy, if you drank the poteen I brought you. Your gospels don't cure unless you drink what we bring you. (*He is going around the wall, uncorking bottles and sniffing at them.*)

PRIEST (*worried*). Mickle, I drank your poteen sweetly – every drop.

MICKLE. I'll know as soon as I bring my nose near it. It was made from the finest bog-water.

PRIEST. Sure all poteen smells alike ... And as for Timmy, God liked him so well that He called him away young.

MICKLE. This is my poteen, and not a mouthful drank out of it!

PRIEST. No, Mickle, that's mountainy poteen.

MICKLE. You can mint lies, like every traitor and murderer. Now I'll make you feel the strength of my bones. I won't leave a spark of sense in you! (*He puts down the bottle beside the open door, cutting off at the same time the priest's escape route through the door. The priest snatches up the chair, and retreats around the table, warding off blows with the chair.*)

PRIEST. You'll lose the luck if you strike a priest.

MICKLE. You're only a traitor priest, and I'll spill your blood like skim milk.

PRIEST. If you do, you'll see your own funeral. You'll be hanged. (PETTICOAT LOOSE *appears in the doorway.*)

PETTICOAT LOOSE. Death alive! Slope his blows, father, and I'll stand fair play for you. (*She takes a bottle from under her shawl, stands it against the wall. She twists her shawl into a rope, and catches an end with each hand. As* MICKLE *comes around the table again in pursuit of the priest, his back is turned to her, and she throws her shawl over his head, and pulls him towards her. The priest drops the chair and grapples with the blinded and impeded* MICKLE. *The trip him and knock him, and the priest wrests the shillelagh away from him.*)

MICKLE. Two against one! Give me Bonaparte's fair play!

PRIEST. In my youth I fought for my family's faction. And if you attack me again, I'll knock you like the scythe knocks grass.

MICKLE (*rising*). Tonight I have to make my son ready for his coffin. On a soon day I'll make ye two ready for your coffins. Then the Divil will enjoy a thousand years blistering your shins. (*He runs out.*)

PRIEST (*mopping his brow*). He shook me with fear. He went as near as amen to killing me.

PETTICOAT LOOSE (*chuckling*). He'd murder the country, only the goodness of God made him weakhanded. (*She closes the door, takes up her bottle, hides it under her shawl.*)

PRIEST. But God comfort him! He'll never straighten his back again after the death of his son. (*He restores his chair to its place, and books knocked off the table.*)

PETTICOAT LOOSE. I may never see my baby again, father, unless you write me a gospel that might spell it back from the fairy forts.

PRIEST. I'll write you a gospel that might cure your baby of whatever ails it. But your own baby is what you have at home, and no latchiko. (*He is sharpening his quill pen with a small knife.*)

PETTICOAT LOOSE. Biddy passed her hands over it again today, and its heart is still ticking like an old person's heart.

PRIEST. Everything that comes into her head she can make ye believe and do. Because she's the highest peak of all the liars of the world. (*He opens his bible, gets ready paper and ink.*)

PETTICOAT LOOSE (*cheerfully*). No, father. There isn't a thing Biddy says, but she knows for true.

PRIEST. Last night was so cold I had to leave the bed and sit at the fire. And tonight's stars are winking for a harder frost still. If you put out your baby on that shovel, it'll be cold meat before morning.

PETTICOAT LOOSE (*with a cunning smile*). Well, father, I'll drive a bargain with you. If you'll write me a gospel out of John's Book, I won't put the latchiko out tonight.

PRIEST. I'll give you a writing from St. John's Gospel every day you promise that. Sew this gospel into a piece of cloth, and hang it around your baby's neck. If it was a fairy latchiko, the gospel would set it spitting and screeching and cursing. But you'll see that your baby won't notice it at all. (*He is writing the "gospel", and she tiptoes to the shelf, and brings back a mug. As she is coming back* PEG ABOVE ALL *peers in the back window, but* PETTICOAT LOOSE *signals to her to go away. She puts the mug on the edge of the table, and uncorks her bottle.*)

PETTICOAT LOOSE. Father, if something else has to die, instead of my baby, ask God to let it be our old goat.

PRIEST (*writing*). Please God nothing will die, unless you let Biddy kill your baby.

PETTICOAT LOOSE (*uneasy*). Father, is it truth or lies, that for one minute of one day every year the Pope knows everything and has power to do what he likes.

PRIEST. The Emperor Napoleon kept the Pope in a French jail for five years, and he wasn't able to get out.

PETTICOAT LOOSE. But they say that for one minute of every year the Pope knows every great sin that's being committed, and can send a curse over that wouldn't leave a toothful in that sinner's carcase!

PRIEST (*smiling*). The Pope hasn't that kind of knowledge, or power, but God Himself has both. (*He folds the "gospel" in triangular shape, and hands it to her.*)

PETTICOAT LOOSE. A thousand thanks, father. And now an empty stomach never helped to make a good bargain. So drink this sup to our good health and glory. (*She is pouring from her bottle into a mug.*)

PRIEST. No, no, Petticoat Loose. I gave God a hard promise to drink no more, and I'll stick to that even if it kills me.

PETTICOAT LOOSE. But what everyone says must be true. Your gospels do no good unless you sup what we bring you.

PRIEST. My blessing on yourself, but my curse on the mouth that taught ye that heresy.

PETTICOAT LOOSE (*wheedling*). Father, take a small sup for the saving of my baby. A little pleases a poor person.

PRIEST. But it's the first drop that destroys. If the drink ever catches me again, I'll go before my God drunk.

PETTICOAT LOOSE. God'll forgive you, when it's needful for saving and curing people.

PRIEST. He never said he would. And the storytellers say the first Petticoat Loose told the priest, who banished her ghost to the Red Sea, that she was damned because she died drunk on a Sunday between two barrels of porter.

PETTICOAT LOOSE (*smiling sadly*). Well, everybody's soul is on their own shoulders. So I must leave your Gospel here, for fear it would put my baby astray. And I must put out the latchiko on the shovel again tonight.

PRIEST. If you do, it'll perish like Harkaway's baby.

PETTICOAT LOOSE (*smiling*). Biddy says it'll die of old age in a year or two anyway. Goodnight, father. (*She sets out for the door.*)

PRIEST. Here, take your bottle. It's no use here.

PETTICOAT LOOSE. I can't bring it, father. It's unlucky to take away anything you'd gift a priest with. (*She goes, closing door. Suddenly the priest becomes shamefaced and agitated.*)

PRIEST. Tarpey, she saved your life tonight! And now you won't save her baby! Now you're disgraced worse than ever. (*He rises, moves about.*) Why didn't I go schoolmastering, instead of curing? Then I wouldn't have to drink myself into the grave! (*He runs to the door, pulls it open.*) Petticoat Loose! Come back! Come back!

PETTICOAT LOOSE (*entering eagerly*). Will you save my baby?

PRIEST. I'll sample your whiskey, but it has a nasty scent off it.

PETTICOAT LOOSE (*closing door*). It's a new and a foreign make of whiskey Dick the Cock gave me. He said you don't like the taste of it first, but soon you grow very fond of it.

PRIEST (*grimly*). It'll be a drink of death for me. Once I taste it, the bush will be out of the gap. (*He drinks.*) The taste is even nastier than the scent. But I'm so sick for a drink that I could drink anything. (*He drinks again deeply.*)

PETTICOAT LOOSE (*pouring more into his mug*). When you have no company, you need the drink.

PRIEST. I have the finest of company – my books! (*He drinks.*)

PETTICOAT LOOSE. Books can't talk to you.

PRIEST (*smiling*). They can answer your questions, if you know how to read them.

PETTICOAT LOOSE. That's no bother to you, and you knowing the seven languages and you the scribe for the country. (*She pours more into his glass.*)

PRIEST. If I drink all that, I won't know my name. Why didn't you let Mickle kill me, while I was fit to die? (*He drinks deeply.*)

PETTICOAT LOOSE. Dick the Cock said that whiskey came foreign with the smugglers. So it has the smell and taste of something God is pleased to grow out foreign.

PRIEST. It has the smell and taste of the graveyard worms. It'll never take in this country.

PETTICOAT LOOSE. A rich lord like Dick the Cock buys only the best of whiskey and everything!

PRIEST. I'm selling my body to this curing, like you're selling your body to Dick the Cock. (*He drinks deeply.*)

PETTICOAT LOOSE (*smiling*). It's a poor bird that doesn't feed its own chicks.

PRIEST. When a child dies of hunger, God takes it into His Heaven, to be happy there for ever and ever.

PETTICOAT LOOSE. It's hard to lose them even to Heaven. . . . (*She pours more into his mug.*) Sup this small drop. Then you'll have well enough drank to save my baby from the forts. (*She takes up the gospel, pockets it carefully.*)

PRIEST. If I drink much more, I won't be able to see a hole in a ladder. (*He drinks again.*)

PETTICOAT LOOSE. Father, a thousand thanks for this gospel. And I give you my word and hand that the latchiko won't be put out tonight. (*She goes to the door.*)

PRIEST. May God and the road go with you!

PETTICOAT LOOSE (*smiling*). The lamb knocks walk out of its mother. Father, may the Virgin herself – (*Suddenly she stops, swings open door, looks out.*) It's freezing heavens hard. (*She goes, closing door.*)

PRIEST (*smiling*). She was going to say, "May the Virgin herself defend you!" But she cut it short, for fear the Virgin'd save me from drinking the rest of her whiskey. (*He sniffs the mug.*) This whiskey'd make a rabbit spit at a dog. (*But he drinks some more of it. There is a timid knock on the door. He looks at it doubtfully.*)

PRIEST. Was that door knocked? Or does this foreign whiskey make living people hear the dead call on their nightly visits to their old homes? And does it make us smell and taste the dead as well as hear them knocking?

(*The door is knocked upon again and more loudly.*)

PRIEST (*half merry*). The dead it is for sure. (*Loudly.*) Lift the latch, dead, and enter.

(*The door opens and* PEG ABOVE ALL *enters limping and*

286

leaning on a stick. She carries a bundle in her other hand. She is dressed much as before, but is better groomed and has benefitted from rest and good feeding. She stands just inside the door, smiling nervously.)

PEG ABOVE ALL. Is this the house of the priest who is gifted by God for curing?

PRIEST (*sternly*). Isn't it well known on the hill and in the hollow that no woman is to call here for gospels after dark? For your own reputation's sake as well as mine.

PEG ABOVE ALL. I never heard that, father. And night caught me on the road.

PRIEST. Where are you from?

PEG ABOVE ALL. The islands of the sea.

PRIEST (*sympathetic*). From there to here was many a twist of the road for a cold foot and a dry throat. Close the door and come in. (*While she closes the door, and comes nearly as far as the fire, he goes to the wall shelf takes a mug, and pours into it from a bottle beside the wall. He comes back, offers the mug.*)

PRIEST. Sup that, and it'll take the cold skin off you! (*He resumes his chair, and begins to sort out his writing materials.*)

PEG ABOVE ALL. I'm thankful to you, father. And may God send you a good ending. (*She drinks a little.*)

PRIEST. Is the gospel for your husband?

PEG ABOVE ALL. No, father. 'Tis for my leg.

PRIEST. So you weren't lamed by your long journey! (*He opens his bible, looks for a passage in St. John's Gospel.*)

PEG ABOVE ALL. No, father. The Good People touched my leg and took my walk off me.

PRIEST. How do you know it was the fairies? Did you see them?

PEG ABOVE ALL. No, father, but I got the touch while I was milking on the wrong side of the cow.

PRIEST (*smiling as he writes*). Why did you do that? Were you tired of your life?

PEG ABOVE ALL. No, father, but there wasn't enough sense in me.

PRIEST. Did you go to any fairy doctor?

PEG ABOVE ALL. Maura the Pet.

PRIEST. Maura the Pet! She's famous. Is she as good as her name?

PEG ABOVE ALL. She can hardly be seen with all that are drawing to her. And the fishermen say she can rise the storm, and fill the boats with seas, or with fish.

PRIEST. After all her spells and herbs you're still hobbling.

PEG ABOVE ALL. She said a stroke by the Queen of a Fort can't be cured by spells or herbs.

PRIEST (*smiling*). The fairy doctor's old excuse, and every time ye believe them. (*He returns to writing his gospel.*)

PEG ABOVE ALL. Still she served me well. She measured me, and found out where the evil was.

PRIEST (*writing busily*). How did she measure you?

(PEG ABOVE ALL *puts her mug down on the edge of the table and, beside it, places a bottle she has been concealing beneath her shawl. She draws up her skirts in front and presses two fingers against a spot in her naked thigh.*)

PEG ABOVE ALL. This way she measured me, with the sprain thread over her thumb.

PRIEST. What way? (*He turns and looks at her, and starts angrily.*) Girl, have you no shame?

PEG ABOVE ALL (*innocently*). You asked how she measured me.

PRIEST. Let down your clothes directly, or I'll put you out without a gospel.

PEG ABOVE ALL (*dropping her clothes with a smile*). Sure priests are holy and no woman could sin their souls.

PRIEST. A priest is a man, and it's an old saying that women are the ruination of men. (*He folds gospel in triangular shape, gives it to her.*) Sew this into a bit of cloth, and hang it around your neck, and don't take it off night, or day, and say a prayer every day until your leg is cured.

PEG ABOVE ALL. God spare you the health, father. (*She pockets the gospel quickly, then takes up her bottle, uncorks it.*) They say our island poteen drinks well.

PRIEST (*ruefully*). So even in the islands of the sea ye think God can't cure without the help of whiskey or poteen.

PEG ABOVE ALL. 'Tis what we see, father. Take a small sup for the curing of my leg. (*She pours some into his mug.*)

PRIEST. Well, God forgive ye! I'll die roaring like O'Kelly's bull. (*He drinks, and his face lights up.*) This is beautiful poteen! A man could live on the smell of it! (*He drinks again, and, as soon as he lays down the mug, she replenishes it.*)

PEG ABOVE ALL (*smiling nervously*). Father, can you foretell like Maura the Pet? Can you foretell things to come, or to happen to you.

PRIEST (*grinning*). I can foretell that if I drink much more of this, I won't know right from left. (*But he drinks again.*)

PEG ABOVE ALL. As I was drawing nigh to your cabin, something passed me and it not noising on the road at all. If it was the

288

Queen of a fort, or the Fool of a fort, would it be safe for me to sleep out tonight?

PRIEST. Sleep out! Aren't you kindly welcome to the bed for the poor that's in every house?

PEG ABOVE ALL (*sadly*). No, father. When they see my mountainy shawl, and see me uneasy on one leg, they fear 'tis the famine fever, so every door is shut against me.

PRIEST. If you sleep out in tonight's frost, you'll be a load for four tomorrow.

PEG ABOVE ALL. And that wind keeps blowing every side of the hedge.

(*The priest rises, takes a hat and cloak from their pegs and puts them on.*)

PRIEST. A half-sir named Shawn Lally lives a cockshout from here. When I tell them you are healthy, they'll welcome you with a smile warm enough to burn you. (*He opens door.*) But hurry! 'Tis after their hour for going to bed.

PEG ABOVE ALL (*feigning alarm*). Father, I'd sooner face the Fool of the Fort than face that cross and awful man again. He took down a gun, and pointed it and said, "I'll give you the contents of my Queen Anne gun, if you ever again poison my doorstep with your diseases".

PRIEST. Then Shawn was out of sorts from drink or fighting. He won't refuse me. I write his letters to his French cousin, Count Lally de Tolendal.

PEG ABOVE ALL. No, father, even if you gave me the three islands of Aran, I wouldn't face that gun again.

PRIEST. But if you sleep out, you'll be dead before morning.

PEG ABOVE ALL. A girl isn't the same as a man. She's sooner die out than be shot.

PRIEST. I must find some roof you can put your head under. You can't wait here. (*Here goes out, closing the door. She quickly pours some more poteen into his mug. She then goes to the bed, feels it, finally sits on the end of the bed nearest the fire, glass in hand. The priest returns, closing the door.*)

PRIEST. I can't see a light anyside. People are going to bed early to kill the hunger, and to baffle the Whiteboys, and the soldiers chasing the Whiteboys.

PEG ABOVE ALL (*limping to the fire*). I'll warm myself here a few minutes. Then I might be able to wear out the night.

(*He looks at her warming herself, still undecided.*)

PRIEST (*at last*). Well, hit or miss. (*He closes and bolts the door,*

289

takes off his cloak, and lays it on the floor near the hearth.) All I can do now is give you the length and breadth of yourself there until morning.

PEG ABOVE ALL (*happy*). Father, I could sleep there as sound as a winter hedgehog.

(*He hangs up his hat, takes down the second cloak, and lays it on top of the first.*)

PRIEST. I hope you haven't too much length in your tongue. If you tell people that you lodged alone with a disgraced priest, you'll never capture a husband. Or if you do, he'll be the leavings of the gallows.

PEG ABOVE ALL (*smiling*). I won't let my tongue cut my throat.

PRIEST. Your throat and mine are at stake, remember. (*He goes back to the fire, takes up first his own, and then her mug.*) Here! You didn't finish your sup of whiskey. (*He holds it out to her, and she comes up quickly and takes it.*)

PEG ABOVE ALL. Thanks, father.

PRIEST. What name do you answer to?

PEG ABOVE ALL. Peg Above All.

PRIEST (*amused*). Peg Above All! Ye use strange names on the islands of the sea. But ye have to, to be heard above the wind and the waves. (*He drinks, and sits in his chair again.*)

PEG ABOVE ALL. Odd times the sea does be glass calm.

PRIEST. How old are you?

PEG ABOVE ALL. I don't know, I never seen the floor of a school. But I'm as big as ever I'll be.

PRIEST. You're too young to make such a long journey alone. But God loves a tryer.

PEG ABOVE ALL. Take another small sup for the curing of my leg. (*She replenishes his mug.*)

PRIEST. Go easy, Peg Above All. A little fire that warms is better than a big fire that burns.

PEG ABOVE ALL. The women say fire is their best friend and their worst enemy.

PRIEST. That's not what the men say. The saints between us and what the men say! (*His recollection of what the men say sobers him a little, and he begins to look a little worried.*) Peg Above All, 'tis after the hour of going to bed; and you'll have to be clear away from here before the neighbours rouse in the morning.

PEG ABOVE ALL. In these longest nights of the year, it's easy to rouse before dawn.

PRIEST. If we give ourselves a good lift of sleep now, we'll waken before Dick the Cock's bell starts calling his workmen. (*He rises, takes a bottle from beside the wall, uncorks it and sniffs at it.*) This is whiskey with carraways in it, so if you drink it well, it could be good for your leg. (*He leaves it beside her bed.*)

PEG ABOVE ALL. Since you gave me the gospel, my lame leg is more inclined to go with the other leg.

PRIEST. That's boiled spuds in the pot there; but it's crying, instead of laughing, the spuds are this year.

PEG ABOVE ALL. It's short since I staunched my hunger from my bundle.

PRIEST. I have my night prayers said. What prayers do you say?

PEG ABOVE ALL. I do say the prayer against the nightmare.

PRIEST. Then we'll say it now.

(*Both go on their knees.*)

BOTH. (*making sign of the cross*). In the name of the Father and of the Son and of the Holy Ghost, Amen.

PEG ABOVE ALL. Anne, mother of Mary; Mary, mother of Christ; Elizabeth the Well-Doer, mother of John the Baptist: these three I put between me and the sickness of the bed, suffocation, drowning or wounding. I put the cross on which Christ died between me and the nightmare until morning. Amen.

BOTH. In the name of the Father and of the Son and of the Holy Ghost, Amen.

(*They both rise. He takes her poteen bottle.*)

PRIEST. I'll need this to cure my sick head in the morning.

PEG ABOVE ALL. The more you sup the better you'll cure me by the power of God.

PRIEST. I'll go to bed first before the drink dies on me. (*He takes the candle, leaves it on the floor beside her bed.*) Don't let this candle wear out. It has to last us until God's light. But don't spare turf or fire, or you'll be too cold to sleep. (*He goes to the bed, sits on the edge of it, sets the bottle on the floor beside the bed. She piles fresh turf on the fire, then sits on the stool with her back turned to him. He hangs his coat and waistcoat on bed posts, then kicks off his shoes. Suddenly he chuckles boozily.*) Peg Above All, did you ever here tell of Phillip Minister?

PEG ABOVE ALL (*looking into fire*). No, father.

PRIEST. Then you're hardly the full score ... Phillip Minister was ordained in Salamanca like myself, and served in his diocese as Father Phil for years. Till a young Protestant whore was bribed to steal into his bed while he was asleep. He was tempted and fell, and, once a man starts that game, he can't rest. So he gave up the Catholic religion, and joined the clergy of the women. (*Teasing.*) I hope the Protestants haven't bribed you to turn me into a Phillip Minister.

PEG ABOVE ALL. Oh, no, father! I wouldn't live and do the like!

PRIEST. I know that well. I was only jesting. The drink was talking. (*He pulls his nightshirt from under the pillows.*) When priests give up the priesthood, it's usually a case of either Punch or Judy, or both. Maybe it was Punch as much as Judy made Phillip Minister join the clergy of the women. (*He is changing into his nightshirt.*) And in his day the French Revolution swept the world with a kind of madness. Priests and nuns left the Church, because the new religion, Democracy, was going to save the world. God wasn't going to be needed any more.

PEG ABOVE ALL (*half-turning*). The young whore – had she much luck after?

PRIEST. Not her. The life of a hare, only shorter. (*Having changed into his nightshirt, he gets into bed. Then having tossed and turned for a few moments, he finds his favourite sleeping posture.*)

PRIEST (*sleepily*). Goodnight, Peg Above All! And the Son of Mary between us and all harm!

PEG ABOVE ALL. Goodnight, father.

(*He seems to fall asleep quickly. She takes from a secret pocket a stick a few inches long. The Spancel of Death, the long strip of human skin wound about it, has loosened; and she rewinds it, and leaves the stick on the stool. She puts more turf on the fire. She listens to his breathing, and tiptoes to the head of the bed. She peers over it for a few moments. She taps the bedhead.*)

PEG ABOVE ALL (*softly*). Father, are your ears asleep?

(*No answer. She tiptoes to the candle, sets it on the sill of the back window, watches the window. Quickly a face appears there; and she beckons it to the door. She unbolts and opens the door, and SHAWN LALLY enters wearing an old battered hat and an old white shirt over his jacket. He carries his shillelagh.*)

SHAWN. You didn't put the spancel of death on him yet! (*He takes it up off the stool.*)

PEG ABOVE ALL (*closing door, but not bolting it*). Not yet, Shawn. You'd need to hold it while I coax the blankets off him.

(*They both go to the foot of the bed.*)

SHAWN. It won't be easy to rouse him. That poteen was made extra strong.

(*She loosens and lifts the bedclothes just enough to expose the priest's ankles.*)

SHAWN. God forgive me! This was my mother's bed that I bestowed on him when he staggered into this country, making for Munster with a backload of books.

PEG ABOVE ALL. You could call it a fine bed! And a sheet above and below.

SHAWN. He was hoping to set up as a hedgeschoolmaster in Munster. But his money and means and strength was gone by the time he got this far, so he was glad to find this cabin empty. The Whiteboys shot as a spy the man who owned this cabin.

PEG ABOVE ALL. After I rouse him, make sure you won't let him see you spying on us through that window.

SHAWN. A couple of peeps will let me know whether the shift of a priest's wife is won.

PEG ABOVE ALL. I have the spancel tied loose, and it's so light he won't notice it at all.
(*They let down and tuck in the blankets. They tiptoe towards the door.*)

PEG ABOVE ALL (*worried*). He's holy enough to kick me out of his bed the minute I rouse him.

SHAWN. He is, but his backbone is well softened now with drink and the coaxiorums.

PEG ABOVE ALL (*more hopeful*). And they say neither man, nor woman, can stand out against the spancel of death.

SHAWN. That's sure. And besides there's the charm God set in a woman's skin. But don't rouse him till your skin is well warmed in the bed. Then you'll find he'll catch you by the shift and a bit of skin, too. (*He opens door.*)

PEG ABOVE ALL (*ruefully*). My skin will be well warmed in Hell.

SHAWN. If we go up, we'll go up. And if we go down, we'll have heat.

PEG ABOVE ALL. If he puts me to death, you'll rear my baby.

SHAWN. That oath is a debt I'll pay.

PEG ABOVE ALL (*fiercely*). If you don't, I'll come back from the dead and burn you!

SHAWN. Biddy's prophecies don't smell any coffin for you tomorrow or soon.
(*He goes, closing door. She bolts the door carefully. She takes the candle from the windowsill, brings it towards the bed. On her way she passes the table, and her glance falls upon the crucifix. She takes it up and stands looking at it; and is obviously undergoing a final struggle with conscience.*)

293

PEG ABOVE ALL (*at last sadly*). Son of the Virgin, and King of the Stars, and Lord of the Judgement Day – farewell till that day on the mountain! (*She puts the crucifix back on the table, and continues on to the bed. She sets the candle on the floor beside the bed. She loosens, and turns back the bedclothes on her side of the bed. She takes off her pampooties. Standing up again, she begins to unbutton her blouse. She stops, and puts her right forearm standing up at right angles to her upper arm, with the fingers at full stretch. She stands looking up at this hand for a few moments.*)

PEG ABOVE ALL (*sadly*). My ghost in the house of pain; and this hand growing up out of my grave! Will my poor baby live to see this hand? And will it live after seeing it? (*Sadly she resumes her undressing.*)

CURTAIN

ACT TWO

Scene Two

The scene is the same, and the nearly burnt out fire indicates that a considerable time has elapsed. The priest is asleep, but lying on the opposite side to that on which we last saw him. PEG ABOVE ALL *is standing beside the bed, finishing dressing. Except for her shift, which is thrown across the foot of the bed. She has undergone a great change in appearance and manner. Now she looks flushed, excited and happy, and her eyes have all the sparkle of the young woman who is really in love. Having dressed, she takes the lighted candle from the floor, and puts it on the window. She stirs up the dying fire, and piles turf on it. But all things she does quietly, as if anxious not to reawaken the priest.*

A man appears at the back window, and taps upon it. She transfers the candle to the table, and unbolts the door. The latch is lifted, and SHAWN LALLY *enters wearing the white shirt as before.*

PEG ABOVE ALL. Talk small, or you'll rouse him. The hardest task ever I got was to coax him back to sleep.

SHAWN. After the long pleasuring ye had, he could hardly be roused by the big gun of Athlone.

(They approach the bed, and look down at the sleeping priest. PEG ABOVE ALL *rolls up her shift, and offers it to* SHAWN.*)*

PEG ABOVE ALL. Give this to Honor, and may this shift of a priest's wife hunt the wicked spell that was binding ye.

SHAWN *(not taking it)*. Peg Above All, never give away your cow at he fair till you're paid for her. Draw to this table. *(He goes to the table, begins to take fistfuls of coins from his pocket, and throw them on the table.)*

PEG ABOVE ALL. I wouldn't mistrust the oldest blood in Ireland.

SHAWN. This'll free you for ever from the straddle of misery. Knock soup and music out of this.

PEG ABOVE ALL *(thrilled)*. Sweet are your fists, Shawn Lally.

295

SHAWN. Can you count to fifty?

PEG ABOVE ALL. Oh, no; but I can count to twenty!

SHAWN. The priest'll count them for you, but give him no glimpse of how you came by this money.

(PEG ABOVE ALL *has taken off her neckerchief, and spread it on the table, then puts the money into it, ties the four corners together.*)

PEG ABOVE ALL (*excited*). Shawn, 'tis the truth what they say: that the heart can get a renewing. I was very lonesome in the heart, and afeard; but now I'm in my best days again, and fear nothing.

SHAWN. When we have money, it makes us uneasy; but it's worse, they say, to have none at all. Now you have the price of a farm, and you can pick your choice of men like Mullee, who're dying down for a wife with a farm.

PEG ABOVE ALL (*happily*). No, Shawn. Now I have a true love, and we're going tramping east to where there is no curse on the crops or the weather.

SHAWN. I hope he isn't some trickster out to rob you and then desert you.

PEG ABOVE ALL. He never will desert me. We love each other better than we love the sun itself. And we need each other every way. (*She approaches bed, and looks down at the priest lovingly.*)

SHAWN. Death and the Divil! D'ye mean to say yourself and that priest mean to harbour together?

PEG ABOVE ALL. When we love each other truly, aren't we better together than not?

SHAWN. What good are a priest's white hands and soft bones on your farm? When it takes two men a day to dig a stone of spuds that aren't rotten?

PEG ABOVE ALL. On the rich lands of Meath half an hour will dig our day's 'nough of spuds.

SHAWN. If you wed him, you'll wed the three virtues of the drunkard: a miserable morning, a dirty coat, and an empty purse.

PEG ABOVE ALL. When we're living happy together, and he hasn't to be curing, he won't need the drink.

SHAWN. Don't go looking for happiness, because it isn't in it. I'm rich and I'm married, so I know.

PEG ABOVE ALL. After tumbling his soul, I'm duty bound to save his body from death by curing and drink.

SHAWN. The man with a family has the most need of drink. And if ye two live together, ye'll draw down a worse curse on the crops, and on myself who put ye lying in the one bed together.

PEG ABOVE ALL. No, ye can blame it away on me. Because Hell is written out for me now; and that nothing can blot.

SHAWN. I'm duty bound to free ye both out of this madness of the bed I flocked ye into. And I promised you beforehand that I would free ye out.

PEG ABOVE ALL. You did, but now I don't want you or anywan to come between us and separate us.

SHAWN. Because you're mad with the madness of the bed. In a fistful of minutes myself and Mullee are coming in here, pretending to be two Whiteboys. And we'll cure the priest with rods of the magic alder tree that nothing bad can stand against. That'll turn him against you and against all women for ever. (*He opens the door.*)

PEG ABOVE ALL. If ye turn him against me, I'll tell him who ye are.

SHAWN. If you do, we'll tell him how you played the man catcher for gold, and parted him from the King of the Saints.

PEG ABOVE ALL. Every knot ye tie against us, I'll open again.

SHAWN. On our side we have the enchantments of Biddy the Tosser. (*He goes, closing the door. She bolts door, and turns towards bed looking very worried.*)

PEG ABOVE ALL. The vexer! ... But Donal won't believe them! You can't catch a wise bird with chaff. (*Smiling she approaches the bed. But suddenly she starts in dismay.*) The spancel of death! He's gone, and we never took off the spancel of death! And if Donal finds it on him, he'll guess eggs where he sees shells. (*She loosens and turns back the bedclothes, exposes the priest's ankles. But just as she is beginning to unwind the spancel, the priest moans loudly, and turns in the bed. She drops the bedclothes over his feet, and retreats out of sight to the fire.*)

PRIEST (*moaning*). Death in drink! – without the graces! My skull is sounding and pounding like seacliffs in a storm. And such nightmares! That a girl was in bed with me. The drunken squireen's nightmare! Thank God, all dreams don't come true. (*He sits up, open his eyes, reaches for the bottle.*) The only cure – a hair of the dog that bit me. (*He takes a swig, then another.*) That's better; you can be a good dog, too.

PEG ABOVE ALL (*coming forward cheerfully*). Now that your head and my leg are cured, two castles can meet!

(*The priest looks at her at first with dismay, and then with joy.*)

PRIEST. Peg! Then it was you and no dream woman that came into my bed!

PEG ABOVE ALL. The banshee's screeches made me, Donal. My two legs were dancing with fear.

PRIEST (*smiling*). It was no banshee you heard. It was a vixen, or cats.

PEG ABOVE ALL. But cats can see the banshee, and she sets them screeching.

PRIEST. The banshee wouldn't even sneeze for one of my family.

PEG ABOVE ALL. Donal, whatever was screeching, there was a jump out of sleep for a year in it.

PRIEST (*smiling ruefully*). And for me there was a jump out of the state of grace and out of my vows.

PEG ABOVE ALL (*untying her neckerchief and showing its contents*). Donal, I was telling you how the landlord's son bestowed on me fifty sovereigns for the rearing of my baby.

PRIEST. Peg, I never saw such a gathering of gold before.

PEG ABOVE ALL. That'll buy the lease of a fine farm beyond the Shannon where the spuds aren't rotting.

PRIEST. If I don't go with you, Peg, it's a drunkard's death for me soon. But if I do go with you, I can save yourself and your baby from robbery on the road and starvation.

PEG ABOVE ALL. If we were living together in our own place, we"d enjoy every tick of the clock.

PRIEST. And there's even a way we could save our children from the name of bastards.

PEG ABOVE ALL. If there is, let us banish that name, because it's shameful enough to turn back a funeral.

PRIEST. We could get wed in church and in law, if we turned Protestant, like Phillip Minister. Then the Protestants'd make me a minister and a magistrate like they made him, and they'd give me a fine house and salary.

PEG ABOVE ALL. Some say there's no difference between Our Lord of the Catholics and Our Lord of the Protestants.

PRIEST. There is no difference, and plenty of Protestants are better Christians and nearer to God than the Catholics.

PEG ABOVE ALL. And the English King pays a high salary to every priest who gives up his religion.

PRIEST. So we'd never have to slave in the mud, sowing and reaping. And as a magistrate I'd be able to help poor Catholics maddened by bad laws.

PEG ABOVE ALL. I'll keep your house as neat as an egg. I never was lazy in my hands.

PRIEST. After tonight, Peg, it'd be against the grain of nature for us to live apart. Come back into bed quick.

PEG ABOVE ALL (*nervous*). Wait till I take a view out. A while back I felt footsteps passing and lights likewise. (*She runs to the windows and peers out.*)

PRIEST (*smiling*). Those lights are natural lights made by the bog. They're the Jack-o-Lantern, what Biddy thinks are fairy hunts and fairy funerals.

PEG ABOVE ALL. But the footsteps I heard! The Whiteboys are going to war again and marching against the rackrenting landlords.

PRIEST. But the Whiteboys never bother me except for a gospel for a comrade wounded, or bad with jail fever.

PEG ABOVE ALL. Their revenge might fall on me if they found me in bed taking his vows off a priest.

(*There is a loud double knock on the door.*)

PEG ABOVE ALL. Whiteboys!

PRIEST. Hide behind the bed; because I'll have to give them admittance.

PEG ABOVE ALL. But I'm sure it was Whiteboys were spying through the window while we were pleasuring. And now maybe they're coming with black spells that'll turn you against me for ever!

PRIEST. There are no such spells, Peg.

PEG ABOVE ALL. There are and sure spells.

(*The knocks are repeated more loudly.*)

PRIEST. In the name of St. Bannon, who's there?

VOICE. Whiteboys!

(*The door is loudly, lashed with sticks.*)

PRIEST. I'll have to open it, or they'll make bits of the door. (*He throws back the bedclothes.*)

PEG ABOVE ALL. No, Donal, I'll open it. (*She unbolts and opens door.* SHAWN LALLY *and* MULLEE *enter masked and wearing old hats and white shirts. Each of them carries a shillelagh in his right hand, and two or three long rods in his left hand. They close the door, and advance upon the bed.*)

PEG ABOVE ALL. Whiteboys, if ye put spells on the priest, I'll put the orphan's curse on ye.

(*But they thrust her aside, and come over behind the bed. One raises his shillelagh as if for a blow, and the priest puts up his arms to save his head. The other Whiteboy pulls back the bedclothes, exposing the priest's upper slopes.*)

MULLEE. May the bark of this magic elder tree convert you to hate Peg Above All and all women for evermore!

(*He begins to tap the priest's body with the rods, while* LALLY'S *shillelagh keeps threatening the priest's head.*)

PEG ABOVE ALL. If ye don't stop, I'll strip and put the curse of my breasts on ye.

PRIEST. If ye don't stop, I'll put on ye St. Columcille's curse that'll make ye too lazy to go to bed in time, or to get up in the morning. (*The Whiteboys retreat quickly to the door, and open it.* BIDDY *is standing there, and enters, and advances between* PEG ABOVE ALL *and the priest. She takes fistfulls of dust from her bag, and scatters it on the ground.*)

BIDDY. I scatter between ye dust from a new made grave. May ye hate one another! May ye be as hateful to each other as bread eaten without a blessing is to God!

PRIEST. May her and me never be as hateful to God as the murderers of babies!

BIDDY. These Whiteboys came here seeking a gospel for a wounded comrade. Through the window they seen you whoring with this orphan girl. They craved me to stop you from bringing down a curse on the crops and the weather.

PRIEST. Whiteboys, that curse is being caused by the murder of babies by Biddy the Tosser.

BIDDY. Fairy latchikoes aren't babies. The sin of a true baby's death was never on me.

PRIEST. No priest ever agreed with that in confessions.

BIDDY. Never think confessions will win pardon for breaking your vow against women. You might as well try to save your soul by walking on your heels. Whiteboys, give me one of your long knives.

(MULLEE *takes a knife from his belt and hands it to* BIDDY.)

BIDDY. This is a sharp edgy knife, and only this, the old remedy, can save your soul now. (*She comes over to the priest, and brandishes the knife near his throat.*) God's vengeance will be satisfied, if you get a true friend to kill you. But he must divide your body into three equal halves, with a knife, an axe and a saw. Anything the knife won't cut, the axe will cut, and anything the axe won't cut, the saw will cut.

PRIEST (*sarcastic*). I have no true friend.

BIDDY. Like every villain. But the Whiteboys have true heroes who'll obey and do anything to lift your curse off the country.

PEG ABOVE ALL. The Whiteboy who murders him, I'll inform on him.

BIDDY. If you do, you'll open your grave with your mouth. (*Turns to priest.*) But the Whiteboys won't make three halves of you, if you'll swear to depart for evermore from this barony.

PRIEST. I'll swear to that if you'll swear never again to command the torture, or the perishing, of babies.

BIDDY. What I never done! Whiteboys, he won't depart and leave us in peace, so I challenge him to deny by the oath on the skull that he has whored with every poor stranger girl who came to him for a gospel!

PRIEST. The oath on the skull! When and where?

BIDDY. At St. Bannon's holy well and graveyard at moonrise next Sunday, the blessed day.

PRIEST. Tell all the ears of the parish I'll be there.

BIDDY. All the ears of the parish will be there ... Whiteboys, your captains are waiting for your word and dispatch. (*She opens the door, looks out, turns back.*) Be aware, priesteen, that next Sunday's moon will be the castrated moon.

PRIEST. The waning moon.

BIDDY. If you swear a lie under the castrated moon, the skull will laugh in your face.

(*She goes, followed by the two Whiteboys.* PEG ABOVE ALL *closes the door, and bolts it. She comes back towards the priest looking anxious. Each realises that their blissful midnight romance has suffered from the intrusion of harsh realities.*)

PEG ABOVE ALL. Donal, I hope their black spells haven't turned you against me.

PRIEST. Not at all, Peg. But don't come back into bed yet. The Whiteboys, after their council of war, may double back.

PEG ABOVE ALL. You'll run into Biddy's snare, if you go to this swearing on the skull.

PRIEST. But if I don't go, I'll be judged guilty of everything Biddy accuses me of.

PEG ABOVE ALL. But why wait to be shamed, when we can be three day's journey away?

PRIEST (*smiling ruefully*). The particle of priesthood that's left in me finds it hard to go without fighting one last battle to break the Devil's grip Biddy has on the people.

PEG ABOVE ALL. But if she strips her evil eye, she'll put a plague of wasting on you.

PRIEST. Before we depart, I'd like to show she has no evil eye.

PEG ABOVE ALL. The morning after the swearing we'll take the road to the rising sun.

PRIEST. If the weather isn't too bad for your baby. And if your leg is well enough.

PEG ABOVE ALL. I'll go with you even if the Whiteboys leave me with only one leg.

PRIEST. Until then don't let the Whiteboys see you calling here. I'll ask a house where there's two women to keep you until then.

PEG ABOVE ALL (*cheerfully, sitting on the bed*). We won't need to give up our own religion altogether, when no Protestants are around, we can say our rosary together.

PRIEST (*ruefully*). We can. But then I'll have to go out to my pulpit, and preach Luther's words that the Mass is a worse sin than all the murders and robberies and all the adulteries and crimes in the world.

PEG ABOVE ALL. If Luther said that, he was mad.

PRIEST. Like all the great heretics, he was a made genius.

PEG ABOVE ALL. But God would know you don't mean what you preach.

PRIEST. But He never said we could preach what we believe to be false. Instead He said, "He who denies Me before men, I will deny him before my Father who is in Heaven."

PEG ABOVE ALL. Then it'd be safer for you not to join the clergy of the women. But to knock out a living on my farm.

PRIEST. It'd be safer for our souls, Peg. He forgave Mary Magdalene for our sin. But He said it would have been better for Judas if he had never been born.

PEG ABOVE ALL (*jumping up off the bed happily*). And if you don't join the clergy of the women, I won't have to learn how to talk English. They say it's double as hard as the Irish tongue.

PRIEST. And if we joined heretics, we'd be excommunicated.

(*There begins an urgent knocking on the door.*)

PEG ABOVE ALL. The Whiteboys!

PRIEST. Hide behind the bed quick!

(*She hides.*)

PRIEST. In the name of St. Bannon, who's there?

VOICE. Petticoat Loose.

PRIEST. Petticoat Loose! She's a well-wisher, Peg, so you can give her admittance.

PEG ABOVE ALL. Thank God it isn't Whiteboys.

(*She opens the door, and* PETTICOAT LOOSE *comes in.*)

PETTICOAT LOOSE. Father, I hope I haven't come too late!

PRIEST. So you put out your baby on the shovel, and it's dying, or dead!

PETTICOAT LOOSE. Not it, father. The fairy latchiko is sleeping snug by the fire. I came to warn you to sup no more of Dick the Cock's whiskey. I found out since he had it dosed with coaxiorums strong enough to make a saint's blood rise against him.

PRIEST. It tasted and smelt that way. If you can find it there, throw it into a boghole.

PETTICOAT LOOSE. I could smell it in a barrel of onions. (*She is uncorking bottles, and sniffing at them.*)

PRIEST. Petticoat Loose, this is a girl from the islands of the sea who came for a gospel. Could she use your bed for the poor for a few nights till her leg is well enough for the long journey home?

PETTICOAT LOOSE. She's as welcome as the first shout of the cuckoo.

PEG ABOVE ALL. I can pay for my eatables.

PETTICOAT LOOSE (*very happy*). Soon myself may be as rich as Lord Damer. Last night I dreamed of finding a crock of gold under a fairy tree.

PRIEST (*smiling*). You might be lucky. They say the Danes buried a lot of money they stole.

PETTICOAT LOOSE. This is Dick the Cock's whiskey. I'll let it go with the stream.

(PEG ABOVE ALL *has put on her shawl, and collected her bundle and her stick.* PETTICOAT LOOSE *gives her a nudge in the back to indicate that she is ready.*)

PEG ABOVE ALL. We might meet again, father.

PRIEST. If your leg needs another gospel.

PETTICOAT LOOSE. I hear Biddy is putting a bad call on you presently. But the man without an enemy is a poor man.

PRIEST (*grinning ruefully*). But the man with an enemy can't afford to do wrong. . . . May the good luck of the year go with ye!

PEG ABOVE ALL. And the same to you, father. (*She goes out.*)

PETTICOAT LOOSE (*sincerely*). And may the Virgin herself defend you! (*She goes, closing door.*)

PRIEST. She left me her full blessing this time. But too late! Too late! . . . But is there something around my leg? (*He draws up his leg, puts down his hands. They re-emerge with the Spancel of Death.*) The Spancel of Death! Biddy the Tosser and Teig of the Tombs! . . . Was it Peg put it on me, so that she'd never lose me? And was it the Spancel of Death and coaxiorums that broke the vow I took on Salamanca's altar? (*He throws the spancel on the floor.*)

CURTAIN

ACT THREE

The time is a few nights later. The scene is the holy well and the holy tree and the surviving end-wall, with its doorway, of the thousand year old monastery of St. Bannon. Irish monasteries of this date often had nearby round towers for refuge during Viking raids. But no round tower would be necessary for the staging of this play.

A typical west of Ireland ancient monastery would be built of large irregular blocks of red sandstone and brown sandstone, with the doorways arching stones and flanking stones all of well-cut bright limestone by way of contrast. Around the ruins would be an ancient but still used, graveyard everybody wishing to be buried in or near the saint's monastery. So ancient forgotten graves are dug up to make room for new burials, and the ancient bones and skulls were flung out, and thrown into corners, or put into holes in walls. In 1822 the gravestones would be crude marking stones.

The monastery wall and doorway are at the back and near the centre of the stage. On the left from the actor's point of view, is the holy well, which originally was, no doubt, simply the monastery well. It is surrounded by a three foot high stone wall, with one entrance narrow enough to keep out cattle. Near the right end of the stage and towards the back is the holy tree an old half withered ash tree. Small rags of many colours are tied to its branches, but most of the colours have faded. Near the tree, but nearer the footlights is a square flat stone, with a smaller round stone placed in its centre. The smaller stone is the much feared cursing stone. A crescent moon can be seen.

The priest comes in from the right. He takes a skull out of a hole in the monastery wall, comes down and sits on the flag supporting the cursing stone. He examines and contemplates the skull. Biddy comes through the church door, carrying a bucket, but seeing the priest, she hides the bucket in a dark corner. She then advances on the priest.

BIDDY. You came early in hopes that Peg Above All would be here before you.

PRIEST. And you came early in hopes that Teig of the Tombs would be here before you.

BIDDY. This night Teig of the Tombs is far away on the plains of Mayo doing people good turns, and enabling them. The people won't believe your oath on the skull unless it's sworn with a white sheet cladding you.

PRIEST. I wasn't told about that. (*He puts down the skull, and rises.*) It'll only take minutes to go home for one.

BIDDY. How could you, a collegian, live with a dyke-tramp's daughter, a creatureen that was only half reared?

PRIEST. She can't live around here, because of my sin. And even a dog would be afraid to face her journey alone.

BIDDY. You waited for tonight's challenge, because you mean vengeance against me. You'd be safer to run from this battle. Peg Above All heard the banshee screeching around your cabin.

PRIEST. If I'm fated soon to die, I'd rather die fighting than running. (*He goes out right. She takes up the skull, examines it quickly.*)

BIDDY. A woman's skull! Not wicked enough! A wicked man's skull will make him confess his guilt.

(*She puts the skull back into a hole in the wall, and takes her pail out of the darkness, and goes inside the well wall. A loud splash is heard; she raises the bucket and rests it on the well-wall.*)

BIDDY (*smiling into the bucket*). Holy fish, I'm hiding you only for the run of an hour, to save your life from that priesteen who thinks you belong to the druids and the Divil. (*She carries the pail through the church door, comes back without it. She raises her eyes Heavenwards.*) St. Bannon, this world is going backwards instead of forwards, and God's priests no longer believe in this holy well that sprung up where a tear fell from your eye. And they don't believe in the holy fish you brought from a bay of the River Jordan. And they don't believe in your holy tree Cuaille that grew from your staff planted in the ground. (*She curtsies to the tree.*) Cuaille that was blessed by the Danes . . . St. Bannon, this priesteen is the worst man since God made the first man out of a horse's rib. He'll quench your holy well the way other priesteens quenched the well of The King of the World. And he'll cut down your holy tree Cuaille the same as wicked priesteens cut down St. Kieran's holy tree that was curing the cows of Connacht. (*She approaches the tree.*) Cuaille, it's a great sin to molest you. But if I break a branch off now, it'll help to banish this priesteen before he cuts you down and burns you. (*She bends a branch.*) If you don't want to lose this branch, make yourself strong, and I won't lean on it too hard . . . (*Anxiously.*) Are you making yourself strong? (*The branch breaks.*) I hope you weren't making yourself strong. Like us all you have to suffer to live. (*She drops the broken branch behind the tree and comes over to the cursing stones.*) St. Bannon, I never turned your cursing stone against a priest before, but I must turn it now against that priesteen to save my people from famine. Nothing is fat now, except the graveyard worms. (*She kneels and lays her hands on the cursing stone, and keeps turning it anti-clockwise during the cursing.*) May the curses of the Fairy Kings, Mananawn and Finvara, fall altogether upon him. May Finvara's Host of the Air fly him to the edge of the sea, and may Mananawn's Host of the Sea flood him out, and sink him as deep as the whales for ever and ever, Amen.

MICKLE (*entering*). Amen, amen. More power to you, Biddy!

BIDDY (*taking a small rough rag doll from her bag*). I have named this dolleen after him. Bury it in his cabbage patch, and my curses will work double as quick.

MICKLE (*taking doll*). The minute I have a prayer said. (*He takes a red rag from his pocket, ties it around a branch of the tree.*) Cuaille, let my grief for my son be fading while this rag is fading. And, St. Bannon, in our hard battle tonight, give us the power of killing without being killed.

BIDDY (*ferociously, turning the stone*). May the curse of an angry Jesus!

MICKLE (*alarmed*). Wait, Biddy, till I'm away! Then give him your full mouthful! (*He runs out in the direction the priest has gone.*)

BIDDY. May the curse of an angry Jesus, and the curse of the friars of Kilroe, and the curse of the friars of Urlaur fall altogether upon him! May their curses dumb his lying tongue and cripple the hand that writes his crooked gospels! May his sins be written on his forehead like they're written on the foreheads of the people of Hell! May the Divil swallow him sideways!

PEG ABOVE ALL (*coming in from the left*). May the prayers fall on the preacher! (*Advancing on Biddy.*) If you don't stop cursing Donal, I'll kick you this way and that. I'll slap your hand about!

BIDDY. If I strip my hidden eye, it'll wither your blood, so that no man will take you.

(PEG ABOVE ALL *snatches up the cursing stone, and holds it over* BIDDY'S *head.*)

PEG ABOVE ALL. If you blink me, I'll whitewash this stone with your brains!

306

BIDDY (*defiant*). I took you up out of the gutter, and put you sitting on a stone! Now you want to make small bits of me!

PEG ABOVE ALL. Donal lost his way of living over you. Now all he has is me. And if you part him and me, before a mile of the road I'll hear an awful saying, 'Your money or your life!'

BIDDY. You'll damn yourselves and us all, if you live with that priesteen!

PEG ABOVE ALL (*fiercely*). I'll see that you'll never again turn the cursing stone against him. This minute I'll drown it in the lake.

(*As she turns to run out through the monastery door, a sad man in his early thirties enters from the left carrying a stout stick. His clothes and his hat and watch and chain indicate prosperity. He looks simple but not stupid.*)

BIDDY. Make a grasp at her! The Divil is on her road!

(HARKAWAY *throws his arms around* PEG ABOVE ALL, *and stops her dead, as she runs past him.*)

HARKAWAY (*sadly*). Are you cursed to drown yourself, too?

BIDDY. She is, Harkaway. And she's the half of a mad woman.

PEG ABOVE ALL. You liary witch! It's the stone I want to drown! (*She is struggling to get free.*)

BIDDY. Don't believe her, Harkaway. The stone is to sink her in the lake. (*She is trying to pull the stone out of* PEG'S *hand.*)

HARKAWAY (*mildly to* PEG). Lady, drowning a stone isn't fit to be believed.

BIDDY. Hold her tight till I call the neighbours. If you free her out, a wake will soon be over her.

HARKAWAY. Harkaway will hold her with the drowning man's grip. (BIDDY *has wrested the cursing stone from* PEG ABOVE ALL.)

BIDDY. If you don't, you'll be named for her death. (*She hurries out through the monastery door with the stone.* PEG *and* HARKAWAY *are still struggling.*)

PEG ABOVE ALL. Wicked is the name for what you are doing.

HARKAWAY (*sadly*). Of late it is surely. I failed to save my wife from drowning herself in that lake, because I trusted her. If I fail to save you, I'll have another drowned face dogging me day and night!

PEG ABOVE ALL. Are you the journeyman tailor Harkaway Walsh whose baby died out on a shovel?

HARKAWAY. I'm Harkaway the journeyman.

PEG ABOVE ALL. And next day your wife drowned herself!

HARKAWAY. Yes. I came from a queer country; and maybe it was that put a curse on me.

PEG ABOVE ALL (*sympathetic*). Whoever cursed us, cursed us well.

HARKAWAY. Who'd put a curse on you, and you having the finest head ever seen on a body?

PEG ABOVE ALL. Our landlord's son done a rape on me, so I have a baby, but I amn't wed.

HARKAWAY. 'Tis a pity the cat didn't eat us when our bones were young and soft.

PEG ABOVE ALL. Biddy declares your wife and child aren't dead all out. They're in the forts.

HARKAWAY. But even if Biddy can spell them back to me, they don't be the same after the forts.

PEG ABOVE ALL. If they come back as wicked as Biddy the Tosser, you'd be better off to leave them in the forts.

HARKAWAY. We're lost birds, between the priests telling us to do one thing, and the fairy doctors telling us to do the opposite. After my wife and child found death by Biddy's advice, I went to Father Donal for a gospel. He said they weren't in the forts, but dead all out. And he said, 'What the grave has, let the grave keep.'

PEG ABOVE ALL (*sympathetic*). So you didn't hire Biddy till their rescue term was over?

HARKAWAY. Their faces were before me night and day craving a rescue, till at long and at last I crossed Biddy's hand with gold. Biddy said, 'It may turn out a poor effort now. The herb that isn't pulled in time doesn't be much good.'

PEG ABOVE ALL. And when a wife is brought back from the forts, she hates her husband, if he didn't rescue her in good time.

HARKAWAY. Yes, dead or alive the women don't like to be kept waiting. So if Biddy can't spell her back to me soon, I'll go away a third part of Ireland from here. They say a fairy wife can't trace her husband that far.

(BIDDY *has appeared unnoticed behind the tree, and stands there listening.*)

PEG ABOVE ALL. Maybe you'd come away tomorrow with my bachelor and me. Three could fight better than one against the highwaymen and the tramps of the road.

HARKAWAY. If my wife and child can't be spelled back to me, ye can lead me through the world with a bridle of snow.

PEG ABOVE ALL. We're tramping east to a good country where the crops didn't fail.

(BIDDY *advances, looking sad.*)

BIDDY. May God comfort you, Tailor Harkaway! I'm after tossing and asking the Good People about your family in the forts. The Good People say my herbs were pulled out of time, so they weren't worth a dog's foot.

HARKAWAY. So my wife and child must go through their years in the forts!

BIDDY. Because that wicked priesteen delayed us.

HARKAWAY. Are they together?

BIDDY. They are, and I got them promoted to a captain fort with a cave in it leading to grandeur and Tir na nog.

HARKAWAY. They'll never ask to leave Tir na nog where there is no death, and come back here, where they'll have to die again.

BIDDY. They gave her to a fairy hurler who won their match against the fairies of Munster.

HARKAWAY. And while he's enjoying her, Harkaway will trudge the long white roads alone. The end of the tailor does be sad.

BIDDY (*mysterious*). When the feeling comes on me, I can't keep the prophecy back. Tailor, if you'd stitch yourself for life to this girl, it'd turn out as lucky as a blacksmith's money.

PEG ABOVE ALL. Leave alone such talk, Biddy. You well know I have a bachelor.

(*But* BIDDY *has taken out her tossing coins, and placed them on her palm.*)

BIDDY. Curra pee and crab's alley! (*She tosses and consults.*) They say ye'll be shovelling the gold, like Dick the Cock; and as happy as Adam and Eve before sin put a load on their backs.

HARKAWAY. But when I hired your prophecy about whether I should wed, you foretold happiness for us, likewise.

BIDDY. And weren't ye happy?

HARKAWAY. The short time she lived. But your prophecy didn't foresee that a beautiful wife does be unlucky.

BIDDY. God said he'd never give knowledge of when people would die to the Good people, or to anyone living. But gold never dies, and this girl has fifty gold sovereigns in her side-pocket.

HARKAWAY. You must come from a good country, not a queer country like me.

PEG ABOVE ALL. The landlord's son gave it to me to help rear the child he made with me.

HARKAWAY. It was nearly worth your while to lose your heel. In all my travels I never heard of a girl so well paid for being put on one heel.

BIDDY. I must leave ye to pick a skull for that priesteen.

HARKAWAY. Can I free her out now?

BIDDY. If you do, the Divil a toe she'll go, but straight into that lake. And, if you lose two women to that lake, God'll never gift you with another.

HARKAWAY. I'll hold her so till the neighbours come. She isn't a heavy handful.

BIDDY. My prophecy says: ye two could enjoy such happiness that it'd feed ye. (*She exits through monastery door.*)

HARKAWAY. Next to curing, matchmaking is the thing Biddy likes to be at.

PEG ABOVE ALL (*curious*). How is your courage for marrying again?

HARKAWAY. After how I was kicked out of marriage last week I swore one marriage was enough. But Biddy's phophecies give people great courage for getting wed.

PEG ABOVE ALL. I hear no one around weds, without first hiring her prophecy.

HARKAWAY. Plenty got wed that never would get a partner, only for Biddy's prophecies.

PEG ABOVE ALL. When it suits her, she can whitewash her mouth.

HARKAWAY. Biddy could very near get a husband for that young wicked hussey, who whored with the priest, and spoiled him.

PEG ABOVE ALL. That wasn't either of their faults. The banshee was their link of misfortune. The priest let this orphan girl sleep in his bed for the poor. In the midnight the banshee came about flaming and screeching, and frightened her into the priest's bed and arms. And there temptation galloped away with them.

HARKAWAY. That was the bad luck of Ireland. And it could happen to the decentest girl and to the blessedest priest.

PEG ABOVE ALL. It happened to me.

HARKAWAY. So you're the orphan girl from the islands of the sea!

PEG ABOVE ALL. Whoever cursed me, cursed me well.

HARKAWAY. And now you're out to drown yourself, because you think no man will take you. But I know a beautiful wife is a very fancy thing to have. No man at all will refuse her, though 'tis said and supposed they're unlucky.

PEG ABOVE ALL. The stone I wanted to drown was the cursing stone of St. Bannon, to stop Biddy from turning it against the priest.

HARKAWAY. But drowning a saint's cursing stone could draw down that saint's curse on you and me.

(MICKLE *comes running in, one hand waving his shillelagh, and the other brandishing a sheet of paper.*)

310

MICKLE (*gloating*). Look what I found nailed to the priesteen's door! The picture of an open coffin!

PEG ABOVE ALL (*alarmed*). That's the Whiteboys' warning!

MICKLE. You tailor of the inches, can you read words as well as inches?

HARKAWAY. I can, though I came from a queer country. (*He takes paper, turns it right way up, and reads.*) 'We can fire high and we can fire low.' 'Rory of the Hill.'

MICKLE. That's the nightboys serving the priesteen with notice to quit!

PEG ABOVE ALL (*bitterly*). He's better than some he'll leave after him around here.

MICKLE (*bullying her*). He's the worst Irishman since an O'Neill captured St. Patrick.

HARKAWAY (*pushing him back from* PEG). And you're a queer eel, as St. Patrick said to the snake.

MICKLE. Tonight, if you try to save that priesteen, I'll make meal of your bones.

HARKAWAY. That's strong talk out of a weak belly. (*Suddenly releasing* PEG ABOVE ALL, *he snatches up his stick.*)

MICKLE. I'll make your rusty needle go easy.

HARKAWAY. I'll wear this stick on you.

(*Both are pulling off their jackets.*)

PEG ABOVE ALL. Have sense, let ye. Isn't every graveyard bursting with broken skulls?

MICKLE (*dancing*). I'm laughing with the joy of killing him!

HARKAWAY. Hi for the tailors! Do you dare tread on the tail of my coat? (*Drawing his jacket along ground.*)

MICKLE (*stepping on* HARKAWAY'S *coat*). Hi for the weavers!

HARKAWAY. For that you'll go down, and an inquest on you!

(*They are circling and sparring for openings.* MULLEE *comes in from right, also carrying a big stick.*)

PEG ABOVE ALL. Mullee, beat a blow on this battle!

MULLEE. Mickle, you're a walking tyrant!

(MULLEE *waits until the circling* MICKLE *has his back turned to him, then he grabs him and trips him, wrests the stick from his hand, and throws it into the right wing.*)

MULLEE. My lucky shillelagh that never lost a fight! If I can't find it, I'll turn the cursing stone against you. (MICKLE *goes out right.*)

PEG ABOVE ALL. Mullee, God bless you till you're better paid.

MULLEE (*picking up his own stick*). I knew it wasn't a mean fight: that ye didn't mean to kill each other.

311

HARKAWAY. Sure I know to within one blow how much beating Mickle can stand.

MULLEE. Petticoat Loose is after finding the price of a farm lease under a fairy tree.

HARKAWAY. I never seen that to happen before though I came from a queer country.

(PETTICOAT LOOSE *comes running in from left, looking very happy.*)

PETTICOAT LOOSE. Mullee, the fairy latchiko is banished away, and my true baby is back from the forts.

MULLEE. Thank God! Was it Biddy's herbs and spells?

PETTICOAT LOOSE. Yes, they put the latchiko into great trouble and fear. Then Biddy stripped it naked, and left it out in the belly of the road.

HARKAWAY. Between the iron cart-wheel tracks!

MULLEE. There's strong virtue in iron.

PETTICOAT LOOSE. It screeched away there, giving out old talk and curses. Till at last it began to give out young talk! Then Biddy passed her hands over it, and found its heart was ticking like a baby's heart, and no longer like an old person's heart.

PEG ABOVE ALL. Thank God, Petticoat Loose!

MULLEE. Now hasn't Biddy the spells and the powers of the Druids?

HARKAWAY. And only for the priest delaying her, she'd have spelled my family back from the forts.

(*Since* MICKLE'S *exit,* PEG ABOVE ALL *has done a good deal of peering anxiously into the darkness into which* BIDDY *retreated.*)

PEG ABOVE ALL. I'm afeard Biddy is in there turning the cursing stone against the priest. Harkaway, will you lend me your company and your courage?

HARKAWAY (*smiling*). Thanks for the asking. I will. Come on.

(*He leads her out through monastery door.* PETTICOAT LOOSE *takes a cloth purse from her pocket and hands it to* MULLEE.)

PETTICOAT LOOSE. Your true baby and mine is back from the forts; and there is fifty gold sovereigns, the price of a farm. Would you like to be man and master over it?

MULLEE (*admiring the money*). I would, and I'll never hide from you a penny I earn.

PETTICOAT LOOSE. When we have our own farm, our mothers can no longer forbid us what they enjoyed themselves.

MULLEE. Once we're tied by a priest, they'll be afeard, maybe, to put on us their widow's curses.

312

PETTICOAT LOOSE. We'll weather out their curses.

MULLEE (*worried*). But 'tis said and supposed the priest is to put his priests' curse on you tonight for dosing him with coaxiorums and the spancel of death. If he curses you, your farm won't grow the grass of a maggot, and I'd sup sorrow if I wed you. (*He hands her back the money, moves away from her.*)

PETTICOAT LOOSE. I doubt he isn't a cursing priest at all.
(PEG ABOVE ALL *and* HARKAWAY *come out through the monastery door.*)

PEG ABOVE ALL. Here's Biddy coming with her pick of the wickedest and the worst skulls in the graveyard!

HARKAWAY. Its sins won't fall on the priest, if he swears no lie.
(MICKLE *comes in from right, waving his stick triumphantly.*)

MULLEE. My lucky stick, found on the stone over the giant's grave!
(BIDDY THE TOSSER *enters through the monastery doorway, followed by* SHAWN LALLY *carrying the cursing stone, which he carefully replaces on its flag. With them comes* HONOR LALLY. *If other actors and actresses are freely available, some could be brought on here for a crowd effect. But no additional actors or crowd are necessary.*)

BIDDY. Is this all that came to witness my challenge and to aid me? After all I saved from the grave and from the forts! And all I suffered for taking cures out of the hand of God!

PETTICOAT LOOSE. Biddy, it isn't that people are thankless towards you. But they're afeard of your hidden eye this night under the castrated moon.

HONOR. And they're afeared of the priest's curse, and his Latin.

ALL. (*murmuring*). Yes. That's how it is.

BIDDY. Neighbours, this evening when the hoop of the sun touched the lake, it blushed blood red, so I tossed and asked the Good People why that was. No puzzle puzzles them long. They said it was because that wicked priesteen stole the holy fish from the holy well, and molested Cuaille, the holy tree.
(*There is general alarm and anger over this.*)

PETTICOAT LOOSE. If he did, nothing can save us, unless Ireland is blessed. (*She runs to examine the holy tree.*)

MULLEE. After that a clean dog wouldn't lick him. (*He goes into examine the well.*)

HONOR. He was whiskey crazy.

SHAWN. He'd drink the Burkes and the Blakes.

PETTICOAT LOOSE (*coming back with branch*). Look! A branch freshly cut off Cuaille!

313

PEG ABOVE ALL. Couldn't plenty do that besides the priest? Are his enemies, the fairies, fit to be believed about him.

BIDDY. He broke that branch off to see whether he could cut down Cuaille and live. If he cuts down Cuaille, he'll leave without shelter your dead friends who're suffering hard their Purgatories under it.

MICKLE. And lepping amongst them could be my Timmy? (*He goes around the tree.*) Timmy, are you hearabouts with your jailors scorching and riddling you?

MULLEE (*emerging from the well*). Biddy has the truth. The holy fish is gone from the well and his duty!

SHAWN. A holy fish who cured when every other cure had failed.

HONOR. That sin could dry the holy well.

PETTICOAT LOOSE. And what'll we do without that holy well of the Breasts?

EILEEN. (*A glamour girl*). We could lose the perfections! (*Or this line could be given to* PEG ABOVE ALL.)

HARKAWAY. That sin could set us crazy, and beaking things.

FURSEY. (*An old man*). Any more what'll cure us from the sickness brought on by storytelling in the daytime? (*Or that line could be given to* SHAWN LALLY?)

BIDDY. That priesteen is worse than what I could tell ye, and double as bad as what ye could tell me. And unless we defeat him now, ye'll be eating rotten spuds and small spuds for ever!

MICKLE. We'll batter in his brains now; then the big spuds will come back.

MULLEE. If we don't, we'll turn into shadows.

(*The crowd, led by* MICKLE, *seems about to set out for the priest's cabin.* PEG ABOVE ALL *runs in front of them.*)

PEG ABOVE ALL. The man who kills him, I'll inform on him.

HARKAWAY (*opposing their advance*). That priest might turn good again, like King David.

(*The advance is checked, so* BIDDY *tries to get it going again.*)

BIDDY. God is slow, but sure. He'll give us good minding in the next world. But in this world it's mostly the Good People that are minding ourselves and our stock and our crops. If ye desert them, they'll desert ye. If ye don't fight their enemy now, ye'll trudge long roads for alms, without a roof-tree to come home to.

(*The priest comes in through the monastery door, carrying a white sheet. The crowd part to allow his advance.*)

PRIEST (*sarcastically*). 'From roaring guns and women's tongues, O

Lord deliver us!'

BIDDY (*turning*). It was time for you to come.

PRIEST. I'm here now. And where are all the people I lost my health in curing?

BIDDY. Where are they? They're under slabs in every graveyard. Women, clad him with the sheet.

(PETTICOAT LOOSE *and* HONOR *hang the sheet around his shoulders, and pin it at his throat.*)

PRIEST (*resignedly*). It's a true saying that the Devil always had a bigger following than God.

BIDDY (*displaying skull proudly*). Take notice, priesteen, that this skull is a big skull, a man's skull, a sinful skull. And this hole and that crack show he died fighting and drunk and murdering. And now he's in the house of pain for ever. (*She hands him the skull.*)

PRIEST. One of the many who come here to pray on the Pattern Day, and end the day challenging and fighting each other.

BIDDY. Cut the sign of the Cross over the skull.

(*The priest makes the sign of the cross over the skull.*)

BIDDY. The skull will laugh if lies are sworn on it under the castrated moon. Did the neighbours learn you the oath on the skull?

PRIEST. They did. (*He kneels on the flag supporting the cursing stone.*)

BIDDY. Sound it out now, without mistake.

PRIEST. I swear to tell nothing but he truth on this skull. If I lie, may the sins of the owner of this skull fall on my soul for ever. And all the punishment due for his sins in this world and the next. And all the punishment due for the sins of his ancestors back to Adam. And may all the misfortunes suffered by the race of this skull fall on my body and soul for ever. And if –

BIDDY (*quickly*). Yes. That'll do.

MICKLE. Sound your charges, Biddy. The rape of Peg Above All! The murder of my son!

PEG ABOVE ALL. Wait, father! They didn't give you time to say the part of the oath that could condemn Biddy herself.

MICKLE (*advancing on* PEG). Stand back, you whore! Or I'll knock a fall out of you!

HARKAWAY (*coming between them*). Stand back you, or I'll leave you black and blue, like a man killed by the fairies!

BIDDY. Priesteen, word out the leavings of the oath on the skull. I never could think they made a pebble's difference.

315

PRIEST. If my accuser accuses me in the wrong, may all the sins and misfortunes of the race of this skull fall on her in this world and in the next.

BIDDY. Neighbours, I accuse this priesteen of whoring with a poor orphan girl who came to him for a gospel.

PRIEST. Now under the oath of the skull you accuse me of whoring. But before you belled it far and wide that I trapped her and raped her.

BIDDY. Through the window the Whiteboys seen ye whoring. But they couldn't hear whether she was laughing or crying.

PRIEST. Neighbours, Biddy has told ye I'm an unbeliever and the father of lies. If I was, I'd swear on the skull that I never sinned with a girl. Because I am a believer I can't swear a lie. So I admit that I did sin with one girl.

BIDDY. You admit it, not because you're a believer, but because the Whiteboys witnessed your sin; and because you're afeard the skull will laugh in your face.

PRIEST. We heard tales of skulls laughing. But who ever witnessed it?

BIDDY. I did, and above once.

PRIEST. Neighbours, Biddy has told ye that I sinned with every stranger girl who came to me for a gospel. I swear on this skull, under the crescent moon, that I sinned with only once such girl.

BIDDY (*contemptous*). He has confessed his guilt – because so many witnessed it. Women, strip the sheet off him! This challenge and swearing it over. (*She takes the skull out of priest's hands. He rises, and* PETTICOAT LOOSE *and* HONOR *come forward to unpin the sheet, take it off and fold it.*)

PETTICOAT LOOSE (*anxiously, with a backward glance at* MULLEE). Father, is it in your mind to put your priest's curse on any of us?

PRIEST. It isn't.

PETTICOAT LOOSE. Now, or ever?

PRIEST. Never. Not even on Biddy the Tosser. 'Vengeance is mine,' said the Lord of Hosts.

(*Smiling happily,* PETTICOAT LOOSE *runs back to* MULLEE.)

BIDDY. Because he knows a whoring priest's curse is dead, like his curing.

PRIEST. Neighbours, Biddy has told ye that the crops and weather are ruined by me denying and defying the fairies.

BIDDY. Maura the Pet and Biddy Nawpla say the same, and every other member of the Good People.

PRIEST. The Church has told us to pray to God and His angels and saints. But it never told us to believe in fairies, or pray to them.

BIDDY. Did Our Lord say it was sinful to believe in them?

PRIEST. He never mentioned them. And He would have, if He wanted us to believe in them.

BIDDY. He was a warm dry country, so they didn't need fairies to keep their stock and crops alive.

PRIEST (*using a rock as a pulpit*). God's book, the Holy Bible, tells us how the Israelites of old turned away from the true God, and worshipped the demon Gods Baal and Moloch, and burned alive their babies in sacrifice to them. Every time the Israelites went after false Gods, and murdered their babies, God sent holy prophets with this message from Himself. 'I will destroy your land, and scatter your amongst the foreigners. Your land shall be a desert and your cities shall be destroyed!' All those punishments did fall on the Israelites of old, and now they are falling on ye, because ye are worshipping fairies and holy trees, and perishing your babies in obedience to Biddy Nawpla and Maura the Pet and Biddy the Tosser.

BIDDY. What babies? Fairy latchikoes! Wasps of things that could be cradled in a child's shoe!

HARKAWAY (*mildly*). Biddy, ours was a fine armful of a baby.

BIDDY. It was before the fairies swept it.

PRIEST. For three centuries schooling for Catholics was forbidden by law in this country. That gave the fairy doctors the time and the chance to bring back their Druid's religion. Now they're making ropes of money out of fear of the fairies and fear of the Evil Eye. But there is no such thing as the Evil Eye. If Biddy had one, she'd have riddled me long since.

MICKLE. Strip it, Biddy, and overlook him! Blink him!

(BIDDY *puts her hand up to her eye-patch, as if about it take it off. General panic ensues. They hide behind the holy well, or the holy tree. They cover their faces. The women hold their rosary beads out between them and the Evil Eye. The men do the same with their knife blades. Only the priest remains standing and confronting* BIDDY.)

SHAWN. Don't, Biddy, or our breed will die out!

HARKAWAY. We'll fall like flies!

MULLEE. Our own dogs won't know us!

PETTICOAT LOOSE. We'll never milk another goat!

PEG ABOVE ALL. Run, father, and live for happy beds!

HONOR. Spare him, Biddy, and us all!

BIDDY. I wouldn't let him live long enough to see the rain fall, but for one danger. As ye know, after a wicked priest dies, he has to roam the world in the likeness of a black dog. And I don't want to be doing my night rounds with a black dog feeling after me.

PRIEST. Neighbours, I came here tonight to do ye a last good turn. To prove that Biddy is lying to ye about her evil eye, like she's lying to ye about the fairies. I'll prove to ye now that she has no evil eye. (*He advances upon* BIDDY, *but as he reaches her, she lifts her eye-patch, pushing it up under her cap. A distorted and evil-looking eye is exposed. The priest retreats hastily, blessing himself.*)

PRIEST. Lord bless us and save us!

BIDDY. Now is it truth or lies that Biddy the Tosser has an Evil Eye descended from King Balor of the Mighty Blows?

(*The general panic increases.* BIDDY *continues to stare at the priest, who is now standing between her and the right hand wing of the stage.*)

SHAWN. Clasp it, Biddy!

MULLEE. Or we'll drink death or long sickness!

HARKAWAY. You'll leave us like men killed by a mad ghost!

PEG ABOVE ALL. Father, run for you life and for the lives that need you!

MICKLE. King Mannanawn, throw the evil on the priest, and away from us!

PETTICOAT LOOSE. The charm of Saints Peter and Paul between us and the Host of the Air!

HONOR. The Charm of Saints Brendan and Enda between us and the Host of the Sea!

EILEEN. We'll be like the bad cows: no man will take us!

FURSEY. We'll turn into shadows, and shadows can't lift anything!

(BIDDY *and the priest are still confronting each other at centre stage, but the priest is regaining confidence.*)

PRIEST (*smiling*). Biddy is staring at me, as if I had two heads. But her evil eye might as well be trying to put a blister on a hedgehog. I'm as sound as Gibraltar!

MICKLE. Wither him, Biddy! Boil the lifesweat out through him!

PRIEST. She can't even knock a sneeze out of me. Because it isn't and evil eye she has, but a diseased eye. If herself, or her fairies, could cure anything, they'd have cured her diseased eye long since. She couldn't win a husband and a farm with such an eye, so she tried her hand as a fairy doctor.

PEG ABOVE ALL (*running up to* BIDDY). The priest has the truth, and Biddy is a liar, with the Divil on her back as a stewart.

HARKAWAY (*advancing on* BIDDY *threateningly*). And Biddy caused the life to leave my wife and child!

FURSEY (*coming up to* BIDDY). Her evil eye is as dead as the tip of a rush.

(*A crowd is now advancing on* BIDDY *threateningly, and she retreats around the back of the well, then runs right, and jumps onto the flag holding the cursing stone. She looks into the distance towards the right, and she smiles triumphantly.*)

BIDDY. I told ye why I wouldn't blink a wicked priest. But I give notice to all the world and to ye that I can blink a wicked priest's cabin, and that I have done. And now his cabin is lit and burnt by fire from the stars!

MICKLE (*delighted*). His cabin is flaming like a limekiln!

PRIEST. My books! Help me to save my books. (*He runs out right. There is great excitement and cries of 'Fire'!*)

MICKLE. Now isn't Biddy holier than any priest?

BIDDY. And that was only half my best. My best wouldn't leave a house standing from here to the Wood of the Flies. (*She has covered her Evil Eye again, and the crowd flock around her with cries of 'More power to you, Biddy!', 'We never doubted you!' 'Hi for the Good People!' 'Hi for Biddy the Tosser!'*)

SHAWN. He couldn't best Biddy even if he stopped up all night!

MULLEE. She can defeat any priest from here to elsewhere!

BIDDY. Only for all the Masses and blessed Aves he said, I'd have him bound under in the worst fort the Good People have.

PEG ABOVE ALL (*urgent*). We're duty bound to save his clothes!

PETTICOAT LOOSE. And his bed!

MULLEE. And his meal and spuds.

HONOR. But have we your leave, Biddy?

SHAWN. And the leave of the Good People?

BIDDY. We grant leave to ye all, except Harkaway and Peg Above All. If they go up there, the fairy host will sweep them into the flames.

PETTICOAT LOOSE. Come on till we save John's book!

(*She runs out, followed by* MULLEE, SHAWN, HONOR *and the crowd − if any.*)

MICKLE. Biddy, would the Good People grudge me a bottle of whiskey plucked from the flames?

BIDDY. You're a well-wisher, Mickle. They won't grudge it to you.

MICKLE. I'll drink to their glory, and to yours. (*Runs out.*)

HARKAWAY (*humbly*). Timely you warned us, Biddy. And we're thankful.

PEG ABOVE ALL (*scared*). And we're sorry for saying against yourself and the Good People.

BIDDY. Biddy will forgive ye. But that priesteen has put ye in a great pity by blasting ye with my hidden eye.

PEG ABOVE ALL. Could the Good People carry me off now? – and my baby?

BIDDY. They could – soon and sudden! Do you feel a cracking in your bones?

PEG ABOVE ALL. No ... (*She walks about uneasily, then sits hunched up on the flag supporting the cursing stone.*) I do a little.

BIDDY. Soon you will a lot, unless you depart a third part of Ireland from here. But not with a man under the curse of a hidden eye, and under the curse of the Good People.

PEG ABOVE ALL. The priest you mean?

BIDDY. Who else? .... (*She turns to* HARKAWAY.) And, Harkaway, unless you get wed soon, the Good People may send you a wife of their own: a fairy hag with two hands colder than the coldest ice that ever froze.

HARKAWAY. Sure I was a lady's man ever, and my trade is bringing in a power more than I can eat myself. So my heart's welcome is for Peg Above All and her baby.

BIDDY. 'Short courting long happiness,

Long courting short happiness.' (*Looking at the skull.*)

Maybe he lost his marriage chance, and that's why he died drunk and fighting and murdering. (*She sets out for the monastery doorway.*)

HARKAWAY (*following her, and handing her a coin*). God bless your heart, and may you have a fine funeral day.

BIDDY. The Good People will look after their own. (*She exits.*)

HARKAWAY (*coming back to* PEG ABOVE ALL *anxiously*). Are they still cracking your bones?

PEG ABOVE ALL. No worse, Harkaway. And I like you as good as any man I met in the islands of the sea, or in Ireland. But the banshee and my sin have left Father Donal without a trade, or a cabin. If he needs my farm and me I'm duty bound to give him both. If he doesn't need me, I'm free.

HARKAWAY. He's sure to come this way on his road to the village.

PEG ABOVE ALL. I'll wait till he comes, but let you go ahead to Shawn Lally's house and judge my baby. If you like my baby, we might marry each other for luck.

HARKAWAY (*thrilled*). I'll run like a hare of two years old. (*He is going, but turns back, and drops his voice.*) This is a queer

320

country – not safe for babies!

PEG ABOVE ALL. There's too many fairy forts and evil eyes in it.

HARKAWAY. I can make a suit for the noble as good as for the ignoble, and earn my living any road. We'll make for the rising sun – away from famine and forts.

PEG ABOVE ALL (*smiling*). There we'll get our breaths again.

HARKAWAY. God keep you! (*He runs out left towards village. She moves towards right, then halts.*)

PEG ABOVE ALL. If I go up there, the fairy host may burn me. Harkaway! (*She runs a few yards after him, then halts again.*) But if I don't go, I may never see Donal again. I'll chance it. There does be good luck on the fool. (*She turns and runs towards right only to meet the priest coming in carrying an armful of books and the crucifix. There is a small bloodstain on his forehead.*)

PEG ABOVE ALL. Donal, how are you?

PRIEST. I'm well, Peg, – if you are! (*He sits on the flag supporting the cursing stone.*)

PEG ABOVE ALL (*anxiously*). You kept us apart until after the swearing. Wasn't that only to save our lives from the Whiteboys?

PRIEST. It hasn't saved my cabin from them. Though maybe it was fired by Teig of the Tombs, and that's why he wasn't here for the challenge.

PEG ABOVE ALL. Have you shelter got for the night?

PRIEST. Yes, Mullee's bed for the poor.

PEG ABOVE ALL. If tomorrow isn't too bad for the long road, I'll call with my baby.

PRIEST. No, Peg, wait here with your baby for a few days till I find a farm with a long lease and a short rent far away, where no one ever heard about you and me.

PEG ABOVE ALL (*happy*). Then you'll need the costs for the farm lease, so take the lot with you. (*She offers him the money.*)

PRIEST (*pushing it back*). No, Peg. Only give me a guinea or two as an earnest for your new landlord, and be showing the rest to your pick of the bachelors around.

PEG ABOVE ALL. What good would that do us?

PRIEST. A million men would wed you for your beauty and for the farm you'll have. Then why live in sin with a priest who can never wed you?

PEG ABOVE ALL. But we were never so happy as when we were in bed together.

PRIEST (*smiling*). They say, 'To sin is human, but to remain in sin is divilish.'

PEG ABOVE ALL. Without my farm you'll die of curing and drink.

PRIEST. No, I'm going south to push my fortune as a hedge-schoolmaster.

PEG ABOVE ALL. But they say the hedge-schoolmaster's end does be the saddest of all.

PRIEST. All ends are sad, Peg. And if hedge-school poverty cures me of the drink, some bishop might give me a half-parish and a bell.

PEG ABOVE ALL. But you said, 'The man who tastes a woman can never rest.'

PRIEST. That isn't always true. Some great rakes became great saints.

PEG ABOVE ALL (*worried*). I'm afeard for you, Donal. If we part now, after your best days are over, you'll be left in a fog.

(*The priest rises with his bundle of books and crucifix, and walks past her a few yards towards the left. Then he stops and turns smiling sadly.*)

PRIEST. Peg, a priest is the only man in all the world, who can't do his day's work unless he's in the state of grace; because he can't say Mass unless he's in the state of grace. You grow to like being in the state of grace: you feel safe. And you realise there can be no real happiness away from God, Our Creator. And after so many years the old dog can't change his trot ... (*He turns to go.*)

PEG ABOVE ALL (*urgently*). If you can't alter your mind before you go now, you'll alter it too late.

PRIEST. In a few years death will turn us into skulls and bones like all the lovers true in there. (*Pointing to graveyard.*) But our souls can live happy with God for evermore.

PEG ABOVE ALL. Then I'll bend with the tree that bends with me: Harkaway the journeyman.

PRIEST. A master tailor, and well able to read a farm lease. He'll buy your farm for you.

PEG ABOVE ALL. Biddy has matched us.

PRIEST. That way she banishes Harkaway as well as you and me. It didn't suit her to have Harkaway telling his customers about how she lost his wife and child. (*He turns to go.*)

PEG ABOVE ALL. We'll meet again?

PRIEST. No, Peg, there's no use in looking at an apple we can't buy. May God keep you and yours! (*He goes out left.*)

PEG ABOVE ALL. May the strength of three be in your journey!

(PEG ABOVE ALL *dabs at her eyes.* MULLEE *and* PETTICOAT LOOSE *enter carrying bedclothes, etc.* PETTICOAT LOOSE *also carries a poteen bottle. Both are in hilarious humour.*)

MULLEE. Peg Above All, you made that priest as crazy as the girl in the lovesong made Friar Cassidy!

PEG ABOVE ALL. Not me!

MULLEE. If he isn't crazy, why did he go saving oul' books, instead of his clothes?

PEG ABOVE ALL. He's to try his hand at schoolmastering.

PETTICOAT LOOSE (*laughing*). Maybe the man who hasn't a woman needs books.

MULLEE. Maybe I'd be safer to take to books than to take you!

PETTICOAT LOOSE. You would not. What a man was used to won't harm him!

PEG ABOVE ALL (*relieved*). Then maybe it won't harm Father Donal to go back to the loneliness he was used to.

PETTICOAT LOOSE (*gaily, waving the bottle*). 'While we can, we'll live in clover. Because when we die, we'll die all over!'

(MULLEE *snatches the bottle out of her hand, and runs out left with that and his bundle of clothes.* PETTICOAT LOOSE *runs after him gaily.*)

PETTICOAT LOOSE. I'll get you hanged for robbery!

(*They go out left, and* PEG ABOVE ALL *is following them out, when suddenly she turns towards the monastery.*)

PEG ABOVE ALL. St. Bannon, ask the One-Son of Mary to gift Harkaway with love for a baby that isn't his, and its mother, the way the Holy Joseph was gifted with love for a baby that wasn't his, and its mother. . . . And, St. Bannon, crave the High King of the Miracles to bestow a Mass-bell soon on Father Donal. And tomorrow I'll pray three hard stations around your holy well.

(BIDDY *comes into the monastery doorway, and* PEG ABOVE ALL *sees, or hears, her approach. She runs out left.* BIDDY *has not seen her. She looks around quickly, and, satisfied that the coast is clear, she returns to the darkness, but is back quickly with the pail. She sets it on the wall of the holy well, and looks into it.*)

BIDDY. Holy fish, your enemy that priesteen is banished for evermore; and all I'm asking in return is a cure for Teig of the Tombs. His hand is lame after a burn it got tonight. Teig is the best man that ever had limbs, for you and for me. (*She carries the bucket into the well, and empties it. She comes out, looks Heavenwards.*) St. Bannon, ask God and the Virgin Everlasting to convert the priests to believe again in the Good People. . . .

How can the priests not see the fairy lights passing from fort to fort by night; and by day the cows puffing, blowing the fairies off the grass? And the fairy winds in the hayfields, and – everywhere! – the tracks of the white fairy blood on the stones? And on the great sea the Death Wave of King Mannanawn, and the Wave of Cleeona, and the sea horses, and the Headless Man, and the High Tide of the Birds? How can the priests not see them? A blind man on a galloping horse could see them. St. Bannon, take from the eyes of the priest whatever pearls are blinding them. (*She approaches the holy tree.*) Cuaille, I'd sooner go eating broken bottles, than break your branch off like I done. But how else could I save you from that priesteen? Odd times the good have to behave cruel to defeat the wicked. To grow a good crop, you have to kill the weeds. (*Half to the tree and half to St. Bannon.*) Good night to ye! (*As she is going out through the monastery doorway, she stops and turns anxiously.*) Saint Bannon, if Maura Harkaway, the tailor's wife is turned into an evil spirit, or a banshee, for corpsing herself, do your best to grow a high hedge between her and me. Already I have my fill of fear. (*She goes.*)

END OF PLAY

The Bachelor's Daughter

A COMEDY IN THREE ACTS

CHARACTERS

Kate
Nan
Rick Duggan
Shagley Cloonan
Ainy
Lacky
Tess
Priest

The Bachelor's Daughter

ACT ONE

*A musical prelude to this play could be the menacing strains of the
"Dies Irae" in one of its orchestral versions, as in the Berlioz
symphony, or in Liszt's "Totentanz Variations". (This tune is used
in Act Two and Act Three.)*

*The year is 1956, and the scene is the kitchen of a small farmhouse
in County Galway. The roof could be thatched but more typically the
thatched roof would have been removed, and replaced by a slated
roof. Electric light has arrived. Two doors lead to bedrooms, and
another in a back wall leads to the ten yards of footpath to the main
road. A plain wooden table and an old, or modern, dresser, and
some chairs, with an old armchair near the fire, complete the
furniture. The fireplace is in the left-hand wall (from the actor's point
of view). On the hearth stands a kettle and a teapot, and in kitchen
corners buckets and pots and pans. KATE is seated at the table eating
shop-cake hastily, and swigging at a bottle of Guinness. She is a
middle-aged or elderly masculine-looking woman, with a cast in one
eye which makes her look even more formidable. Her smile is rare
and warped, her manner is domineering and rough, and her grey
hair is untidy. Her clothes are rough and ready. She wears a battered
man's cap with the peak turned behind her head.*

KATE. Was it a rat, or Nan, took this pinch out of my shopcake?
(A banging noise is heard off-stage. She jumps up.)
KATE. The bitch is back and banging again on the butt of the
window. I'll enjoy these when she's gone to bed hungry.
*(Hurriedly she carries her supper into the bedroom on the left.
The front door opens, and NAN enters, bent under the weight of a
bag of turf, and leaning on a strong stick. She limps to the
fireplace, and drops the bag of turf against the wall. She looks
anywhere between eighteen and twenty-three years of age: pale
and rather thin and nervous. But when she becomes merry there
is something childlike and innocent about her gaiety. She takes*

327

off an old topcoat and beret. Her clothes are neat, but old and patched. KATE *comes out, goes straight to the front door, closes and bolts it.*)

KATE. You never close a door. It's easy known you were born in a field.

NAN. I couldn't, mam. The bag was staggering me.

KATE. You were able to go banging on the butt of the window!

NAN. Oh, no, mam. I was in a hurry – afeard my blood would come entirely! (*She points to the back of her leg.*)

KATE. You're bleeding like a pig, you dirty thing!

NAN. A dog came behind and bit me as I was stealing his master's turf.

KATE. Why didn't you give him stick?

NAN. I didn't see him until he made the bound. Then I lashed him off my leg.

KATE. You never do anything right.

NAN. Can I bandage it now?

KATE. You can, but don't tear anything belonging to me.

NAN. Sure my room is full of rags. Can I put Dettol on it?

KATE. There's no need. A dog's bite is healthy, not like a rat's. (NAN *limps into her bedroom, and* KATE *examines the bag of turf.*)

KATE. This is soft bad turf with no lasting in it. When the village is well asleep, you'll have to go again on the same errand. (*Two or three loud bangs sound in* NAN'S *bedroom.*)

KATE. Stop that mad sulking and noising, or I'll soon sign you over to the mental hospital doctors. (NAN *comes out with a bandage in her hand.*)

NAN. Mam, that wasn't me noising. On my oath and soul!

KATE. That noise never comes around the house except when you're in the house, or near it.

NAN. These Galway rats are noisy freaky kind of rats, and maybe they hate me for trapping them. (*She bandages her leg.*)

KATE. Set the rat traps right tonight.

NAN. Maybe they caught none last night, because all the rats were dead.

KATE. If they are dead, it must be you that's banging tonight.

NAN. No, mam. More rats could creep in from the bog and the haggards.

KATE. You that's noising to make me believe this house is haunted, and make me sell out again and go back to Mayo.

NAN. In Mayo they don't want us back, because we were bad thiefs. (*She is at the table setting the rat-traps.*)

328

KATE. The old people stole turf and spuds in their hour of need, and still they got the heavens.

NAN. Can I get the supper soon?

KATE. No, I amn't hungry yet. You must have the eating diabetes. You're always hungry.

NAN (*sadly*). Before meals mostly. (*The front door is knocked upon.*)

NAN (*hastily*). That wasn't me, mam.

KATE (*going to door*). Who's there?

MAN'S VOICE. Rickard Duggan.

KATE. Are you a drunken tinker, or a neighbour?

RICK. A neighbour.

KATE. Who's that fellow with you? (*To* NAN.) The slasher!

RICK. I'm by myself. (NAN *runs into* KATE'S *bedroom.*)

KATE. Is that dog cross?

RICK. My dog is locked up. (NAN *comes out with a bill-hook, or slasher. She takes the heavy tongs from the hearth, gives them to* KATE.)

KATE. What is your business?

RICK. To give ye a bag of good turf.

KATE (*to* NAN). I smell a tinker's plot here. Hide behind the door, and if they attack, split them down to their shoes.

NAN (*nervous*). Yes, mam.

(NAN *blesses herself hastily, and stands behind the door with upraised slasher.* KATE *unbolts the door, and retreats behind the table with the tongs at the ready.*)

KATE. Come in if you're good looking.

(*The door is opened, and* RICK DUGGAN *comes in, carrying a big bag of turf on his back. He is thirty, or a little over, tall and strong-looking and intelligent. He wears wellingtons and his work-a-day clothes have nothing shabby about them.*)

RICK (*cheerful*). Where'll I leave it?

KATE. Where it hangs, until you say how much you'll charge for it.

RICK. Not a cent. The summer being so fine I cut and reared enough turf to roast me for two years.

KATE. You aren't a bad man ... Leave it against the hob wall. (RICK *does as directed.* NAN *closes and bolts the door.*)

KATE. We're ordering turf as fast as we can.

RICK. I'll keep ye going until it comes.

KATE. And I won't let Nan of the Leaves murder you. She's mentally affected as you can see. (*To* NAN *sternly.*) Give me that weapon.

NAN (*meekly*). Yes, mam. (*She gives* KATE *the slasher.*)

329

KATE. In place of murdering this decent man, get a glass, and put a little drink in it for him.

NAN. Yes, mam. (*She takes a glass from the dresser.*)

RICK. Don't bother, Nan. I work on the dry battery mostly . . .

NAN. What'll I do, mam?

KATE. What I told you. (NAN *goes into the bedroom.*)

KATE. Sit down, and wear away a while with us.

RICK. How do ye like your new farm and house? (*He sits.*)

KATE. It'll do . . . Why hadn't I to pay more for it?

RICK (*evasive*). You struck a lucky day . . . And the old bachelors that died out on this farm were a lonesome odd people. They never went to Mass, only to holy wells on pattern days. So the old people said their land would be unlucky – full of fairies.

KATE. Why did the last buyers, the Cullinanes, sell it again so soon and sudden?

RICK. Their telling was that a blood cousin died, and left them a bigger farm in their own country.

KATE. Our mearing fences show as many gaps as an oul' man's teeth. Were land-greedy neighbours knocking those gaps, to bully the Cullinanes into selling their farm again?

RICK (*smiling – evasive*). A bachelor like me, has no one to disturb his sleep. So how neighbours pass the night he doesn't know. (*Two or three loud bangs sound in* NAN'S *room.* RICK *is very interested, but he merely looks at* KATE *for her reaction, and makes no comment.* KATE *rises from her chair, and moves towards* NAN'S *room.*)

KATE. Has Galway a new breed of rats, as noisy as aeroplanes?

RICK. Some say there is a new breed of rats, as big as loaves of bread.

KATE. But Nan of the Leaves is cracked enough to be banging them noises.

RICK. 'Tis a nice name: Nan of the Leaves.

KATE. She was made by some side of the road manufacturer. And her mother left her amongst the leaves, and there my married sister found her.

RICK. They say God looks after orphans, and they turn out the finest people in the world. (NAN *comes out with a half empty glass of stout.*)

KATE. That's only a drink for a dwarf!

NAN. The rest got spilled when the rats began noising near me.

KATE. You drank it yourself sweetly, and then banged the table as an excuse.

330

NAN (*giving the glass to* RICK). Has my breath the scent of porter? (*She brings her mouth near to his nose.*)

RICK (*smiling*). My nostrils can't catch a taste of porter. (*He raises his glass.*) Here's long life and happiness to ye in your new home! (*He drinks.*)

NAN (*smiling*). And the same to you? (*She resumes the task of setting the rat-traps, baiting them with bits of bacon.*)

KATE. Is this village noted for neighbours trespassing and colliding?

RICK. No, but long ago it was noted for a ghost called Clurheen.

KATE. All them old ghost stories were invented by parents to keep their daughters in at night.

RICK. Around here when children 'd behave noisy their parents 'd say to them 'Ye're as noisy as Clurheen'.

NAN. Was he as noisy as the big Galway rats? (*She is adjusting the baits.*)

RICK. Clurheen used to be up in the loft in O'Loughlin's noising, and tossing down little stones.

KATE. If they set their rat traps right, they wouldn't hear any noises. (*She comes over to inspect and adjust the rat traps.*)

NAN. Is O'Loughlin's house alive yet?

RICK. No, the O'Loughlins died or emigrated long ago.

NAN. Maybe fear made them emigrate. Was Clurheen seen?

RICK. No, he was never seen, but he learned to talk from all the talk in O'Loughlin's visiting house. And he helped the young servant boy at picking the spuds, and driving the cows home.

KATE. All ignorant lies that grew out of darkness, when the only light was the fire, or the rush candle, and never enough of either. (*Having readjusted the baits, she returns to her armchair.*)

RICK. But Clurheen killed Sling Godfrey, smashed his skull in with Godfrey's stick. And to this day Godfrey's descendants don't deny it.

KATE. Stick fighting was going greatly that time. Some other fighter killed Godfrey, and put the blame on Clurheen.

RICK. But it was Clurheen himself told the people at O'Loughlin's visiting house that he had killed Sling Godfrey by the roadside with Godfrey's stick. And next morning Sling's body was found where Clurheen said it was.

KATE. There never was, and never will be, any ghost to be had.

NAN. Why did Clurheen kill Sling Godfrey?

RICK. Because Sling tried to bully and banish Clurheen.

KATE. Sling's murderers invented Clurheen to clear themselves.

RICK. Sling's stick was found beside his head, with his own hair and blood stuck to it.

NAN. What happened to the young servant boy?

RICK. He was courting a neighbour's daughter, and Clurheen was jealous, and played every trick to stop them from meeting or marrying.

NAN. Did the poor things die unwed?

RICK. The old people couldn't remember that. When Clurheen killed Sling Godfrey a very holy priest, or friar, was sent for, and he banished Clurheen.

(*"Sling" is a nickname which used to be given to tall powerful looking men.*) (*The front door is struck a couple of violent blows with a stick. They start.*)

NAN (*hastily*). That wasn't me, mam.

KATE. Take the slasher, and stand behind the door.

(NAN *takes the slasher reluctantly, and stands behind the door.* KATE *takes the tongs, and approaches the door.*)

KATE. Who's there?

VOICE (*angry*). Shagley. Open up there!

KATE. D'ye know the whore?

RICK (*grinning*). Who doesn't? An old bachelor farmer living in the farthest house into the bog.

KATE. Is he mad and bad like that lady there?

RICK. He's a wild tribe of a man, but his bark is worse than his bite.

KATE (*to* NAN). If worse than yourself comes in, split him down to his shoes. (*She goes to door, unbolts it, shouts out.*) Come in! – but civil!

(*She retreats behind the table, tongs in hand. The door knob is turned, and the door is kicked wide open.* 'SHAGLEY' CLOONAN *appears. He is a tall bony elderly man with melancholy slightly mad eyes, jet black hair and bushy eyebrows and dark unwashed skin. He wears no collar or tie, and his shirt has never been washed since he bought it many months ago. His clothes are patched and dirt stained, and he wears wellingtons and an old cap or hat. He carries a big stick, and is in a blazing rage.*)

SHAGLEY. Ye two thiefs from Mayo's lowest tinker hill! I have traced your bloodstains to here (*pointing to floor.*) There's a thief's blood! And here. (*He comes to* NAN'S *bag of turf.*) And on this bag. (*Looks into bag.*) And I'd know my cut and turf at the bottom of the ocean.

KATE. A penny worth of law will make you deny that charge.

SHAGLEY. Look at your daughter's leg where my dog defended his own!

KATE. Nan, tell him how barbed wire gave your leg a rip today.

NAN (*weakly*). Yes, that's how it happened.

SHAGLEY. I heard you screeching as my dog bit you, and him howling when you struck him. He came home with blood on him, and I found my turf rick broached at the wrong end.

RICK. Your ass could broach it by rubbing his head against it.

SHAGLEY. Nothing was stealing in this village until these tinkers came into it. Buying up our land with whore's money and rogue's money. They'll not rob Shagley. (*He pulls the bag of turf towards the door.*)

KATE. Nan, dash his skull in pieces!

NAN (*sadly*). I'm ordered to split you.

(*She raises the slasher half-heartedly.* KATE *advances with tongs.* RICK *interposes himself between* KATE *and* SHAGLEY.)

RICK. Shagley, watch out. Steel goes to the heart!

KATE (*struggling with* RICK). Let me go, or I'll crown yourself!

SHAGLEY (*raising stick and retreating*). I defy all women from Kathleen Mavourneen to Mother Machree.

RICK. Let ye be warning, but not striking.

KATE. You bitch, why don't you split the whore?

NAN. He won't wait near enough.

RICK. Nan, give me that, and I'll talk sense into Shagley.

NAN (*giving him slasher*). I feel giddy and in a mist. (*She goes into her bedroom.*)

KATE. We'll send Shagley a letter from the wickedest and worst lawyer in Ireland.

RICK. If ye go to law, this row won't die out until yourselves die out. Unknownt to the law be in it.

(SHAGLEY *takes up the bag of his turf, and throws it against a sidewall contemptuously.*)

SHAGLEY. I have leavings of turf, but I want to convert them out of thievery and badness. (*Some loud bangs come from* NAN'S *room.*)

SHAGLEY (*suspicious*). Who's that noising?

KATE. Nan is hammering new feet into a stool. (NAN *comes running out scared.*)

NAN. That wasn't me, mam.

KATE. Liar and lunatic! (*The banging is repeated*).

RICK. That isn't Nan.

KATE. It's the big new breed of rats.

SHAGLEY. It isn't. It's some noise beyond nature.

KATE. You haven't much between your two ears, if you believe it's

333

ghosts.

SHAGLEY. The Cullinanes believed it wasn't worldly, whether it's a good thing or a bad.

KATE. It's easy to see what you are: a landgrabber out to frighten us out of our new farm.

SHAGLEY. I'm an old bachelor, walking slow and going fast. Not able to look after the few bog gardens I have.

RICK. The Cullinanes believed bad neighbours were banging on the butts of the windows to scare them into selling again.

KATE. Nan of the Leaves, take a rabbits run around the house, and see if you can catch anyone.

NAN (*nervous*). Its dark night now, and hard to tell a ghost from a person. (*She moves to the front door, but* SHAGLEY *stops her there.*)

SHAGLEY. If they run away, you won't see who they are. If they make a stand, a darkness blow could blind you, or kill you.

RICK. Yes, the darkness blow is the worst, because you can't see it, and they can't aim it right.

NAN (*relieved*). They won't let me go, mam.

KATE. Because they know their landgrabber friends are out there noising.

SHAGLEY. Why did the Cullinanes bring a priest to read Mass in this kitchen?

KATE. That's often done when people move into a new house.

RICK. But the priest bought that height of books about a class of ghost called a poltergeist, and he gave them to the Cullinanes.

SHAGLEY. And from the Cullinanes them books got scattered about the village.

KATE. Paper can't refuse ink, and ghost books are as liary as the telephone.

(*Two or three loud bangs come from* NAN'S *room.*)

NAN. There's something that isn't right in there.

SHAGLEY. The priest classed this ghost as a poltergeist. They're never seen, but they make noise and throw things

KATE. If the Cullinanes went to the police, they'd soon catch these land greedy ghosts.

RICK. The priest will tell you the truth, because he can never buy your land.

KATE. He can earn soft money by pretending to banish ghosts.

SHAGLEY. He charged the Cullinanes nothing at all.

RICK. Priests don't want that job. They reckon its dangerous.

NAN. We never heard it preached that there is such a thing as

334

ghosts.

RICK. The priest said the Church left everyone free to believe, or not to believe, in ghosts.

SHAGLEY (*to* KATE). Will you let me do what I witnessed the curate doing: cross question this ghost?

KATE (*cynical*). Go ahead. Chance your arm and break your leg.

SHAGLEY. The priest learned this way from the books he bought about poltergeists.

RICK. And he called this ghost Clurheen because he read cases where a poltergeist came back to where he was before.

(SHAGLEY *has opened the ghost room door, and stands facing it. He puts his two hands into his jacket pockets.*)

KATE. The ghost books have softened your brains into believing anything.

SHAGLEY. Clurheen, or whoever you are, I have fingers closed and fingers spread. Beat a blow for every finger spread . . . Clurheen, or whoever you are!

RICK. They don't answer until you ask the third time.

SHAGLEY. Beat one blow for every finger spread.

(*Five clear strong bangs follow.* SHAGLEY *takes out his hands, showing the fingers of one hand closed and the other hands fingers spread.*)

KATE. Even Nan of the Leaves, that part lunatic, can see through what you done. After counting the blows, you opened five fingers.

SHAGLEY. You wouldn't trust the Pope, the next man to God.

KATE. I don't trust land grabbers.

SHAGLEY. This time I'll do it another way the priest done it. (*He closes ghost room door, faces it, and puts his hands behind his back.*) Count my fingers spread, but don't tell Clurheen.

KATE. We have them counted.

SHAGLEY. Clurheen, beat a blow for every finger spread. (*Three blows sound.*)

RICK. That's no rat. That's a professor!

NAN. And he's answering to his name – Clurheen!

(KATE *snatches up the bill-hook, and sets out for the door.*)

KATE. Shagley told them his numbers, or they're spying them through that window. (*She opens the door suddenly, runs out.*)

RICK. Nan, is her bite as bad as her bark?

SHAGLEY. Is she as bad as the venom in her nose?

NAN (*smiling*). She cant help that. Her breed were rough, and she was reared by oul' bachelors.

RICK. Shagley, did you tell a certain pair of brothers how many blows to beat?

SHAGLEY. I did not. If they want to win a wife with a farm, they'll have to win her without help from Shagley.

NAN. Odd times I do feel something pulling at my blankets and pillows.

RICK (*smiling*). Odd times we all have nightmares like that.

(KATE *enters, and closes and bolts the door.*)

SHAGLEY (*sarcastic*). Which had you to kill? Ghosts or land-grabbers?

KATE. Neither. But I heard steps running. (*She leaves bill-hook against the wall.*)

RICK. Dogs or foxes.

KATE. I'm long enough walking to know the voice of a person's footsteps.

SHAGLEY. Cross examine this noise maker yourself.

KATE. That's what I will do. And I'll try to see any landgrabbers spying through that window.

(*She stands with her back to ghost room door, so that she can see the window. She closes all her fingers except one.*)

KATE. Clurheen, I have fingers spread and fingers closed. Beat a blow for every finger spread. (*One blow sounds.*)

RICK. Like the Yanks they're good guessers.

KATE. Clurheen, I have fingers closed, and fingers spread. Beat a blow for every finger spread.

(*She has opened six fingers, and soon six clear blows sound.*)

SHAGLEY. A spirit can see through a wall as easy as we can see through glass.

KATE. No, but it's easier for landgrabbers out in the darkness to see us than for us to see them. (*She goes to window, peers out.*)

RICK. Can you see them?

KATE. No, they seen my move, and ducked away.

NAN. Ask Clurheen is he the Clurheen that killed a man long ago.

SHAGLEY. Clurheen, are you the ghost that was around here long ago? Beat one blow if you are. (*Several blows sound.*)

RICK. No murderer wants to be caught by his tongue.

(*A few angry bangs follow.*)

NAN. Rick, he doesn't like what you said.

SHAGLEY. Clurheen, do you need any clothes, or riggings, or a hat for your head? If you don't, beat one blow.

(*One blow sounds.*)

SHAGLEY. Clurheen, did you live and die a bachelor wondering about women? And is that why you were following the Cullinane girl last year? Beat one blow for yes.

(*Several blows sound.*)

NAN. Thank God he isn't after women!

KATE. Even the dead wouldn't be seen dead with you.

SHAGLEY. Are you here because you weren't good enough for Heaven, or bad enough for Hell? Beat one blow for yes.

(*Two or three blows sound.*)

RICK. The ghost books say poltergeists don't be great discussers.

KATE *snatches up the slasher, runs to the door and out.*)

SHAGLEY. Some night she'll kill some innocent neighbour calling about trespass.

NAN. Or he'll kill her. Then two ghosts will be dogging me!

RICK. It's uncivilised to make a girl sleep in a room with a ghost that killed a man.

NAN. She wouldn't let me shift my bed out to the kitchen. She said rats never killed anyone.

SHAGLEY. If she slept like me in the barns of Lincolnshire and Yorkshire, she'd hear cases where rats killed people.

RICK. Come on, Nan, and we'll have your bed out before she comes back. (*He goes towards ghost room door.*)

NAN. If I do, she'll tongue lash me and blacken me.

RICK. You'll heal out of a beating, but not out of a murder by a ghost.

NAN. Come on so.

(*She runs into her bedroom followed by* RICK. SHAGLEY *goes towards front door, and meets* KATE *coming in.*)

SHAGLEY. Did you feel any footsteps?

KATE. No, but I felt clods or stones flying past my lugs.

SHAGLEY. The two Clurheens were pelting things: the old and the new.

KATE. Fairy tales!

SHAGLEY. Read the books on poltergeists the curate bought. They're around the village. Noising and throwing things: that's the poltergeist's dish.

(KATE *closes, and bolts the front door.*)

KATE. Where are that pair?

SHAGLEY. They're stripping her bed to bring it out here.

KATE. No, but they're stripping themselves to make a child. (*She goes to ghost room with bill-hook.*) Come out here, or I'll make four halves of ye.

(RICK *comes out, and calmly looks up at the upraised bill-hook.*)

337

RICK. If you hit me, it'll cost you more than your new farm did.

KATE. I can't let her sleep near me, because she's dangerous insane.

SHAGLEY. She can't be insane, when she's afeard of ghosts. The old people knew a lot, and they said the insane never fear ghosts.

RICK. She isn't cracked yet, but sleeping with a ghost 'd crack the Queen of England.

(*Loud banging is heard in the ghost room.*)

KATE. D'ye hear the lunatic at her contrary noise again?)

RICK. I'll see who's sounding. (*He runs into the bedroom.*)

KATE. There's no sounding except when that bitch is hereabouts.

SHAGLEY. It was the same when the Cullinane girl was here.

KATE. Was she another mad disturber?

SHAGLEY. No, but she turned a bit simple. It was said and supposed that Clurheen made her simple by enchantment.

KATE. So now he's enchanting Nan out of the little sense she had!

SHAGLEY. The ghost books print that poltergeists get their energy and power to noise and pelt things from a secret power some girls have before they get wed.

KATE. Them books were written by poisonous old bachelors like you who were let down by all women.

SHAGLEY. 'If a man lives single, he'll rue it sore,
If he marries a wife, he'll rue it more.'
A wife won't let you spit into the fire.

KATE. Was there a young unwed daughter in the house of the old Clurheen?

SHAGLEY. No, but there was a young unwed servant boy. Poltergeists can draw energy and powers from youths too.

KATE. All youths and girls are fond of tricks and divilment. They're the poltergeists.

(RICK *appears excitedly.*)

RICK. Shagley, a big rat is crawling under the blankets. I'll tuck in the blankets, and trap him.

SHAGLEY (*snatching his stick off the table*). And I'll make a dead rat of him.

(RICK *and* SHAGLEY *run into* NAN'S *room.*)

KATE. It'll come to law if ye damage that bed.

(NAN *comes running out.*)

NAN. They said a wounded rat will attack and never let go!

KATE. Maybe they're landgrabbers out to set fire to our house. So they want you out of their way. (*She moves towards ghost room.*)

NAN. But I seen the big rat moving under the blankets.

338

KATE. Every lunatic sees what isn't there.
(*Shouts are heard off stage.*)
RICK. Hit him!
SHAGLEY. Take that! And that! And that!
KATE. Do you smell fire?
NAN. Not yet.
(RICK *and* SHAGLEY *come out looking crestfallen.*)
RICK. We missed him, because there was nothing there.
KATE. Ye were so slow and cowardly he escaped the far side.
RICK. He couldn't escape through tucked in blankets.
SHAGLEY. And I made bits of his body and bones with every blow.
RICK. But when we lifted the blankets there wasn't a speck of blood or bones.
NAN. Clurheen can bulge the blankets in the shape of a rat, but when you lift them there's nothing there.
KATE. Ye have planned these lies to evict me from my farm.
RICK (*excitedly*). And Clurheen was growing bigger and smaller under the blankets!
SHAGLEY. And moving a way no rat can move!
KATE. There's no way a rat can't move. And there's no smoke without fire. (*Sniffing she goes into the ghost's room.*)
(*Some angry bangs come from the bedroom.*)
RICK (*to* SHAGLEY). Clurheen is vexed because we tried to kill him.
SHAGLEY. And it was for that the old Clurheen murdered Sling Godfrey.
(KATE *comes out looking puzzled.*)
KATE. It's hard to trace whether that noise is from inside or outside. But I'd say outside.
SHAGLEY. The thing we want to believe – that's the only thing we will believe.
RICK. The night is passing away. Come on, Nan, till we dismantle your bed. (*He goes into bedroom, followed by* NAN, *who glances nervously at* KATE *as she goes.*)
KATE (*shouting after them*). If ye break that bed between ye, she'll have to sleep on the ground – where she was made and born.
SHAGLEY. That man is a contractor who built his own house and many a house. As well as stocking his own farm.
KATE. When he has the bird cage, why hasn't he a wife?
SHAGLEY. He's sweethearting with a staff nurse that has a high salary.
KATE. Why is there such a greed for land in this townland?
SHAGLEY. There were no landlords' demesnes, or big grazing farms

for dividing by the Government.

KATE. So while Ireland became a land of plenty, ye barely kept a living.

(NAN *comes out carrying a bundle of blankets. She is followed by* RICK *carrying some sections of an old iron bed.*)

SHAGLEY. Nan, who tore your bib?

NAN. Something pulled at my clothes.

KATE. That young blackguard did.

RICK. Somebody slapped my face.

KATE. Nan did.

NAN. I couldn't, mam, because the width of the bed was between us.

SHAGLEY. Clurheen done both to make them enemies. He's jealous.

(RICK *moves the table from centre stage to the right-hand wall, where it will remain until page 384. He clears a space under the window for the bed.* KATE *takes an old notebook and pencil from the mantelpiece.*)

KATE. This is the cows' and the bulls' date book. I want your full name, because I'm booking down the day and date you were alone in there with Nan of the Leaves.

RICK (*smiling*). My name is Richard Donegan, but the neighbours shorten it to Rick.

KATE (*writing at table*). Making a man's name small isn't nice. But making a child with an insane girl is a criminal offence.

RICK (*to* KATE, *smiling*). I'm fond of girls, but so was your father, or you wouldn't be here.

(*He goes into the bedroom, followed by* NAN.)

SHAGLEY. Her eye doesn't look mad, or wicked.

KATE. Wait till you see her when her face is twisted with madness. The mental doctors said she's dangerous insane.

SHAGLEY. Them doctors do be half mad themselves. Why do you keep her if she's dangerous?

KATE. I'm too old to manage sheep and cattle without help.

SHAGLEY. If Clurheen maddens her worse, she may kill you.

KATE (*complacently*). I couldn't rear her without beating her, so she's afeard of me. (*She puts the Cow's book back on the mantelpiece.*)

SHAGLEY. How will you get rid of this poltergeist?

KATE. I cursed out a bad husband, so that he never came back until he was sent home in a box.

SHAGLEY. So now you own the worst curse of all: the widow's curse.

KATE. And I have enough holy water in there to banish any demon or spirit.

(*She goes into her bedroom.* RICK *and* NAN *come out with more bed parts, and set to work to reconstruct the bed.*)

NAN. Maybe Clurheen will follow me out here.

SHAGLEY. No, your room must be built on a fairy path; and that's why Clurheen housed himself in there.

(KATE *comes out with a lemonade bottle full of holy water, and she sprinkles herself and the kitchen with a goose feather.*)

RICK (*smiling*). Ye'll never have peace until ye knock that room, and build another on the east side.

KATE (*suspicious*). That's why your pals are noising outside: to win this contract for yourself!

RICK (*grinning*). That'd be the first contract ever won by a ghost.

KATE. Two cursers would have a better chance of banishing Clurheen. Shagley, have you a dirty tongue?

SHAGLEY. I have curses that couldn't be printed in a newspaper.

NAN. And you're old enough to have the orphan's curse!

RICK. And old enough to know the Curse of the Nine Blind McDonnells.

SHAGLEY. The priest failed because he cursed Clurheen in Latin, and Clurheen thought he was praising him.

KATE. He must be an uneducated priest. Barely ever he scraped the collar around him.

SHAGLEY. We know as many curses as any priest.

KATE (*sprinkling* SHAGLEY *with holy water*). This shower of holy water will survive you.

SHAGLEY. Stop that! Water washes all the proof and goodness out of clothes, and out of the skin. (*He is brushing it off his clothes.*)

KATE. Like all the bachelors, you wipe the dishes with the tail of the cat. And the shirt on your back is as black as a beetle.

SHAGLEY. The washed and clean are in the graveyard, but I'm still here.

NAN. Don't curse Clurheen into a cruel lonesome place.

KATE (*advancing on ghost room*). Shagley, are you following me?

SHAGLEY. Like a chicken following a hen.

RICK. Shagley, the old Clurheen killed a man with his own stick.

SHAGLEY. True, Here, hold my stick safe you.

(*An angry, or a frightened, drumming begins in the ghost room.*)

KATE (*sprinkling holy water*). Clurheen, you escaped jailbird from Purgatory, or Limbo, or Hell. May this holy water be petrol to drive you back to wherever you broke out of.

341

SHAGLEY. Clurheen, you ghost of a walking anti-Christ from Mayo.

KATE (*turning on him*). Liar! Clurheen was a Galway whore! (*She splashes him with holy water.*)

SHAGLEY. There never was a Galway whore until you invaded us.

KATE. I got the sacrament of matrimony what you never did.

SHAGLEY. I never was a blackguard low enough to need a wife.

KATE. The lowest women ever wouldn't dirty her blood with you.

(RICK *forces his way between them.*)

RICK. Hold on there!

SHAGLEY. Hold on never built a railroad.

RICK. Ye won't have a drop of water, or a curse, left for Clurheen.

KATE. If he broke his mother's heart, he won't break mine.

SHAGLEY. The mother that didn't strangle you was fond of children.

(KATE *has turned back towards the ghost room.*)

KATE. Clurheen, you disturber from the earth, or the sky. May my widow's curse, and the curse of the bad planets banish you behind the moon now and forever. (*She goes to the ghost room.* SHAGLEY *follows her to the door.*)

SHAGLEY. Clurheen, you mongrel born out of a banshee and a leprehawn! If you don't vanish away, our curses will condemn you to shovel the sand of Galway Bay for seven years and a day. (*He goes into the ghost room. Drumming breaks out again.* RICK *closes the ghost room door.*)

RICK. Let them lash at it!

NAN (*smiling*). They'd be better pleased fighting than not. (*He has resumed work on the bed. She helps him with the mattress and bedclothes.*)

NAN. The blessing of God on you!

RICK. Nobody but you could put up with her. And I'd venture to say she'd work the hind legs of an ass.

NAN (*smiling*). Patience is the best plaster for what can't be cured.

RICK. But your case could be easy cured.

NAN. Evermore she gave me a home, and let me live on her pocket.

RICK. The bachelor farmers around 'd be glad to give you a wedding ring and every comfort.

NAN. Kate says doctors examined me when I was a baby, and diagnosed me as insane and unmarriageable ever.

RICK. Maybe she invented that tale to keep you as a slave for herself.

NAN. I have no memory of the doctors.

RICK. How did she capture you first?

342

(*They are working away as they talk.*)

NAN. I was a bachelor's daughter, and my mother left me amongst the leaves, and ran away to England for fear she'd be arrested to find out if she had breast milk.

RICK. Like us all, you were born from two human beings. ... My girl friend is a staff nurse in a mental hospital, and she may be able to tell you whether you are uneven in the head, or as wise as Solomon.

NAN. Tell her to call Friday, the day Kate goes for her pension.

RICK. She'll call as soon as she has a day off on a Friday.

NAN. Will ye get wed soon?

RICK (*gloomily*). Soon – or never. She wants me to sell my farm and concentrate on the building trade. And build a new home for us near her hospital job.

NAN. They say the good-looking do be unlucky, but it won't be so with you.

RICK. There's a bad slump in the building trade. If I sell my farm, I could be as idle as the cat in the ashes.

NAN. They say its better to be sorry and stay, than to be sorry and go away.

RICK. My heart and soul is in my farm and new house and in the neighbours. But she's a deserter from the land of Ireland, like all the women around.

NAN (*smiling*). If she is, it'd be a pity to have you wasted with her.

RICK. What girl would wed into my farm between a bog and a river? Would you?

NAN (*smiling*). I would – if I wasn't mad.

RICK. We'll prove Kate is mad and you're sane.

NAN. If ye can do that, it'll be a bigger miracle than Clurheen.

KATE (*coming from room*). I have dumbed Clurheen, and banished him for evermore,

RICK. Clurheen comes and goes like the bad weather.

SHAGLEY (*returning*). You have all the good and proof washed out of my clothes.

KATE. You were always in the way like all the men?

SHAGLEY. All my life I'm warning women against water, but I might as well be telling it to the bull.

KATE. You obey your own catechism. You're the picture of dirt.

RICK (*worried*). Shagley, did you curse Clurheen all out?

SHAGLEY. I did. I haven't a curse left that'd blush a nun.

RICK. Maybe now Clurheen is in ambush on our road home to batter us to death the same way as he done to Sling Godfrey.

343

KATE. Live or die, ye can't spend the night here.

SHAGLEY. Salt or a black-handled knife sometimes save a person from ghosts and spirits.

KATE. Give them a grain of salt
(NAN *goes to the dresser for salt.*)

RICK. We'll wait till we finish Nan's bed.

KATE. No, we can do that ourselves at our dead ease.

NAN. Can I lend them the black-handled knife?

KATE (*grimly*). You may as well, seeing that you were so forward in your tongue about it.
(NAN *gives the black-handled knife to* RICK, *and pours some salt into his palm.* SHAGLEY *has picked up his stick.* NAN *pours some salt into his palm.*)

SHAGLEY. Rick, which of us'll walk on the left, the side the wicked ghosts appear?

RICK. I took Nan away from Clurheen's room, and for that he may never forgive me.

SHAGLEY. But I cursed him into the pits, and you have the black-handled knife.

RICK. Very well. And we won't walk on the side of the road like Sling Godfrey did.

SHAGLEY. We'll stick to the middle of the road, between the iron wheel marks. There's strong magic in iron.
(*They open the front door.*)

KATE. In the morning I'll send out Nan of the Leaves to see if ye're on the ground.

SHAGLEY. In good time before the rats and the scaldcrows make breakfasts of our faces.

RICK. Good night, Nan.

NAN. Good night, Rick.
(*They go, closing the door.* NAN *quickly bolts it.*)

NAN. Can I get the supper now?

KATE. No. A late supper helps the breakfast.
(*She takes a sharpening stone from the table drawer, and sharpens the bill-hook. Suddenly a banging noise is heard.*)

NAN. Clurheen is back!

KATE. No, but them landgrabbers are banging the butt of the window again. (*She goes to the front door with the bill-hook.*) Get the pig sticking knife, and join me the minute I shout, "Doras!"
(KATE *goes out closing door.* NAN *takes the knife from the dresser drawer.*)

NAN. God grant I won't have to stick anyone.

KATE. Doras! Doras!

(*The front door opens, and a man retreats in, wearing a hat and mask and carrying a stick. He is very lively, but not very big. He wears wellington boots.*)

NAN. You can't come in here.

AINY. If I don't, she'll massacree me. Don't stab me. I'm a true friend.

NAN. If you are, why have you a false face on?

(*He dodges past* NAN, *holding his stick defensively.* KATE *enters, and closes and bolts the front door.* AINY *retreats to near the ghost room door, and there turns.*)

AINY. I was only proving to ye that this house is haunted, so ye need a man who understands ghosts and knows how to manage them and humour them. And myself needs a wife with a farm and a hearthstone.

KATE. Take off that false face, or I'll wear out this slasher on you.

AINY. I can't take it off tonight, because I'm a little in breach of the law.

KATE. Take it off, or we'll turn you into a real ghost!

AINY. I could jump ye, and break your eyes with the eye and chin hold . . . But I don't want to hurt any part of ye.

KATE (*advancing*). I'll knock his brains out, and you'll let his puddings out.

(*As they advance,* AINY *turns and runs into the ghost room, and shuts the door.* KATE *tries to force the door open, but fails.*)

KATE. Nan, fetch the sledge from the barn, and we'll break down this door.

NAN. Yes, mam.

(*Reluctantly she opens the front door, and finds herself confronted by a big powerful looking man wearing a mask and hood, and holding a shotgun at the ready.* LACKY (*short for Malachy*) *has a powerful voice, and his gestures are rather wild.* NAN *retreats from his gun.*)

NAN. I amn't able to go, mam.

KATE. Are you letting on to be falling with the hunger? You'd kill yourself if you got enough to eat.

LACKY (*bull-voiced*). Leave that innocent man alone!

(KATE *looks back.*)

KATE. What have we here? Two tinkers out robbing, or raping, or murdering?

LACKY. The guilty mind suspects everyone. Give that innocent man

345

a free road, and no bad thing will happen to ye.

KATE. The sergeant is to call here any minute, and no tinkers ever yet got away with robbery or rape or murder. (*She joins* NAN *behind the table, and the two women stand at bay.*)

LACKY. Come out now innocent man. (LACKY *closes the front door,* AINY *comes out.*)

AINY (*mildly*). If ye don't know yet, ye'll soon know, what all know, that this house is haunted. ... So your daughter needs a husband who knows how to humour ghosts.

LACKY. Is your daughter to be let with the farm?

KATE. She's to be let alone. She isn't a drop's blood to me. I was a missed ewe.

AINY. She's very good looking, and well put together.

LACKY. We can see your washing, and a washing without a man's shirt in it is very lonesome.

KATE. So ye're out to change the name on my ass-cart!

AINY. That fellow was the nest-egg, so he has a house and a farm of his own. But wherever I put down my suitcase – that's my address!

LACKY. Where else can I get a girl who's humble enough to wed into a farm between a bog and a river? You know black women who'd wed oul' men without teeth?

KATE. She can't go to bed with a farm, or fall in love with faces she can't see.

AINY. We'll call another night barefaced and civil. And I'm no tinker. I can sow them and dig them; and my savings would give ye a great lift in the world. (*He joins* LACKY *at the door.*)

LACKY. If Clurheen keeps ye awake until cockcrow here, ye could sleep like corncrakes in my house. (*He opens the front door.*)

KATE. We were going to bleed ye, but we'll pray for ye, instead.

AINY. Ghosts is like onions: you love them, or you hate them. I love ghosts, so Clurheen and me could get on forever.

LACKY. Miss, a horse of a man is the best man in the double bed, or in the harvest field.

AINY. Goodnight, mam and miss. (*He goes.*)

NAN. Goodnight.

LACKY (*shouting after him*). Watch out, or the briars will cut your throat! (*Turns.*) Ye'll need my land, if bad times turn out again. (*He goes.*)

KATE. When ye're out, out is the place to leave ye. (*She closes, and bolts the door.*)

NAN. Can I get the supper soon?

346

KATE. It's too late now for supper. Tonight we'll do with the soldier's supper: a p- and go to bed.

(*Banging resumes off-stage.*)

NAN. They're at it again.

KATE. Tomorrow I'll report them to the police.

NAN (*worried*). But if you do, they'll report us as thiefs.

KATE. True ... I'll sell a beast, and buy a shotgun. "What Justice can't do, the bullet can do" as the Moonlighters said.

CURTAIN

ACT TWO

The scene is the same, and it is a week later in the afternoon. NAN *enters wearily, carrying a hammer, pliers, and a small tin box. These she puts on the top of the dresser. She puts some turf on the fire, shakes the kettle, and hangs it on the crane.*

NAN. Mam, are you back from the town? . . . Now I can rest my four bones for a while.
(She sits in the armchair and closes her eyes. Two or three playful, or flirtatious whistles ring out. She opens her eyes.)
NAN. Clurheen, did you blow them whistles? Or was it one of the lads? I'm too tired to go out and see.
(The whistles are repeated.)
NAN. Clurheen, if you're any the better for being warned, Kate is gone for her widow's pension, and for priests to banish you. If they banish you, I hope we'll meet in Heaven, or some other promotion some day.
(Again she closes her eyes, and a bar or two of "An Cailin Ruadh" by Clurheen produces no reaction. Neither does a mild knock on the door. The door opens and AINY *enters, carrying a book. He is the smaller of the masked intruders in Act One. He looks to be in his middle, or late thirties, very suntanned and fit. He is curiously shy and mild for a man who worked abroad most of his life; and his accent is unchanged, because he never wanted to change it.)*
AINY. Nan, I seen you drawing for home, and this is a book about poltergeists the priest left in the village last year. . . . *(Getting no reply he smiles.)* They say a sleep in the chair is the sweetest . . . *(Alarmed.)* Nan, you're as bent as a rainbow, and as white as a hound's tooth. It's a fainting spell! *(He gets a cup from the dresser and water from a bucket, and holds it to her lips.)* Sup this, Nan.
(She drinks and her eyes open.)

348

NAN. Ainy, was I sleeping, or learning to die?

AINY. A nod of sleep, Nan, that'll keep you rosy and goodlooking.

NAN. I was fencing, and greatly sweated from sledging and hammering and straining the barbed wire.

AINY. Why didn't you call on me?

NAN. I can't be bothering you every day.

AINY. Sure my muscles are on fire to help you, and Lacky doesn't need me. He's working like a horse around his farm from dark to dark every day.

NAN. Odd times since we came to this farm, I get as tired as a hawker's ass. Kate reckons I'm ate with consumption, but I have no cough.

AINY. Kate is taking the skin off you with work. But, according to this book about poltergeists, its Clurheen that's running you down.

NAN. That couldn't be so, Ainy. Since I got used to Clurheen, he's the same to me as a thrush or a blackbird I'd hear singing.

AINY. But these books say the poltergeist draws his power to whistle and bang and throw things from some unwed person in the house, and that has to be you.

NAN. And Clurheen is growing stronger. This morning he roused me with a whistle that'd knock stones off a wall.

AINY. And he's learning more skills. And the more he learns the weaker that may leave you.

(NAN *is sipping water, and growing stronger. He watches her, or consults his book.*)

NAN. I'd never grudge Clurheen a share of my strength so long as my limbs can do all I want them to do.

AINY. These ghost books say once you're wed, Clurheen couldn't draw power from you at all.

NAN (*smiling*). Kate says no man could live with me, because I'm mad and haunted.

AINY. It isn't you that's mad: it's Kate: She's the wrongest woman that ever lived.

NAN. She didn't half let me go to school. Instead she'd make me go stealing turf in the bogs.

AINY. If you got education, you'd never want to marry on the land. And I won't buy this farm, unless I can win you along with it.

NAN. I'm shabby and rough, because I had no father, or mother. But this is a nice soft farm, with plenty of turf and water. (*She goes towards the door, looks out.*)

AINY. She'll have to sell out this farm, because she's making no shape to get on with Clurheen.

NAN. It'll take an awful batch of foreign earnings to buy this farm.

AINY. I wrought and saved hard in the wars and out foreign. Here are bars of chocolate and a new girl's belt. (*He produces them from pockets.*) To tighten your belt is great for killing the hunger.

NAN (*accepting them*). Ainy, you must be as rich as a Lord.

AINY. I could bestow a good living on you. And my money is no good to me, if the graveyard growth is in you.

NAN. I'll hide them in Clurheen's room.

AINY. Maybe he'll pelt them out to Kate!

NAN. Oh, no. He never betrays me. (*She runs into Clurheen's room.*)

AINY. Clurheen knows we're his wellwishers, not like Rick. Rick doesn't trust anyone.

(NAN *comes running out excitedly.*)

NAN. Is it Rick's car has stopped on the broad road? (*She looks out.*) It isn't Rick's.

AINY (*looking through window*). It's the car of his staff nurse girlfriend. And he's in it with her!

NAN. He was to bring her here to test me for insanity.

AINY. Rick is a coward who's afeard of insanity, and afeard of Clurheen. I amn't afeard of either.

NAN. It'd be ease to my mind to know whether I am insane.

AINY. She might need to test you alone. So I'll leave you alone for a while.

NAN (*at front door, happily*). Rick, you'll live for another year, because you came just as we were talking of you!

RICK (*cheerful*). Who was talking? (*Seeing* AINY *he becomes grim.*) Ainy, Kate was seen going into the barracks today. If I was a blackguard scamp, guilty of haunting women, I'd take the air back to Chicago.

AINY (*doggedly*). It wasn't me. And he who flings mud is losing ground. (*He moves towards the front door.*)

RICK. You wouldn't find Chicago too quiet and lonesome, if you cracked an odd dollar on a cocktail, or on a dance-hall ticket.

AINY. Courting two women will land you in jail for bigamy. Nan, I'm off to buy a new roll of barbed wire for you. (*He goes*).

NAN. If I had Ainy's help a bit longer, we'd have fences a racehorse couldn't go over.

RICK. His mother used to tell everyone she had two sons, and Lacky was a great success, but Ainy was a failure. She should know.

NAN. He'll buy this farm, or your farm, if your nurse makes you sell.

RICK. If he's that rich, why hasn't he the four wheels? Some say he done nothing but hoboing about out foreign.

NAN. Has your nurse come to test my insanity?

RICK. She has, Nan, but she said not to tell people. It's a doctor's job.

NAN. But if she's jealous of me and you, she'll report me as mad enough to kill all Ireland.

RICK. She can't report you because you don't belong to her hospital area. And it's more likely that she wants to get rid of me by matching me with you.

NAN (*pleased*). Bring her in so, Rick.

RICK. She'll prove Kate a liar. (*He goes to door.*)

NAN. Rick, before you go, kiss me again. I love that!

RICK. Ditto here, Nan. But out of her view!

(*They leave the doorway, and kiss and embrace. Suddenly a bottle smashes on the floor opposite the front door.*)

NAN. Clurheen!

RICK. No, Ainy! I'll make a rag ball of that blackguard! (*He runs out front door. NAN goes to the ghost room door.*)

NAN. Clurheen, if you banged that bottle, you have no need to be so jealous of Rick. He's afeard of ghosts, because he's living alone. But if he had a wife that liked you well, he'd get used to you, too, and he'd have welcome and the good word for you.

(*TESS, the nurse, has arrived in the doorway, and she stands silently watching NAN. She is a woman of thirty, strongly built and vigorous, intelligent and accustomed to command, but sympathetic. She wears her off-duty clothes.*)

NAN. Clurheen, keep as mute as you can while Rick's nurse is here. Some people can't hear you at all, and if she doesn't, she'd say I was hearing you because every screw in my head is loose, except the screw holding it on. Her verdict might part me and you for life. Maybe she's more jealous of me and fonder of Rick than Rick thinks. Rick thinks herself and himself are like an orphan lamb you'd be trying to put with a ewe.

(*TESS coughs deliberately, and NAN turns and smiles innocently.*)

NAN. Are you Rick's nurse?

TESS. I am a nurse, Nan. Who were you talking to?

NAN. Our ghost – Clurheen.

TESS. Can he hear you?

NAN. He can hear as good as a person (worried). Did Rick catch Ainy?

TESS. I didn't see him catch anyone. He's outside now watching out

351

for Kate.

NAN. What sign is it to hear a ghost? (*She takes sweeping brush from the corner.*)

TESS. It's a sign you're not deaf – if there is a ghost!

NAN. Are all of us mad that hear him? (*She sweeps broken bottle fragments together.*)

TESS. You're all suffering from collective hallucinations.

NAN. Can they be cured?

TESS. Usually they can. They're temporary delusions. . . . Can I take your pulse, Nan?

NAN (*cheerful*). They say anything worth asking is worth taking.

(TESS *takes* NAN'S *pulse, timing it by her wrist-watch.*)

NAN. On account of this farm being haunted and deserted, its fences got as gapped as the head of a rake. And all the repairs fall on me.

TESS. You have a heart as strong as a diesel engine . . . Nan, can you tell me what day and date this is. (*She walks away from* NAN, *looks at the bed.*)

NAN. It's Friday the third of March 1956.

TESS. Correct . . . Nan, do you suffer nightmares?

NAN. An odd night. When I sleep on my back mostly.

TESS. Do you ever hear voices?

NAN. No, only Clurheen noising.

TESS. Does he frighten you?

NAN. Not since I got used to him.

TESS. Do you ever feel depressed?

NAN. Does that mean sad and worried?

TESS. And hopeless and helpless.

NAN. An odd time I do.

TESS. Do you ever be tempted to kill yourself?

NAN. Why would I? If the dead have a better way of living than us, Clurheen wouldn't come back to a hole in a wall.

(*She has swept the bottle fragments together, and fire shovelled them into the ash bucket.*)

TESS. Do you ever be tempted to stay in bed all day?

NAN. Only if I had the bad flu.

TESS. Do you like to collect things?

NAN. I don't have the price of a button.

TESS. Do you collect and keep any rubbish: old papers, or rags, or anything?

NAN (*smiling*). Not me! That'd be daft.

TESS. Nan, we all have bosses over us, and often we hate them. Do you hate Kate?

NAN. How could I? She gave me a home.

TESS. Still, some say she bullies you, and doesn't give you enough to eat. Do you ever be tempted to attack her?

NAN. Fighting belongs to the men. A girl makes herself very low, if she fights. Unless she's ordered to.

TESS. If our boss is a walking tyrant, we'd sometimes be tempted to poison them, though we'd never do it, of course. Were you ever tempted to poison Kate?

NAN. No, that'd be a big sin and a crime.

TESS. When did the doctors diagnose you as insane?

NAN. I have no memory of them at all. Kate says it happened when I was a baby.

TESS. Then it never happened, Nan. A baby can't be diagnosed as mad, because a baby has no sense anyway. (*She looks into the ghost room.*)

NAN. Maybe I'm marriageable so?

TESS. You're as marriageable as any who think they hear Clurheen.

NAN. The curate heard Clurheen.

TESS. Priests can suffer from delusions, too. But don't tell him I said so. He was nice to my father on his death bed.

NAN. That's great: when good people are nice, instead of cross.

(TESS *turns back from the ghost room door, and is struck by an old pillow in the back, and mocked by whistles and a bang or two.*)

TESS. Hell and the Devil! What was that? (*She runs to fireplace.*)

NAN (*smiling*). That was Clurheen telling you I amn't mad.

(*She picks up the pillow, throws it back into the ghost room.*)

TESS. I can't believe it! There's some playboy in there.

(*She goes into the ghost-room.*)

NAN (*urgently*). Don't scold Clurheen, or try to banish him! One Sling Godfrey was killed over that, they say.

TESS (*coming out*). Nan, you're not mad. There's something beyond the power of man in that room.

(RICK *comes hurrying in.*)

RICK. Kate is dawning over Pollanoister Hill! And, Nan, Merrigan's ass will soon be up to his tail in your haystack!

NAN (*taking a stick from the corner*). When we're up to our necks in hot water, let us be like the kettle and sing! (*She runs out.*)

RICK. Is she insane?

TESS. No, but Kate's rough, and cruel rearing may leave her emotionally disturbed for life.

353

RICK. Would marriage cure that?

TESS. It might. . . . Or marriage might make it worse.

RICK. Is this draper still pestering you?

TESS. He is and saying 'Leave him while you're good-looking'. His shop is thirty yards from my hospital. Your farm is thirty miles.

RICK. Housebuilding is in a slump. If I sell my farm, I may turn into a lazy idler, or an alcoholic.

TESS. People keep growing up, falling in love and needing new houses. Farming is for people who have no skill at anything else.

RICK. Give me another few days. That delay won't spoil your beauty.

TESS. Unless I meet some drunken driver on my sixty miles a day.

(KATE *enters carrying a shopping bag. She stops and stares at* TESS.)

KATE. Is this another busybody looking for ghosts?

RICK. She's a neighbour's daughter looking for me.

KATE. Have you looked at him long enough?

TESS (*smiling*). No, but I'll see him again. (*She moves to the door.*)

KATE. Tell your friends the only ghosts out now are live ones.

TESS. Everybody says that, so it must be true. (*She goes.*)

RICK. Are the priests coming?

KATE. The parish priest said, 'Get a black cat. A white cat is no good, because the rats can see him.'

(*She goes into her bedroom with her shopping bag, leaving the door open.*)

RICK. He knows it's safer to believe there's no ghost. His priest uncle banished a spirit from a house in Lisheennaheltia. Two months after he fell from his horse and was killed.

(KATE *comes out without her hat and cloak, or the shopping bag.*)

KATE. The curate said, 'I failed before to banish Clurheen.'

RICK. They say only one priest in a hundred has power to banish them.

KATE. I told him plump and plain, 'If you don't try again, I'll turn to a Protestant, and a bloody black Protestant!'

RICK (*grinning*). Competition is the life of trade, and of religion.

KATE. The priest said, 'I'll go, but when we take risks, risks often take us.'

RICK. I hear a car! (*Goes to door.*) He's landed. . . . But according to the poltergeist books, the safest way to banish Clurheen is to get Nan married.

KATE. That's all ye men want: the seven day licence and a child every nine months.

(*The* PRIEST *appears in the doorway, bareheaded and wearing his soutane, and carrying a small suitcase and a few books. He is a pale, shy, bespectacled man; and the combination of books and spectacles suggest the scholarly bibliophile type of priest.*)

PRIEST. God bless! (*He knocks on the open door.*)

KATE. Come in, father.

PRIEST. I see some of my old poltergeist books have survived. (*He unloads his books onto the table, also his suitcase.*)

RICK. The case of the old Clurheen isn't in any of them.

PRIEST. Probably ninety per cent of all poltergeist hauntings have never been reported, or recorded.

KATE. Some say our poltergeist is bad neighbours.

PRIEST. Get the police to check up on that. But there's a mountain of evidence of poltergeist hauntings around the world.

(*The* PRIEST *takes a small bottle and a sprinkler from his bag, goes to the ghost room door, and opens it wide. He blesses himself, sprinkles some holy water into the room, waits for a reaction.*)

PRIEST. He doesn't seem to be in residence at the moment. (*He returns to table.*)

RICK. What do the scientists say?

PRIEST. They don't agree, but many of them say the poltergeist is the only ghost there is clear scientific evidence of.

(*The* PRIEST *takes out his surplice and stole, his Rituale Romanum book and crucifix.*)

KATE. Were them books written by Catholics?

PRIEST. No. But poltergeists have been recorded from every religion and from every country as far back as records go.

KATE. They say a waterfall and a Divil out of Hell are two things that can't rest.

PRIEST. As a rule poltergeists don't do anything very wicked. They have been called the juvenile delinquents of the spirit world.

RICK. When the apple ripens it falls, and when the poltergeist ripens, does it have to go away again?

PRIEST. Usually they do, after a few months. But some have remained for years, and some have gone away for years, and returned. (*He puts on the surplice and stole.*)

KATE. Did they ever commit murders?

PRIEST. I have marked the chapter on the Bell poltergeist in Tennessee. He poisoned and killed farmer Bell, because bell tried to banish him.

KATE. Like the old tale about Clurheen killing Sling Godfrey.

355

PRIEST. And a poltergeist may have been responsible for the suicide of two students in the ghost room of Maynooth College.

RICK. A suicide pact?

PRIEST. No, the first suicide was in 1843, and the second in 1860, but in the same bedroom. They were young students.

RICK. Teenagers, the age poltergeists have most power over!

PRIEST. After the second suicide that bedroom was turned into an oratory of St. Joseph, the patron saint of a happy death. It's still an oratory.

(*The front door is struck a couple of violent blows with a stick, and is then kicked open.* SHAGLEY *comes in raging, and brandishing a big stick. He advances on* KATE.)

SHAGLEY. You murderer! You poisoned and killed my sheepdog, because he was making it hard for ye to rob me.

KATE (*retreating behind table*). That's all a cod, as the cow said to the bull. You let him die of hunger.

SHAGLEY. Would I starve the greatest and the only comrade ever I had? And my hot water bottle – he always slept across my feet.

RICK. It's lambing time when farmers put out poison for stray dogs.

SHAGLEY. That dog never strayed a yard.

KATE. He had to stray for a bite to eat.

PRIEST. You tried to banish Clurheen, so maybe he poisoned your dog.

SHAGLEY. How could a ghost poison anything?

PRIEST. Read this chapter about the Bell poltergeist poisoning farmer Bell. Bell's doctor and his family testified to that.

(*He hands book to* SHAGLEY).

RICK. Tomorrow Vet Keane is coming to test my cattle. Get him to find out what your dog died of.

SHAGLEY. I will even if it costs me my own burial money.

KATE (*taking up* PRIEST'S *crucifix*). I didn't poison your dog. I swear that without fearing for my mouth.

SHAGLEY. Then your haunted Nan of the Leaves poisoned him, because he bit her leg.

RICK. She's evicting Merrigan's ass.

(SHAGLEY *sets out for the door.*)

KATE. Call herself and Clurheen home.

PRIEST. We can't banish Clurheen, unless he's here.

SHAGLEY. I'll flock the two murderers home. (*He goes.*)

KATE. Father, the Divil must be in Nan, when she's Clurheen's favourite and his customer.

PRIEST. A poltergeist has no body, and we can't prove he has any

356

connection with the Devil.

KATE. Back in the room I have holy water well fired with whiskey. So it might explode Clurheen into sparks and ashes. (*She goes into her bedroom.*)

RICK. Your books tell about poltergeists beating and bullying girls until they broke off their engagements.

PRIEST. And the book of Tobias in the old Testament tells of Asmodeus the spirit, who was in love with Sarah. So he murdered every man she married on the wedding night, as each man entered the bridal chamber.

RICK. That poltergeist was no more jealous than Clurheen is.

PRIEST. Sarah's prayers were answered at last, just as she was about to marry Tobias. The angel Raphael was sent from Heaven, and he banished Asmodeus to a desert in Egypt and chained him there.

(SHAGLEY *enters.*)

SHAGLEY. Father, don't make the mistake of not banishing Clurheen far enough away.

PRIEST. They say the old Clurheen wasn't banished far enough away.

(KATE *returns with her water bottle.*)

SHAGLEY. After Clurheen was banished a neighbour was watering his horse in the stream beyond. Clurheen screamed from the river bed, 'Your horse is standing on me.'

RICK. Clurheen has murdered a man for less!

SHAGLEY. The horseman saved himself by sending Clurheen to Shawn Maura's house. And Clurheen was there until he banished himself.

(NAN *enters smiling eagerly.*)

NAN. Is Clurheen here?

KATE. He isn't noising whatever.

NAN. He was in the field tossing sticks and stones about, but I lost track of him when Shagley scolded me.

PRIEST. Maybe we can find out if Clurheen is here. . . . Nan, would you mind lying on the bed for a moment?

NAN. Can I take off my wellingtons?

PRIEST. Of course. (*He pulls the quilt off the bed, and offers it to* RICK.) Would you mind spreading this over her and tucking it in?

RICK. I'll lap it around Nan. But duck your heads. Clurheen may fly something at us.

PRIEST. Then we'll know he's here.

(*Having kicked off her wellingtons, Nan lies on the bed, shyly amused,* RICK *spreads the quilt over her, and tucks it in. A bottle smashes near the front door.* NAN *ducks her head under the quilt, and* RICK *retreats from the bed.* KATE *runs into her bedroom.*)

RICK. Father, does that prove it'd be suicide for me and Nan to wed?

PRIEST. It proves Clurheen is back. You can leave the bed, Nan.

(KATE *comes running out with an old shotgun.*)

KATE. Every time they fire at me, I'll fire at them. (*She runs out front door.*)

RICK. Kate, that was Clurheen! (*He runs out.* SHAGLEY *follows him to the door.*)

SHAGLEY. Come back you fool! It's safer to be in front of Kate's gun than to be behind it.

(*A shot rings out.*)

NAN. She has shot Ainy! (*She puts on her wellingtons.*)

SHAGLEY. Not likely! That cheap oul' secondhand gun she bought is as crooked as the hind leg of a dog.

PRIEST. It's dangerous to keep a gun in the house where there's a poltergeist.

(KATE *enters, and proceeds to reload the gun.*)

KATE. The bottle shooter dodged behind a mearing bush, but I sent a shot through it. May he have a tea wake and weak tea!

NAN. Any more we'll have two ghosts sounding! Was it Ainy?

RICK (*entering*). I seen no corpse along his mearing?

NAN. Then Ainy is still amongst the living! Thank God!

PRIEST (*lighting candle*). Shagley, will you carry this, and relight it every time Clurheen blows it out?

SHAGLEY. I will, but it's time ye invented a blessed electric torch. (*He accepts the candle and box of matches.*)

PRIEST (*to* KATE). Mam, will you keep sprinkling the holy water?

KATE (*accepting bottle and sprinkler*). I done it before, and lived. But that oul' bachelor needs washing as well as blessing. (*She sprinkles* SHAGLEY *liberally, but he hastily retreats out of range.*)

SHAGLEY. Father, it's time ye invented some blessing that won't rot our clothes.

KATE (*sprinkling* PRIEST). The nails you drive with your Latin curses, we'll clinch with our English curses.

SHAGLEY. And then maybe Clurheen will see your Latin isn't praising him.

PRIEST. Prayers, and not curses, we need now, to succeed, and to be safe.

(*Holding the crucifix aloft in his right hand and the open Rituale in*

(A Mearing was the fence, or wall separating two farms).

358

his other hand, the PRIEST *advances on the ghost-room.*)
PRIEST. In nomine Patris et Filii et Spiritus Sancti, Amen.
(*He is interrupted by a burst of whistling and drumming, and then staggered and knocked by flying pillows,* KATE *next in line, turns to* SHAGLEY.)
KATE. Shagley, help the priest up.
SHAGLEY. I won't, even if he never got up. It's very unlucky to help a priest up, or lay hands on him at all.
(*A flying garment wraps itself around his head, and quenches his candle.*)
KATE. You coward, you quenched the candle to delay yourself.
SHAGLEY. After you banished your husband, he died of happiness.
PRIEST (*rising*). Exorciso te, immundissime spiritus, omne phantasme, omnis legio, in nomine Domini Jesu Christi ... (*He goes into room.*)
KATE (*following priest*). Clurheen, my widow's curse on you forever and a day!
(RICK *is helping* SHAGLEY *to free himself from the flung garment, and relight his candle.*)
SHAGLEY. Rick, we'll need your help in there.
RICK. If I go in, he'll start flying bottles.
SHAGLEY. And bleed us to death! Stay where you are so. (*Goes to room door.*) Clurheen, may my seven thousand curses rout you out of here for ever.
(*He goes into room, and* RICK *closes the door.*)
RICK. We're safer with that door closed.
NAN. Clurheen, may harm someone over these curses.
RICK (*Urgently*). Nan, you could save my farm and my home, and I could save you, if we got wed.
NAN. But Clurheen is against anything between you and me.
RICK. He hates me out of jealousy and because I rescued you from his room.
NAN. Clurheen doesn't mind Ainy at all!
RICK. Because he knows you wouldn't bless your bones with Ainy. Nan, I have a sister married a few miles away, and I asked her if you could sleep in her house tonight.
NAN. But Clurheen allows us a fair share of sleep lately.
NAN. I want to find out if Clurheen will follow you to my sister's house. If he follows you that far, he's sure to follow you to my house a hen's kick from here.
NAN. But Kate will never let me sleep out.
RICK. I'll call for you late when she's well asleep, and bring you home

359

before she rouses in the morning.

NAN. If Clurheen follows me to your house, he could kill or maim you!

RICK. And kill and maim yourself.

NAN (*excitedly*). I'll light a candle on that window as soon as Kate is snoring.

RICK. Yes, as soon as her whiskey talks.

(*The front door is flung open, and* LACKY *runs in carrying a bill-hook. He no longer wears his mask and hood of Act One. Instead he wears an old hat at an eccentric angle, and farm clothes and wellingtons. There is something wild-looking and odd and innocent about* LACKY, *and he seems a few years older than his brother* AINY. *His wild appearance is accentuated by bloodstains on his right ear and cheek and on his hands. He is in a rage.*)

LACKY. Where is Kate, that murdering she-male? That's her gun whatever. I'll break it into inches. (*Leaving his bill-hook against the wall, he takes up the gun, checks it to see if it is loaded.*)

NAN (*anxiously*). Lacky is that your own blood, or your brother Ainy's?

LACKY. It's a true hero's blood, the blood of the only farmer around who's mighty enough to flatten while cutting turf with a slane. Nan, it'll never be the day with you until you wed me and my farm. In summer you'll lie close to me for love and in winter for heat.

NAN. Talk small. The priest is banishing Clurheen!

RICK. So go home, Lacky; and come back civilised.

LACKY. If I go home, she'll shoot and kill and hurt more with badness. (*Shotgun at the ready he advances on the ghost room door, kicks it open, shouts in.*) You hag of the Divil, come out to your fate!

(*The priest can be heard declaiming in Latin, with* KATE *and* SHAGLEY *calling names to Clurheen, or to each other. Suddenly all this ceases.*)

NAN. It's murder to shoot her, Lacky.

LACKY. She thinks no more of shooting us, than of killing a hen.

(*The priest appears holding the crucifix high.*)

PRIEST. Malachy, have respect for the great saint whose name you bear.

LACKY. Who would you respect, if she shot blood out of your lug?

KATE (*appearing behind priest*). Why did you half kill me with a bottle?

LACKY. I never did.

360

KATE. Then why did you dodge and hide behind the mearing bush?

LACKY. I was cutting trimmings for the mearing fence. My slasher is there.

PRIEST. Both sides were innocent, so, Malachy, put away that old gun. A museum is the only place that might be safe in.

LACKY. Only it's as crooked as her eye, I'd be asking the road to Purgatory or Hell by now,

(*He goes towards the front door with the gun. The* PRIEST *and* KATE *move towards the table.*)

KATE. Where do you think you're going with my gun?

LACKY. Home, because my mare lost a foal before over a start she got from a gunshot. So I'm holding your gun until she foals again in a fortnight's time.

KATE. Tomorrow the Guards will call on you with their red note summonsing you for robbery with violence.

LACKY. Their red note will cost me less than a dead foal and mare.

KATE. Who'll pull the foal when you're in jail for robbery?

LACKY. Father, make her allow Nan of the Leaves to get wed. When marriage isn't allowed, that's when scandal is committed.

PRIEST. Nan's marriage would be the safest and surest way of getting rid of Clurheen.

KATE. He's banished already – this time for good.

LACKY. Nan of the Leaves, I have my own fine house where you won't have to live with a mother-in-law, cat and mouse, paw and claw. . . . Don't wed Rick, a contractor who's going down, instead of up, with his contracts.

RICK (*sarcastic*). So our bank manager tells you everything!

LACKY. Nan of the Leaves, don't wed Ainy who disgraced our classical family by harvesting and tramping with the spalpeens in England. Even if you put an S-O-S in the newspapers, you won't get a better husband than Lacky.

(LACKY *goes off with his bill-hook and* KATE'S *gun.*)

KATE. Snow to his heels. Empty vessels make a loud noise.

(*The* PRIEST *is taking off his surplice and stole.*)

RICK. Father, Clurheen stops noising to make us believe he's banished.

PRIEST. I know that, but there's nothing more we can do today.

(SHAGLEY *comes out of ghost room, and blows out his candle.*)

SHAGLEY. Any more I resign from this war.

KATE. Coward and traitor!

SHAGLEY. The old people had a saying, 'Praise God, but don't blackguard the Divil!'

361

PRIEST (*packing his suitcase*). So far Clurheen hasn't done anything diabolical. (*Smiling.*) Like Shagley he doesn't like holy water.

KATE. It isn't for anything good Clurheen came.

PRIEST. We can't be certain about that. These ghost books tell about a poltergeist who haunted the home of a thirteen-year-old English boy named John Wesley. That boy grew up to be the greatest Christian preacher of his century. Perhaps it was that poltergeist who gave him such a burning conviction about the existence of the supernatural.

KATE. That's as much as to say God doesn't want us to banish Clurheen.

PRIEST. That is possible. Maybe Clurheen will be recalled when he has done what he was sent to do.

KATE. Madden us and murder us all!

PRIEST. Nan and Rick, if you come as far as my car, I'll tell you more about how Tobais and Sarah were saved from the Poltergeist Asmodeus. (*He goes out.*)

RICK. That's what we need to know. Come on, Nan. (*He goes out.*)

NAN. Mam, can I go?

KATE. Don't delay. A lot of jobs are calling.

NAN. I'll be back before three minutes are over,

(NAN *runs out.* SHAGLEY *moves towards door.*)

KATE. The cowardice is running you home.

SHAGLEY. My funeral expenses are buried in a secret place. I must dig them up before Clurheen makes me ready for my coffin.

KATE. We won't be left on top. If they won't bury us for love, they'll bury us for stink.

SHAGLEY. Too many of my people were buried in poor-house coffins a child could drive his fist through. I'm the last of my family and race, so I'm going to be buried in a safe coffin.

KATE. The coward wants a very safe coffin.

SHAGLEY. And I'm going to have a dead Mass, with four priests singing Latin hymns to save my soul from Clurheen's gang.

KATE. If the women wash you before they coffin you, you'll melt like mud and disappear.

SHAGLEY. We'll all disappear, and we won't come whistling back in an hour's time like Clurheen. (*He goes.*)

KATE. If we don't die, the undertaker can't live. And the priest marked out my fate in this book. (*She takes up the book which the* PRIEST *had left open, and reads laboriously.*)

KATE. The Bell poltergeist in Tennessee. Poisons and kills farmer Bell. Doctor's report.

362

(*She sits in the armchair, and settles down to read, her lips moving, her voice murmuring or droning, for she has never learned to read silently. Suddenly from the ghost room begins a whistled version of the Dies Irae, accompanied by a funeral beat as of a muffled drum.*)

KATE. You're back! Damn and blast you!

(*As the whistling continues and she recognises the tune, she springs to her feet, allowing the book to fall on the floor.*)

KATE (*scared*). The Dead Mass hymn! . . . So murder is what you have in your heart for me! Don't dare to follow me into my room. I have the Blessed Virgin's statue, and God's picture, and a stone from the holiest well in Mayo!

(*The Dies Irae and its accompaniment grow louder and more menacing. She snatches her holy water bottle off the table, and blesses herself, retreating until she comes to her bedroom door. She runs in, and bangs the door shut, but it is flung open again. There is a crash, followed by a thud.*)

CURTAIN

ACT TWO

Scene 2

The scene is the same and the time is near midnight on the same day. NAN *is sitting up in bed, reading a book by the light of the candle. A chair moves jerkily from the ghost room, across the kitchen.* NAN *smiles.*

NAN. Clurheen, this book says poltergeists are useful only for moving the furniture. Stop it before it hits Kate's door!
(KATE'S *door opens, and the chair moves towards the doorway.* NAN *springs out of bed and stops the disappearing chair. She listens at* KATE'S *door for a few moments.* NAN *closes* KATE'S *door, carries the chair back to the opposite wall. She goes to the ghost room door.*)

NAN. Clurheen, at long and at last she's doing what I was waiting for: she's snoring like a pig that'd be full up. Don't rouse her, or she'll scald you with holy water and widow's curses. (*She runs back to the bed, pulls on her stockings. She already wears her skirt and slip. Her jumper is on the chair beside the bed and it takes flight in the direction of* KATE'S *door.* NAN *stops it in time and turns good-humouredly.*) Clurheen, have manners! You're as bad as the lads, and I doubt you were a lad when you were alive. (*She dons the jumper, puts the lighted candle on the window-sill. She tidies her hair. Low whistles sound.*)

NAN. Rick! (*She is running towards the front door, when a doubt assails her.*) Or Clurheen, was it you? Whistle twice if it was you.
(*Two quick whistles sound.*)

NAN (*sad*). So it was you! Rick is gone home tired by now, sure I lost courage and was gone to sleep. And maybe it's as well for him and for me. (*She removes the candle from the window to the chair. As she is closing the window curtains,* RICK *taps on the*

364

window.)

NAN (*thrilled*). Rick! Clurheen, near sent you astray on me! (*She runs to the door, unbolts it, and* RICK *enters in his Sunday best.*)

RICK. Did you not hear my whistles?

NAN. Clurheen said they were his.

RICK. And I suppose he told you I lost your address.

(NAN *has closed and bolted the door.*)

NAN. Don't say a word to vex him, or he'll rouse Kate. (*She is putting on her cloak, and putting her nightshirt into a paper shopping bag.*)

RICK. And unless we keep far asunder from each other he'll rouse Kate.

NAN. For fear he'll rouse her, I'll put a dummy into my bed.

(*She runs into the ghost room and* RICK *listens at* KATE'S *door.* NAN *comes out with pillows and cushions, which she puts under her blankets.*)

RICK. The stars of the sky make no noise, but Kate's whiskey makes a fine snore.

NAN (*chuckling*). At midnight the silent mouth is the sweetest to hear, they say.

(RICK *leaves the door and looks serious.*)

RICK. Nan, if Clurheen does follow you to my sister's house, tell them he won't stay there, because their children aren't teenagers.

NAN. If Clurheen follows me miles to their house, he'd be sure to follow me to your house.

RICK. And you heard the priest tell about how the poltergeist Asmodeus killed Sarah's husbands on their wedding nights. And that's in the Bible.

NAN (*scared*). Leave that story in darkness. Clurheen hears everything!

(RICK *opens the front door.* NAN, *having put on her topcoat, moves towards it. Suddenly a loud burst of whistling and drumming begins. The door bangs shut again through no human agency.* NAN *retreats.* KATE'S *door opens. The fierce drumming and whistling rises to a climax, and suddenly stops.*)

NAN. Clurheen has opened her door and roused her. I can't go now, Rick.

RICK. If you don't, I'll have to wed Tess. This is your last chance to escape from slavery and starvation.

NAN. I can't go. I feel weak of a sudden.

RICK. Starvation and Clurheen is sapping you. You'll begin with a

365

cough, and end with a coffin, if you wait here.

NAN. If I go, Kate will sign me over to the mental doctors.

(RICK *runs over and grabs her.*)

RICK. Chance that and chance everything. Put a stout heart to steep hill!

NAN. Well, hit or miss, I will.

(*He hurries her out the door, barely waiting to close it. Another fierce burst of whistling and banging develops. Car lights can be seen passing the window.* KATE *appears wearing an old cloak over her night shirt, and carrying a whiskey bottle and her holy water bottle. A strip of sticking plaster adorns her temple.* KATE *blesses herself with holy water, then takes a long slug out of the whiskey bottle. The ghostly noises cease.*)

KATE (*fiercely*). Clurheen, you stab from the dark, and then run away like every cowardly blackguard. And every time I have to lean on this bottle to sleep again. The whiskey is killing me, and robbing me, and that's what you want you whore. (*She drinks again.*) But every time you rouse me, I'll scald you with curses and holy water. Nan, rouse up there, and back me up with your orphan's curses. Waken up, or I'll beat a blow on you that'd sicken an ass! You bloody drone you! (KATE *hits her a mighty blow.*) What's here? (*She pulls back the blankets.*) A dummy woman! She has hopped it like a magpie with some blackguard scamp! Because she's too well fed, and it's putting too much heat into her! I'll soon cool her down on one meal a day. That'll make a nun out of her.

(*She has reached the front door, when a disturbing thought occurs to her. She turns back.*)

KATE. But maybe Clurheen maddened her into suicide the way the two Maynooth students were maddened into suicide. . . . I get a scent of blood from in there. (*She goes into the ghost room, can be heard moving about. She comes out carrying the chocolate bars given by* AINY *to* NAN.) The blackguards gave her these to put hotter and wickeder heat into her. . . . They know I'm trying to cool her with hunger. (*She hides them in secret pockets.*)

KATE. Now she's outside man-struck and shameless with a bachelor as low as a dog. (*She throws open the front door, listens, and then begins to shout.*) Nan of the Leaves, come in out of that! I can hear you well out there, screeching like a jennet and scandalising. And I can hear your ram talking the clothes off you. If you aren't afeard of the ram, be afeard of the lamb. . . . In nine month's time you'll be crying tonight's fun. . . . Soon

366

you'll be called Sweepstake, because every man has a share in you. . . . I well know your ram, and I'll see he gets twelve calendar months in jail for making a child with a girl who's insane. Come in Nan, or I'll tell priests, parsons, and press about ye. . . . (*Suddenly she goes to* NAN'S *bed, and rummages.*) Her night-shirt is gone! So she's gone for the night, or for ever, with some low bachelor who'd sleep with a corpse! (*She goes back to the front door, closes it, and bolts it.*) And now I'm left alone to be a victim and a jeer and a mock for Clurheen! (*She goes back to the whiskey bottle, takes another slug, gives herself another sprinkle of holy water.*) Clurheen, if you'll let me live, and let me sleep enough, or near enough, I'll let you live here uncursed and unscalded. Knock once if you agree, and twice if you won't agree. (*Two loud knocks sound.*) So war it has to be. Well, Kate is fighting all her days, and she was never defeated yet.

(*The door knocks are repeated.* KATE *goes to the front door.*)

KATE. Is there anyone there?

VOICE. Ainy!

KATE. Ainy! I thought you were Clurheen. Wait till I get the key.

(*She goes into the bedroom, comes out with the bill-hook. She unbolts the door, and stands with upraised slasher where the door will conceal her as it opens.*)

KATE. Come in, Ainy!

(*He comes in, sees no one about, advances towards the table.*)

AINY. Are you living or dead?

(KATE *bangs the door shut, and advances on* AINY *with the upraised bill-hook. He takes a quick look back, runs to the hearth, picks up the tongs, runs to the far side of the table.*)

AINY. Before I smash the light, what is your argument?

KATE. What did you do with Nan?

AINY. I witnessed her being stolen away by Rick in his car.

KATE. To his own house?

AINY. No, the opposite direction.

KATE (*lowering bill-hook*). No priest'd wed them at this hour. I'll give you a sup of whiskey. You were perished out there. (*She gets a cup or a glass from the dresser.*)

AINY. And at this hour they won't be taken in most hotels.

KATE. Clurheen is gone with them, and going or coming he'll crash Rick's car. (*She pours whiskey into cup, gives it to* AINY.)

AINY. Any minute Nan could be carried in here broken and bleeding!

367

KATE. Then you could run for the ambulance, or it's first cousin the hearse.

AINY. I could, so I'll wait a while.

KATE. Wait the night and sleep in her bed.

AINY. I'd give you what you paid for this farm. Then you could have a dry foot and a lady's life in town.

KATE. Have you that much money? They say you were in America; or most of the way.

AINY. I had to go all the way. The whales hadn't a spare bed.

KATE. If I lose Nan, I'll have to sell.

AINY. And if I lose Nan, I won't buy.

KATE. The women say they marry because they're too shy to say no. That's lies. They're out to hobble ye, and they do, because ye have to go running after them some way.

AINY. Maybe both of us have lost Nan to a wolf in cheap clothing.

KATE. Let us enjoy a nod of sleep while Clurheen is gone. (*Taking her bottles of whiskey and holy water, she sets out for her bedroom.*)

AINY. Should I bolt the front door?

KATE. Do, but there's no law or order in this house. The doors won't stay either open, or shut. (*She goes into her bedroom, closing door.* AINY *bolts the front door, then goes to the ghost room door.*)

AINY. Clurheen, I guess you're gone with Nan. But like God and the radios maybe you can hear words said miles away. And maybe you know how I suffered amongst strangers: bulldozing through the London blitz, smothered in dust in summer, and stuck in the mud in winter. And then through America, a land of adventure, walking for jobs, and fighting for jobs. So I fear no ghosts; and if you bring Nan home safe, and help me to wed her, you can reign here for evermore. If Nan isn't rescued from Kate, she'll die. That's as sure as you're a poltergeist, or whatever the dead are pleased to call you. (*He goes to the bed, kneels against it, makes the sign of the cross. He springs to his feet again, hurries back to the ghost room door.*)

AINY (*urgently and grim*). Clurheen, I give you fair warning. I'm going praying now until my knees are like rusty hinges. Asking God for one thing only. His curse for ever, and the curse of my seven deadly sins for ever on you, Clurheen, if you crash Rick's car, and murder Nan. Maybe it's a sinful prayer, but I'll keep praying it until Nan comes home safe, or until you make a dead man of myself. . . . Rick is too cowardly ever to wed a haunted girl, so let them live. If you do, that could win you promotion into the Heavens, and out of that queer ghostly room the spiders have deserted.

(*He goes back to the bed, kneels against it, makes the sign of the cross.*)

AINY. In the name of the Father and of the Son and of the Holy Ghost.

CURTAIN

ACT THREE

The scene is the same, and the time is the following morning. The window curtains are closed, and the kitchen is in semi-darkness. AINY *is asleep on his knees with his head resting on the bed. A few mild whistles and bangs from the ghost room fail to waken him. A cushion comes sailing across the room, and wakens* AINY. *He springs up anxiously.*

AINY. Clurheen, you're back! Did you crash Rick's car? Are Nan and Rick dead. or alive, or half alive? You would'nt be back, if Nan wasn't here, or near, dead or alive. (*He unbolts the front door, looks out.*) I see no car parked, or car lights coming! So it must be Nan's ghost that's near, or here! (*He closes the door, becomes very disturbed.*) Clurheen, did you crash Rick's car and kill them? Beat one blow if you did . . .

(*The "Dies Irae" is whistled off-stage.*)

AINY (*bitterly*). This is no time for flute playing. . . . (*He recognises the tune.*) The Dead Mass hymn! So you did crash the car! And Nan is no more! (*Bitterly.*) God and the Blessed Virgin why didn't ye save her? I prayed for her long enough and hard enough, and it was tiredness, not laziness, made me drop asleep. . . . What good is my money to me now? (*He takes deposit books from his pockets, throws them on the ground.*) My blood and sweat and tears! And the new clothes I measured Nan for, and bought for her! Clothes as fancy as a doll's. Will Kate grudge to let Nan wear them in her coffin?

(*He is moving about, calming down a little. The "Dies Irae" continues to be whistled, but less loudly.*)

AINY. Nan, are you still on trial before the Judgement Seat? May you get a good verdict if you are. Maybe you're here already, looking on at me from the air, the same as Clurheen. If I could see you now, maybe I wouldn't know you. If you are here now, I'll tell you a secret. Out foreign an old Irish priest told me why

370

Irish girls have such lovely eyes. He learned me the Latin name for it, the vultus Christi, the face of Christ. He said Irish girls who received Holy Communion often and right got the vultus Christ, the look of Christ. The first minute I seen you, Nan, I said, 'That's a true Irish girl, and she has the vultus Christi. . . . But I was never worthy of a true Irish girl with the vultus Christi. . . . Maybe that's why God let Clurheen kill you . . . (*Moving about.*) Nan, if you can give me a sign that you're happy where you are now. Any sign at all, but different from Clurheen's signs? (*He looks into the ghost room.*) Clurheen is still hymning for you, like as if he's sorry for killing you. It was Rick he hated, foul or fair. . . . Nan, I know you're doing your best to give me a sign, but only one in a million are allowed to give a sign. . . . Because we're duty bound to believe what we can't see. And if we could see everything, we couldn't be true believers at all.

(*The front door opens, and* NAN *appears. Seeing* AINY *she stands open-mouthed.*)

AINY. Nan, is it yourself, or your ghost?

NAN. Myself, but my ghost Clurheen is following me everywhere like a sheepdog.

AINY. I was afeard Clurheen 'd crash Rick's car.

NAN. He didn't crash it last night whatever. (*She closes the door, takes off her cloak and beret.*)

AINY. Thank God you belong to the living!

NAN (*Sadly*). I might be as well off belonging to the dead. (*She pokes the fire, puts fresh turf on it, hangs the kettle.*)

AINY. Why so? Did he not treat you right?

NAN. He disgraced me for evermore. (*She goes to* KATE'S *door, listens.*)

AINY. And then left you to paw it home alone like a tinker's dog!

NAN. Does Kate know I slept out last night?

AINY. She does. That's why she made me wait the night, afeard of Clurheen.

NAN. Rick brought me to his married sister's house. To test whether Clurheen would follow me to his own house, if we were wed.

AINY. Last night Clurheen went rambling somewhere.

NAN. He followed me to Rick's sister's house. And they weren't used to his capers. At first light they threw me out, saying I had seven divils in me the same as Mary Magdalene!

AINY. After her own brother disgracing you!

NAN. Rick never disgraced me. It was Clurheen, by following me to another house.

AINY. Rick will never wed you now. He's a lonesome man and afeard of ghosts.

AINY. And he heard the priest tell how the poltergeist in the Bible killed Sara's husbands on their wedding nights, as they entered the bride's room.

AINY. I disobeyed the Mafia, and lived. And I'll disobey Clurheen, and wed you.

NAN (*scared*). Don't talk so venturesome! Clurheen hears everything.

AINY. Did Clurheen ever forbid you to wed me?

NAN. Oh, no, thank God, he never did. But it takes an awful capital to buy a house and a farm these times.

AINY. I'll show you my blood money. . . . Blood and sweat and tears as the man said. (*He picks his deposit books off the floor, shows them to her.*)

NAN. Ainy, it's a big miracle that you weren't blinded by so much money! . . . Why does Lacky call you a failure?

AINY. Because he was mightier than me, and had rougher bones.

NAN (*handing back books*). But I'd rather die out a stale maid than be the cause of Clurheen killing you.

AINY. Let us ask him straight and fair whether he'll let us live together. (*He moves towards the ghost room door.*)

NAN (*following him*). He doesn't turn contrary when you call here, when you help me on the land.

(*They arrive at the ghost room door.*)

AINY. Let you ask him, Nan. Ye know each other greatly.

NAN (*gravely*). But we know how he greets me. We'd like to know how he greets you.

AINY. Maybe I haven't a head for talking to ghosts. If I say anything wrong, give me a bruise.

NAN. I will.

AINY. Clurheen, if Nan isn't rescued from Kate soon, she'll die. And after death she'll be sent maybe to some Limbo for bachelor's daughters. A secret place cut off from all views and news, so you'll never know whether Nan is happy for ever, or miserable for ever.

NAN. And tell him we need his help soon, before the bad luck gives us the last shove.

AINY. Clurheen, I can rescue Nan from Kate and from Limbo by buying this house and farm from Kate. . . . If Kate can be made to sell.

NAN (*prompting*). And then by wedding me.

AINY. And then by wedding Nan. No other way can we live together.

NAN. Ask will he allow that.

AINY. Clurheen, will you allow us to live together?

NAN. As man and wife.

AINY. As man and wife?

NAN. Tell him he'll get the height of justice as long as we last.

AINY. Clurheen, my mother knew about the two worlds, and evermore she said, 'A ghost is the luckiest thing ever you had in your house, if it's treated right'.

NAN. Give him his numbers now.

AINY. Clurheen, if you'll let us live together as man and wife, beat one blow. If you won't, beat two blows.

(*Two loud knocks sound.*)

AINY. He's afeard your marriage will banish himself, as the ghost books foretell.

LACKY (*flinging open front door*). Even heavy knocks these females won't answer! (*Shouting at* AINY.) You foreign mongrel! Half Yank, and half John Bull! Here you passed the night, sleeping between two women, and you not strong enough for one!

NAN. Lacky, I spent the night at the home of Rick's sister.

LACKY. So this foreigner slept with the widow! The cheap way of winning a farm!

AINY. I slept in Nan's bed.

LACKY. Nan, don't believe marriage promises from this mongrel foreigner. He's like the flea: when you think you have him, you haven't him.

AINY. Our family was a classical family, and we shouldn't let it die out, or go down.

LACKY. Plenty of girls I liked, bit I didn't like to own them.

AINY. Don't wait till you're no good for work or marriage.

LACKY. Nan and me should wed, and keep the family farm alive. And let you take the air back to the black women of Chicago.

AINY. In Chicago you can grow homesick for Hell.

KATE (*screaming off-stage*). Fire! Fire! Fire!

NAN (*running to* KATE'S *door*). The fire is in good bloom, mam!

KATE (*off stage*). Fire! Fire!

AINY. That isn't a command! It's a news! (*He runs to* KATE'S *door, opens it.*) The room is on fire!

NAN. The spring water buckets are here.

(NAN *and* AINY *run to the corner, carry the water buckets into the bedroom.* LACKY *looks in the door.*)

LACKY. Kate was too boozed to quench her cigarettes. It's a true saying that a drunken man is a terrible curse, but a drunken woman is twice as worse. (KATE *comes out coughing, and clutching her bottle of whiskey.*)

KATE. I'd be a grilled herring, if that fire started while I was asleep.

LACKY. No fire could start while you were asleep. You had to drop a match, or a cigarette butt.

KATE. I done neither, and I hid all matches since I read that poltergeists can start fires.

LACKY. If Clurheen brought that fire from Hell, Galway Bay won't quench it. (*He looks into room.*)

KATE. Clurheen killed Shagley's dog, because Shagley cursed him. Now Clurheen is out to do a murder on me. (*She swigs at the whiskey.*)

LACKY. It can't be Hell fire. They have it quenched down to the smoking.

KATE. Tonight we'll go to sleep, and wake up to find ourselves smothered, or roasted.

(NAN *comes out with empty buckets, which she returns to their corners.*)

NAN. Tonight fear will keep us awake. We'll be shivering like whipped dogs.

KATE. Maybe the doctor can inject us with insomnia. Then we could watch out for fires.

AINY (*appearing with bucket*). Clurheen's first fire is out. But he'll improve with practice! (*He returns the bucket to its corner.*)

LACKY. Kate, let Nan wed me this day. Then the two of ye can sleep safe in my house.

NAN (*dismayed*). Oh, no, no. How can we wed when we never courted?

LACKY. That's soon remedied. Kate, send Nan out to the barn now for an hour, or two, sweethearting with me.

NAN. Oh, no, no.

KATE. Would you rather be roasted than courted?

NAN. No, but I had no breakfast, and they say it isn't right for a full belly to be courting an empty belly.

KATE. Your parents were blackguards, so cooled down by an empty belly is the safest way to send you courting.

AINY. Mam, you might as well give her up to a field of tinkers.

LACKY. You may thank you're my only brother, or you'd get my hospital clout for that.

KATE. Lacky, there's nothing for nothing. What'll you pay me for an hour's courting with Nan?

LACKY. What is she worth? She's like the thistle: it's hard to get near her.

KATE. You're going to win a wife. And I'm going to lose a servant. So a hundred pounds, neither more nor less!

LACKY. A hundred pounds! Her fee is high. Did she win prizes at the Shows? Like Durkan's bull?

KATE. She could have unknown to me.

LACKY (*searching pockets*). I haven't that much money on me.

KATE. Go home, and plough it up. It's time it got fresh air.

LACKY. If I go, this mongrel foreigner will run away with her.

KATE. She won't be let run away with any man who hasn't a farm, and a hearthstone.

LACKY. If she does, she'll soon grow a whisker from misery.

(*He goes,* NAN *closes the front door quickly.*)

NAN. I'll bolt the door against his back and overs.

KATE. You will not. Go in and sweep up that fire.

NAN. Yes, mam. (*She goes into bedroom with a fire-shovel, and a brush.*)

AINY. Clurheen followed Nan five miles last night. What'll stop him from roasting ye alive in Lacky's house, an ass's roar from here.

KATE (*bitterly*). Nothing can stop him, when God won't stop him. This house is upside down from too much liberty. (*She swigs at the whiskey.*)

AINY. Before night you can be living safe a hundred miles away. I'll run in to a safe lawyer for a farm transfer deed. And my banks will give you safe cheques. (*He shows deposit books.*)

KATE. Then I can go home to my own Mayo again. There's nothing in Galway but a mouthful of 'Give me!', and a fistful of 'Have you?'

(NAN *comes out of bedroom, and empties the fire debris into the grate.* AINY *hurries to the front door, turns.*)

AINY. You won't send Nan out with Lacky now!

KATE. Why wouldn't I? I never refuse money.

AINY. But lacky is a wild arab of a man. He knows no end.

KATE. It's time some man rummaged a bit of life into her, and she a sleepy lazy bitch.

AINY. Nan, if you see him coming, make for the furze ditch or the bog.

NAN. I will, if I'm allowed.

AINY. Here's Shagley with some news or programme, but I can't wait. (*He goes.*)

KATE (*contemptuously*). Give a clown a choice, and he'll choose the worst. Three clowns have chosen the bachelor's daughter. But the wild duck never laid a tame egg.

NAN. Can I get the breakfast now?

KATE. You cannot. You're safer courting Lacky with an empty belly.

NAN (*worried*). Would a girl be safe with Lacky. if she got a fainting spell from hunger?

KATE. Lacky isn't the full shilling. But he isn't bad and mad like you.

NAN. If Lacky and me are mad, is it safe to put us together?

(SHAGLEY *appears, looking scared.*)

KATE. You're as pale as a pock-marked cat.

SHAGLEY. The dead bell is ringing for me and for you. The Vet says my dog died of a broken neck.

NAN. A shoulder from a passing car.

SHAGLEY. The vet could see no cut, or bruise. And just before Clurheen killed him, my dog put his head between my legs with fear.

KATE. So Clurheen broke his neck by enchantment!

NAN. Because he bit me!

SHAGLEY. Ainy is after telling me about Clurheen setting fire to your house.

KATE. Nan, go in quick you, and ask Clurheen's pardon for our curses.

SHAGLEY. And tell him we'll curse him and scald him no more, no matter what he does.

NAN. I'll tell him, if he's there. (*She goes into the ghost room.*)

SHAGLEY (*going to ghost room door*). Nan, ghosts are as slow as God, and have to be asked as many times. So keep asking, as often as a rosary. (*He closes door, comes back to* KATE.) I have a plan made, but it'll fail, if Nan hears it.

KATE. What's it about? (*Sceptical.*)

SHAGLEY. Our only hope of living until we die of shortness of breath, is to find a new parking place for Clurheen and Nan forty mile from here.

KATE. The Mental Hospital you mean?

SHAGLEY. Let you hire a car, and sign her over to the Mental doctors this very day.

KATE. But if they're low blackguards of men, they'd side with a young goodlooking bitch like Nan.

SHAGLEY. And say it's yourself that's crazy!

KATE. The old name for the mental doctors, was the mad doctors, and it was true.

SHAGLEY. If we could convert Nan to believe she'll get great feeding and rest in the Mental Hospital, and it'd be worth her while to talk and behave crazy for a few days.

KATE. I'm cooling her down with hunger, to save her from the starved bachelors around here.

(*The ghost room opens, and* NAN *comes out.*)

NAN. I doubt Clurheen is gone for a fresh air. So can I get the breakfast now?

KATE. It's too late now for breakfast. Wash the spuds, and we might have an early dinner.

(*Wearily* NAN *takes a bucket, and sets out for the front door.*)

KATE. Shagley, does she deserve any dinner? Last night she was an outlier: out all night scandalising.

NAN. No, Rick left me at his sister's house to see if Clurheen would follow me there?

SHAGLEY. And did he?

NAN. He did.

KATE. If any man weds a haunted thing like her, he'll suicide himself in a week, or cut her throat.

SHAGLEY. Sure even the best of wives – their men can hardly put with them.

(*Sadly* NAN *goes out with her bucket.*)

KATE (*smiling*). She's worn out after all yesterday in the clay.

SHAGLEY. And the poor thing is wobbling with the hunger.

KATE. She'd go to Hell and the Divil for a few days rest and feeding. So tell her you were in hospital, and got great rest and feeding in it. (*She opens one of the ghost books.* SHAGLEY *is perusing another.*)

SHAGLEY. That was facts. I was in hospital, and they had better cooks than me. They cooked things you couldn't name, and you could eat them, too, if you were hungry.

(NAN *comes in with a bucket of water which she sets on a chair.* NAN *proceeds to wash the potatoes.*)

NAN. On account we had no breakfast can I put down two or three spuds extra?

KATE. Two ... Shagley this is a true book by a sure author: about an American girl who got haunted by a poltergeist until her health and nerves went down at last.

SHAGLEY. The same thing happened to the haunted girl over against Lough Corrib. At last her jacket was able to fit her as a topcoat.

KATE. This American girl surrendered herself to the doctors and to the hospital at last. The poltergeist vanished for ever the day she entered the hospital, and the great feeding and rest in the hospital made her rosy and goodlooking and marriageable again.

SHAGLEY. The doctors told me my belly was to explode sometime, and kill me, unless I had this operation. So I surrendered to hospital.

KATE. Did they give ye enough to eat?

SHAGLEY. Not a man in Ireland could eat all we got of rashers and sausages and beef and mutton and hens, and jellies and sweetcake.

KATE. Had ye to work hard for that?

SHAGLEY. Not a stroke. The nurses done all work, while we lied in bed and idled all day and all night.

(NAN *has been washing potatoes, and taking an increasing interest in this conversation.*)

NAN. Would I be taken in that hospital?

KATE. What's wrong with you?

NAN. Odd times my heart does be walking out of my mouth with weakness.

KATE. But have you a bad pain, or a big swelling anywhere?

NAN. No.

KATE. Then you won't be taken in an ordinary hospital. What you have is dirty water in the brain.

SHAGLEY. I heard the highest doctor in Galway say dirty water between the two lugs is very serious. . . . Water is bad inside or outside, or anywhere.

KATE. The Mental Hospital is the only place they can cure that disease.

NAN. Do they get two or three meals a day in the Mental Hospital?

SHAGLEY. Patients were sent to our hospital from the mental hospital and they said the food and the rest was twice better in the Mental Hospital.

NAN. Maybe they said that because they were insane.

SHAGLEY. They weren't insane at all, but able dealers. So they behaved giddy before the doctors, and talked cuckoo, and earned themselves a lovely holiday in the mental hospital.

NAN. But maybe now they'll never be allowed out again?

SHAGLEY. They said they'd be ordered out home the first day they behaved sensible.

NAN. If I don't go somewhere, I'll soon be six foot down.

KATE (*rising briskly*). If you'd like a few days rest and feeding in the Mental Hospital, I'll hire Merrigan's car.

NAN (*coming over*). Will the doctors hold a court on me?

SHAGLEY. They will, and you'll need to behave giddy, and answer crazy.

NAN (*smiling*). Rick's nurse told me the questions they'll ask.

KATE. When they ask your name answer Nan of the Leaves before any other name.

NAN. And when they ask my age I'll say I'm four hundred years and fifteen months.

SHAGLEY. And the mother of King Brian Boru. I'll bolt this door against spies and long tongues. (*He bolts front door.*)

KATE (*pouring a glass of whiskey*). Here, drain this. And tell the doctors you're drinking whiskey like ducks drinking water.

NAN. They'll ask what day and date this is.

SHAGLEY. Tell them it's Christmas Day and the middle of October.

NAN. They'll ask whether I like to stay in bed all day.

KATE. Tell them you wouldn't work to keep yourself warm.

NAN. They'll ask about suicide, and I'll say I mean to keep drinking water until it drowns my insides.

SHAGLEY. Don't say much about that. Mocking is catching, and water is dangerous.

NAN. They'll ask whether I hear voices.

KATE. Say you hear Arrah, the Divil's mother, arguing with Musha, the Divil's father.

NAN. And I'll tell how I hear Clurheen.

SHAGLEY. But tell them nobody else hears him.

KATE. And tell them the Divil has commanded you to kill three.

SHAGLEY. No, seven was the Irish number, and the lucky number.

NAN (*cheerful*). I'll say the neighbours class me as fit to kill all in the village.

(*Somebody tries to open the front door, and then knocks on it urgently.*)

NAN. God save me! That's Lacky back with my fee!

SHAGLEY. He's gone daft for a wife ever since you came into his views.

KATE. Nan, don't let Lacky, or anyone except us three, know you're only shamming mad.

NAN. Why so?

KATE. Long tongues and begrudgers could report you for

shamming mad. Then you'd get jail.

NAN. I'll hide from Lacky so. (*She runs towards ghost room.*)

KATE. My room is safer.

(NAN *comes back.*)

SHAGLEY. Lacky will search every room, and we aren't bullies fit to stop him.

KATE. Nan, pull the slasher from under my mattress, and hold it on high with a mad dog's face.

NAN (*smiling*). To cancel his courting, I'll prove a nettle could be a twin sister to me. (*She runs into* KATE'S *room, closing door.*)

SHAGLEY (*worried*). But they say God looks after orphans, so maybe He'll rescue her from our plot.

KATE. You're an orphan. Did He look after you?

SHAGLEY (*bitterly*). No. He made no match for me.

KATE. No one could. You're as odd as an ass at a Horseshow.

SHAGLEY. But I was an old fashioned orphan; and a divil for wine, women and Woodbines. But nan is as holy as a sieve.

KATE. No, she's gone mad after men now.

SHAGLEY (*brightening up*). Well, if she's tuning the men into bad scholars, God will let us jail her.

(LACKY *is banging noisily on the door.* SHAGLEY *unbolts, and opens the door.*)

SHAGLEY. Lacky, you're as noisy as Clurheen.

LACKY (*loudly happy*). I'm after seeing a very lucky token: a cow licking herself the wrong way!

KATE. Then you're soon getting wed.

LACKY. Yes, I'm leaving the Cape of Good Hope, and entering the United States. Is Nan bidding farewell to her ghost in the wall? (*He goes into ghost room.* KATE *takes out a purse, and gives* SHAGLEY *money.*)

KATE. Let you run to Merrigan, and hire his car for the Mental Hospital.

SHAGLEY. If I fall, I won't wait to get up.

(LACKY *comes out of ghost room roaring with rage.*)

LACKY (*to* KATE). You cally-fed hag! You let her run away with that foreign mongrel and failure! And me having her full fee here!

KATE. No, Lacky. She's in my room.

SHAGLEY. But if you go near her, she'll put an itch in your head.

LACKY. Liar! There's no flea in her. (*He throws open* KATE'S *door.*) Nan! For why have you the slasher? I don't practise the bull's religion like these mongrel foreigners.

KATE. Nan is gone out of her wits again.

SHAGLEY. Nothing goes right with a motherless child.

LACKY. It's too much farmwork! When I'm doing all her farmwork, and she has a belly like a bay window, her good sense will come back again.

KATE. It's better to live naked than to live in fear. In your sleep she'd mob you and murder you.

LACKY. I'm able to hold a twelve hundredweight bullock by his lug and his nose. I'd have poor courage if I couldn't hold a ten stone girl by her lug and her nose.

SHAGLEY. Kate, give Nan a sup of whiskey. What whiskey, or butter won't cure, there's no cure for.

KATE. True. (*She pours a glass of whiskey.*)

LACKY. We often heard about people going mad with joy. And Nan has gone mad with joy over the prospects of marriage with me. Shagley, no woman ever went mad with joy over you!

SHAGLEY. No, but there isn't many veins in a woman I don't know, or where they're running to.

(NAN *appears with upraised bill-hook, and acting mad.*)

NAN. The Divil has commanded me to kill seven.

LACKY. Nan, I'm Lacky that has gradh machree for you. And I wouldn't need a radio, if I had a wife to bring me the news from Mass.

NAN. I won't hurt you much. No good butcher is cruel.

(LACKY *shouting and pointing.*)

LACKY. Look at Clurheen! Behind you!

NAN (*turning*). Where? I don't see Clurheen, or his shadow.

(LACKY *grabs her from behind, and* SHAGLEY *takes the bill-hook from her.*)

LACKY (*happily*). At last I have her. The mother of my family! You'll have Christmas all times in my house.

(KATE *runs into her bedroom.* NAN *pretends to struggle against* LACKY *and* SHAGLEY.)

NAN. It's a big sin to disobey the Divil.

SHAGLEY. He'll never be disobeyed until it is made a sin.

(KATE *comes out with a rope.*)

KATE. Here, put the cross cow's tie on her, while I bundle her clothes together for the hospital.

(*She gives them the rope, and goes into the ghost room. They tie* NAN'S *hands together.*)

NAN. It'd be ease to my bones to be dead.

SHAGLEY. A few days rest and feeding will bring back your right

381

mind.

LACKY. Shagley, have you a right mind?

SHAGLEY (*grimly*). No man could grow a right mind in the bogland where I was bred born and starved.

LACKY. Still you never lost a trick, or threw out a wrong card.

(KATE *returns with an old battered suitcase.*)

KATE. Shagley, give Lacky the car hire for Merrigan. He has younger legs than you.

SHAGLEY (*giving money to Lacky*). Tell him Nan will never see another day, if he don't hurry her to the hospital.

LACKY. Merrigan's best side is out, but he'll do anything for money.

(LACKY *goes.*)

NAN (*smiling*). Did I behave a true madcap?

SHAGLEY. Be more savage: grinding your teeth.

KATE. And in fits and starts, like an ass harrowing.

(*A couple of angry whistles ring out.*)

NAN (*startled*). Clurheen is back, and vexed over something! (*She runs to the window*). Rick's car is halted, and he's letting himself out. I'll hide my madness. (*She runs towards* KATE'S *room.*)

KATE. If Rick doesn't see you behaving mad, his nurse will report you for false pretences.

NAN. But I amn't going to her hospital.

KATE. Them hospitals phone each other every day.

SHAGLEY. And the man who gives a quick love, gives a quick hatred. So don't trust Rick.

(NAN *returns sadly to the armchair.*)

NAN. I'll dumb myself. But I won't let Rick see me talking insane.

(RICK *appears, looking worried.*)

RICK. Is Nan here?

KATE. She's here, but she isn't all there.

RICK. Nan, I called at my sister's house, but you were gone.

SHAGLEY. And now she's gone in the head, too. That's why she's tied.

KATE. She tried to kill us with the slasher.

RICK. She looks in a sleepy kind of condition. But not mad.

SHAGLEY. Lacky is gone for Merrigan's car to bring Kate and Nan to the doctors and the mental hospital.

RICK. Nan, let me bring you. I'll tell the doctors you're the gentlest girl that ever laced a shoe.

KATE. Merrigan's car is ordered now, and I'll not make an enemy by cancelling him.

RICK. He'll charge a hatful of money. I'll charge nothing.

KATE. I never trust anything I'm offered for nothing.

RICK. And some never trust an honest man. Nan, don't let them rail you until I come back. I'll stand fair play for you before the doctors. (*He goes*).

KATE. Rick'd tell the doctors what'd make them throw you out without bite or sup, or a minute's rest.

NAN (*sadly*). Rick doesn't know how hungry and weary I am.

KATE. Hide in my room before he comes back.

SHAGLEY. And I'll tell him ye're gone already.

NAN. Can I lie on your bed? Clurheen was very restless in a strange house last night.

KATE (*giving her a glass of whiskey*). Drink this, and it'll give you a great nod of sleep.

NAN. I could sleep on rocks this minute.

(NAN *takes the glass into* KATE'S *room.* KATE *closes the door.*)

KATE. Stupid drunk! – that's the way we need to have her.

SHAGLEY. The same way they got rid of the poltergeist over against Lough Corrib. But their poor orphan servant girl never got out of the asylum alive.

KATE. Nan will get better treatment from the lunatics than you and me will get from Clurheen and the dead.

SHAGLEY (*grimly*). A lot of the dead were mean and cruel while they were alive.

(LACKY *comes in looking cheerful.*)

LACKY. Merrigan is coming the minute he gets on his clothes for state days and bonfire nights. And Ainy is after landing from town, and he's coming over to see you.

KATE. He's coming to buy my farm, but he won't buy it if he hears Nan has a nervous downfall.

SHAGLEY. And if he doesn't buy it, this farm will never fall to you Lacky, if Ainy dies out an old bachelor.

LACKY. Ainy is sure to die out soon, because he's battered out from too much work and wars and weathers in England and America.

KATE. Ainy met the same fate as Shagley: his wife's mother died an old maid. (*She is giving glasses of whiskey to* LACKEY *and* SHAGLEY.)

LACKY. But where is my girl?

KATE. Nan is in my room hiding from Ainy. We'll tell Ainy she's gone to the bog, seeking a stray bullock.

SHAGLEY. And by the time Ainy has the bog searched for her, Nan will be forty mile away.

LACKY (*laughing loudly*). Only for the fools, the clever couldn't make a living.

SHAGLEY. Here's a health to Nan and Lacky and their two fine farms.

LACKY. And to the Baby Ford we'll buy that'll splash bad neighbours every wet Sunday coming from Mass!

(*They touch glasses and drink.* AINY *comes in carrying a new and well-filled shopping bag and a large parcel.*)

AINY. Where's Nan?

KATE. Searching the bog for a stray bullock.

AINY (*disappointed*). I told ye to sell that cross bullock before he gets drowned in the bog.

(*He places his shopping bag and parcel on, or near the table.*)

SHAGLEY. This time of year a strong dog couldn't walk safe in that bog.

AINY (*handing documents to* KATE). The transfer deed and the cheques are here, and while you're judging them I'll run to the bog for Nan, (*He sets out for front door.*)

KATE. We don't need Nan. Shagley and Lacky can sign as witnesses.

AINY. I'm buying this farm for Nan, so I want her to see the signing.

KATE. It's unlucky to postpone weddings and sales.

AINY. Them oul pishrogues aren't worth a cuckoo spit.

LACKY. Our old people said, 'Those old rules shouldn't be overruled'. And you're talking like an ignorant foreigner.

KATE. Unless you sign now, I'll give the sale to an auctioneer.

AINY. Very well.

(*He brings the table from the side-wall to centre stage. He takes a pen from his pocket, signs, and hands the pen to* KATE.)

KATE. That isn't the name you answer to.

AINY. Ainy is short for Aeneas. We're descended from a Munster scholar who came here as a hedge school master.

LACKY. Some say too much learning drove us mad.

KATE (*signing*). Katherine Rainey – ex-farmer – thank God! Here are the keys of your house and stables. (*Gives keys to* AINY).

AINY. You can live here until you get lodgings, and I'll live in Lacky's until the wedding.

KATE. By the time you come back from the bog, I'll be gone for ever. I'll send an auctioneer to sell the stock and the furniture.

AINY. I'll bid for both. It's a wonder Nan didn't bring her ashplant. (*He takes a stick from the corner*). I'll fetch it to her now.

KATE. And now I'll fill my suitcases for a journey Clurheen will never see the end of.

(*She goes into her bedroom.* AINY *takes a bottle of whiskey from his shopping bag.*)

AINY. Let ye be drinking good luck to my new home and farm.

LACKY. New kings make new rules. Never again let anyone curse Clurheen.

AINY. Mother always said the dead can't bear cursing in a new house.

(*He gives the uncorked whiskey bottle to* SHAGLEY, *and goes to the front door with* NAN'S *stick. But as he reaches the door he is stopped by a fierce outburst of whistling and banging from the ghost room. It stops as suddenly as it began.*)

AINY (*dismayed*). Is Clurheen vexed because I bought his house and farm? (*He crosses to the ghost room door.*) Clurheen, beat one blow if you're vexed because I bought your house and farm. Beat two blows if you aren't vexed.

(*Two clear blows sound.*)

AINY. Thank God you aren't vexed. Beat one blow if you're glad.

(*One blow sounds*).

SHAGLEY. Run to the bog before Nan is drowned.

LACKY. She doesn't know the over-grown drains ten foot deep.

AINY. I'll run like a hound.

(*He hurries to the front door, but again he is stopped by an urgent outbreak of whistling and banging.*)

AINY (*mystified*). For all the world as if he doesn't want me to go!

SHAGLEY. Maybe he wants Nan to join the dead!

LACKY. Like the politicians, the dead want everyone to join themselves.

(AINY *crosses to ghost room door.*)

AINY. Clurheen, is Nan in danger? Beat one blow if she is.

(*One blow sounds.*)

AINY. Is she in danger from the bog.

(*Two or three blows sound.*)

AINY. She isn't in danger from the bog.

LACKY. What else would he say, if he's out to drown her?

AINY. But then why did he tell me she was in danger?

SHAGLEY. To delay you here questioning and wondering while he's drowning her.

(KATE *comes out of her bedroom wearing her hat and cloak, and carrying a big suitcase.*)

KATE. You're here yet! You'd be a good messenger to send for the death.

AINY. How can Clurheen noise so loud, if Nan is so far away?

385

SHAGLEY. Clurheen was heard noising as loud when he lived alone here.

AINY. I'll see is Nan drawing near? (*He goes out.*)

LACKY (*to* KATE). Clurheen is playing every trick to keep Ainy here.

KATE. If Ainy comes back, let one of ye set out for the bog.

SHAGLEY. Yes that'll shame him into going with me.

(*As he moves towards door,* AINY *comes in looking worried.*)

AINY. Are ye sure Nan went towards the bog? I can't see her that side.

SHAGLEY. A bad sign that she's up to her neck in a bog hole. Come on quick.

(*He hurries out. As* AINY *follows him there is another burst of whistling and banging.* AINY *waits until it subsides.*)

AINY (*bitterly*). Clurheen, if you drown Nan, I'll burn this house over your head, or whatever you have in place of a head. (*He hurries out.*)

KATE. Lacky, you'll lose Nan to Ainy if you don't hurry Merrigan's car.

LACKY (*suddenly furious*). Merrigan is a proper buck, as bad as the cat's father! I'll throw him into the well of his car. I'll beat a blow on him. I'll knuckle him!

(*He storms out* KATE *hastens to the ghost room door.*)

KATE (*conciliatory*). Clurheen, Nan has to go for a cure to the Mental Hospital. And she'll be awful lost for you, if you don't go with her. In the hospital you'll have ten times more company than here, and ten times more rooms for your games. And bright lights night and day, like Heaven, but no prayers or holy water, or Latin curses. You can dance, diddle and sing there all hours, and the lunatics won't wonder at you at all. And the nurses and doctors will think it's the lunatics are noising and pelting things. So you can reign there happy for ever, like the poltergeist from over against Lough Corrib. He's there near fifty years, and he wouldn't leave it even if he got the Heavens. And Nan will be there fifty years, because no-one will claim out a haunted thing like her. With the men out of sight is out of mind, and love is only as thick as a finger. The man isn't baptised yet that'll marry her.

(*Some happy whistles come from Clurheen.*)

KATE. Clurheen, you're pleased! My news and advice suits you! You'll never get better advice. The living haven't much power, but we know a lot.

(*A louder burst of celebratory whistles and bangs from Clurheen.*)

AINY *comes in, takes a parcel off the table.* KATE *is stunned, but quickly recovers.*)

KATE. Ainy! Clurheen has confessed that Nan is up to her neck in a bog hole.

AINY. She's in your room wearing your cast offs. But now she'll put on this new dress. Nan! (*He goes into room.*)

KATE. The wives men get from God do be contrary enough. So what class of a wife will you get from Clurheen and the Divil? (SHAGLEY *and* RICK *enter looking grim.* SHAGLEY'S *shirt collar is torn.*)

SHAGLEY. Did Ainy not twist the neck off you, the way he near strangled myself?

KATE. The dead man's shroud on all traitors! It was yourself, or Lacky betrayed me. Neither of ye is a patch on a good man. Clurheen will roast ye tonight.

RICK. Kate, It was myself let your cat out of its bag.

KATE. You couldn't, because you didn't know.

RICK. As I was coming back, I met them going, and Ainy asked if I seen Nan. I told him I seen her here tied like a criminal, waiting to be transported to the Mental Hospital.

SHAGLEY. Ainy made a bound at my throat, and if I didn't tell him all, I'd be in Clurheen's country by now.

KATE. Soon your houses will be bonfires, and ye'll all be in Clurheen's country, while Kate will be over the hills and far away. (LACKY *appears.*)

LACKY. Merrigan's car is out on the broad road.

KATE. Nan isn't going, but I am, and back never. (*She takes up her suitcases.*)

LACKY (*shocked*). You're not leaving us without an American wake, and a half barrel rolling down!

KATE. I am, and I have only one present to leave ye: Clurheen! May he be as everlasting as Shagley's britches! (*She goes out.* SHAGLEY *shouts after her.*)

SHAGLEY. May you go so far away that it'll cost you a hundred pounds to post us a letter.

KATE. May ye all be kicked around like a football in Kerry. (KATE *goes.* AINY *comes from* KATE'S *room, closing door after him.*)

LACKY. I want to see Nan.

AINY. You can't see her yet. She's changing her dress.

LACKY. Is she still mad with joy over me?

AINY. When Kate failed to madden her, nothing will ever madden her.

RICK (*sadly*). Lacky, Clurheen is the new matchmaker around here, and his word is law.

AINY. They say the two happiest days in a man's life are the day he sells his wool, and the day he gets wed.

(*He is pouring out drinks and giving them to the men.* NAN *comes out fingering her new dress.*)

NAN. Does this look as nice as it feels?

SHAGLEY. You'll never wear anything as nice again until you're wearing your child's arm around your neck.

RICK. Nan, don't forget the Angel Raphael's advice that saved Tobias and Sara from the ghost who loved Sara.

NAN (*sadly*). The lesson we suffer over we never forget.

AINY. Men, drink a toast to Nan and myself.

SHAGLEY. I know only the old toast. Here's a health to the men, and may the women live for ever!

RICK. May ye be in God's hand!

LACKY. And may he never close his fist too tight on ye!

(*They drink.* RICK *puts his glass on the table.*)

RICK. Unless I phone my girl, I'll miss that boat, too. (*He sets out for the front door.*)

AINY. If she makes you sell your farm, I'll give you as good a bid as any.

RICK (*sadly*). One out and another in was ever the way on the farms. But the land is going into big ranches again, while the people are emigrating away. Good luck to ye!

SHAGLEY. Nan, tell Clurheen I'll will my farm to you, if Clurheen lets me live until God wants me.

NAN. I'll tell him.

SHAGLEY. And tell him I never cursed the dead until Kate led me astray.

NAN. I'll tell him.

SHAGLEY. And tell him I'll never again be guilty of obeying a woman in anything.

NAN (*smiling*). I'll tell him.

(SHAGLEY *goes to the door, and turns.*)

SHAGLEY. Tonight if ye see a St. John's bonfire where my shack was, ye'll know Shagley is gone, shoes or no shoes. It's misting rain, but not enough to quench Clurheen's fires (*He goes.*)

(AINY *is taking groceries from his shopping bag, and* NAN *is admiring some unaccustomed luxuries.*)

AINY. Lacky, will you forgive us for getting wed?

LACKY. The old rhyme said:
"If you want to be praised, die,
If you want to be blamed, marry."
But I'll never blame ye for bringing new life and land to our classical family.

AINY. We'll ask Clurheen to find out a wife for you.

LACKY. Tell him my oul' dog and cat are sick and tired of my oul' chat. (*He sets out for the door.*)

NAN. Did you never give your hand to a fortune teller?

LACKY. I did, and they all said there was a wife for me. So she's sitting on a hob somewhere, gathering dust. If Clurheen was able to rake you out of the wilds of Mayo, he should be able to prod my lady out of her hob.

NAN. We'll tell him.

LACKY. Tell her I'm the full of the bed, and it'll do her heart good to see me. And I never waste time in bed, or out of it. So I bid ye good day. (*He goes, closing door.*)

NAN (*happily*). Thank God, and thank Clurheen, and thank you, Ainy!

AINY (*opening parcels*). A few cakes and jellies and beef.

NAN. You have yourself robbed.

AINY. And rashers and sausages to take the rust off Kate's pan.

NAN (*smiling*). And her shamrock tea – three leaves! But first we must save Shagley from death by fire. (*She goes to ghost room door.*) Clurheen, Shagley said he'd will his farm to us, if you'll spare his life and his home. He'd never have cursed you only for Kate; and he has made a faithful vow never again to obey a woman in anything.

(AINY *takes a coloured child's ball from his shopping bag, and gives it to* NAN.)

AINY. Clurheen might get fun out of hopping and throwing this.

NAN. Ainy, you think of everything! Clurheen, this'll rise your heart, and make you grow two inches.

(*She tosses the ball into the room. It is received with some merry whistles.*)

NAN (*coming back*). A house without a ghost does be too quiet.

AINY. There doesn't be enough life in it.

(*From the room comes a referee style whistle, and the ball comes bouncing back.* AINY *fields it, and tosses it to* NAN, *who throws it back into the ghost room.*)

NAN (*merry*). Hi for Clurheen the best player in Ireland!

AINY (*merry*). We three will be a match for any three players, dead or alive!

(*Suddenly* NAN *looks grave.*)

NAN. Ainy, you're a foreigner, so I want you to promise me one thing.

AINY (*smiling*). Anything short of murder.

NAN. Promise that you'll never send me stealing from anyone.

AINY. I swear by the Sacred Heart of God.

AINY. Apart from that I'll wear out my shoes for you. (*She goes to chair, sits down.*)

AINY. Which do you need first and most: a meal, or a sleep?

NAN. Ainy, kiss me again. I love that.

AINY. There's no other way to have fun without laughing.

(AINY *takes a chair, and sits facing her. They embrace and kiss. The ball rolls out of the ghost room, and stops near them.*)

NAN (*smiling*). Ainy, I have to sleep a while, or die.

AINY. Sleep away, Nan. They say sleep is very good for the brain.

(NAN *rests her head on the table, closes her eyes.* AINY *picks up the ball, goes to the ghost room door, throws the ball in.*)

AINY. Clurheen, Nan needs sleep, and a sleepy tune could be a remedy.

(*He goes to the front door, listens. Clurheen begins to whistle "The Castle of Dromore", or a Connemara lullaby.* AINY *gets two buckets and a tin mug. He goes to the ghost room door.*)

AINY (*softly*). Clurheen, Kate's cows are lowing and roaring to be milked. Their tits are bursting. When we lose an hour in the morning, we're chasing it all day.

(*He hurries out.* NAN *seems asleep. The lullaby continues. Quick curtain.*)

CURTAIN

BIBLIOGRAPHICAL CHECKLIST

PLAYS

The King of Friday's Men, James Duffy, Dublin, 1953.
First published in *Plays of the Year, 1949–1950*, chosen by J. C. Trewin, Paul Elek, London, 1950, pp. 307–436.

The Paddy Pedlar, James Duffy, Dublin, 1954.
Also published in *A Prose and Verse Anthology of Modern Irish Writing*, ed. Grattan Freyer, Irish Humanities Centre, Dublin, 1979, pp. 181–202.

The Will and the Way, P. J. Bourke, Dublin, 1957.

Old Road, Progress House, Dublin, 1961.

The Wood of the Whispering, Progress House, Dublin, 1961.

Daughter from Over the Water, Progress House, Dublin, 1963.

The Bitter Pill, in *Irish Countrywomen's Association Prizewinning Plays of 1964*, Progress House, Dublin, and Brandon Press, Boston (Mass.), 1965, pp. 53–80.

The Visiting House, in *Seven Irish Plays 1946–1964*, ed. Robert Hogan, University of Minnesota Press, Minneapolis, 1967, pp. 32–95.

Petticoat Loose, Proscenium Press, Newark (Delaware), and Society of Irish Playwrights, Dublin, 1982.

The Bachelor's Daughter. First published in this volume.

COLLECTION

Three Plays (The King of Friday's Men, The Paddy Pedlar, The Wood of the Whispering), Proscenium Press, Newark (Delaware), 1975.

PROSE

'The Making of Folk Plays' in *Literature and Folk Culture: Ireland and Newfoundland*, eds. Alison Feder and Bernice Schrank, Memorial University of Newfoundland, St. John's, 1977, pp. 58–80.

INTERVIEW

'Molloy holds true to old ideals of play writing' by Eithne Tynan, in *The Herald* (Dublin), 11 March 1989, p. 3.

UNPUBLISHED WORKS
PLAYS

Tess Leitrim, unperformed (at various times during its writing, called *Knight Errant, Alluring Minx* and *Scandalous Minx*).

The Right Rose Tree, performed Abbey Theatre, Dublin, 27 October 1958.

The Wooing of Duvesa, performed Abbey Theatre, Dublin, 21 September 1964.
The Bride of Fontebranda, unperformed.
Delilah (1982), unperformed.
The Runaways (1987), performed Tuam Theatre Guild, 1989.
The Fateful Princess (1993), unperformed.

PROSE
The Visiting House , an collection of folklore.

For a biographical sketch on M. J. Molloy, see his brother Christy Molloy's *Milltown Sketches*, Lurgan Publications (Inverin, Co. Galway), 1995, pp. 250–253.

IRISH DRAMA SELECTIONS

ISSN 0260–7962

1. SELECTED PLAYS OF LENNOX ROBINSON
   Chosen and introduced by Christopher Murray
   Contains *Patriots*, *The Whiteheaded Boy*, *Crabbed Youth and Age*, *The Big House*, *Drama at Inish*, *Church Street*, Bibliographical Checklist.

2. SELECTED PLAYS OF DENIS JOHNSTON
   Chosen and introduced by Joseph Ronsley
   Contains *The Old Lady Says 'No!'*, *The Moon in the Yellow River*, *The Golden Cuckoo*, *The Dreaming Dust*, *The Scythe and the Sunset*, Bibliographical Checklist.

3. SELECTED PLAYS OF LADY GREGORY
   Foreword Sean O'Casey
   Chosen and introduced by Mary Fitzgerald
   Contains *The Travelling Man*, *Spreading the News*, *Kincora*, *Hyacinth Halvey*, *The Doctor In Spite of Himself*, *The Goal Gate*, *The Rising of the Moon*, *Dervorgilla*, *The Workhouse Ward*, *Grania*, *The Golden Apple*, *The Story Brought by Brigit*, *Dave*, Lady Gregory on Playwriting and her Plays, Bibliographical Checklist.

4. SELECTED PLAYS OF DION BOUCICAULT
   Chosen and introduced by Andrew Parkin
   Contains *London Assurance*, *The Corsican Brothers*, *The Octoroon*, *The Colleen Bawn*, *The Shaughraun*, *Robert Emmet*, Bibliographical Checklist.

5. SELECTED PLAYS OF ST JOHN ERVINE
   Chosen and introduced by John Cronin
   Contains *Mixed Marriage*, *Jane Clegg*, *John Ferguson*, *Boyd's Shop*, *Friends and Relations*, prose extracts, Bibliographical Checklist.

6. SELECTED PLAYS OF BRIAN FRIEL
   Chosen and introduced by Seamus Deane
   Contains *Philadelphia, Here I come*, *Translations*, *The Freedom of the City*, *Living Quarters*, *Faith Healer*, *Aristocrats*, Bibliographical Checklist.
   Our edition of this title is only for sale in North America

7. SELECTED PLAYS OF DOUGLAS HYDE
   Chosen and introduced by Janet Egleson Dunleavy
   and Gareth Dunleavy
   Contains *The Twisting of the Rope*, *The Marriage*, *The Lost Saint*, *The Nativity*, *King James*, *The Bursting of the Bubble*, *The Tinker and the Sheeog*, *The Matchmaking*, *The Schoolmaster*, Bibliographical Checklist. This volume publishes the original Irish language texts with Lady Gregory's translations.

8. SELECTED PLAYS OF GEORGE MOORE
   AND EDWARD MARTIN
   Chosen and introduced by David B. Eakin and Michael Case
   Contains *The Strike at Arlingford*, *The Bending of the Bough*, *The Coming of Gabrielle*, *The Passing of the Essenes;* and *The Heather Field*, *Maeve*, *The Tale of a Town*. Bibliographical Checklist.

9. SELECTED PLAYS OF HUGH LEONARD
   Chosen and introduced by S. F. Gallagher
   Contains *The Au Pair Man*, *The Patrick Pearse Motel*, *Da*, *Summer*, *A Life*, *Kill*. Bibliographical Checklist.

10. SELECTED PLAYS OF T. C. MURRAY
    Chosen and introduced by Richard Allen Cave
    Will contain *Sovereign Love*, *Birthright*, *Maurice Harte*, *The Briery Gap*, *Autumn Fire*, *The Pipe in the Fields*.
    Bibliographical Checklist.

11. SELECTED PLAYS OF MICHEÁL mac LIAMMÓIR
    Chosen and introduced by John Barrett
    Contains *Where Stars Walk*, *Ill Met by Moonlight*, *The Mountains Look Different*, *The Liar*, *Prelude in Kazbek Street*, On Plays and Players (essay by mac Liammóir), Bibliographical Checklist.

12. SELECTED PLAYS OF M. J. MOLLOY
    Chosen and introduced by Robert O'Driscoll
    Will contain *The King of Friday's Men*, *The Paddy Pedlar*, *The Wood of the Whispering*, *Daughter from Over the Water*, *Petticoat Loose*, and *The Bachelor's Daughter*. Bibliographical Checklist.